Lecture Notes in Artificial Inte

Subseries of Lecture Notes in Computer S
Edited by J. G. Carbonell and J. Siekmann

Lecture Notes in Computer Science

Edited by G. Goos, J. Hartmanis, and J. van Leeuwen

Springer
Berlin
Heidelberg
New York
Barcelona
Hong Kong
London
Milan
Paris
Tokyo

Alessandro Armando (Ed.)

Frontiers of Combining Systems

4th International Workshop, FroCoS 2002
Santa Margherita Ligure, Italy, April 8-10, 2002
Proceedings

 Springer

Series Editors

Jaime G. Carbonell, Carnegie Mellon University, Pittsburgh, PA, USA
Jörg Siekmann, University of Saarland, Saarbrücken, Germany

Volume Editor

Alessandro Armando
DIST – Università di Genova
Viale Causa 13, 15145 Genova, Italy
E-mail: armando@dist.unige.it

Cataloging-in-Publication Data applied for

Die Deutsche Bibliothek - CIP-Einheitsaufnahme

Frontiers of combining systems : 4th international workshop ; proceedings /
FroCoS 2002, Santa Margherita Ligure, Italy, April 8 - 10, 2002. Alessandro
Armando (ed.). - Berlin ; Heidelberg ; New York ; Barcelona ; Hong Kong ;
London ; Milan ; Paris ; Tokyo : Springer, 2002
(Lecture notes in computer science ; Vol. 2309 : Lecture notes in
artificial intelligence)
ISBN 3-540-43381-3

CR Subject Classification (1998): I.2.3, F.4.1, F.4

ISSN 0302-9743
ISBN 3-540-43381-3 Springer-Verlag Berlin Heidelberg New York

Springer-Verlag Berlin Heidelberg New York
a member of BertelsmannSpringer Science+Business Media GmbH

http://www.springer.de

© Springer-Verlag Berlin Heidelberg 2002
Printed in Germany

Typesetting: Camera-ready by author, data conversion by Steingräber Satztechnik GmbH, Heidelberg
Printed on acid-free paper   SPIN: 10846555   06/3142   5 4 3 2 1 0

Preface

This volume contains the proceedings of FroCoS 2002, the 4th International Workshop on Frontiers of Combining Systems, held April 8-10, 2002 in Santa Margherita Ligure (near Genova), Italy. Like its predecessors, organized in Munich (1996), Amsterdam (1998), and Nancy (2000), FroCoS 2002 offered a common forum for the presentation and discussion of research activities on the combination and integration of systems in various areas of computer science, such as logic, computation, program development and proof, artificial intelligence, mechanical verification, and symbolic computation.

There were 35 submissions of high quality, authored by researchers from countries including Australia, Belgium, Brazil, Finland, France, Germany, Italy, Portugal, Spain, Singapore, United Kingdom, United States of America, and Yugoslavia. All the submissions were thoroughly evaluated on the basis of at least three referee reports, and an electronic program committee meeting was held through the Internet. The program committee selected 14 research contributions. The topics covered by the selected papers include: combination of logics, combination of constraint solving techniques, combination of decision procedures, combination problems in verification, modular properties of theorem proving, integration of decision procedures and other solving processes into constraint programming and deduction systems.

The workshop program was enriched by four invited talks by Greg Nelson on "Foundations of a Constraint-Based Illustrator", Alessandro Cimatti on "Integrating BDD-based and SAT-based Symbolic Model Checking", Deepak Kapur on "A Rewrite Rule based Framework for Combining Decision Procedures", and Tom F. Melham on "An Investigation into Software Architecture for Embedded Proof Engines", and one tutorial by Thom Fruehwirth and Slim Abdennadher on "Reasoning with, about, and for Constraint Handling Rules".

I would like to thank the many people who made FroCoS 2002 possible. I am grateful to: the members of the program committee and the additional referees named on the following pages for reviewing the papers in a very short time and maintaining the very high standard of FroCoS workshops; the other members of the FroCoS Steering Committee for their advice and encouragement; the invited speakers; and last, but by no means least, Silvio Ranise for handling the software for our web-based reviewing procedure and Luca Compagna for his help in the local organization of the workshop.

January 2002   Alessandro Armando

Workshop Chair

Alessandro Armando (DIST, University of Genova)

Program Committee

Alessandro Armando (U. Genova)
David Basin (U. Freiburg)
Frederic Benhamou (U. Nantes)
Jacques Calmet (U. Karlsruhe)
Giorgio Delzanno (U. Genova)
Bernhard Gramlich (T.U. Wien)
Deepak Kapur (U. New Mexico)
Hélène Kirchner (LORIA Nancy)

Michael Kohlhase (CMU)
Christophe Ringeissen (LORIA Nancy)
Michael Rusinowitch (LORIA Nancy)
Klaus Schulz (LMU München)
Roberto Sebastiani (U. Trento)
Cesare Tinelli (U. Iowa)
Luca Viganò (U. Freiburg)
Frank Wolter (U. Leipzig)

Local Organization

Alessandro Armando
Luca Compagna
Silvio Ranise

Additional Reviewers

Rafael Accorsi
Marco Aiello
Alexander Bockmayr
Chad E. Brown
Walter A. Carnielli
Luca Compagna
Alessandro Coglio
Pasquale Delucia
Eric Domenjoud
Hubert Dubois
Chiara Ghidini
Silvio Ghilardi

Paolo Giorgini
Isabelle Gnaedig
Frédéric Goualard
Laurent Granvilliers
Timothy J Hickey
Dieter Hutter
François Lamarche
Steffen Lange
Francisco Lopez-Fraguas
Michael Marte
Richard Mayr
Eric Monfroy

Julien Musset
Silvio Ranise
Michel Rueher
Luciano Serafini
Frieder Stolzenburg
Juergen Stuber
Ashish Tiwari
Heinrich Wansing
Michael Zakharyaschev
Hantao Zhang

Sponsoring Institutions

University of Genova
Dipartimento di Informatica, Sistemistica e Telematica (DIST), University of
Genova

Table of Contents

Foundations of a Constraint-Based Illustrator

Greg Nelson

COMPAQ Systems Research Center
130 Lytton Avenue, Palo Alto, CA 94301

Abstract. The talk describes some of the formal foundations of Juno-2, a constraint-based graphical illustrator implemented by Allan Heydon and Greg Nelson and available over the web in source form.

The first idea underlying Juno-2 is that constraint-based programming is obtained from ordinary imperative programming not by adding a feature but by subtracting a restriction: specifically by dropping the law of the excluded miracle from the calculus of guarded commands of Edsger W. Dijkstra. Dropping this law introduces "partial commands" (sometimes called "miracles"), which, when combined with conventional local variable introductions ("VAR statements") creates a highly principled constraint solving primitive that is beautifully orthogonal to the conventional imperative features of the language.

The second idea is that the "combination of decision procedures technique" that has been widely used in the automatic theorem-proving community for the last two decades can also be used to combine constraint solvers for two logical theories into a single constraint solver for the combination of the theories. Juno-2 uses this idea to combine a simple solver for the theory of a pairing function (which amounts only to an implementation of unification closure) with a sophisticated numerical solver for the theory of the real numbers to produce a powerful constraint solver that is useful for producing accurate technical illustrations and animations. The talk will include a demonstration of Juno-2, weather permitting.

References

1. Allan Heydon and Greg Nelson. The Juno-2 Contraint-based Drawing Editor. Research Report 131a. Digital Equipment Corporation Systems Research Center, Palo Alto, CA 1994.
2. The Juno-2 Home Page. `http://research.compaq.com/SRC/juno-2`
3. Greg Nelson. Juno, A Constraint-based Graphics System. In Proceedings of the ACM Siggraph conference, pp 235–43, July 1985.
4. Greg Nelson. A Generalization of Dijkstra's Calculus. ACM TOPLAS 11(4). October 1989, pp 517–61.
5. Greg Nelson. Combining Satisfiability Pocedures by Equality-sharing. In "Automatic Theorem Proving: after 25 years" edited by W. W. Bledsoe and D. W. Loveland. (vol 29 of "Contemporary Mathematics") American Mathematical Society 1983. pp 201–11.

A. Armando (Ed.): FroCoS 2002, LNAI 2309, p. 1, 2002.
© Springer-Verlag Berlin Heidelberg 2002

Integrating HOL-CASL
into the Development Graph Manager MAYA

Serge Autexier[1] and Till Mossakowski[2]

[1] FR 6.2 Informatik, Saarland University,
P.O. Box 15 11 50, D 66041 Saarbrücken,
`Autexier@ags.uni-sb.de`, Fax: +49 681 302 2235
[2] BISS, University of Bremen,
P.O. Box 330 440, D 28334 Bremen,
`till@tzi.de`, Fax: +49 421 218 3054

Abstract. For the recently developed specification language CASL, there exist two different kinds of proof support: While HOL-CASL has its strength in proofs about specifications in-the-small, MAYA has been designed for management of proofs in (CASL) specifications in-the-large, within an evolutionary formal software development process involving changes of specifications. In this work, we discuss our integration of HOL-CASL and MAYA into a powerful system providing tool support for CASL, which will also serve as a basis for the integration of further proof tools.

1 Introduction

The specification of large software systems is only manageable if specifications are built in a structured manner. Specification languages, like CASL [4], provide various mechanisms to combine basic specifications to structured specifications. Analogously, verification tools must be able to represent the logical content of specifications in a structured way. This needs to be more than the pure logical content of the specification, since the status, proven or open, of proof obligations must be represented in order to keep the whole development in a consistent state. Attempts to prove some proof obligation may fail, revealing errors in the specification, which is subsequently changed. Hence specification and verification of software are intertwined, until we finally obtain a version of the specification, whose proof obligations can all be proved. In practice, it is indispensable to deal in an efficient manner with the effects of correcting flaws in the specification. This is mainly to be able to determine which proofs remain valid, since a lot of proof effort, i.e. development time, has gone into creating those proofs.

Industrial strength formal software development systems like VSE [9] have been designed to deal with the evolutionary character of the software development process. The main differences between those systems and usual theorem provers is on the one hand that they accommodate the need to provide tool support to exploit the structure of specifications to ease their verification. On the other hand, they provide tool support to administrate the status of the development. The development graph manager MAYA [13,8] has been designed to make

A. Armando (Ed.): FroCoS 2002, LNAI 2309, pp. 2–17, 2002.

the ability of development administration and management of change accessible to existing (semi-)automated theorem provers. It incorporates a mechanism to reason about the structure of specifications, and thus provides tool-support for the verification of specifications *in-the-large*. Doing so, it organizes and minimizes the overall verification task, and leaves the task to prove theorems from a set of axioms – i.e. the verification of specifications *in-the-small* – to the theorem provers, which is what they are usually designed for.

MAYA provides a uniform interface to parsers of specification languages, and the CATS-parser [15] for the Common Algebraic Specification Language (CASL) has already been integrated into MAYA, using a transformation from CASL to development graphs (see [1]). From this integration resulted the need for strong proof support for specific theorems arising during the verification of CASL specifications. The HOL-CASL-system [15] provides such CASL specific tool support of verification *in-the-small*, but lacks the abilities required for verification *in-the-large*. The two systems, MAYA and HOL-CASL have complementary features, and thus there is a need to integrate them to obtain a strong tool support for formal software development with CASL.

In this paper we present this integration of HOL-CASL with MAYA and it is organized as follows: In Sect. 2 we present the development graph manager MAYA and briefly introduce its basics. In Sect. 3 we describe the HOL-CASL-system and its graphical user interface IsaWin. A discussion of possible integration scenarios, followed by a detailed description of the chosen scenario and its implementation is presented in Sect. 4. Before concluding in Sect. 6, we also give an account on some related work in Sect. 5.

2   Development Graph Manager MAYA

The development graph as presented in [13,8] has been developed to mediate between parsers for specifications and theorem provers to deal with all evolutionary aspects of formal software development. Software is usually specified in a structured manner in order to allow for the reuse of software components. Various structuring mechanisms have been proposed to this end (e.g. [6,20,21]). Besides the definition of software systems, the system requirements are specified (e.g. safety or liveness properties) in requirement specifications. Those must be fulfilled by the specified system and this is represented by postulating entailment relations between the requirement specifications and the system specification. Some of the postulated relations can be discharged just by exploiting the structure of the specification. Recognizing those subsumption relations saves a lot of proof effort, and hence development time. From the remaining postulated relations arise the proof obligations which must be tackled using some interactive or automated theorem prover. The existing theorem provers that can be used to tackle proof obligations *often do not support the structuring mechanisms*, or only simple structuring mechanisms. In order to allow for their use in the context of formal software development, it is necessary to determine, for each proof obligation, *the set of axioms that can be used to prove the proof obligation*.

```
spec LIST [sort Elem] =
  free  type List[Elem]  ::= [] | _ :: _(Elem; List[Elem])
  ops  _++_  :  List[Elem] × List[Elem] → List[Elem];
       reverse  :  List[Elem] → List[Elem];
  pred  null  :  List[Elem]
  ∀   x, y  :  Elem;
      K, L  :  List[Elem]
      . [] ++K = K                            %(concat_nil_List)%
      . (x :: L) ++K = x :: (L ++K)           %(concat_NeList_List)%
      . reverse([]) = []                      %(reverse_nil)%
      . reverse(x :: L) = reverse(L) ++(x :: [])  %(reverse_NeList)%
      . null(L) ⇔ L = []                       %(null)%
  then  %implies
      ∀ K,L : List[Elem]  . reverse(K ++L) = reverse(L) ++reverse(K)
                          . null(reverse(L)) ⇔ null(L)
end

spec MONOID =
  sort Elem
  ops  e    :  Elem;
       _*_  :  Elem × Elem → Elem, assoc, unit e
end

view MONOIDASLIST : MONOID to LIST[sort Elem] =
       Elem  ↦  List[Elem],
       e     ↦  [],
       _*_   ↦  _++_
end
```

Fig. 1. A CASL specification that lists with append form a monoid.

The whole formal software development process is evolutionary in nature, as failing to establish some proof obligation may lead to changes in the actual specification which again may affect subsumption properties and already proven proof obligations. The minimization of the effects of changes is a major issue, since it saves a lot of accomplished proof efforts. To achieve this the structure of the specifications can, again, be exploited.

The development graph, as introduced in [13,8], is a uniform formalism to represent structured theories. In order to illustrate its description we use the example CASL-specification viewed in Fig. 1. This specification consists of a specification LIST composed of a specification of lists over arbitrary elements (of type Elem), which are enriched by an append function _ ++_ and a reverse function *reverse*. This can be seen as the *system specification*. The second specification MONOID specifies monoids and can be seen as the *requirement specification*, which is then linked to LIST by the **view** MONOIDASLIST.

Formally, a development graph is an acyclic, directed graph, where each node represents a theory like for instance LIST, its different parts structured by

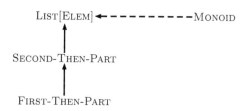

Fig. 2. Development Graph for the running example

then, or MONOID in CASL. Each node contains a *local signature* and a set of *local axioms*. E.g. the local signature of the second **then**-part of LIST are the functions $\_\_ ++ \_\_$ and *reverse* and its local axioms are the axioms defining those functions. The so-called *definition links* of the graph are directed links between two nodes. They define how the theory of the target node is built upon the theory of the source node. Those links can be compared roughly to the **then** structuring mechanisms, but also **and** (i.e. unions of specifications), depending on the number of definition links that go into some node. There are three kinds of definition links:

1. **Global definition links**, that intuitively export the whole visible signature and axioms of the source node to the target node,
2. **Local definition links**, whose intuitive semantics is that they export only the local signature and the local axioms of the source node to the target node,
3. and **Hiding definition links**, that export the visible signature except the hidden symbols. Those are used to encode the hiding of signature symbols in specification language. Examples are local functions, which are encapsulated by some module and invisible to the outside.

Intuitively, global and hiding definition links are used to represent the structure of the specification, e.g. the CASL-specification in Fig. 1. Global and hiding definition links are decomposed into various local definition links, which allows for a granular and thus efficient analysis of the effects due to changes of the specification (cf. [1] for an example). For a formal definition of the development graph and a detailed account on how links are decomposed we refer to [8,13].

In addition to definition links, there are *theorem links*, which are used to represent proof-obligations arising from the original specification. In contrast to definition links, which are *assumed* relationships, theorem links *postulate* relationships and also come in three kinds:

1. **Global theorem links** postulate that all visible axioms of the source node must be theorems in the target node,
2. **Local theorem links** postulate that only the local axioms of the source node must be theorems in the target node, and
3. **Hiding theorem links** are global theorem links from a *subtheory of the source* to the target (i.e. some of the symbols in the source may be hidden and therefore need not be mapped into the target signature).

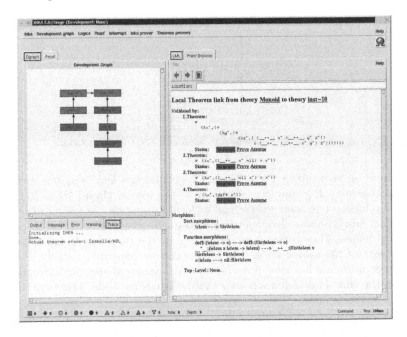

Fig. 3. The development graph manager MAYA

The global theorem links are mainly used to encode the postulated entailment relations between specifications. Similarly to definition links, global theorem links are decomposed into local theorem links. This allows on the one hand to recognize those parts of the global theorem link that are subsumed by the other relations between theories. On the other hand, it allows for a granular and thus efficient analysis of changes in the specification. During the decomposition, hiding theorem links are used to represent intermediate states of the decomposition process.

The development graph for the running example is viewed in Fig. 2. Leaves in the graph correspond to basic specifications, which do not make use of other theories (like MONOID or the first **then**-part of the structured specification LIST). Inner nodes correspond to structured specifications which define theories using other theories (like LIST or its second **then**-part). The structuring mechanisms like **then** are encoded into definition links in the graph. Postulated relationships are encoded into the global *theorem links*. E.g. the **view**-part of name MONOIDASLIST of the CASL-specification postulates that "list with append form a monoid structure". This is expressed by a global theorem link from MONOID to LIST annotated by the morphism σ, that maps the type *Elem* to the type *List*, and the functions e and $\_\ast\_$ to $[]$ and $\_++\_$, respectively. The actual proof obligations arising from this theorem link are to prove that the axioms from MONOID mapped by σ are theorems in the theory of LIST.

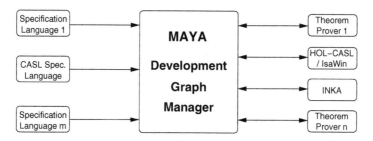

Fig. 4. The vision of the development graph manager MAYA

The development graph manager MAYA is an implementation of the development graph and provides tool support for the various aspects of an evolutionary formal software development process:

- It allows the encoding of structured specifications in a uniform and structured representation.
- The bookkeeping about proven and pending proof obligations is supported in order to keep the whole development in a consistent state.
- The decomposition and subsumption algorithms provide an efficient and reliable tool support to recognize those parts of postulated relationships, that are subsumed by the graph structure.
- It performs a detailed analysis of changes in the specification and minimizes their effects on existing proofs of established proof obligations by exploiting the decomposition of global relationships into local relationships.

The core of MAYA is implemented in Allegro Common Lisp and its graphical user interface (see Fig. 3) in MOZART (www.mozart-oz.org). The vision of the development graph manager is that it serves as a uniform mediator between on the one hand different specification languages and different theorem provers on the other hand (see Fig. 4). The vision gives rise to several requirements that need to be addressed during the design of the development graph manager: First, it should be as easy as possible to connect a specification language. To do so, only a parser must be supplied for the specification language as well as a translation from the specification language's logic and structuring mechanisms into those of the development graph. This allows to represent the specifications in the development graph structure and MAYA provides tool support to determine changes between different specification revisions. The validity of this design goal has been showed by implementing a connection from CASL to MAYA and has been reported in [1]. Secondly, it should be as easy as possible to connect an existing theorem prover to MAYA, in order to use it to prove the arising conjectures. There are several possible integration scenarios, which are discussed in Sect. 4, as well as the scenario chosen to integrate the HOL-CASL-system.

The logic underlying the implemented development graph currently is higher-order logic (HOL) with polymorphism and type constructors. We have chosen

HOL since it is general and flexible enough to encode nearly all logics used in practice. Moreover, there are good theorem provers supporting HOL. However, it should be stressed that the choice of the logic is entirely orthogonal to the structuring mechanisms of the development graph. Presently, MAYA not only supports HOL, but also an extension of HOL with a temporal logic of actions. In the future, we plan to allow heterogeneous development graphs over a given arbitrary but fixed graph of logics, see [16].

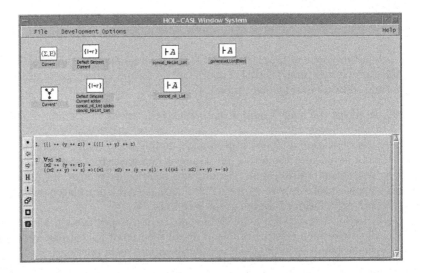

Fig. 5. The HOL-CASL instantiation of the IsaWin system

3   HOL-CASL and IsaWin

CASL is a specification language combining first-order logic and induction principles with subsorting and partiality. Now most theorem provers do neither support subsorting nor partiality, and therefore it also does not make much sense to have them in the logic of the development graph. Therefore, in order to do theorem proving for CASL specifications, we need to code out these features. The encoding of CASL into higher-order logic (HOL) is done by encoding partiality via error elements living in a supersort, encoding subsorting via injections, and encoding sort generation constraints as induction axioms (see [14,15]). These encodings are not only translations of syntax, but also have a model-theoretic counterpart, which provides an implicit soundness and completeness proof for the re-use of HOL-theorem provers for theorem proving in the CASL logic, which is also known as the "borrowing" technique of Cerioli and Meseguer [3].

HOL-CASL now is an interface from CASL to Isabelle/HOL based on this encoding. We have chosen Isabelle [18] because it has a very small core guaranteeing correctness. Furthermore, there is over ten years of experience with it (several mathematical textbooks have partially been verified with Isabelle).

IsaWin is a generic graphical interface, which can be set on top of Isabelle [12,11]. We have instantiated IsaWin with our HOL-CASL encoding of CASL into Isabelle/HOL. In Fig. 5, you can see a typical IsaWin window. The icon labeled with (Σ, E) denotes a CASL specification (more precisely, its encoding in HOL). The icon labeled with a tree is an open proof goal. By double-clicking on it, you can perform proof steps with this goal. This is done by dragging either already proven theorems (those icons marked with $\vdash A$) or simplifier sets (icons marked with $\{l \rightarrow r\}$) onto the goal. The effect is the (one-step) resolution of the goal with the selected theorem, or the (multi-step) rewriting of the goal with the chosen simplifier set. After the proof of a goal is finished, it turns into a theorem. You can then use it in proofs of other theorems, or, if it has the form of a rewrite rule, add it to a simplifier set.

4   Integrating HOL-CASL and IsaWin into MAYA

The development graph manager MAYA has a connection to the specification language CASL (see [1]). Hence, it provides tool support for the administration of formal software developments with CASL specifications and especially an efficient management of change. Conceptually, this provides a kind of proof engine for the verification of CASL specifications *in-the-large*, and it lacks a proof engine for verification *in-the-small*, to actually prove the conjectures arising during formal software development.

The HOL-CASL-system is an instance of the Isabelle/HOL generic theorem prover for CASL. It incorporates specialized proof support to tackle theorem proving problems arising in the domain of CASL-specification. However, it lacks a sophisticated administration of whole developments as well as an efficient management of change. In contrast to MAYA, it thus provides strong tool support for CASL-specification and verification in-the-small, but is weak for CASL-specification and verification in-the-large.

In comparison, the two systems have complementary strengths and thus there is a need to integrate both systems to overcome the weaknesses of the stand-alone systems.

4.1   Spectrum of Integration Scenarios

The overall principle of the integration of MAYA with some theorem prover is as follows: MAYA deals with all *in-the-large* aspects of formal software development, while the theorem prover is used to deal with the *in-the-small* aspects, i.e. to actually prove a conjecture w.r.t. some set of axioms.

However, there is a large scale as of to which degree the integration of MAYA and some theorem prover can be realised. The looser the integration is, the simpler it is to realise, but also the less efficient it is in practice, and vice versa. The loosest possible coupling would be that whenever there is a conjecture to prove w.r.t. the theory of some node, all the axioms defining the theory of this node are determined from the development graph structure. All those axioms are sent to the theorem prover together with the request to prove the conjecture. As a result, the theorem prover returns whether it could prove the conjecture or not. However, such a loose integration has some severe drawbacks in practice: On the one hand, in practice the number of axioms can be rather huge and it is very inefficient to send always all axioms together with a conjecture, even if the set of usable axioms for the current conjecture is the same than those for the previous theorem. On the other hand, if the theorem prover returns only the information whether it could prove a conjecture or not, there is no information about the axioms actually used during that proof. Subsequently, MAYA must assume, that *any* usable axioms could have been used. Hence, the status of this proof depends on *all* usable axioms, and the proof gets invalid – from MAYA's point of view – as soon as one of those is deleted due to some change of the original specification. This is another strong loss in efficiency for the management of change.

In contrast to this loosest integration, the tightest integration would be to determine all nodes in the development graph, w.r.t. whose theories the actual conjectures must be proven. For each such *proof node*, an instance of the theorem prover is created and initialized with the theory of this node. Besides the logical content of a node in the development graph, each node could contain information about domain specific reasoning procedures. Those are e.g. domain specific tactics for some tactical theorem prover. Those specific reasoning procedures could be handled over to the theorem prover, in order to reach a high degree of automation for proof search. After setting up all theorem prover instances in this manner, each is requested to prove the conjectures associated to its proof node. The theorem prover returns for every conjecture whether it could prove it or not. In case it could prove a conjecture, it returns a proof object in some logical calculus, which is stored in the development graph. Whenever the specification is changed, MAYA can exploit the structure of the development graph to determine on a granular level how the theories of proof nodes are affected, and subsequently only send the differences to the associated instances of the theorem prover. This consists of inserting resp. deleting single types, constants, or axioms in the theorem prover, and prevents having to send always the whole theory after some change. Furthermore, the proof objects stored for some theorem can be analysed, whether the axioms used during that proof are still present or not. If so, the proof is still valid. If not, then we can try to patch the proof using the various proof reuse or proof patching techniques.

Besides this very efficient management of change, the tight integration also allows to support incremental software development methods, i.e. a development strategy that begins with developing the core of a system and adds features incrementally. Those methods change or extend the specification in a determined manner, such that the effects on proof objects are predictable. Again, specific proof patching techniques can be used to try to patch the affected proof objects, which would prevent to have to redo the proofs. Examples for such incremental formal software development methods can be found in [22].

4.2   Integration Scenario for HOL-CASL

From this scale of possible integration scenarios, we chose the following: According to the ideal tight integration scenario, there should be in each *proof node* an instance of the HOL-CASL-system. In practice, there may be a large number of those *proof nodes*, and it is technically infeasible to run several instances of HOL-CASL in parallel. Therefore the approach is to have one instance of the HOL-CASL-system and to literally "move" it around between the proof nodes. If the HOL-CASL-system is initialized w.r.t. a specific proof node, MAYA provides all the axioms visible in that node (i.e. the theory of this node) that can be used to prove that conjecture. To actually prove a conjecture w.r.t. this node, MAYA sends a request to the HOL-CASL-system. When it comes to prove a conjecture w.r.t. a different proof node, the HOL-CASL-system must be initialized w.r.t. the new proof node. To this end, MAYA exploits the structure of the development graph in order to compute the differences between the theories of the old and the new proof node. Subsequently, only the differences are sent to HOL-CASL prover, which results in a gain in efficiency in practice. The latter is expected to hold a single theory (called Current, see Fig. 5), that contains all usable types, constants and axioms. The presented integration scenario is realised on top of seven basic interface functions from MAYA to the HOL-CASL-system:

- Insertion and deletion of types
- Insertion and deletion of constants
- Insertion and deletion of axioms.
- Request to prove some conjecture.

A theorem proving request returns whether the cojecture could be proven or not, and this information is incorporated into the *in-the-large* process of the development graph manager. In case it could be proven, information about the axioms used to prove that theorem (this can be extracted from proof trees) is returned as well as two file names, one for the proof tree and one for the tactic script of the proof. The information about used axioms is included into MAYA and serves to determine whether or not a proof remains valid after a change of the specification. If a proof has been invalidated, we can try to reprove the theorem by using the tactic script contained in the stored file. The other file with the proof tree can be used to run a proof-checker. At the moment, proof trees have a prover specific format; however, we plan to make the format prover independent, such that MAYA can construct a large proof tree out of the individual trees, which can then be fed into a proof checker in order to double-check the correctness of proofs in the integrated system.

Since both the actual MAYA-system and the HOL-CASL-system are based on higher-order logic, there was no need to define logic morphisms.

4.3   Theorem Prover Design Requirements

The functionality exhibited by the basic functions has implications on the design of the theorem prover. The problem arises from the non-monotonic update of its theory. Usually, theorem provers are designed such that their theories can be enriched, but lack the ability to change or remove parts of its theory. The theorem prover must have at least a weak truth maintenance system, in order to track dependencies between axioms and derived information, like e.g. simplifier rules, induction rules or orderings among constants. The derived information might be more complex: Consider as an example the classification of some rewrite rule, where the left-hand side must be greater than the right-hand side w.r.t. a term ordering on top of the ordering among constants. The latter may be induced by bits of ordering relations between constants, which result from the analysis of axioms. It is necessary to know which ordering bits have been used to determine whether some term is greater than another, in order to know which axioms this comparison depends on. Subsequently, the rewrite rule depends on those axioms as well as the original axiom this rule stems from. Those dependencies are even more complex in case rewrite rules are derived from other rewrite rules, by e.g. some completion procedure.

In plain Isabelle, the derivation of simplifier sets is not that sophisticated — Isabelle follows a conservative extension paradigm and automatically generates simplifier sets only along conservative extensions. Therefore, Isabelle is not so well-suited for the integration with MAYA, since MAYA always sends sets of arbitrary axioms, which need not to follow the conservative extension paradigm. We have solved this problem by adding some heuristics for the automatic computation of simplifiers to HOL-CASL, e.g. by adding all axioms in Horn form. This needs to be further improved in the future (see also the section about future work).

For the HOL-CASL-system, the functions implying a monotonic change (i.e. insertion of types, constants and axioms) of its current theory could also be easily realised. A major problem were the functions entailing a non-monotonic change, i.e. a modification of the current theory. Indeed, those modifications conflict with Isabelle's LCF-style approach of guaranteeing correctness by restricting the access to the core proof engine by means of the Standard ML type system in a way that no unsound proof is possible. This restriction of access also means that it is not possible to delete parts of theories. Further, it is not even possible to copy those parts of a theory that should be kept. Therefore, we had to change the Isabelle kernel by removing some of the access restrictions. Of course, in general such a manipulative surgery sacrifices Isabelle's puristic philosophy. However, in this case, correctness cannot be ensured by Isabelle alone any longer, but results from an interplay with MAYA and Isabelle — a view that in principle is also shared by the developers of Isabelle [17].

4.4   Technical Integration

On a technical level, the integration is realised such that the HOL-CASL-system is called as a subprocess from Lisp, the programming language used for MAYA. The commands from MAYA to HOL-CASL are sent via a Unix pipe to the HOL-CASL-system using a refinement of the XML-RPC protocol (`www.xml-rpc.org`). The complete DTD of the used exchange format can be found on the MAYA webpage (`www.dfki.de/~inka/maya.html`). The commands are processed by the HOL-CASL system and acknowledged according to the XML-RPC standard.

However, it should be stressed that the XML format is essentially theorem prover independent and can be used for any prover supporting proofs in higher-order logic (HOL). The prover is expected to hold one theory (called the current theory). Via the protocol, MAYA can tell the prover to enrich the current theory (by adding types, constants and axioms) as well as to modify it (by deleting types, constants and axioms). The protocol also allows to ask the prover to prove a formula. The prover must return the formula plus possibly a number of lemmas needed in the proof. Both the original formula and the lemmas each come along with a proof status. The proof status may either be "proved", "disproved" or "open". In the case of "proved", also the list of axioms used in the proof must be supplied. Finally, the names of the two files containing the tactic script, that generated the proof, and the proof object may be returned as well.

4.5   Example

As a very small example, consider the specification in Fig. 1. Suppose that we have erroneously specified the axiom

$$reverse(x :: L) = reverse(L) + +[\,].$$

We can then prove without difficulty the proof obligations corresponding to the view from Monoid to List (which then will change its colour from red to green in the MAYA user interface, see Fig. 3), and also the first of the two formulas that have been specified to be implied, namely

$$reverse(K + +L) = reverse(L) + +reverse(K).$$

However, when attempting to prove

$$null(reverse(L)) \iff null(L)$$

we will fail. When looking at the specification, we (manually) can trace this back to the erroneous axiom and correct it into

$$reverse(x :: L) = reverse(L) + +(x :: [\,]).$$

After this, MAYA recomputes the development graph. The view from Monoid to List still has green colour, indicating that its proof still remains valid. However, the proof of

$$reverse(K + +L) = reverse(L) + +reverse(K)$$

is now invalidated and has to be replayed. Fortunately, in this case the tactic script need not be changed, because in contrast to plain Isabelle, HOL-CASL computes simplifier sets containing axioms from the specification. Finally, we now also can prove

$$null(reverse(L)) \iff null(L).$$

The main benefit in this small example was to avoid the replay of the tactic script for the proof of the view. The full power of the integration of MAYA with HOL-CASL shows up in more complex examples, where the structure of the specification changes and even where for some theorems that remain valid after the change, a replay of tactic scripts would not be possible, because e.g. simplifier sets in HOL-CASL have changed.

5   Related Work

Recently, a number of approaches of integrating different theorem provers and exchange formats for logical entities have been developed, among them the MATH-WEB project [7], the OMDOC [10] format, the HOL-CLAM project [2] and the PROSPER toolkit [5]. Typically, these approaches define an interchange format for logical entities and/or provide a central core proof engine, which serves as the basis to integrate different theorem provers. The approach presented here is new with respect to the emphasis on theorem proving and management of change in *structured* specifications. That is, MAYA can be regarded as a kind of core proof engine, but not at the level of specification in-the-small, but at the level of specification-in-the-large: Many proof obligations can be discharged and proofs can be re-used (after change of the specification) by an analysis of the structure of the specification (here represented as development graph). A similar approach is taken in the VSE system [9] and the KIV system [19]. However, those systems are not built in a way as modular as our system, but are instead monolithic, which hampers the integration of theorem provers different from the integrated one. Moreover, our system is suitable for extensions allowing for theorem proving across different logics (see [16]).

6   Conclusion

In this paper we reported on the integration of the development graph manager MAYA with the HOL-CASL and IsaWin system. The major outcomings of this work are twofold: First, this work is a proof of principle of the validity of the design issues of MAYA as a mediator between parsers of specification languages and state of the art theorem provers. While [1] showed that the interface of the development graph to parsers is adequate to integrate those, the work presented in this paper demonstrates the adequacy of the interface of the development graph tool to theorem provers. The major difficulty encountered during the integration of HOL-CASL was getting the underlying Isabelle/HOL system to accept non-monotonic changes of its theories.

The second major benefit is that the HOL-CASL-system has been extended to a verification tool that handles in an efficient manner the management and bookkeeping tasks due to the *evolutionary* character of formal software development. One should note that normally, Isabelle proofs are carried out in a rather *static* environment, that is, the theory is not expected to change - and when it changes, it is sometimes very tedious to adapt proof scripts accordingly, especially if the structure of the specification changes and simplifier sets do no longer work in the expected way. Using Isabelle's information about used axioms in some Isabelle/HOL proof, MAYA allows for a more efficient management of change. Changes in the specification can be analysed and only the local effects are propagated to the theorem prover.

A third achievement is that a prover with only limited *in-the-large* structuring mechanisms (such as Isabelle/HOL) can now be used for proofs in complex structured specifications. This is important especially for the verification of large software systems. In a future extension, it might be desirable to exploit Isabelle's limited structuring mechanisms (extension and union) whenever possible. This would mean that a local proof would take place not in a flattened theory as now, but rather in a structured theory limited to extension and union.

As a by-product of this integration, there is now a simple XML based exchange format to exchange logical information like signatures and axioms between systems. It is designed to communicate single entities of unstructured pure logical information, and by this is less verbose than other encodings like [10]. This uniform format together with the general integration scenario should allow to integrate any tactic-based LCF-style theorem prover, provided that it supports non-monotonic updates of its database. The Lisp sources of MAYA as well as the binaries of HOL-CASL can be obtained from the MAYA-webpage www.dfki.de/~inka/maya.html.

Future work will consist in using the sketched verification environment to perform case studies using CASL as the specification language to specify software systems. With respect to the MAYA system, future work is concerned with providing a full support for hiding. Also, we plan to connect more provers to the prover independent XML interface. In connection with this, it is desirable to make the analysis techniques of the Inka theorem prover, which can compute simplifier sets in a sophisticated way using termination orderings, also available to HOL-CASL. For this end, MAYA would need to be extended to be able also to communicate information about simplifier sets. Finally, MAYA shall be extended with a generic mechanism for definition of logics and logic morphisms, such that multi-logic development graphs [16] can be processed. With a definition of a logic, not only its syntax, but also a format for proof trees shall be provided. In this way, proof patching techniques, re-use of proofs and proof checking will become available.

References

1. S. Autexier, D. Hutter, H. Mantel, and A. Schairer. Towards an evolutionary formal software-development using CASL. In C. Choppy, D. Bert, and P. Mosses, (Eds.), *WADT'99*, LNAI 1827, 73–88, Springer-Verlag, 2000.

2. R. Boulton, K. Slind, A. Bundy, and M. Gordon: An Interface between CLAM and HOL, In J. Grundy and M. Newey (editors), *Proceedings of TPHOLs'98*, LNAI 1479, 87-104, Springer, Canberra, Australia, September/October 1998.
3. M. Cerioli and J. Meseguer. May I borrow your logic? (transporting logical structures along maps). *Theoretical Computer Science*, 173:311–347, 1997.
4. CoFI Language Design Task Group. *The Common Algebraic Specification Language (CASL) – Summary*, Version 1.0 and additional Note S-9 on Semantics, available from http://www.cofi.info, 1998.
5. L. A. Dennis, G. Collins, M. Norrish, R. Boulton, K. Slind, G. Robinson, M. Gordon, and T. Melham. The PROSPER toolkit. In S. Graf and M. Schwartbach, editors, *Tools and Algorithms for Constructing Systems, TACAS, Berlin, Germany*, LNAI 1785, 78–92. Springer-Verlag, 2000.
6. R. Diaconescu, J. Goguen, P. Stefaneas. Logical support for modularization, In G. Huet, G. Plotkin, (Eds), *Logical Environments*, 83–130, Cambridge Press 1991.
7. A. Franke, M. Kohlhase: System Description: MathWeb, an Agent-Based Communication Layer for Distributed Automated Theorem Proving, In H. Ganzinger (Ed.) *Proceedings of the 16th conference on automated deduction (CADE-16)*, Trento, Italy. LNAI 1632, 217–221, Springer 1999.
8. D. Hutter: Management of change in structured verification, In *Proceedings Automated Software Engineering (ASE-2000)*, IEEE, 2000.
9. D. Hutter et. al. Verification Support Environment (VSE), *Journal of High Integrity Systems*, Vol. 1, 523–530, 1996.
10. M. Kohlhase: OMDOC: Towards an OPENMATH Representation of Mathematical Documents, SEKI-Report SR-00-02, FR Informatik, Saarland University, 2000, www.mathweb.org/omdoc.
11. C. Lüth, H. Tej, Kolyang, and B. Krieg-Brückner. TAS and IsaWin: Tools for transformational program development and theorem proving. In J.-P. Finance, editor, *Fundamental Approaches to Software Engineering FASE'99. Joint European Conferences on Theory and Practice of Software ETAPS'99*, LNAI 1577, 239–243. Springer Verlag, 1999.
12. C. Lüth and B. Wolff. Functional design and implementation of graphical user interfaces for theorem provers. *Journal of Functional Programming*, 9(2):167–189, March. 1999.
13. T. Mossakowski, S. Autexier, and D. Hutter: Extending Development Graphs With Hiding. In H. Hußmann (Ed.), *Proceedings of Fundamental Approaches to Software Engineering (FASE 2001)*, Genova, Italy. LNAI 2029, 269–283. Springer, 2001.
14. T. Mossakowski, Kolyang, and B. Krieg-Brückner. Static semantic analysis and theorem proving for CASL. In F. Parisi Presicce, editor, *WADT 1997*, LNAI 1376, 333–348. Springer, 1998.
15. T. Mossakowski. CASL: From semantics to tools. In S. Graf and M. Schwartzbach, editors, *TACAS 2000*, LNAI 1785, 93–108. Springer-Verlag, 2000.
16. T. Mossakowski. Heterogeneous development graphs and heterogeneous borrowing. In M. Nielsen (Ed.) Proceedings of *Foundations of Software Science and Computation Structures (FOSSACS02)*, Grenoble, France, Springer LNAI, 2002.
17. T. Nipkow. Personal communication.
18. L. C. Paulson. *Isabelle - A Generic Theorem Prover*. LNAI 828. Springer, 1994.
19. Wolfgang Reif: The KIV-approach to Software Verification, In *KORSO: Methods, Languages, and Tools for the Construction of Correct Software - Final Report*, LNAI 1009, 339-368. Springer, 1995.
20. D. Sannella, A. Tarlecki. Specifications in an arbitrary institution, *Information and Computation*, 76(2-3):165-210, 1988.

21. D. Sannella, A. Tarlecki. Towards Formal Development of Programs from Algebraic Specifications: Model-Theoretic Foundations, *19th ICALP*, Springer, LNAI 623, 656–671, Springer-Verlag, 1992.
22. A. Schairer, D. Hutter: Short Paper: Towards an Evolutionary Formal Software Development, In *Proceedings of ASE 2001*, IEEE, November, 2001.

Monads and Modularity

Christoph Lüth[1] and Neil Ghani[2]

[1] FB 3 — Mathematik und Informatik, Universität Bremen
`cxl@informatik.uni-bremen.de`
[2] Department of Mathematics and Computer Science, University of Leicester
`ng13@mcs.le.ac.uk`

Abstract. This paper argues that the core of modularity problems is an understanding of how individual components of a large system interact with each other, and that this interaction can be described by a *layer structure*. We propose a uniform treatment of layers based upon the concept of a *monad*. The combination of different systems can be described by the *coproduct* of monads.

Concretely, we give a construction of the coproduct of two monads and show how the layer structure in the coproduct monad can be used to analyse layer structures in three different application areas, namely term rewriting, denotational semantics and functional programming.

1 Introduction

When reasoning about complex systems (such as specifications of large systems, or semantics of rich languages with many different features), modularity and compositionality are crucial properties: *compositionality* allows a large problem to be broken down into parts which can be reasoned about separately, while *modularity* finds criteria under which results concerning these parts combine into results about the overall system.

A prerequisite for modular reasoning is an understanding of how individual components of a large system interact with each other. In modular term rewriting, the key concept is the *layer structure* on the terms of the combined rewrite system, i.e. we can decompose the combined system into *layers* from the component systems. Our basic observation is that this methodology can be generalized by moving to a categorical framework, where layers become the basic concept, described by *monads*, which describe a far wider class of systems than just term rewriting systems, as demonstrated by the examples below. The combination of smaller systems into a larger one is in general described by colimits, but in this paper, we restrict ourselves a natural first step, the *coproduct*.

Monads have been used to describe various formal systems from term rewriting [10,11] to higher-order logic [3] and arbitrary computations [13], just as colimits have been used to describe the combination of specifications and theories [16,17]. A construction of the colimit of monads was given by Kelly [7, Chapter VIII] but the generality of the construction is reflected in its complexity which can be detering even for experienced category theorists, and hence limits the applicability of the construction to modularity problems.

A. Armando (Ed.): FroCoS 2002, LNAI 2309, pp. 18–32, 2002.

Our contribution is to provide alternative constructions which, by restricting ourselves to special cases, are significantly simpler and hence easier to apply in practice. We describe how monads correspond to algebraic structures, coproducts correspond to disjoint unions and how the layer structure in the coproduct monad models the layer structure in the combined system, and apply these ideas to three settings: modular rewriting, modular denotational semantics, and the functional programming language Haskell.

Generality requires abstraction and, as we shall argue later, the use of monads is appropriate for our abstract treatment of layers. We are aware that our categorical meta-language may make our work less accessible to those members of the FroCoS community who are not proficient in category theory. Nevertheless, we have written this paper with the general FroCoS audience in mind, by focusing on ideas, intuitions and concrete examples; proofs using much category theory have been relegated to the appendix. Our overall aim is to apply our general ideas to specific modularity problems and for that we require an exchange of ideas; we hope this paper can serve as a basis for this interaction.

The rest of this paper is structured as follows: we first give a general account of monads and motivate the construction of their coproducts. We examine particular special cases, for which we can give a simplified account. We finish by detailing our three application areas.

2   An Introduction to Monads

In this section, we introduce monads, describe their applications and explain their relevance to a general treatment of layers. Since this is standard material, we refer the reader to general texts [12] for more details. We start with the canonical example of term algebras which we will use throughout the rest of the paper.

Definition 1 (Signature). *A (single-sorted)* signature *consists of a function* $\Sigma : \mathbb{N} \to \textbf{Set}$. *The set of n-ary* operators *of Σ is defined $\Sigma_n = \Sigma(n)$.*

Definition 2 (Term Algebra). *Given a signature Σ and a set of variables X, the* term algebra $T_\Sigma(X)$ *is defined inductively:*

$$\frac{x \in X}{'x \in T_\Sigma(X)} \qquad \frac{f \in \Sigma_n \quad t_1, \ldots t_n \in T_\Sigma(X)}{f(t_1, \ldots, t_n) \in T_\Sigma(X)}$$

Quotes are used to distinguish a variable $x \in X$ from the term $'x \in T_\Sigma(X)$. For every set X, the term algebra $T_\Sigma(X)$ is also a set — categorically $T_\Sigma : \textbf{Set} \to \textbf{Set}$ is a functor over the category of sets. In addition, for every set of variables X, there is a function $X \to T_\Sigma(X)$ sending each variable to the associated term. Lastly, substitution takes terms built over terms and flattens them, as described by a function $T_\Sigma(T_\Sigma(X)) \to T_\Sigma(X)$. These three pieces of data, namely the construction of a theory from a set of variables, the embedding of variables as terms and the operation of substitution are axiomatised as a monad:

Definition 3 (Monads). *A monad* $T = \langle T, \eta, \mu \rangle$ *on a category* C *is given by an endofunctor* $T : C \to C$, *called the* action, *and two natural transformations,* $\eta : 1 \Rightarrow T$, *called the* unit, *and* $\mu : TT \Rightarrow T$, *called the* multiplication *of the monad, satisfying the* monad laws: $\mu \cdot T\eta = 1 = \mu \cdot \eta_T$, *and* $\mu \cdot T\mu = \mu \cdot \mu_T$.

We have already sketched how the term algebra construction T_Σ has an associated unit and multiplication. The equations of a monad correspond to substitution being well behaved, in particular being associative with the variables forming left and right units. In terms of layers, we think of $T_\Sigma(X)$ as a layer of terms over X, the unit converts each variable into a trivial layer and the multiplication allows us to collapse two layers of the same type into a single layer. Monads model a number of other interesting structures in computer science:

Example 1 (More Complex Syntax). Given an algebraic theory $A = \langle \Sigma, E \rangle$, the free algebra construction defined by $T_A(X) = T_\Sigma(X)/{\sim_E}$, where $\sim_E$ is the equivalence relation induced by the equations E, is a monad over **Set**.

A many-sorted algebraic theory $A = \langle S, \Sigma, E \rangle$, where S is a set of sorts, gives rise to a monad on the base category **Set**^{S} which is the category of S-indexed families of sets and S-indexed families of functions between them.

Calculi with variable binders such as the λ-calculus, can be modeled as a monad over **Set**$^{\mathcal{F}}$ which is the category of functors from the category $\mathcal{F}$ of finite ordinals and monotone functions between them, into the category **Set** [4].

Example 2 (Term Rewriting Systems). Term rewriting systems (TRSs) arise as monads over the category **Pre** of preorders, while labelled TRSs arise as monads over the category **Cat** of categories [10,11].

Example 3 (Computational Monads). Moggi proposed the use of monads to structure denotational semantics where TX is thought of as the computations over basic values X [13]; see Sect. 5 below.

Example 4 (Infinitary Structures). Final coalgebras have recently become popular as a model for infinitary structures. The term algebra from Def. 2 is the initial algebra of the functor T_Σ, and just as initial algebras form a monad, so do final coalgebras: for the signature Σ, the mapping T_Σ^∞ sending a set X to the set of finite and infinite terms built over X is a monad [5].

From the perspective of modularity, we regard $T(X)$ as an abstraction of a layer. In the examples above, layers are terms, rewrites, or computations; the monad approach allows us to abstract from their particular properties and concentrate on their interaction. Monads provide an abstract calculus for such layers where the actual layer, the empty layers, and the collapsing of two layers of the same type are are taken as primitive concepts.

3   Coproducts of Monads

Recall our aim is to understand the layer structure in modularity problems by understanding the layer structure in the coproduct of monads. The construction of the coproduct of monads is rather complex and so we motivate our general construction by considering a simple case, namely the coproduct of two term algebra monads. Given two signatures Σ, Ω with corresponding term algebra monads $\mathsf{T}_\Sigma, \mathsf{T}_\Omega$, the coproduct $\mathsf{T}_\Sigma + \mathsf{T}_\Omega$ should calculate the terms built over the disjoint union $\Sigma + \Omega$, i.e. $\mathsf{T}_\Sigma + \mathsf{T}_\Omega = \mathsf{T}_{\Sigma+\Omega}$.[1]

Terms in $T_{\Sigma+\Omega}(X)$ have an inherent notion of layer: a term in $T_{\Sigma+\Omega}$ decomposes into a term from T_Σ (or T_Ω), and strictly smaller subterms whose head symbols are from Ω (or Σ). This suggests that we can build the action of the coproduct $T_{\Sigma+\Omega}(X)$ by successively applying the two actions (T_Σ and T_Ω):

$$T_\Sigma + T_\Omega(X) = \begin{aligned} X + T_\Sigma(X) + T_\Omega(X) + T_\Sigma T_\Sigma(X) + T_\Sigma T_\Omega(X) + \\ T_\Omega T_\Sigma(X) + T_\Omega T_\Omega(X) + T_\Sigma T_\Omega T_\Sigma(X) + \dots \end{aligned} \tag{1}$$

Crucially, theories are built over variables, and the instantiation of variables builds layered terms. The quotes of Def. 2 can now be seen as encoding layer information within the syntax. For example, if $\Sigma = \{\texttt{F}, \texttt{G}\}$ then the term $\texttt{G'G'x}$ is an element of $T_\Sigma(T_\Sigma(X))$ and hence has two Σ-layers. This is different from the term $\texttt{GG'x}$ which is an element of $T_\Sigma(X)$ and hence has only one Σ-layer.

Equation (1) is actually too simple. In particular there are different elements of the sum which represent the same element of the coproduct monad, and we therefore need to quotient the sum.

Firstly, consider a variable $x \in X$. Then $x \in X$, $\texttt{'}x \in T_\Sigma(X)$, $\texttt{''}x \in T_\Omega T_\Sigma(X)$. By identifying a layered term with its image under the two units, one can identify these layered terms; we call this the η-quotient.

Secondly, if $\Omega = \{\texttt{H}\}$ is another signature, the layered terms $t_1 = \texttt{GG'x} \in T_\Sigma(X)$ and $t_2 = \texttt{G'G'x} \in T_\Sigma(T_\Sigma(X))$ are both layered versions of $\texttt{GG'x} \in T_{\Sigma+\Omega}(X)$. By identifying a layered term containing a repeated layer with the result of collapsing the layer, one identifies these terms (μ-quotient).

Finally, in all elements of the sum (1), descending from the root to a leaf in any path we pass through the same number of quotes. Thus, layered terms such as $\texttt{F(G'x,'H'x)}$ do not exist in the sum. However, this term is an element of $T_\Sigma(X + T_\Omega(X))$ which indicates that the layer structure of (1) is not the only possible layer structure. In fact, there are a number of different layer structures which we propose, each with uses in different modularity problems.

Summing up, the coproduct monad $\mathsf{T} + \mathsf{R}$ should be constructed pointwise for any set X of variables as a quotient of layered terms. Layered terms are formed solely by constructions over the component monads. This is crucial, as the construction of the coproduct is compositional, and hence properties of T and R can be lifted to $\mathsf{T} + \mathsf{R}$. The equations are essentially given by the unit and multiplication of the components.

For the rest of this paper, we have to make certain technical assumptions about the two monads and the base category (see Appendix A).

---

[1] This relies on the fact that the mapping of signatures to monads preserves the coproduct, which it does because it is a left adjoint.

3.1   Pointed Functors

A functor $S : \mathcal{C} \to \mathcal{C}$ with a natural transformation $\sigma : 1 \Rightarrow S$ is called *pointed*. Every monad is pointed, so taking the coproduct of pointed functors is a first step towards the construction of the coproduct of monads. In the term algebra example, the natural transformation $\eta_T : 1 \Rightarrow T_\Sigma$ models the variables, and the coproduct of two pointed functors S, T should be the functor which for any given set X returns the union of TX and SX with the variables identified. This construction therefore implements the η-quotient from above.

In **Set**, we identify elements of a set by taking the quotient. Thus, for example to share the variables from X in $T_\Sigma(X) + T_\Omega(X)$, we quotient the set by the equivalence relation generated by ${}'x \sim {}'y$ (note how the term on the left is an element of $T_\Sigma(X)$, whereas the term on the right is an element of $T_\Omega(X)$). Categorically, this process is modelled by a *pushout*:

Definition 4 (Pointed Coproduct). *Given two pointed functors $\langle T, \eta_T \rangle$ and $\langle S, \eta_S \rangle$, their coproduct is given by the functor $Q : \mathcal{C} \to \mathcal{C}$ which maps every object X in $\mathcal{C}$ to the colimit in (2) with the obvious extension of Q to morphisms. Q*

$$
\begin{array}{ccc}
X & \xrightarrow{\;\eta_T\;} & TX \\[2pt]
{\scriptstyle \eta_R}\big\downarrow & & \big\downarrow{\scriptstyle \sigma_T} \\[2pt]
RX & \xrightarrow[\;\sigma_R\;]{} & QX
\end{array}
\tag{2}
$$

is pointed with $\sigma : 1 \Rightarrow Q$ given by $\sigma_X = \sigma_R \cdot \eta_R = \sigma_T \cdot \eta_T$.

3.2   Non-collapsing Monads

An algebraic theory $\mathcal{A} = \langle \Sigma, E \rangle$ is non-collapsing if none of the equations has a variable as its left or right-hand side. Generalising this to monads, this means that TX can be decomposed into the variables X and non-variable terms $T_0 X$, i.e. $TX = X + T_0 X$ for some T_0. More succinctly, this decomposition can be written as an equation on functors, i.e. $T = 1 + T_0$.

Definition 5 (Non-Collapsing Monads). *A monad $T = \langle T, \eta, \mu \rangle$ is non-collapsing iff $T = 1 + T_0$, with the unit the inclusion $in_1 : 1 \Rightarrow T$ and the other inclusion written $\alpha_T : T_0 \Rightarrow T$. In addition, there is a natural transformation $\mu_0 : T_0 T \Rightarrow T_0$ such that $\alpha \cdot \mu_0 = \mu \cdot \alpha_T$.*

Given a signature Σ, the term monad T_Σ is non-collapsing, since every term is either a variable or an operation (applied to subterms). More generally, given an algebraic theory $\langle \Sigma, E \rangle$, the representing monad $\mathsf{T}_{\langle \Sigma, E \rangle}$ is non-collapsing iff neither the left or right hand sides of any equation is a variable.

Lemma 1. *In any category, the pushout of the inclusions $in_1 : 1 \Rightarrow 1 + X$ and $in_1 : 1 \Rightarrow 1 + Y$ is $1 + X + Y$. Given two non-collapsing monads $1 + T_0$ and $1 + R_0$, their pointed coproduct is (Q, q) with $Q = 1 + T_0 + R_0$ and $q : 1 \Rightarrow Q$.*

Proof. The first part can be proved by a simple diagram chase. The second part follows since in a non-collapsing monad the units are the inclusions.   □

3.3   Layer Structure 1: Alternating Layers

Our first axiomatisation of layer structure is based upon the idea that, in the coproduct monad, layers alternate between T-layers and R-layers. Since we can decompose the layers of the non-collapsing monads into the variables and the terms, we share the variables between the two monads and only build new non-variable layers on top of other non-variable layers.

Definition 6 (Alternating Layers). *Define the series of functors $A_{T,n}$ and $A_{R,n}$ as follows:*

$$A_{T,0} = 1 \quad A_{T,n+1} = 1 + T_0 A_{R,n} \quad A_{R,0} = 1 \quad A_{R,n+1} = 1 + R_0 A_{T,n}$$

Define natural transformations $a_{T,n} : A_{T,n} \to A_{T,n+1}$ and $a_{R,n} : A_{R,n} \to A_{R,n+1}$

$$a_{T,0} = in_1 \quad a_{T,n+1} = 1 + T_0 a_{R,n} \quad a_{R,0} = in_1 \quad a_{R,n+1} = 1 + R_0 a_{T,n}$$

Finally, define A_R and A_T as the colimits of the chains:

$$A_R = \underset{n<\omega}{colim} \; A_{R,n} \qquad A_T = \underset{n<\omega}{colim} \; A_{T,n}$$

We then have $e_T : 1 \Rightarrow A_T$ and $e_R : 1 \Rightarrow A_R$ defined by the inclusion of $A_{T,0}$ into A_T and A as the pushout:

$$
\begin{array}{ccc}
1 & \overset{e_T}{\longrightarrow} & A_T \\
{\scriptstyle e_R}\downarrow & & \downarrow \\
A_R & \longrightarrow & A
\end{array}
\qquad (3)
$$

The functor $A_{T,n}$ can be thought of as alternating, non-variable layers of depth at most n, starting with a T-layer. Thus $A_{T,n+1} = 1 + T_0 A_{R,n}$ says that an alternating, top T-layer term of depth at most $n + 1$ is either a variable or contains a non-variable layer T_0 on top of an alternating, top R-layer term of depth at most n. A_R and A_T are alternating layers of arbitrary depth, starting with a R and T-layer, respectively. A contains all alternating layers, starting with either R or T, with the variables shared as we saw in the pointed coproduct construction. That A is (isomorphic to) the coproduct is shown in Sect. A.1.

3.4   Layer Construction 2: Quotiented Layers

In certain situations, the alternating layers will not be appropriate as, for example, one may not want to have to explicitly enforce the alternating criteria on layers. An alternative construction starts with the pointed coproduct of monads $1 + T_0$ and $1 + R_0$ given by $Q = 1 + T_0 + R_0$ with $q : 1 \Rightarrow Q$ given by Lemma 1.

Definition 7 (Q-layers). *With (Q,q) given by Lemma 1, let $Q^* = \underset{n<\omega}{colim}\ Q^n$ be the colimit of the ω-chain Q^n with maps $q_n : Q^n \Rightarrow Q^{n+1}$ given by $q_0 = q$ and $q_{n+1} = Q^n q$.*

Of course, Q^* is not the coproduct; it has η-quotienting built in, but no μ-quotienting. For this, we define a map $v^* : Q^*X \to (\mathsf{T}+\mathsf{R})X$ which tells us when two elements of Q^* represent the same element of the coproduct monad, and then we construct normal forms for this equivalence relation. Technically, the map v^* is defined by a family of maps $v_n : Q^n X \to (\mathsf{T}+\mathsf{R})X$ which commute with the q^n (i.e. $v_n \cdot q_n = v_{n-1}$); such a family is called a *cone*. The precise definition of v_n and the quotienting, along with a proof of correctness, can be found in Sect. A.2.

3.5   Layer Structure 3: Non-alternating Layers

A third axiomatisation of layers follows from the observation that every term in the coproduct is either a variable, a T_0-layer over sublayers or an R_0-layer over sublayers. Thus one defines

$$L_0 = 1 \qquad L_{n+1} = 1 + T_0 L_n + R_0 L_n$$

As the arguments are similar to those for the quotiented layers, and with space considerations in mind, we only sketch the details. We define $L^* = \underset{n<\omega}{colim}\ L_n$, and uses the inclusions of T_0 and R_0 into $\mathsf{T}+\mathsf{R}$ to define a natural transformation $w^* : L^* \Rightarrow \mathsf{T}+\mathsf{R}$ which indicates when two layered term represent the same term in the coproduct monad.

We then define a right inverse for w^* by embedding the alternating layers monad into L^*, which allows us to conclude that the quotient of L^* by the kernel of w^* defines the coproduct monad. The right inverse can be used to construct representatives for each equivalence class of the kernel.

3.6   Collapsing Monads

We have given a number three constructions of the coproduct on non-collapsing monads, each with a different layer structure. Kelly [7, Sect. 27] has shown the construction of colimits of monads, from which we can deduce coproducts of arbitrary monads as a special case. The coproduct is constructed pointwise; given two monads $\mathsf{T} = \langle T, \eta_T, \mu_T \rangle$ and $\mathsf{R} = \langle R, \eta_R, \mu_R \rangle$, the coproduct monad $\mathsf{T}+\mathsf{R}$ maps every object X to the colimit of sequence X_β defined as follows:

$$T+R(X) = \underset{\beta<\omega}{colim}\ X_\beta \qquad X_0 = X \qquad X_1 = QX \qquad X_{\beta+1} = colim(D_\beta)$$

where Q, σ_T, σ_R are given by Def. 4, and D_β by the diagram in Fig. 1 with the colimiting morphism $x_\beta : D_\beta \to X_{\beta+1}$ which given the shape of the diagram is a single morphism $x_\beta : QX_\beta \to X_{\beta+1}$ making all arrows in the diagram commute. In principle, D_β defines another layer structure for terms in the coproduct monad but in practice the shape, size and contents of this diagram makes it difficult to reason with directly.

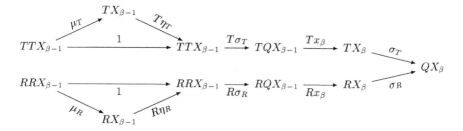

Fig. 1. The diagram defining the coproduct of two monads.

An alternative is to return to the quotiented layers. We can still define a chain Q_n as in Def. 7, together with a map $k^* : Q^n X \to (\mathsf{T} + \mathsf{R})X$; unfortunately, in the absence of the non-collapsing assumption we cannot go further and provide canonical representatives of each equivalence class.

A final, very simple special case is when there is a natural transformation $m : QQ \Rightarrow Q$ which commutes with μ_T and μ_R

$$\sigma_T \cdot \mu_T = m \cdot (\sigma_R * \sigma_R) \qquad \sigma_R \cdot \mu_E = m \cdot (\sigma_R * \sigma_R) \qquad \sigma \cdot m = 1_{QX} \qquad (4)$$

then Q is the coproduct, and m its multiplication.

4 Applications I: Modular Rewriting

In this section, we sketch the application of our analysis to modular term rewriting. The results in this section have been presented elsewhere before [10], but the alternating layer presentation from Sect. 3.3 further simplifies our arguments.

The prerequisite of monadic rewriting is the representation of a TRS as a monad. The action of this monad is given by the term reduction algebra:

Definition 8 (Term Reduction Algebra). *For a term rewriting system* $\mathcal{R} = \langle \Sigma, R \rangle$, *the* term reduction algebra $T_{\mathcal{R}}(X)$ *built over a preorder* X *has as underlying set the term algebra* $T_{\Sigma}(X)$ *and as order the least preorder including all instantiations of rules* $r \in R$ *and the order on* X *such that all operations* $f \in \Sigma$ *are monotone.*

The mapping of X to $T_{\mathcal{R}}(X)$ gives rise to a functor $T_{\mathcal{R}} : \mathbf{Pre} \to \mathbf{Pre}$ on the category of preorders. To make this into a monad, we add unit and multiplication as in the case of signatures (see Sect. 2), except that we further have to show that they are monotone. Since the monadic semantics is *compositional*, i.e. $T_{\mathcal{R}+\mathcal{S}} \cong T_{\mathcal{R}} + T_{\mathcal{S}}$, we can prove properties about the disjoint union of TRSs by proving them for the coproduct monad. Of course we also have to translate properties P of a TRS into an equivalent property P' of monads. The obvious way is to require that the action of the monad preserves P.

Definition 9 (Monadic SN). *A monad* $\mathcal{T} = \langle T, \eta, \mu \rangle$ *on* **Pre** *is strongly normalising iff whenever the irreflexive part of* X *is strongly normalising, then so is the irreflexive part of* TX.

To show that this definition makes sense, we show that a TRS $\mathcal{R}$ is SN iff its representing monad $\mathsf{T}_\mathcal{R}$ is SN in the sense of Def. 9; see [10, Prop. 5.1.5]. We can now prove modularity of strong normalisation for non-collapsing TRS [15]. The main lemma will be that the coproduct of two non-collapsing monads $\mathsf{T}+\mathsf{R}$ is SN if T and R are. For this, recall the alternating layers A from Def. 6.

Lemma 2 (Modularity of SN for non-collapsing monads). *Let* T, R *be non-collapsing, strongly normalising monads, then the monad* $\mathsf{T}+\mathsf{R}$ *is SN.*

Proof. We use the fact that $T + R(X) = AX$, and show that AX is SN. We first show that A_R and A_T are SN, i.e. that if X is SN so is $A_R X$. Since $A_R = \underset{n<\omega}{colim}\ A_{R,n}$ this is done by induction over n: the base case is the assumption; for the inductive step, $A_{R,n}X$ is SN by the induction hypothesis, $T_0 A_{R,n}$ is SN since T_0 preserves SN preorders and hence $A_{T,n+1}X = X + T_0 A_{R,n}$ is SN since the disjoint union of SN preorders is SN. Now, $AX \cong TA_R X$, and since A_R is SN, and by assumption T is SN, so is AX.   □

Proposition 1 (Modularity of Strong Normalisation). *Strong normalisation is modular for non-collapsing term rewriting systems.*

Proof. Given two strongly normalising TRSs $\mathcal{R}$ and $\mathcal{S}$, then $\mathsf{T}_\mathcal{R}$ and $\mathsf{T}_\mathcal{S}$ are SN. By Lemma 2 it follows that AX is SN whenever X is, and since $AX \cong (\mathsf{T}_\mathcal{R} + \mathsf{T}_\mathcal{S})X$, $\mathsf{T}+\mathsf{R}$ is SN. By compositionality, this means that $\mathsf{T}_{\mathcal{R}+\mathcal{S}}$ is SN, and hence $\mathcal{R}+\mathcal{S}$ is SN, as required.   □

The advantage of using monads here is that the main lemma does not talk about term rewriting systems anymore, but about monads. Thus, the theorem applies to any structure which can be modelled by a monad as well, for example if we allow equations as well as rewrite rules.

5   Applications II: Computational Monads

Computational monads [13] provide a categorical framework for expressing computational features independent of the specific computational model we have in mind. The base category provides a basic model of computation, and the computational monad builds additional features, such as exceptions, state and non-determinism:

Example 5 (Exceptions). Let E be an object of $\mathcal{C}$, which are the exceptions. The *exception monad* is given as

$$Ex_E(X) = E + X \qquad \eta_E = in_2 \qquad \mu_E = [in_1, 1]$$

As a second example, consider a monad adding state dependency. In an abstract view, state is just an object $S \in \mathcal{C}$ of our base category:

Example 6 (The State Transformer Monad). Let S be an object of $\mathcal{C}$. The monad $\mathsf{St}_S = \langle St_S, \eta_S, \mu_S \rangle$ is defined as

$$St_S(X) = S \rightarrow S \times X \qquad \eta_{S,X}(x) = \lambda s.x \qquad \mu_{S,X}(c) = \lambda s.\mathit{let} \; \langle f, x \rangle = cs \; \mathit{in} \; f\,x$$

A stateful computation maps a state to a successor state and a value. The multiplication composes two stateful computations by inserting the successor state of the first computation as input into the second. The overall result is the result of the second computation.

Finally, if we have a finite powerset functor $\mathbb{P}_{\mathit{fin}} : \mathcal{C} \rightarrow \mathcal{C}$ in our base category (e.g. if $\mathcal{C} = \mathbf{Set}$), then we can incorporate non-determinism to our set of models:

Example 7 (The non-determinism monad). The monad $\mathsf{P} = \langle \mathbb{P}_{\mathit{fin}}, \eta_P, \mu_P \rangle$ has the finite powerset functor as its action, with the unit and multiplication defined as follows:

$$\eta_P(X) = \{X\} \qquad \mu_P(X) = \cup_{X_0 \in X} X_0$$

The exception monad does not build any new layers, it only adds constants. Thus, exceptions only ever occur in the lowest layer:

Lemma 3. *The coproduct of Ex_E with any monad $R = \langle R, \eta_R, \mu_R \rangle$ is given by*

$$SX = R(E + X)$$

The proof of Lemma+3 can be found in the appendix (Sect. A.3). Lemma 3 allows us to combine exceptions with statefulness, leading to $Ex_E + St_S = (S \rightarrow S \times (X + E))$, and with non-determinism, resulting in $\mathbb{P}_{\mathit{fin}} + Ex_E = \mathbb{P}_{\mathit{fin}}(X + E)$. Further, we can combine non-determinism with stateful computations. One might think that the action of the combination would be $Q(X) = S \rightarrow (S \times \mathbb{P}_{\mathit{fin}}X)$, but this is slightly wrong, since it does not allow non-deterministic computations not depending on the state S; the correct action is given by first calculating $Q(X) = (S \rightarrow S \times X) + \mathbb{P}_{\mathit{fin}}X/\sim$ where $\lambda s.\langle s, X \rangle \sim \{X\}$. In other words, every computation is either stateful or non-deterministic. In the coproduct, this is closed under composition, i.e. the computations are interleaved sequences of stateful and non-deterministic computations (appropriately quotiented).

The combination of computational monads has been investigated before, but mainly for special cases [6,8]. Monad transformers have been suggested as a means to combine monads [14,9], but they serve as an organisational tool rather than a general semantic construction like the coproduct described here.

6   Applications III: Haskell

Monads are used extensively in Haskell, which provides the built-in monad `IO a` as well as user-defined ones. The Haskell types are our objects, and the terms our morphisms. Thus, a type constructor t forms a *functor* if for any function `f::a->`

b there is a function fmap :: t a-> t b, and it is a *monad* if additionally
there are functions eta :: a -> t a and mu :: t (t a) -> t a for all types
a. These overloaded functions are handled by type classes. Building upon the
class Functor from Haskell's standard prelude [1, Appx. A], we define

```
class Functor t=> Triple t where
   eta  :: a-> t a
   mu   :: t (t a) -> t a
```

The monad laws cannot be expressed within Haskell, so the tacit assumption
is that they are verified externally. In the implementation of the coproduct,
we face the difficulty that Haskell does not allow us to write down equations
on types. Hence, we representing the equivalence classes, making eta and mu
operate directly on the representatives, which are modelled as follows:

```
data Plus t1 t2 a = T1 (t1 (Plus t1 t2 a))  -- top-T1 layer
                  | T2 (t2 (Plus t1 t2 a))  -- top-T2 layer
                  | Var a                   -- a mere variable
```

Note how this datatype corresponds to the functor L^* from Sect. 3.5. We have
to make the type constructor Plus t1 t2 into a monad by first making it into a
functor, and then giving the unit and multiplication. For this, we implement the
decision procedure mentioned in Sect. 3.5. Essentially, we recursively collapse
adjacent layers wherever possible:

```
instance (Triple t1, Triple t2)=> Triple (Plus t1 t2) where
   eta x       = Var x
   mu (Var t) = t
   mu (T1 t)  = T1 (mu (fmap lift1 (fmap mu t))) where
     lift1 :: Plus t1 t2 x-> t1 (Plus t1 t2 x)
     lift1 (T1 t) = t
     lift1 t      = eta t
   mu (T2 t)  = ... -- analogous to mu (T1 t)
```

Finally, we need the two injections into the coproduct; we only show one:

```
inl :: Triple t1=> t1 a-> Plus t1 t2 a
inl t = T1 (fmap Var t)
```

We can now implement exceptions, state and so on as monads, and compose
their computations in the coproduct. This is different from using the built-in IO
monad, since the type of an expression will be contain precisely those monads
the computational features of which are used in this expression.

Technically, monads as implemented by Haskell (in particular the monad
IO) define a monad by its *Kleisli-category* [12, Sect. VI.5], hence our own type
class Triple above, rather than the standard Monad. One can easily adapt our
construction to cover this case. Note that the code above requires extensions to
the Haskell 98 standard, such as multi-parameter type classes.

7   Conclusion

The basic hypothesis of this paper has been that when we combine different formal systems, be they algebraic theories, models of computations, or programs, their interaction can be described in terms of their *layers*. We have given an abstract characterisation of layers by monads, and shown how the combination of different monads can be modelled by the coproduct.

We have complimented the general construction of the colimit of monads with alternative, specialised constructions. In particular, we have constructed the coproduct monad based on alternating layers, quotiented layers and non-alternating layers, and employed these constructions for modular term rewriting, modular denotational semantics, and modular functional programming.

Obviously, this work is just the beginning. What needs to be done is to extend our construction to cover e.g. non-collapsing monads, to augment the applications (in particular with regards to Haskell) and to investigate in how far other applications can be covered by our methodology.

References

1. Haskell 98: A non-strict, purely functional language. Available at http://www.haskell.org, January 1999.
2. J. Adamek and J. Rosický. *Locally Presentable and Accessible Categories*. LMS Lecture Notes 189, Cambridge University Press, 1994.
3. E. J. Dubuc and G. M. Kelly. A presentation of topoi as algebraic relative to categories or graphs. *Journal for Algebra*, 81:420–433, 1983.
4. M. Fiore, G. Plotkin, and D. Turi. Abstract syntax and variable binding. In *Proc. LICS'99*, pages 193–202. IEEE Computer Society Press, 1999.
5. N. Ghani, C. Lüth, F. de Marchi, and J. Power. Algebras, coalgebras, monads and comonads. Proc. CMCS'01, *ENTCS* 44:1, 2001.
6. M. Jones and L. Duponcheel. Composing monads. Technical Report YALEU/DCS/RR-1004, Yale University, Dept. Comp. Sci, Dec 1993.
7. G. M. Kelly. A unified treatment of transfinite constructions for free algebras, free monoids, colimits, associated sheaves and so on. *Bulletins of the Australian Mathematical Society*, 22:1–83, 1980.
8. D. King and P. Wadler. Combining monads. In J. Launchbury and P.M. Samson, editors, *Functional Programming*, Workshops in Computing, 1993.
9. S. Liang, P. Hudak, and M. Jones. Monad transformers and modular interpreters. In *Proc. of the 22nd ACM Symposium on Principles of Programming Languages*. ACM Press, Jan 1995.
10. C. Lüth. *Categorical Term Rewriting: Monads and Modularity*. PhD thesis, University of Edinburgh, 1998.
11. C. Lüth and N. Ghani. Monads and modular term rewriting. In *CTCS'97*, LNAI 1290, pages 69–86. Springer, Sep 1997.
12. S. Mac Lane. *Categories for the Working Mathematician, Graduate Texts in Mathematics* 5. Springer, 1971.
13. E. Moggi. Computational lambda-calculus and monads. In *Proc. LICS'89*. IEEE, Computer Society Press, June 1989.

14. E. Moggi. An abstract view of programming languages. Technical Report ECS-LFCS-90-113, LFCS, 1990.
15. M. Rusinowitch. On the termination of the direct sum of term-rewriting systems. *Information Processing Letters*, 26(2):65–70, 1987.
16. D. T. Sannella and R. M. Burstall. Structured theories in LCF. In 8th *Colloquium on Trees in Algebra and Programming*, LNAI 159, pages 377– 391. Springer, 1983.
17. D. T. Sannella and A. Tarlecki. Specifications in an arbitrary institution. *Information and Computation*, 76(2/3):165–210, Feb/Mar 1988.

A   Correctness Proofs

As blanket assumptions, we assume that the base category is locally finitely presentable (lfp) [2], which in particular means it has all colimits, and that the monads in question are finitary.

If we claim that a construction defines the coproduct monad, how can we to prove this? The answer is that just as one can understand an algebraic theory through its models, one can understand a monad through its *algebras*:

Definition 10 (Algebras for a monad). *An algebra* (X, h) *for a monad* $T = \langle T, \eta, \mu \rangle$ *on a category* C *is given by an object* X *in* C, *and a morphism* $h : TX \to X$ *which commutes with the unit and multiplication of the monad, i.e.* $\eta_X = h \cdot \eta_{TX}$ *and* $h \cdot \mu_X = h \cdot Th$.

The category of algebras for T *and morphisms between them is called* $T-\textbf{Alg}$.

We think of a T-algebra (X, h) as being a model with carrier X. The map h ensures that if one builds terms over a such a model, then these terms can be reinterpreted within the model. This is exactly what one is doing in the term algebra case where one assigns to every function symbol f of arity n an interpretation $[\![f]\!] : X^n \to X$. Since monads construct free algebras, we can prove a functor to be equal to a monad if we can prove that the functor constructs free algebras. In particular, we can prove a functor to be the coproduct monad if we can prove it constructs free $T + R$-algebras which are defined as follows:

Definition 11 (T+R-algebras). *The category* $T+R\text{-}\textbf{Alg}$ *has as objects triples* (A, h_t, h_r) *where* (A, h_t) *is a* T-algebra *and* (A, h_r) *is an* R-algebra. *A morphism from* (A, h_t, h_r) *to* (A', h'_t, h'_r) *consists of a map* $f : A \to A'$ *which commutes with the* T *and* R-algebra structures on A and A'.

There is an obvious forgetful functor $U : T+R\text{-}\textbf{Alg} \to C$, which takes a $T + R$-algebra to its underlying object, and we have the following:

Proposition 2 ([7, Propn. 26.4]). *If the forgetful functor* $U : T+R\text{-}\textbf{Alg} \to C$ *functor has a left adjoint* $F : C \to T+R\text{-}\textbf{Alg}$, *i.e. if for every object in* C *there is a free* $T + R$-algebra, *then the monad resulting from this adjunction is the coproduct of* T *and* R.

Thus to show that a functor S is the coproduct $T + R$, we can show that for every object X, SX is a $T+R$-algebra and, moreover, it is the free $T+R$-algebra.

A.1   Correctness of the Alternating Layer Construction

Lemma 4. *We have the following isomorphisms:*

$$A_T \cong 1 + T_0 A_R, \qquad A_R \cong 1 + R_0 A_T \tag{5}$$

$$A \cong T A_R, \qquad A \cong R A_T \tag{6}$$

Proof. Isomorphism (5) is shown as follows:

$$A_T = \underset{n<\omega}{colim}\ A_{T,n} = \underset{n<\omega}{colim}\ 1 + T_0 A_{R,n-1}$$
$$\cong 1 + \underset{n<\omega}{colim}\ T_0 A_{R,n-1} \cong 1 + T_0 \underset{n<\omega}{colim}\ A_{R,n-1} = 1 + T_0 A_R Q Q$$

Here, we use interchange of colimits (in the second line) and the fact that T_0 is finitary (which means it preserves colimits of chains).

Since $T A_R = A_R + T_0 A_R$, isomorphism (6) is proven by showing that $A_R + T_0 A_R$ is the pushout of diagram (3). The morphism $A_R \to A_R + T_0 A_R$ is given by the left inclusion; the morphism $m : A_T \to A_R + T_0 A_R$ is given by $e_R + 1$, since by (5) $A_T = 1 + T_0 A_R$. The diagram commutes since e_T is the inclusion $1 \to A_T = 1 + T_0 A_R$. Given any other X and morphisms $g : A_T \to X$, $f : A_R \to X$, we have a unique morphism $!_{f,g} : A_R + T_0 A_R$ given by $!_{f,g} = [f, g_2]$, where g_2 is g on $T_0 A_R$.   □

We will now prove that A is the coproduct $\mathsf{T} + \mathsf{R}$, using Proposition 2, by showing that A is the free $\mathsf{T} + \mathsf{R}$-algebra.

Lemma 5 (A is a $\mathsf{T} + \mathsf{R}$-algebra). *For any $X \in \mathcal{C}$, AX is a $\mathsf{T} + \mathsf{R}$-algebra.*

Proof. We have to show that there are morphism $h_t^A : T A X \to A X$ and $h_r^A : R A X \to A X$ which satisfy the equations from Def. 10. By (6), we may define h_t^A as

$$T A X \quad = \quad T T A_R X \xrightarrow{\mu_{T,A_R X}} T A_R X \quad = \quad A X$$

and similarly, set $h_r^A = \mu_R$. That h_t^A and h_r^A commute with the unit and multiplication of T and R respectively is easy.   □

Lemma 6 (A is the free $\mathsf{T} + \mathsf{R}$-algebra). *The functor $\mathcal{A} : \mathcal{C} \to \mathsf{T}+\mathsf{R}$-**Alg**, mapping X to (AX, h_t^A, h_r^A), is a left adjoint to $U : \mathsf{T}+\mathsf{R}$-**Alg** $\to \mathcal{C}$.*

Proof. We prove that $e_{A,X} : X \to A X$ is universal to U. That is, given any other $T + R$-algebra (Y, h_t, h_r) and map $f : X \to Y$ in $\mathcal{C}$, there is a unique $T + R$ algebra morphism $f^* : (AX, h_t^A, h_r^A) \to (Y, h_t, h_r)$ such that $U(f^*) \cdot e_{A,X} = f$.

To define a map $f^* : A X \to Y$, it suffices to define maps $f_T : A_T X \to Y$ and $f_R : A_R X \to Y$ such that $f_R \cdot e_R = f_T \cdot e_T$. With $A_T X$ the colimit of $A_{T,n}$, this means f_T is given by a cone $f_{T,n} : A_{T,n} \to Y$ for $n < \omega$. Setting $f_{T,0} = f$ and, with $A_{T,n+1} X = X + T_0 A_{R,n}$, we set $f_{T,n+1} = [f, h_{t,0} \cdot T_0 f_{R,n}]$ where $h_{t,0}$ is the restriction of h to $T_0 Y$. That f_T and f_R are cones is proven by induction while they both clearly equal to f when restricted along e_T and e_R. Thus f^* is well defined. That f^* is an algebra morphism is a routine inductive argument using the fact that h_t and h_r commute with μ_T and μ_R. Finally the equation $f^* \cdot e_{A,X} = f$ has already been commented upon while uniqueness of f^* follows by the uniqueness property of mediating morphisms out of the pushout.   □

A.2   Correctness Proofs for the Quotiented Layers

First note we can define a map $v : QX \to (\mathsf{T} + \mathsf{R})X$ by sending TX to its inclusion in $(\mathsf{T}+\mathsf{R})X$ and similarly for RX. Now to define $v_n : Q^n X \to (\mathsf{T}+\mathsf{R})X$ by $v_n = \mu^n_{T+R} \cdot v^n$ where μ^n_{T+R} is the n-fold iteration of multiplication in the coproduct and v^n is the n-fold iteration of v. This clearly forms a cone and hence gives a map $v^* : Q^* X \to (\mathsf{T} + \mathsf{R})X$.

We claim that the quotient of Q^* by the kernel of v^* is the coproduct $\mathsf{T} + \mathsf{R}$. We have already mapped Q^* into $\mathsf{T} + \mathsf{R}$ via v^*. Now we embedd $\mathsf{T}+\mathsf{R}$ in Q^* via A which we have already seen to be $\mathsf{T} + \mathsf{R}$. This embedding effectively decides the kernel of v^*.

First we define maps $s_{T,n} : A_{T,n} \Rightarrow Q^n$ and $s_{R,n} : A_{R,n} \Rightarrow Q^n$ by setting $s_{T,0} = s_{R,0} = 1$ and $s_{T,n+1}$ by

$$A_{T,n+1} = 1 + T_0 A_{R,n} \xrightarrow{[in_1 \cdot q^n, \; in_2 \cdot T_0(s_{R,n})]} Q^n + T_0 Q^n + R_0 Q^n = Q^{n+1}$$

That these maps form cones is easily verified and hence we get a map $s : A \Rightarrow Q^*$. By unwinding these definitions, we obtain $v^* \cdot s = 1$.

Lemma 7. *The quotient of Q^* by the kernel of v^* defines the coproduct monad. Each equivalence class of this quotient has a canonical representative.*

Proof. The existence of s means that v^* is a split epimorphism and hence the quotient of Q^* by the kernel of v^* is the codomain of v^* and hence is $\mathsf{T} + \mathsf{R}$. If $t \in Q^*$, then we define its representative to be $s(v^*(t))$. Thus t is related to u in the kernel of v^* iff $v^*(t) = v^*(u)$ which implies that $s(v^*(t)) = s(v^*(u))$, ie they have the same representative. □

A.3   Proof of Lemma 3

By Prop. 2, it is sufficient to show that SX is the free $Ex_E + \mathsf{R}$-algebra.

Showing that SX is an R-algebra is simple, with the structure map given by μ_R. The structure map $[1, \alpha] : ESX \to SX$ making SX into an Ex_E-algebra is given by $\alpha = Rin_1 \cdot \eta_R$.

The unit of the adjunction is given by $\eta_S = Rin_2 \cdot \eta_R$. To show it is universality from U, assume there is a $R + E$-algebra Y with $\delta : E \to Y$ and $\beta : RY \to Y$, and a morphism $f : X \to Y$. Then we define $!_f : R(E + X) \to Y$, defined as $!_f = \beta \cdot R[\delta, f]$. A simple diagram chase shows that $!_f \cdot \eta_X = f$. □

A Modular Approach to Proving Confluence

Michael Marte[*]

Institut für Informatik, Universität München
Oettingenstr. 67, 80538 München, Germany
`marte@informatik.uni-muenchen.de`

Abstract. We are interested in investigating the confluence properties of cooperating constraint solvers. To this end, we model solvers as reductions that transform constraint networks, we define the notion of *insensitivity* to a superset relation, and show that, if each solver of a given set of solvers is *insensitive* to the same terminating superset relation, then any combination of these solvers is confluent. By means of this modular approach, we study the relationship between confluence and maintaining certain levels of local consistency and we demonstrate the confluence of a solver for a global finite-domain constraint that consists of several reductions.

1 Introduction

We are interested in investigating the confluence properties of cooperating constraint solvers. If a system of constraint solvers is confluent, then the result of constraint propagation does not depend on how the solvers are scheduled. If it is either known to diverge or if its neither known to be confluent nor to diverge, then the question arises which scheduling strategy will perform best. This is inconvenient in application development as it potentially adds another dimension to the design space.

To establish confluence properties, we model solvers as reductions that transform constraint networks, we define the notion of *insensitivity* to a superset relation, and show that, if each solver of a given set of solvers is *insensitive* to the same terminating superset relation, then any combination of these solvers is confluent.

As a first application of our approach, we study the relationship between confluence and maintaining certain levels of local consistency. In particular, we investigate domain and interval consistency as defined by van Hentenryck et al. [6] in the context of finite-domain constraint solving. It turns out that any combination of solvers where each solver maintains either level of local consistency is confluent.

Second, we apply our approach to a solver for a global finite-domain constraint that has been designed to model and solve track parallelization problems. This kind of problem occurs in school timetabling and consists in parallelizing

---

[*] This work was supported by the German Research Council (DFG).

A. Armando (Ed.): FroCoS 2002, LNAI 2309, pp. 33–48, 2002.

the execution of task sets [4]. The solver consists of several reductions and we demonstrate its confluence and the confluence of any subset of its reductions with a number of proofs linear in the number of reductions.

This paper is organized as follows. Section 2 introduces some terminology. Section 3 introduces the concept of insensitivity and relates it to the concept of strong commutation. Section 4 presents our method for proving confluence. In Section 5, we provide a reduction system that captures the process of solving finite-domain constraints. Section 6 studies the relationship between local consistency and confluence. In Section 7, we present our solver for track parallelization and investigate its confluence properties. In Section 8, we present related work and compare to it. Section 9 summarizes and closes with perspectives for future work. Proofs that have been left out for reasons of space are given in [5].

2   Preliminaries

A *reduction system* is a pair $(A, \rightarrow)$ where A is a set and $\rightarrow \subseteq A \times A$. $\rightarrow^=$ denotes the reflexive closure of $\rightarrow$. $\rightarrow^+$ denotes the transitive closure of $\rightarrow$. $\rightarrow^*$ denotes the reflexive transitive closure of $\rightarrow$. x is called *reducible* iff $\exists y. \; x \rightarrow y$. x is called *in normal form (irreducible)* iff it is not reducible. y is called *a normal form of* x iff $x \rightarrow^* y$ and y is in normal form. We say that y is a *direct successor* of x iff $x \rightarrow y$. We say that y is a *successor* of x iff $x \rightarrow^+ y$. $x, y \in A$ are called *joinable* iff $\exists z. \; x \rightarrow^* z \leftarrow^* y$. We write $x \downarrow y$ to denote that x and y are joinable. $\rightarrow$ is called *terminating* iff there is no chain $a_0 \rightarrow a_1 \rightarrow \ldots$ that descends infinitely. It is called *confluent* iff $y \leftarrow^* x \rightarrow^* z$ implies $y \downarrow z$. It is called *locally confluent* iff $y \leftarrow x \rightarrow z$ implies $y \downarrow z$. It is called *convergent* iff it is terminating and confluent. Let $(A, \rightarrow_1)$ and $(A, \rightarrow_2)$ be reduction systems. We say that $\rightarrow_1$ and $\rightarrow_2$ *commute* iff $y \leftarrow_1^* x \rightarrow_2^* z$ implies $\exists u. \; y \rightarrow_2^* u \leftarrow_1^* z$. We say that $\rightarrow_1$ and $\rightarrow_2$ *commute strongly* iff $y \leftarrow_1 x \rightarrow_2 z$ implies $\exists u. \; y \rightarrow_2^= u \leftarrow_1^* z$.

3   Insensitivity

Intuitively, $\rightarrow_1$ is insensitive to $\rightarrow_2$, if the inference capabilities of $\rightarrow_1$ are preserved under application of $\rightarrow_2$.

Definition 1. *Let $(A, \rightarrow_1)$ and $(A, \rightarrow_2)$ be reduction systems. We say that $\rightarrow_1$ is insensitive to $\rightarrow_2$ iff the following requirements are satisfied.*

1. *If $y \leftarrow_1 x \rightarrow_2 z$, $y \neq z$, and $z \rightarrow_2 y$, then $z \rightarrow_1 y$.*

2. If $y \leftarrow_1 x \rightarrow_2 z$, $y \neq z$, $y \not\rightarrow_2 z$, and $z \not\rightarrow_2 y$, then $u \in A$ exists s.t.
$y \rightarrow_2 u \leftarrow_1 z$.

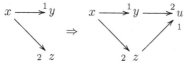

Corollary 1. If $\rightarrow_1$ and $\rightarrow_2$ are insensitive to $\rightarrow_3$, then $\rightarrow_1 \cup \rightarrow_2$ is insensitive to $\rightarrow_3$.

Corollary 2. Let $(A, \rightarrow)$ be a reduction system. If $\rightarrow$ is insensitive to itself, then it is locally confluent.

The following propositions show that the concepts of insensitivity and strong commutation are related but not equivalent.

Proposition 1. Let $(A, \rightarrow_1)$ and $(A, \rightarrow_2)$ be reduction systems. If $\rightarrow_1$ is insensitive to $\rightarrow_2$, then $\rightarrow_1$ and $\rightarrow_2$ commute strongly.

Proof. We have to show that $y \leftarrow_1 x \rightarrow_2 z$ implies $\exists u.\ y \rightarrow_2^= u \leftarrow_1^* z$. If $y = z$, we are done. Otherwise, there are three cases. If $y \rightarrow_2 z$, we are done. If $z \rightarrow_2 y$, then $z \rightarrow_1 y$ because $\rightarrow_1$ is insensitive to $\rightarrow_2$. If neither $y \rightarrow_2 z$ nor $z \rightarrow_2 y$, then $u \in A$ exists s.t. $y \rightarrow_2 u \leftarrow_1 z$ because $\rightarrow_1$ is insensitive to $\rightarrow_2$.   □

Proposition 2. Let $(A, \rightarrow_2)$ be a reduction system and let $\rightarrow_1 \subseteq \rightarrow_2$ be a transitive reduction s.t. $\rightarrow_1$ and $\rightarrow_2$ commute strongly. If $y \leftarrow_1 x \rightarrow_2 z$, $y \neq z$, $y \not\rightarrow_2 z$, and $z \not\rightarrow_2 y$, then $u \in A$ exists s.t. $y \rightarrow_2 u \leftarrow_1 z$.

Proof. By strong commutation, we know that $u \in A$ exists s.t. $y \rightarrow_2^= u \leftarrow_1^* z$. Suppose $u = z$. Then $y \rightarrow_2^= z$. Because $y \neq z$, $y \rightarrow_2 z$. This contradicts the premise and thus $z \rightarrow_1^+ u$. Because $\rightarrow_1$ is transitive, $z \rightarrow_1 u$. Suppose $u = y$. Then $z \rightarrow_1 y$ and thus $z \rightarrow_2 y$ because $\rightarrow_1 \subseteq \rightarrow_2$. This contradicts the premise and thus $y \rightarrow_2 u$.   □

4   Confluence through Insensitivity

Theorem 1. Let $(A, \rightarrow_2)$ be a terminating reduction system. If $\rightarrow_1 \subseteq \rightarrow_2$ is insensitive to $\rightarrow_2$, then $\rightarrow_1$ is locally confluent.

Proof. For each pair $(y, z) \in A \times A$ s.t. $\exists x.\ y \leftarrow_1 x \rightarrow_2 z$, $\exists x.\ y \leftarrow_2 x \rightarrow_1 z$, $y \neq z$, $y \not\rightarrow_2 z$, and $z \not\rightarrow_2 y$, choose a pair $(\hat{y}, \hat{z}) \in A \times A$ s.t. $y \rightarrow_2 \hat{y} \leftarrow_1 z$ and $z \rightarrow_2 \hat{z} \leftarrow_1 y$. This is possible because $\rightarrow_1$ is insensitive to $\rightarrow_2$.

Let $(x_2, y_2) \prec (x_1, y_1)$ iff $x_1 \rightarrow_2 x_2$. $\prec$ is well-founded because $\rightarrow_2$ is terminating. By well-founded recursion on $\prec$, we define $s(y, z)$ for all (y, z) that satisfy $\exists x.\ y \leftarrow_1 x \rightarrow_2 z$ and $\exists x.\ y \leftarrow_2 x \rightarrow_1 z$:

$$s(y, z) = \begin{cases} (y, z), & \text{if } y = z,\ y \rightarrow_2 z,\ \text{or } z \rightarrow_2 y \\ (y, z), s(\hat{y}, \hat{z}) & \text{otherwise} \end{cases}$$

In the second case, $s(\hat{y}, \hat{z})$ is well-defined because $(\hat{y}, \hat{z})$ exists, $\hat{y} \leftarrow_1 z \rightarrow_2 \hat{z}$, and $\hat{y} \leftarrow_2 y \rightarrow_1 \hat{z}$. Since s is defined by well-founded recursion on $\prec$, $s(y, z)$ is finite for all (y, z) that s is defined for.

Let $y_1 \leftarrow_1 x \rightarrow_1 z_1$. $s(y_1, z_1)$ is well-defined because $\rightarrow_1 \subseteq \rightarrow_2$ and thus $y_1 \leftarrow_1 x \rightarrow_2 z_1$ and $y_1 \leftarrow_2 x \rightarrow_1 z_1$. Let $n > 0$ s.t. $s(y_1, z_1) = (y_1, z_1), \ldots, (y_n, z_n)$. We observe that, for all $1 \le k < n$, $y_k \rightarrow_2 y_{k+1} \leftarrow_1 z_k$ and $z_k \rightarrow_2 z_{k+1} \leftarrow_1 y_k$, and that $y_n = z_n$, $y_n \rightarrow_2 z_n$, or $y_n \leftarrow_2 z_n$. The following figure shows a situation where $n \ge 5$.

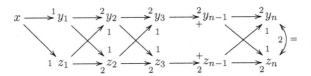

It remains to show that $y_1 \downarrow_1 z_1$. If n is odd, then $y_1 \rightarrow_1^* y_n$ and $z_1 \rightarrow_1^* z_n$. If n is even, then $y_1 \rightarrow_1^* z_n$ and $z_1 \rightarrow_1^* y_n$. If $y_n = z_n$, we are done. If $y_n \rightarrow_2 z_n$, then $y_n \rightarrow_1 z_n$ because $y_n \leftarrow_2 y_{n-1} \rightarrow_1 z_n$ and $\rightarrow_1$ is insensitive to $\rightarrow_2$. If $z_n \rightarrow_2 y_n$, then $z_n \rightarrow_1 y_n$ because $z_n \leftarrow_2 z_{n-1} \rightarrow_1 y_n$ and $\rightarrow_1$ is insensitive to $\rightarrow_2$.   □

The following result is obtained by applying Newman's Lemma. Newman's Lemma states that a terminating reduction is confluent iff it is locally confluent.

Corollary 3. *Let $(A, \rightarrow_2)$ be a terminating reduction system. If $\rightarrow_1 \subseteq \rightarrow_2$ is insensitive to $\rightarrow_2$, then $\rightarrow_1$ is confluent.*

5   A Model of Finite-Domain Constraint Solving

To apply our method to finite-domain (FD) constraint solvers, it is necessary to provide a reduction system that captures the process of solving FD constraints. We use a reduction system where reduction steps transform finite constraint networks by pruning values from domains. Neither the addition nor the removal of variables and constraints is supported.

On the conceptual level, a *finite constraint network* (FCN) is a finite (hyper-)graph with variables as nodes and constraints as (hyper-)arcs. Given a FCN, the corresponding *finite constraint satisfaction problem* (FCSP) consists in finding a variable valuation that satisfies all the constraints. We will not distinguish between a FCN and its FCSP.

Let P be a FCSP with variables X and constraints C. We assume that there is a unary constraint for each variable that specifies its set of admissible values. P will be represented by a triple (X, δ, C) where δ is a total function on X (the *domain function* of P) that associates each variable with its set of admissible values (its *domain*). We say that P is *ground* iff all its variables have singleton domains. We say that P is *failed* iff at least one of its variables has an empty domain. We use scope(P) and store(P) to denote the variables and constraints of P, respectively. If c is a constraint, scope(c) denotes the set of variables constrained by c.

Frequently, we will refer to domain functions that have not been declared explicitly. However, in such a case, there will a FCSP the domain function belongs to according to the following naming scheme: If P, P_i, R, R_i, Γ, and Σ denote FCSPs, then δ, δ_i, ρ, ρ_i, γ, and σ are their respective domain functions.

We will consider FCSPs with integer domains only. If a and b are integers, we write $[a, b]$ to denote the set of integers i with $a \leq i \leq b$.

Definition 2. *Let $P_0 = (X_0, \delta_0, C_0)$ and $P_1 = (X_1, \delta_1, C_1)$ be FCSPs.*

1. $P_0 \to_{FD} P_1$ *iff* $X_1 = X_0$, $C_1 = C_0$, $\delta_1 \neq \delta_0$, *and* $\delta_1(x) \subseteq \delta_0(x)$ *for all* $x \in X$.

2. $P_1 \in gs(P_0)$ *(P_1 is a ground successor of P_0) iff* $P_0 \to_{FD} P_1$ *and* P_1 *is ground.*

3. $P_1 \in sol(P_0)$ *(P_1 solves P_0) iff* $P_1 \in gs(P_0)$ *and* δ_1 *simultaneously satisfies all* $c \in C$.

4. $P_0 \equiv P_1$ *(P_0 and P_1 are equivalent) iff* $sol(P_0) = sol(P_1)$.

Corollary 4. $\to_{FD}$ *is strict and convergent.*

Corollary 5. *Let* $P_0 = (X, \delta_0, C) \to_{FD} P_1$.

1. *Lower (Upper) bounds of domains grow (shrink) monotonically, i.e.*
   $\min \delta_0(x) \leq \min \delta_1(x) \leq \max \delta_1(x) \leq \max \delta_0(x)$ *for all* $x \in X$.

2. *Sets of ground successors shrink monotonically, i.e.* $gs(P_0) \supseteq gs(P_1)$.

3. *Solution sets shrink monotonically, i.e.* $sol(P_0) \supseteq sol(P_1)$.

Definition 3. $\to_r \subseteq \to_{FD}$ *is called correct iff, for all* $P_0 \to_r P_1$, $P_0 \equiv P_1$.

Definition 4. $\to_C = \bigcup \{\to_r \subseteq \to_{FD} : \to_r \text{ is correct}\}$

$\to_{FD}$ allows for arbitrary domain reductions while $\to_C \subseteq \to_{FD}$ only allows for domain reductions that preserve solutions.

Corollary 6. $\to_C$ *is terminating and correct.*

Lemma 1. *Let* $P_0 = (X, \delta_0, C) \to_{FD} P_1$ *and* $Y = \{y_1, \ldots, y_n\} \subseteq X$ *s.t.* $\delta_1(x) = \delta_0(x)$ *for all* $x \in X - Y$.

1. *If* $P_0 \to_{FD} P_2 \to_{FD} P_1$, *then*

$$\delta_1(y_1) \times \ldots \times \delta_1(y_n) \subset \delta_2(y_1) \times \ldots \times \delta_2(y_n) \subset \delta_0(y_1) \times \ldots \times \delta_0(y_n).$$

2. *If* $P_0 \to_{FD} P_2$, $P_1 \not\to_{FD} P_2$, $P_2 \not\to_{FD} P_1$, *and* $P_1 \neq P_2$, *then*

$$\delta_2(y_1) \times \ldots \times \delta_2(y_n) \not\subseteq \delta_1(y_1) \times \ldots \times \delta_1(y_n).$$

Lemma 2. *If* $P_0 \to_C P_1$ *and* $P_0 \to_{FD}^{=} P_2 \to_{FD}^{=} P_1$, *then* $sol(P_0) = sol(P_2) = sol(P_1)$.

6   Insensitivity through Local Consistency

Suppose a constraint solver is known to maintain a certain level of local consistency. Then we have a performance guarantee: Whatever input state the solver is applied to, the output state will satisfy an invariant specific to the level of local consistency considered. The question arises whether this specific guarantee entails insensitivity to some suitable superset relation.

In particular, we consider domain and interval consistency [6] as both notions are important in FD constraint solving. Indeed, as we show in the following, if a solver maintains domain or interval consistency, then it is insensitive to $\to_{FD}$. In consequence, any combination of solvers where each solver maintains either level of local consistency is confluent.

6.1   Domain Consistency

Suppose $P = (X, \delta, C)$ is a FCSP and $c(x_1, \dots, x_n) \in C$. According to van Hentenryck et al. [6], c is *domain-consistent*, if, for each variable x_i and for each value $v_i \in \delta(x_i)$, there exist values $v_1, \dots, v_{i-1}, v_{i+1}, \dots, v_n$ in $\delta(x_1), \dots, \delta(x_{i-1})$, $\delta(x_{i+1}), \dots, \delta(x_n)$ s.t. $c(v_1, \dots, v_n)$ holds.

Suppose c is a constraint. For each $x \in \text{scope}(c)$, we define the transition $\to_{DC(c,x)}$ (cf. Definition 5). This transition eliminates exactly those values from the domain of x that do not have support according to the definition of c. To be more precise, if $P_0 \to_{DC(c,x)} P_1$, then $\delta_1(x) \subset \delta_0(x)$, each value in $\delta_1(x)$ occurs in a solution to the relaxation $P_0|_{\{c\}} = (X, \delta_0, \{c\})$ of P_0, and no predecessor of P_1 wrt. $\to_{FD}$ satisfies these conditions. We proceed by showing that $\to_{DC(c,x)}$ is correct and insensitive to $\to_{FD}$. In consequence, $\to_{DC(c)} = \bigcup_{x \in \text{scope}(c)} \to_{DC(c,x)}$ is correct and insensitive to $\to_{FD}$. Quite obviously, $\to_{DC(c)}$ maintains domain consistency for c.

Corollary 7. *If $P_0 \to_{FD} P_1$ and $c \in \text{store}(P_0)$, then $P_0|_{\{c\}} \to_{FD} P_1|_{\{c\}}$.*

Definition 5. *We say that $P_0 \to_{DC(c,x)} P_1$ iff $P_0 \to_{FD} P_1$, $c \in \text{store}(P_0)$, $x \in \text{scope}(c)$, and $\delta_1 = \delta_0$ except for*

$$\delta_1(x) = \{a \in \delta_0(x) : \exists \Sigma \in \text{sol}(P_0|_{\{c\}}). \, x\sigma = a\}.$$

Proposition 3. *Let c be a constraint and $x \in \text{scope}(c)$. $\to_{DC(c,x)}$ is correct.*

Lemma 3. *If $P_0 \to_{DC(c,x)} P_1$, then $P_0|_{\{c\}} \to_{DC(c,x)} P_1|_{\{c\}}$.*

Proposition 4. *If $P_0 \to_{DC(c,x)} P_1$ and $P_0 \to_{FD} P_2 \to_{FD} P_1$, then $P_2 \to_{DC(c,x)} P_1$.*

Proof. Let $R_i = P_i|_{\{c\}}$. By Definition 5,

$$\delta_1(x) = \{a \in \delta_0(x) : \exists \Sigma \in \text{sol}(R_0). \, x\sigma = a\}$$

By Lemma 3, $R_0 \to_{DC(c,x)} R_1$ and, by Corollary 7, $R_0 \to_{FD} R_2 \to_{FD} R_1$. Hence, by Lemma 2, $\text{sol}(R_0) = \text{sol}(R_2)$. Furthermore, by Lemma 1, $\delta_1(x) \subset \delta_2(x) \subset \delta_0(x)$. As a simple consequence from these facts,

$$\delta_1(x) = \{a \in \delta_2(x) : \exists \Sigma \in \text{sol}(R_2). \, x\sigma = a\}\,.$$

and thus, by Definition 5, $P_2 \to_{DC(c,x)} P_1$. □

Proposition 5. *If* $P_0 \to_{DC(c,x)} P_1$, $P_0 \to_{FD} P_2$, $P_1 \not\to_{FD} P_2$, $P_2 \not\to_{FD} P_1$, *and* $P_1 \neq P_2$, *then a FCSP* P_3 *exists s.t.* $P_1 \to_{FD} P_3$ *and* $P_2 \to_{DC(c,x)} P_3$.

Proof. Let $R_i = P_i|_{\{c\}}$. By Definition 5,

$$\delta_1(x) = \{a \in \delta_0(x) : \exists \Sigma \in \text{sol}(R_0). \, x\sigma = a\}$$

Let $X = \text{scope}(P_0)$, $C = \text{store}(P_0)$, and $P_3 = (X, \delta_3, C)$ with $\delta_3 = \delta_2$ except for

$$\delta_3(x) = \{a \in \delta_2(x) : \exists \Sigma \in \text{sol}(R_2). \, x\sigma = a\}\,.$$

We note that, by Corollary 7, $R_0 \to_{FD} R_2$ and thus, by Corollary 5, $\text{sol}(R_2) \subseteq \text{sol}(R_0)$.

$P_2 \to_{FD} P_3$: By Lemma 1, $\delta_2(x) \not\subseteq \delta_1(x)$, or equivalently, $a \in \delta_0(x)$ exists s.t. $a \in \delta_2(x)$ and $a \notin \delta_1(x)$. By $a \notin \delta_1(x)$, $x\sigma \neq a$ for all $\Sigma \in \text{sol}(R_0)$. Since $\text{sol}(R_2) \subseteq \text{sol}(R_0)$, $a \notin \delta_3(x)$ and thus $\delta_3(x) \subset \delta_2(x)$.

$P_1 \to_{FD} P_3$: $P_3 \neq P_1$ because otherwise $P_2 \to_{FD} P_1$. For all $y \in X - \{x\}$, $\delta_1(y) = \delta_0(y) \supseteq \delta_2(y) = \delta_3(y)$ because $P_1 \leftarrow_{DC(c,x)} P_0 \to_{FD} P_2 \to_{DC(c,x)} P_3$. Suppose $\delta_3(x) \not\subseteq \delta_1(x)$, or equivalently, $a \in \delta_0(x)$ exists s.t. $a \in \delta_3(x)$ and $a \notin \delta_1(x)$. By $a \notin \delta_1(x)$, $x\sigma \neq a$ for all $\Sigma \in \text{sol}(R_0)$. Since $\text{sol}(R_2) \subseteq \text{sol}(R_0)$, $a \notin \delta_3(x)$. □

Corollary 8. *Let* c *be a constraint and* $x \in \text{scope}(c)$. $\to_{DC(c,x)}$ *is insensitive to* $\to_{FD}$.

6.2 Interval Consistency

Suppose $P = (X, \delta, C)$ is a FCSP and $c(x_1, \ldots, x_n) \in C$. Let $B(x) = \{\min \delta(x), \max \delta(x)\}$, if $\delta(x) \neq \emptyset$, and $\emptyset$ otherwise. Let $\rho(x) = [\min \delta(x), \max \delta(x)]$, if $\delta(x) \neq \emptyset$, and $\emptyset$ otherwise. We say that c is *interval-consistent*, if, for each variable x_i and for each value v_i of $B(x_i)$, there exist values $v_1, \ldots, v_{i-1}, v_{i+1}, \ldots, v_n$ in $\rho(x_1), \ldots, \rho(x_{i-1}), \rho(x_{i+1}), \ldots, \rho(x_n)$ s.t. $c(v_1, \ldots, v_n)$ holds. This definition coincides with the original definition by van Hentenryck et al. [6] except for that it also applies to constraints with a variable that has an empty domain.

Suppose c is a constraint. For each $x \in \text{scope}(c)$, we define the transition $\to_{IC(c,x)}$ (cf. Definitions 6 and 7). This transition tightens the bounds of the domain of x according to the definition of c. To be more precise, if $P_0 \to_{IC(c,x)} P_1$, then $\delta_1(x) \subset \delta_0(x)$, both $\min \delta_1(x)$ and $\max \delta_1(x)$ occur in solutions to the relaxation $\text{ir}(P_0|_{\{c\}}, x)$ of P_0 that does not touch the domain of x but relaxes all other domains according to [6], and no predecessor of P_1 wrt. $\to_{FD}$ satisfies these conditions. We proceed by showing that $\to_{IC(c,x)}$ is correct and insensitive to $\to_{FD}$. In consequence, $\to_{IC(c)} = \bigcup_{x \in scope(c)} \to_{IC(c,x)}$ is correct and insensitive to $\to_{FD}$. Quite obviously, $\to_{IC(c)}$ maintains interval consistency for c.

Definition 6. *Suppose* $P = (X, \delta, C)$ *is a FCSP with* $x \in X$. *Then* $ir(P, x) = (X, \rho, C)$ *with*

$$\rho(y) = \begin{cases} \delta(y), & \text{if } y = x \text{ or } \delta(y) = \emptyset \\ [\min \delta(y), \max \delta(y)] & \text{otherwise.} \end{cases}$$

Corollary 9. *Suppose* $P_0 = (X, \delta_0, C) \to_{FD} P_1$.

1. *If* $x \in X$, *then* $ir(P_0, x) \to_{\overline{FD}} ir(P_1, x)$.

2. *If* $x \in X$ *and* $c \in C$, *then* $ir(P_0|_{\{c\}}, x) \to_{\overline{FD}} ir(P_1|_{\{c\}}, x)$.

Definition 7. *We say that* $P_0 \to_{IC(c,x)} P_1$ *iff* $P_0 \to_{FD} P_1$, $c \in store(P_0)$, $x \in scope(c)$, *and* $\delta_1 = \delta_0$ *except for*

$$\delta_1(x) = \begin{cases} \emptyset, & \text{if } S = \emptyset \\ \{a \in \delta_0(x) : l \le a \le u\} & \text{otherwise} \end{cases}$$

where $S = sol(ir(P_0|_{\{c\}}, x))$, $l = \min\{x\sigma : \Sigma \in S\}$, *and* $u = \max\{x\sigma : \Sigma \in S\}$.

Proposition 6. *Let* c *be a constraint and* $x \in scope(c)$. $\to_{IC(c,x)}$ *is correct.*

Lemma 4. *If* $P_0 \to_{IC(c,x)} P_1$, *then* $ir(P_0|_{\{c\}}, x) \to_{IC(c,x)} ir(P_1|_{\{c\}}, x)$.

Proposition 7. *If* $P_0 \to_{IC(c,x)} P_1$ *and* $P_0 \to_{FD} P_2 \to_{FD} P_1$, *then* $P_2 \to_{IC(c,x)} P_1$.

Proof. Let $R_i = ir(P_i|_{\{c\}}, x)$, $S_i = sol(R_i)$, $l_i = \min\{x\sigma : \Sigma \in S_i\}$, and $u_i = \max\{x\sigma : \Sigma \in S_i\}$. By Definition 7,

$$\delta_1(x) = \begin{cases} \emptyset, & \text{if } S_0 = \emptyset \\ \{a \in \delta_0(x) : l_0 \le a \le u_0\} & \text{otherwise.} \end{cases}$$

By Lemma 4, $R_0 \to_{IC(c,x)} R_1$ and, by Corollary 9, $R_0 \to_{\overline{FD}} R_2 \to_{\overline{FD}} R_1$. Hence, by Lemma 2, $S_0 = S_2$ and thus $l_0 = l_2$ and $u_0 = u_2$. Furthermore, by Lemma 1, $\delta_1(x) \subset \delta_2(x) \subset \delta_0(x)$. As a simple consequence from these facts,

$$\delta_1(x) = \begin{cases} \emptyset, & \text{if } S_2 = \emptyset \\ \{a \in \delta_2(x) : l_2 \le a \le u_2\} & \text{otherwise.} \end{cases}$$

and thus, by Definition 7, $P_2 \to_{IC(c,x)} P_1$. $\qquad\square$

Proposition 8. *If $P_0 \rightarrow_{\text{IC}(c,x)} P_1$, $P_0 \rightarrow_{\text{FD}} P_2$, $P_1 \nrightarrow_{\text{FD}} P_2$, $P_2 \nrightarrow_{\text{FD}} P_1$, and $P_1 \neq P_2$, then a FCSP P_3 exists s.t. $P_1 \rightarrow_{\text{FD}} P_3$ and $P_2 \rightarrow_{\text{IC}(c,x)} P_3$.*

Proof. Let $R_i = \text{ir}(P_i|_{\{c\}}, x)$, $S_i = \text{sol}(R_i)$, $l_i = \min\{x\sigma : \Sigma \in S_i\}$, and $u_i = \max\{x\sigma : \Sigma \in S_i\}$. By Definition 7,

$$\delta_1(x) = \begin{cases} \emptyset, & \text{if } S_0 = \emptyset \\ \{a \in \delta_0(x) : l_0 \le a \le u_0\} & \text{otherwise.} \end{cases}$$

Let $X = \text{scope}(P_0)$, $C = \text{store}(P_0)$, and $P_3 = (X, \delta_3, C)$ with $\delta_3 = \delta_2$ except for

$$\delta_3(x) = \begin{cases} \emptyset, & \text{if } S_2 = \emptyset \\ \{a \in \delta_2(x) : l_2 \le a \le u_2\} & \text{otherwise.} \end{cases}$$

If $S_2 \neq \emptyset$, then $l_0 \le l_2$ and $u_2 \le u_0$: We note that, by Corollary 9, $R_0 \rightarrow_{\overline{\text{FD}}}^= R_2$ and thus, by Corollary 5, $S_2 \subseteq S_0$.

$P_2 \rightarrow_{\text{FD}} P_3$: By Lemma 1, $\delta_2(x) \not\subseteq \delta_1(x)$, or equivalently, $a \in \delta_0(x)$ exists s.t. $a \in \delta_2(x)$ and $a \notin \delta_1(x)$. If $S_2 = \emptyset$, then $\emptyset = \delta_3(x) \subset \delta_2(x) \ni a$. Otherwise, by $a \notin \delta_1(x)$, $a < l_0$ or $a > u_0$ and thus $a < l_2$ or $a > u_2$. Hence $a \notin \delta_3(x)$ and thus $\delta_3(x) \subset \delta_2(x)$.

$P_1 \rightarrow_{\text{FD}} P_3$: $P_3 \neq P_1$ because otherwise $P_2 \rightarrow_{\text{FD}} P_1$. For all $y \in X - \{x\}$, $\delta_1(y) = \delta_0(y) \supseteq \delta_2(y) = \delta_3(y)$ because $P_1 \leftarrow_{\text{IC}(c,x)} P_0 \rightarrow_{\text{FD}} P_2 \rightarrow_{\text{IC}(c,x)} P_3$. Suppose $\delta_3(x) \not\subseteq \delta_1(x)$, or equivalently, $a \in \delta_0(x)$ exists s.t. $a \in \delta_3(x)$ and $a \notin \delta_1(x)$. If $S_2 = \emptyset$, then $\delta_3(x) = \emptyset$ contradicts $a \in \delta_3(x)$. Otherwise, by $a \notin \delta_1(x)$, $a < l_0$ or $a > u_0$ and thus $a < l_2$ or $a > u_2$. Hence $a \notin \delta_3(x)$.   □

Corollary 10. *Let c be a constraint and $x \in \text{scope}(c)$. $\rightarrow_{\text{IC}(c,x)}$ is insensitive to $\rightarrow_{\text{FD}}$.*

7   Application to a Finite-Domain Constraint Solver

A *track parallelization problem* (TPP) [4] consists in parallelizing the execution of task sets. A TPP is specified by a set of tracks where each track is a set of tasks. Solving a TPP requires to find a schedule for each track s.t. the schedules cover the same set of time slots. TPPs occur in school timetabling, especially in problem settings where options and official regulations imply the need to parallelize the education of pupils from several classes of the same grade [4].

We proceed as follows. In Section 7.1, we define TPP constraints in terms of syntax and semantics. In Section 7.2, we describe a TPP solver consisting of several reductions. In Section 7.3, we show that the solver and any subset of its reductions are confluent.

7.1   Syntax and Semantics of TPP Constraints

A TPP constraint is written as $\text{tpp}(\mathcal{T})$ where $|\mathcal{T}| > 1$ and, for all $T \in \mathcal{T}$, T is a non-empty set of pairs of FD variables. Each pair (S, P) of FD variables is intended to model a task in terms of its *start time* S and its *processing time* P. Fixed start or processing times may be modeled by means of variables with singleton domains. We assume that processing times are greater than 0.

If P is a FCSP with $\mathrm{tpp}(\mathcal{T}) \in \mathrm{store}(P)$, $T \in \mathcal{T}$, and $t = (\mathrm{S}, \mathrm{P}) \in T$, we write $\delta(t)$ instead of $\delta(\mathrm{S}) \times \delta(\mathrm{P})$.

Definition 8. *Let P be a FCSP with $\mathrm{tpp}(\mathcal{T}) \in \mathrm{store}(P)$. Let $T \in \mathcal{T}$ and $t = (\mathrm{S}, \mathrm{P}) \in T$.*

1. *Value covers:*

$$\mathrm{vc}(t, \delta) = \bigcap_{(s,p) \in \delta(t)} [s, s{+}p{-}1], \ \ \mathrm{vc}(T, \delta) = \bigcup_{t \in T} \mathrm{vc}(t, \delta), \ \ \mathrm{vc}(\mathcal{T}, \delta) = \bigcup_{T \in \mathcal{T}} \mathrm{vc}(T, \delta)$$

2. *Value supplies:*

$$\mathrm{vs}(t, \delta) = \bigcup_{(s,p) \in \delta(t)} [s, s{+}p{-}1], \ \ \mathrm{vs}(T, \delta) = \bigcup_{t \in T} \mathrm{vs}(t, \delta), \ \ \mathrm{vs}(\mathcal{T}, \delta) = \bigcap_{T \in \mathcal{T}} \mathrm{vs}(T, \delta)$$

The following figure illustrates the concept of parallel execution. We consider the ground problem $(X, \gamma, \{\mathrm{tpp}(\{T_0, T_1, T_2\})\})$. Tracks T_0 and T_1 are executed in parallel because their schedules cover the same value set. In contrast, the schedule of T_3 covers values that the other schedules do not cover; it is not executed in parallel to the other tracks.

Definition 9. *Let P be a ground FCSP with $\mathrm{tpp}(\mathcal{T}) \in \mathrm{store}(P)$. δ satisfies $\mathrm{tpp}(\mathcal{T})$ iff*

$$|\{\mathrm{vc}(T, \delta) : T \in \mathcal{T}\}| = 1,$$

i.e. iff the track schedules cover the same value set.

Lemma 5. *Suppose $P_0 \to_{\mathrm{FD}} P_1$ and $\mathrm{tpp}(\mathcal{T}) \in \mathrm{store}(P_0)$. Let $T \in \mathcal{T}$ and $t \in T$.*

1. *Value supplies shrink monotonically, i.e.*
   $\mathrm{vs}(t, \delta_0) \supseteq \mathrm{vs}(t, \delta_1)$, $\mathrm{vs}(T, \delta_0) \supseteq \mathrm{vs}(T, \delta_1)$, *and* $\mathrm{vs}(\mathcal{T}, \delta_0) \supseteq \mathrm{vs}(\mathcal{T}, \delta_1)$.

2. *Value covers grow monotonically, i.e.*
   $\mathrm{vc}(t, \delta_0) \subseteq \mathrm{vc}(t, \delta_1)$, $\mathrm{vc}(T, \delta_0) \subseteq \mathrm{vc}(T, \delta_1)$, *and* $\mathrm{vc}(\mathcal{T}, \delta_0) \subseteq \mathrm{vc}(\mathcal{T}, \delta_1)$.

Proof. All properties follow immediately from Corollary 5.   □

Lemma 6. *Suppose Γ is a ground FCSP with $\mathrm{tpp}(\mathcal{T}) \in \mathrm{store}(\Gamma)$. Let $T \in \mathcal{T}$ and $t \in T$.*

1. *In general, $\mathrm{vs}(t, \gamma) = \mathrm{vc}(t, \gamma)$ and $\mathrm{vs}(T, \gamma) = \mathrm{vc}(T, \gamma)$.*

2. *Furthermore, if γ satisfies $\mathrm{tpp}(\mathcal{T})$, then $\mathrm{vc}(T, \gamma) = \mathrm{vs}(\mathcal{T}, \gamma) = \mathrm{vc}(\mathcal{T}, \gamma)$.*

Proof. See [4].   □

7.2 Solving TPP Constraints

We propose three reductions for solving TPP constraints. ([5] has another one.) $\rightarrow_{\text{PVS}}$ identifies and prunes all start and processing times that entail the covering of values that are not element of the value supply of the track set. $\rightarrow_{\text{IPT}}$ reveals inconsistencies by comparing bounds on the processing times of tracks. $\rightarrow_{\text{NC}}$ reveals inconsistencies by identifying situations where values that have to be covered cannot be covered.

Definition 10. *We say that $P_0 \rightarrow_{\text{PVS}} P_1$ iff $P_0 \rightarrow_{\text{FD}} P_1$ and $\text{tpp}(\mathcal{T}) \in \text{store}(P_0)$, $T \in \mathcal{T}$, $t = (\text{S}, \text{P}) \in T$, and $a \in \text{vs}(t, \delta_0)$ exist s.t. $a \notin \text{vs}(\mathcal{T}, \delta_0)$ and $\delta_1 = \delta_0$ except for*
$$\delta_1(t) = \{(s, p) \in \delta_0(t) : a \notin [s, s + p - 1]\}.$$

The following figure illustrates the effects of applying $\rightarrow_{\text{PVS}}$. We consider the problem $P_0 = (X, \delta_0, \{\text{tpp}(\{T_0, T_1\})\})$ and its normal form $P_1 = P_0 \downarrow_{\text{PVS}}$.

Definition 11. *We say that $P_0 \rightarrow_{\text{IPT}} P_1$ iff $P_0 \rightarrow_{\text{FD}} P_1$, P_1 is failed, and $\text{tpp}(\mathcal{T}) \in \text{store}(P_0)$, $T_0, T_1 \in \mathcal{T}$, and $l, u \geq 0$ exist s.t., for all $\Gamma \in \text{gs}(P_0)$, l is a lower bound on $|\text{vc}(T_0, \gamma)|$, u is an upper bound on $|\text{vc}(T_1, \gamma)|$, and $u < l$.*

For example, consider the problem $(X, \delta, \{\text{tpp}(\{T_0, T_1\})\})$ with $T_0 = \{t_{00}, t_{01}\}$ and $T_1 = \{t_{10}, t_{11}\}$ where $t_{00} = (\{0, 5\}, \{2\})$, $t_{01} = (\{2, 6\}, \{1, 2, 3\})$, $t_{10} = (\{2, 3\}, \{4, 5\})$, and $t_{11} = (\{0, 6\}, \{2, 3\})$ (For simplicity, we replaced the variables by their domains.) We note that $\text{vs}(T_0, \delta) = \text{vs}(T_1, \delta) = [0, 8]$ and that T_0 cannot cover more than five values. Since T_0 and T_1 are supplied the same values, $\rightarrow_{\text{PVS}}$ does not apply. If the tasks of T_1 are allowed to overlap, T_1 has a schedule covering five values and $\rightarrow_{\text{IPT}}$ does not apply either. However, if a disjunctive schedule[1] is required for T_1, any schedule of T_1 covers at least six values. In consequence, the tracks cannot be executed in parallel. $\rightarrow_{\text{IPT}}$ will reveal this inconsistency if the demand for disjunctiveness is considered when computing the minimum number of values any schedule of T_1 covers.

Definition 12. *Let $P = (X, \delta, C)$ be a FCSP with $\text{tpp}(\mathcal{T}) \in C$. If $T = \{t_1, \ldots t_n\} \in \mathcal{T}$, then $\text{vcg}(\mathcal{T}, T, \delta)$ denotes the bipartite graph (U, V, E) with*

$$- \; U = \bigcup_{\substack{1 \leq i \leq n \\ \delta(\text{P}_i) \neq \emptyset}} \left\{ u_i^j : 0 \leq j < \max \delta(\text{P}_i) \right\},$$

$$- \; V = \text{vc}(\mathcal{T}, \delta), \; \text{and}$$

---

[1] In a disjunctive schedule, tasks do not overlap.

$$- E = \left\{ (u_i^j, a) : u_i^j \in U \, \wedge \, a \in V \, \wedge \, \exists s \in \delta(\mathsf{S}_i). \, s + j = a \right\}.$$

We call this structure value-cover graph.

Definition 13. *We say that* $P_0 \rightarrow_{\mathrm{NC}} P_1$ *iff* $P_0 \rightarrow_{\mathrm{FD}} P_1$, P_1 *is failed, and* $\mathrm{tpp}(\mathcal{T}) \in \mathrm{store}(P_0)$ *and* $T \in \mathcal{T}$ *exist s.t.* $\mathrm{vcg}(\mathcal{T}, T, \delta_0) = (U, V, E)$ *does not have a matching*[2] M *with* $|M| = |V|$.

For example, consider the problem $(X, \delta, \{\mathrm{tpp}(\{T_0, T_1\})\})$ with $\mathrm{vc}(T_0, \delta) = [1, 4]$, $\mathrm{vs}(T_0, \delta) = \mathrm{vc}(T_0, \delta)$, and $T_1 = \{t_1, t_2, t_3\}$ where $t_1 = (\{1, 2\}, \{1\})$, $t_2 = (\{3\}, \{2\})$, and $t_3 = (\{3, 4\}, \{1\})$. (For simplicity, we replaced the variables by their domains.) We note that $\mathrm{vs}(T_1, \delta) = [1, 4]$. Hence $\rightarrow_{\mathrm{PVS}}$ does not apply. $\rightarrow_{\mathrm{IPT}}$ does not apply either if starting times are not considered. Now consider the value-cover graph $\mathrm{vcg}(\{T_0, T_1\}, T_1, \delta)$:

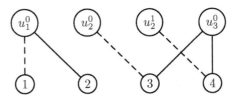

The dotted edges constitute a matching of cardinality 3 and it is easy to verify that it has maximum cardinality. Hence only three values out of $[1, 4]$ can be covered simultaneously. $\rightarrow_{\mathrm{NC}}$ detects this inconsistency and signals a failure.

Proposition 9. $\rightarrow_{\mathrm{PVS}}$, $\rightarrow_{\mathrm{IPT}}$, *and* $\rightarrow_{\mathrm{NC}}$ *are correct.*

Proof. See [4]. □

7.3   Confluence Properties of the TPP Solver

We show that $\rightarrow_{\mathrm{PVS}}$, $\rightarrow_{\mathrm{IPT}}$, and $\rightarrow_{\mathrm{NC}}$ are insensitive to $\rightarrow_{\mathrm{FD}}$ (cf. Corollaries 11, 12, and 13). Thus, by Corollary 1, each combination of $\rightarrow_{\mathrm{PVS}}$, $\rightarrow_{\mathrm{IPT}}$, and $\rightarrow_{\mathrm{NC}}$ is insensitive to $\rightarrow_{\mathrm{FD}}$ and, by Corollary 3, each combination of $\rightarrow_{\mathrm{PVS}}$, $\rightarrow_{\mathrm{IPT}}$, and $\rightarrow_{\mathrm{NC}}$ is confluent.

Proposition 10. *If* $P_0 \rightarrow_{\mathrm{PVS}} P_1$ *and* $P_0 \rightarrow_{\mathrm{FD}} P_2 \rightarrow_{\mathrm{FD}} P_1$, *then* $P_2 \rightarrow_{\mathrm{PVS}} P_1$.

Proof. Let $\mathrm{tpp}(\mathcal{T}) \in \mathrm{store}(P_0)$, $T \in \mathcal{T}$, $t = (\mathsf{S}, \mathsf{P}) \in T$, and $a \in \mathrm{vs}(t, \delta_0)$ s.t. $a \notin \mathrm{vs}(\mathcal{T}, \delta_0)$ and $\delta_1 = \delta_0$ except for

$$\delta_1(t) = \{(s, p) \in \delta_0(t) : a \notin [s, s + p - 1]\}.$$

By Lemma 1, $\delta_1(t) \subset \delta_2(t) \subset \delta_0(t)$. As a consequence,

$$\delta_1(t) = \{(s, p) \in \delta_2(t) : a \notin [s, s + p - 1]\}.$$

---

[2] Given a bipartite graph (U, V, E), a *matching* is a subset of edges $M \subseteq E$ s.t., for all vertices $v \in U \cup V$, at most one edge of M is incident on v.

Let $\Delta = \delta_2(t) - \delta_1(t)$. We observe that

$$\emptyset \neq \Delta \subset \delta_0(t) - \delta_1(t) = \{(s,p) \in \delta_0(t) : a \in [s, s+p-1]\}.$$

It follows that

$$a \in \bigcup_{(s,p) \in \Delta} [s, s+p-1] \subseteq \bigcup_{(s,p) \in \delta_2(t)} [s, s+p-1] = \mathrm{vs}(t, \delta_2).$$

Furthermore, by Lemma 5, $a \notin \mathrm{vs}(\mathcal{T}, \delta_2)$. We conclude that $P_2 \rightarrow_{\mathrm{PVS}} P_1$. $\square$

Proposition 11. *If $P_0 \rightarrow_{\mathrm{PVS}} P_1$, $P_0 \rightarrow_{\mathrm{FD}} P_2$, $P_1 \not\rightarrow_{\mathrm{FD}} P_2$, $P_2 \not\rightarrow_{\mathrm{FD}} P_1$, and $P_1 \neq P_2$, then a FCSP P_3 exists s.t. $P_1 \rightarrow_{\mathrm{FD}} P_3$ and $P_2 \rightarrow_{\mathrm{PVS}} P_3$.*

Proof. Let $X = \mathrm{scope}(P_0)$ and $C = \mathrm{store}(P_0)$. Let $\mathrm{tpp}(\mathcal{T}) \in C$, $T \in \mathcal{T}$, $t = (\mathsf{S}, \mathsf{P}) \in T$, and $a \in \mathrm{vs}(t, \delta_0)$ s.t. $a \notin \mathrm{vs}(\mathcal{T}, \delta_0)$ and $\delta_1 = \delta_0$ except for

$$\delta_1(t) = \{(s,p) \in \delta_0(t) : a \notin [s, s+p-1]\}.$$

Let $P_3 = (X, \delta_3, C)$ with $\delta_3 = \delta_2$ except for

$$\delta_3(t) = \{(s,p) \in \delta_2(t) : a \notin [s, s+p-1]\}.$$

First, we show that $P_2 \rightarrow_{\mathrm{PVS}} P_3$. By Lemma 1, $\delta_2(t) \not\subseteq \delta_1(t)$, or equivalently, $(s,p) \in \delta_0(t)$ exists s.t. $(s,p) \in \delta_2(t)$ and $(s,p) \notin \delta_1(t)$. We conclude that $a \in [s, s+p-1]$ and thus $(s,p) \notin \delta_3(t)$. Hence $\delta_3(t) \subset \delta_2(t)$ and thus $P_2 \rightarrow_{\mathrm{FD}} P_3$. Furthermore, $a \in \mathrm{vs}(t, \delta_2)$ and, by Lemma 5, $a \notin \mathrm{vs}(\mathcal{T}, \delta_2)$. It follows that $P_2 \rightarrow_{\mathrm{PVS}} P_3$.

It remains to show that $P_1 \rightarrow_{\mathrm{FD}} P_3$. $P_3 \neq P_1$ because otherwise $P_2 \rightarrow_{\mathrm{FD}} P_1$. For all $x \in X - \{\mathsf{S}, \mathsf{P}\}$, $\delta_1(x) = \delta_0(x) \supseteq \delta_2(x) = \delta_3(x)$ because $P_1 \leftarrow_{\mathrm{PVS}} P_0 \rightarrow_{\mathrm{FD}} P_2 \rightarrow_{\mathrm{PVS}} P_3$. Suppose $\delta_3(t) \not\subseteq \delta_1(t)$, or equivalently, $(s,p) \in \delta_0(t)$ exists s.t. $(s,p) \in \delta_3(t)$ and $(s,p) \notin \delta_1(t)$. We conclude that $a \in [s, s+p-1]$ and thus $(s,p) \notin \delta_3(t)$. $\square$

Corollary 11. $\rightarrow_{\mathrm{PVS}}$ *is insensitive to* $\rightarrow_{\mathrm{FD}}$.

Proposition 12. *If $P_0 \rightarrow_{\mathrm{IPT}} P_1$ and $P_0 \rightarrow_{\mathrm{FD}} P_2 \rightarrow_{\mathrm{FD}} P_1$, then $P_2 \rightarrow_{\mathrm{IPT}} P_1$.*

Proof. Let $\mathrm{tpp}(\mathcal{T}) \in \mathrm{store}(P_0)$, $T_0, T_1 \in \mathcal{T}$, and $l, u \geq 0$ s.t., for all $\Gamma \in \mathrm{gs}(P_0)$, l is a lower bound on $|\mathrm{vc}(T_0, \gamma)|$, u is an upper bound on $|\mathrm{vc}(T_1, \gamma)|$, and $u < l$. By Corollary 5, $\mathrm{gs}(P_2) \subseteq \mathrm{gs}(P_0)$. Let $\Gamma \in \mathrm{gs}(P_2)$. Because $\Gamma \in \mathrm{gs}(P_0)$, we know that l is a lower bound on $|\mathrm{vc}(T_0, \gamma)|$, u is an upper bound on $|\mathrm{vc}(T_1, \gamma)|$, and $u < l$. Furthermore, P_1 is failed because $P_0 \rightarrow_{\mathrm{IPT}} P_1$. We conclude that $P_2 \rightarrow_{\mathrm{IPT}} P_1$. $\square$

Proposition 13. *If $P_0 \rightarrow_{\mathrm{IPT}} P_1$, $P_0 \rightarrow_{\mathrm{FD}} P_2$, $P_1 \not\rightarrow_{\mathrm{FD}} P_2$, $P_2 \not\rightarrow_{\mathrm{FD}} P_1$, and $P_1 \neq P_2$, then a FCSP P_3 exists s.t. $P_1 \rightarrow_{\mathrm{FD}} P_3$ and $P_2 \rightarrow_{\mathrm{IPT}} P_3$.*

Proof. Let $X = \text{scope}(P_0)$ and $C = \text{store}(P_0)$. Let $\texttt{tpp}(\mathcal{T}) \in C$, $T_0, T_1 \in \mathcal{T}$, and $l, u \geq 0$ s.t., for all $\Gamma \in \text{gs}(P_0)$, l is a lower bound on $|\text{vc}(T_0, \gamma)|$, u is an upper bound on $|\text{vc}(T_1, \gamma)|$, and $u < l$. Let $P_3 = (X, \delta_3, C)$ with $\delta_3(x) = \delta_1(x) \cap \delta_2(x)$ for all $x \in X$. P_3 is failed because P_1 is failed.

Suppose $P_1 \not\rightarrow_{\text{FD}} P_3$. Then either $\delta_1 = \delta_3$ or $x \in X$ exists s.t. $\delta_3(x) \not\subseteq \delta_1(x)$. The latter case contradicts the construction of P_3. If $\delta_1 = \delta_3$, then $\delta_1(x) \subseteq \delta_2(x)$ for all $x \in X$ and thus either $P_1 = P_2$ or $P_2 \rightarrow_{\text{FD}} P_1$.

Suppose $P_2 \not\rightarrow_{\text{FD}} P_3$. Then either $\delta_2 = \delta_3$ and thus $P_2 = P_3$ or $x \in X$ exists s.t. $\delta_3(x) \not\subseteq \delta_2(x)$. The former case contradicts $P_1 \not\rightarrow_{\text{FD}} P_2$, the latter case contradicts the construction of P_3.

Furthermore, by Corollary 5, $\text{gs}(P_2) \subseteq \text{gs}(P_0)$. Let $\Gamma \in \text{gs}(P_2)$. Because $\Gamma \in \text{gs}(P_0)$, we know that l is a lower bound on $|\text{vc}(T_0, \gamma)|$, u is an upper bound on $|\text{vc}(T_1, \gamma)|$, and $u < l$.

We conclude that $P_2 \rightarrow_{\text{IPT}} P_3$. □

Corollary 12. $\rightarrow_{\text{IPT}}$ *is insensitive to* $\rightarrow_{\text{FD}}$.

Proposition 14. *If* $P_0 \rightarrow_{\text{NC}} P_1$ *and* $P_0 \rightarrow_{\text{FD}} P_2 \rightarrow_{\text{FD}} P_1$, *then* $P_2 \rightarrow_{\text{NC}} P_1$.

Proof. Let $\texttt{tpp}(\mathcal{T}) \in \text{store}(P_0)$ and $T \in \mathcal{T}$ s.t. $G_0 = (U_0, V_0, E_0) = \text{vcg}(\mathcal{T}, T, \delta_0)$ does not have a matching M_0 with $|M_0| = |V_0|$. Suppose $G_2 = (U_2, V_2, E_2) = \text{vcg}(\mathcal{T}, T, \delta_2)$ has a matching M_2 with $|M_2| = |V_2|$. Let $M_0 = \left\{ (u_i^j, a) \in M_2 : a \in V_0 \right\}$. We will show that M_0 is a matching in G_0 and that $|M_0| = |V_0|$.

1. M_0 is a matching because $M_0 \subseteq M_2$.

2. $M_0 \subseteq E_0$: Let $(u_i^j, a) \in M_0$. We know that $u_i^j \in U_2$, $a \in V_0$, and that $s \in \delta_2(S_i)$ exists s.t. $s + j = a$. Let $s \in \delta_2(S_i)$ s.t. $s + j = a$. $u_i^j \in U_0$ and $s \in \delta_0(S_i)$ because $P_0 \rightarrow_{\text{FD}} P_2$.

3. $|M_0| = |V_0|$ because, for all $a \in V_2$, a is matched by M_2 and, by Lemma 5, $V_0 = \text{vc}(\mathcal{T}, \delta_0) \subseteq \text{vc}(\mathcal{T}, \delta_2) = V_2$.

Furthermore, P_1 is failed because $P_0 \rightarrow_{\text{NC}} P_1$. We conclude that $P_2 \rightarrow_{\text{NC}} P_1$. □

Proposition 15. *If* $P_0 \rightarrow_{\text{NC}} P_1$, $P_0 \rightarrow_{\text{FD}} P_2$, $P_1 \not\rightarrow_{\text{FD}} P_2$, $P_2 \not\rightarrow_{\text{FD}} P_1$, *and* $P_1 \neq P_2$, *then a FCSP* P_3 *exists s.t.* $P_1 \rightarrow_{\text{FD}} P_3$ *and* $P_2 \rightarrow_{\text{NC}} P_3$.

Proof. Similar to the proof of Proposition 13 by exploiting the fact that $(U_2, V_2, E_2) = \text{vcg}(\mathcal{T}, T, \delta_2)$ with $\texttt{tpp}(\mathcal{T}) \in \text{store}(P_0)$ and $T \in \mathcal{T}$ does not have a matching M_2 with $|M_2| = |V_2|$ as shown in the proof of Proposition 14. □

Corollary 13. $\rightarrow_{\text{NC}}$ *is insensitive to* $\rightarrow_{\text{FD}}$.

Corollary 14. *If* $R \subseteq \{\rightarrow_{\text{PVS}}, \rightarrow_{\text{IPT}}, \rightarrow_{\text{NC}}\}$ *and* $\rightarrow_r = \bigcup R$, *then* $\rightarrow_r$ *is terminating, insensitive to* $\rightarrow_C$, *locally confluent, and confluent.*

8 Related Work

The Commutative Union Lemma [2] (CUL) is a well-known tool to prove confluence. It states that the union of two reductions is confluent if both reductions are confluent and commute. In the following, we compare our method to the method suggested by the CUL. We are interested in how to proceed in different situations: when proving the confluence of a reduction from scratch and when proving the confluence of a reduction that has been obtained by extending or reducing a confluent reduction.

Let $(A, \bigcup_{1 \leq i \leq n} \to_i)$ be a reduction system. To show that $\bigcup_{1 \leq i \leq n} \to_i$ is confluent, the CUL suggests to show that each $\to_i$, $1 \leq i \leq n$, is confluent and that, for each $1 < i \leq n$, $\to_i$ and $\bigcup_{1 \leq k < i} \to_k$ commute. Our approach requires n proofs of insensitivity to $\bigcup_{1 \leq i \leq n} \to_i$, one for each $\to_i$, $1 \leq i \leq n$. In general, each proof of insensitivity has to consider n cases, one for each $\to_i$, $1 \leq i \leq n$, except for it is possible to characterize $\bigcup_{1 \leq i \leq n} \to_i$ or some superset relation in a way that facilitates to deal with all cases in one sweep. In our application to FD constraint solving, we proved insensitivity to $\to_{FD}$. This way it was possible to prove the confluence of the TPP solver with a number of proofs linear in the number of reductions.

Let $\to_{n+1} \in A \times A$. Suppose $\bigcup_{1 \leq i \leq n} \to_i$ is known to be confluent. To show that $\bigcup_{1 \leq i \leq n+1} \to_i$ is confluent, the CUL obliges to show that $\to_{n+1}$ is confluent and that $\to_{n+1}$ and $\bigcup_{1 \leq i \leq n} \to_i$ commute. In the worst case, our approach obliges to show that, for all $1 \leq i \leq n+1$, $\to_i$ is insensitive to $\bigcup_{1 \leq i \leq n+1} \to_i$. This amounts to proving confluence from scratch. However, if we can characterize a superset relation that contains all reductions we might wish to investigate, it is possible to reuse all prior proofs of insensitivity: Suppose we know that $\bigcup_{1 \leq i \leq n} \to_i$ is insensitive to the superset relation, then it is sufficient to show that $\to_{n+1}$ is insensitive to the superset relation. In our application to FD constraint solving, we used $\to_{FD}$ as superset relation. If we wished to extend the TPP solver, it was sufficient to show that the extension is insensitive to $\to_{FD}$.

Suppose $\bigcup_{1 \leq i \leq n} \to_i$ is known to be confluent. Let $1 \leq k \leq n$. Is $\bigcup_{1 \leq i \leq n, i \neq k} \to_i$ confluent? If the CUL has been applied, then, for each $k < l \leq n$, it is necessary to prove that $\to_l$ and $\bigcup_{1 \leq i < l, i \neq k}$ commute. If our approach has been used, no proof obligations arise, independent of whether insensitivity has been proved to $\bigcup_{1 \leq i \leq n} \to_i$ or to some superset relation.

Suppose $\bigcup_{1 \leq i \leq n} \to_i$ is known to be confluent. Let $I \subset [1, \ldots, n]$. Is $\bigcup_{i \in I} \to_i$ confluent? The answers to this question are similar to those to the previous question. In particular, if our approach has been used to prove the confluence of $\bigcup_{1 \leq i \leq n} \to_i$, no proof obligations arise.

Another well-known but less general approach to proving confluence is based on so-called critical pairs. Basically, a critical pair is a pair of states obtained from the parallel application of two interfering rewrite rules to a common and minimal ancestor state. Typically, a set of rewrite rules is locally confluent iff all its critical pairs are joinable. Critical pairs are vital for establishing confluence in different domains, e.g. in term-rewriting systems [2] and in rule-based constraint solving [1]. We did not consider the critical-pair approach for two reasons. First, it has not yet been transfered to our setting. Second, there is not very much motivation to do so because the resulting method would not be modular.

9   Conclusion

We developed a sufficient condition for local confluence and demonstrated that it is very well suited to study the behaviour of cooperating constraint solvers. First, we showed that any combination of solvers where each solver maintains either domain or interval consistency is confluent. Second, we studied a solver for track parallelization and showed that any combination of its reductions is confluent.

We call our approach modular because removing reductions does not affect confluence and because proving confluence after adding a reduction requires only a single proof that, if a superset relation is used, does not require to reconsider any other reduction. Our approach is suitable for the study of constraint solvers because superset relations are available that comprise all conceivable solvers.

Our future research interests include the application of our method to techniques that are important in scheduling like edge-finding and energetic reasoning [3].

References

1. S. Abdennadher, T. Frühwirth, and H. Meuss. Confluence and semantics of constraint simplification rules. *Constraints*, 4(2):133–165, 1999.
2. F. Baader and T. Nipkow. *Term Rewriting and All That.* Cambridge University Press, 1998.
3. P. Baptiste, C. L. Pape, and W. Nuijten. Satisfiability tests and time-bound adjustments for cumulative scheduling problems. *Annals of Operations Research*, 92:305–333, 1999.
4. M. Marte. A global constraint for parallelizing the execution of task sets. Technical Report PMS-FB-2001-13, Institut für Informatik der Universität München, 2001.
5. M. Marte. A modular approach to proving confluence. Technical Report PMS-FB-2001-18, Institut für Informatik der Universität München, 2001.
6. P. Van Hentenryck, V. Saraswat, and Y. Deville. Design, implementation, and evaluation of the constraint language cc(FD). *Journal of Logic Programming*, 37(2):139–164, 1998.

Integrating BDD-Based and SAT-Based Symbolic Model Checking

Alessandro Cimatti[1], Enrico Giunchiglia[2], Marco Pistore[1], Marco Roveri[1],
Roberto Sebastiani[3], and Armando Tacchella[2]

[1] ITC-IRST, Via Sommarive 18, 38050 Trento, Italy
{cimatti,pistore,roveri}@irst.itc.it
[2] DIST – Università di Genova, Viale Causa 13, 16145 Genova, Italy
{enrico,tac}@mrg.dist.unige.it
[3] Università di Trento, Via Sommarive 14, 38050 Trento, Italy
rseba@science.unitn.it

Abstract. Symbolic model checking is a very successful formal verification technique, classically based on Binary Decision Diagrams (BDDs). Recently, propositional satisfiability (SAT) techniques have been proposed as a computational basis for symbolic model checking, and proved to be an effective alternative to BDD-based techniques. In this paper we show how BDD-based and SAT-based techniques have been effectively integrated within the NuSMV symbolic model checker.

1 Introduction

Model checking [11,20] is a formal technique for the verification of finite state systems. The system being analyzed is represented as a Finite State Machine (FSM), while the requirements to be satisfied are expressed in temporal logics, e.g. Computation Tree Logic (CTL), or Linear Temporal Logic (LTL). Model checking algorithms are based on the exhaustive analysis of the state space of the FSM. They are able to prove that the system satisfies the requirement, or, more importantly, are able to produce a counterexample, i.e. a behaviour of the FSM that violates the requirements. Model Checking is an extremely effective debugging technique, and is being applied in several application domains, ranging from the analysis of telecommunication protocols to reactive controllers to hardware designs.

Originally, model checking was implemented by means of "explicit-state" techniques, where single states of the FSM are analyzed and stored. One of the most notable examples of explicit-state model checking is SPIN [17], that is very effective in the analysis of asynchronous systems. In general, for many application domains, the large amount of computational resources needed to analyze real-size designs (the so-called state-explosion problem) may be a significant limitation. The introduction of *Symbolic* Model Checking [18] made it possible to explore state spaces of extremely large size. In symbolic model checking, instead of manipulating individual states, the algorithms manipulate *sets* of states. These are compactly represented and efficiently constructed by means of Binary Decision

A. Armando (Ed.): FroCoS 2002, LNAI 2309, pp. 49–56, 2002.

Diagrams [6] (BDDs), that are canonical forms for propositional formulae. Since the seminal work of McMillan [18], several mechanisms for a partitioned representation of finite state machines and different exploration styles [7,22,13] have allowed to increase the applicability of BDD-based model checking. Recently, a new form of symbolic model checking, commonly known as Bounded Model Checking [4], has been introduced. Bounded Model Checking is based on the encoding of a model checking problem into a propositional satisfiability (SAT) problem, and on the application of efficient SAT solvers. This approach, in the following called SAT-based model checking, relies on the enormous progress in the field of propositional satisfiability [19]. The approach is currently enjoying a substantial success in several industrial fields (see, e.g., [12], but also [5]), and opens up new research directions.

BDD-based and SAT-based model checking are often able to solve different classes of problems, and can therefore be seen as complementary techniques. The effective integration of BDD-based and SAT-based model checking techniques is very important to widen the spectrum of applicability of symbolic model checkers. Goal of this paper is to describe how the BDD-based and SAT-based approaches to symbolic model checking have been successfully integrated within the NuSMV model checker. In Section 2 we outline the NuSMV project. In Section 3 and 4 we describe the functionalities and the architecture of Nu-SMV2. In Section 5 we discuss some results and outline directions for future development.

2   The NuSMV Symbolic Model Checker

NuSMV is a symbolic model checker originated from the reengineering, reimplementation and extension of SMV [18], the original BDD-based model checker developed by McMillan et al. at CMU (SMV from now on). The NuSMV project aims at the development of a state-of-the-art symbolic model checker, designed to be applicable in technology transfer projects: it is a well structured, open, flexible and documented platform for model checking, and is robust and close to industrial systems standards [8].

The first version of NuSMV, called NuSMV1 in the following, basically implements BDD-based symbolic model checking. The second version of NuSMV (NuSMV2 in the following), inherits all the functionalities and the implementation style of the previous version. However, NuSMV2 significantly extends the functionalities of NuSMV1, and its internal structure departs from the one of NuSMV1. The main novelty in NuSMV2 is the integration of model checking techniques based on propositional satisfiability. Remarkably, the integration covers the whole input language of NuSMV. NuSMV2 is currently the only publicly available system that allows for both BDD-based and SAT-based model checking. In order to integrate SAT-based and BDD-based model checking, a major architectural redesign was carried out in NuSMV2, in order to make as many functionalities as possible independent of the actual model checking engine used. An example of this are the services provided by the modules implementing the preprocessing and reduction of the model to be analyzed. This allowed for the effective integration of the new SAT-based engine, and opens up toward the implementation of other model checking procedures.

NuSMV2 is the result of a cooperative project. IRST and the University of Trento carried out the activities related to model checking, while the University of Genova provided a package implementing reduced boolean circuits [1] and the state of the art SIM SAT solver [16]. The SIM solver is particularly effective in tackling problems arising from bounded model checking [12]. NuSMV2 is publicly available, under the GNU Lesser General Public License (LGPL), at http://nusmv.irst.itc.it/.

3   System Functionalities

NuSMV is able to process files written in an extension of the SMV language. In this language, it is possible to describe finite state machines by means of declaration and instantiation mechanisms for modules and processes, corresponding to synchronous and asynchronous composition, and to express a set of requirements in CTL and LTL. NuSMV can work batch or interactively, with a textual interaction shell.

An SMV file is processed in several phases. The first phases require the analysis of the input file, in order to construct an internal representation of the system to be analyzed. NuSMV2 neatly separates the input language in different layers, of increasing simplicity, that are incrementally eliminated. The first step, called *flattening*, performs the instantiation of module types, thus creating modules and processes, and produces a synchronous, flat model, where each variable is given an absolute name. The second step, called *boolean encoding*, maps a flat model into a boolean model, thus eliminating scalar variables. This second step takes into account the whole SMV language, including the encoding of bounded integers, and the set-theoretic and arithmetic functions and predicates. It is possible to print out the different levels of the input file, thus using NuSMV2 as a flattener. The same reduction steps are applied to the requirements. In addition, by means of the cone of influence reduction [2], it is possible to restrict the analysis of each property to the relevant parts of the model. This reduction can be extremely effective in tackling the state explosion problem.

The preprocessing is carried out independently from the model checking engine to be used for verification. After this, the user can choose whether to apply BDD-based or SAT-based model checking. In the case of BDD-based model checking, a BDD-based representation of the the Finite State Machine is constructed. In this step, different partitioning methods and strategies [21] can be used. Then, different forms of analysis can be applied: reachability analysis, fair CTL model checking, LTL model checking via reduction to CTL model checking, computation of quantitative characteristics of the model.

In the case of SAT-based model checking, NuSMV2 constructs an internal representation of the model based on Reduced Boolean Circuit (RBC), a representation mechanism for propositional formulae. Then, it is possible to perform

SAT-based bounded model checking of LTL formulae. Given a bound on the length of the counterexample, a LTL model checking problem is encoded into a SAT problem. If a propositional model is found, it corresponds to a counterexample of the original model checking problem. With respect to the tableau construction in [4], enhancements have been carried out that can significantly improve the performances of the SAT checker. The system enters a loop, interleaving problem generation and solution attempt via a call to the SAT solver, and iterates until a solution is found or the specified bound is reached. Dual techniques for invariant checking [3] can be applied to invariant properties.

The properties are handled and shown to the user by a property manager, that is independent of the model checking engine used for the verification. This means that it is possible for the user to decide what solution method to adopt for each property. Furthermore, the counterexample traces being generated by both model checking modules are presented and stored into a unique format. Similarly, the user can simulate the behaviour of the specified system, by generating traces either interactively or randomly. Simulation can be carried out both via BDD-based or SAT-based techniques.

4   System Architecture

In the development of NuSMV, particular care is directed to the architectural design, in order to obtain an open architecture that can be integrated within different design environments, and customized depending on the application domain. Therefore, the architecture of NuSMV2 has been deeply revised and extended with respect to NuSMV1, in order to allow for a clean and effective integration of SAT-based techniques and to overcome some limitations of NuSMV1. A high level view of the internal structure of NuSMV2 is reported in Figure 1. The architecture is composed of the following main modules.

Flattening: The Flattening module implements the parsing of the model, some consistency checks to guarantee the well foundedness of the definitions, and eliminates processes and modules, producing a flat, scalar model, and a set of flat properties.

Encoding: The Encoding is responsible for mapping the flat, scalar model into a boolean model. This requires the introduction of the suitable boolean variables, depending on the range of the scalar variables being manipulated. For instance, for a bounded integer variable x, ranging from 0 to 255, 8 boolean variables $x_1, \ldots, x_8$ are defined. Furthermore, an encoding that associates each of the proposition $x = v$ into a corresponding assignment to $x_1, \ldots, x_8$ is constructed. Then, for each atomic proposition in the program, the corresponding boolean expression is constructed. For instance, the atomic proposition $(x+y) \leq z$ would be associated with a boolean expression in the boolean variables associated with x, y and z. This operation is carried out by means of Algebraic Decision Diagrams, particular forms of Decision Diagrams with non-boolean leaves.

Cone of Influence. This module implements the routines to restrict the analysis to a reduced FSM, containing only the relevant variables for each prop-

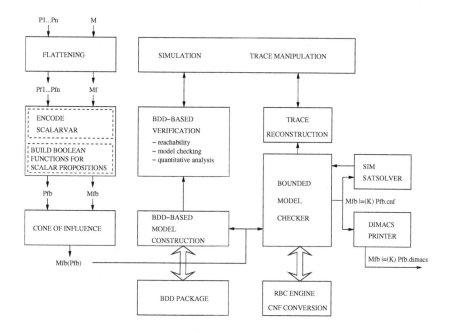

Fig. 1. The internal structure of NuSMV2.

erty. This reduction is amenable both for BDD-based and SAT-based model checking.

BDD-Based Model Construction: The BDD-based model construction module implements the Finite State Machine corresponding to the input file in terms of BDDs. An explicit data structure for FSM's is provided, that allows to encapsulate the actual construction/partitioning method applied. It is therefore possible to have different FSM's associated to different verification problems.

BDD-Based Verification: The BDD-based verification routines implement reachability analysis, LTL and CTL model checking, and quantitative analysis, in terms of the FSM data structures provided by BDD-based model construction. CTL model checking is implemented directly, while LTL model checking is reduced to a CTL model checking problems by means of a tableau construction, as described in [9]. The analysis of quantitative properties, such as the computation of the least distance between the occurrence of two given events, is carried by dedicated algorithms. All the operations only rely on image and preimage computations, and are independent of the actual partitioning mechanism.

BDD Package: The functionalities for the manipulation and storage of BDDs is provided by the BDD module. This module is based on the state-of-the-art Colorado University Decision Diagram (CUDD) package developed by Fabio Somenzi [24]. An additional layer encapsulates the CUDD functionalities in order to provide a uniform interface that hides low-level issues related to garbage collection of BDDs.

Bounded Model Checker: The Bounded Model Checker module provides the SAT-based model checking functionalities. It interacts with the RBC package to generate a RBC-based model representation. At the lowest level, an association between state variables at different time instants and the corresponding RBC variables is defined. The construction is optimized by means of memoizing techniques, in order to avoid the recomputation of frequently used RBCs. The variable association schema is implemented in such a way that full blown parallel substitution can be replaced by a shifting operation. Once the internal representation of the model is complete, the Bounded Model Checker can generate the SAT problems corresponding to a given formula, with a construction that extends the one in [4]. In particular, the construction takes into account all the components of the model (e.g., fairness constraints, invariants). Several encodings of the property are possible, depending if we are checking for a violation occurring exactly at step k or at a step $\leq k$, and with different loop-back structures for the counterexample. The problem is generated as an RBC, that is then converted in CNF format and provided in input to the SIM solver. If a model is found, then it is returned to the Bounded Model Checker, whose final step it to activate the trace reconstruction of the counterexample. The produced model checking problems can also be printed out in the standard DIMACS format, thus allowing for the stand-alone use of other SAT solvers.

Reduced Boolean Circuit (RBC): The RBC package implements a simplified version of the RBC data structure and the associated primitives for storing and manipulating propositional formulas, see [1]. The RBC package comes with a depth-first traversal routine, which allows to search the RBC, applying a given function (passed as a parameter) to each node being visited either in-order, pre-order, or post-order. This function is at the basis of the CNF converter. The CNF converter generates an equi-satisfiable formula obtained from the RBC by applying a structure-preserving transformation. The CNF converter also marks the variables occurring in the RBC. The ability to distinguish between the "independent" variables (i.e., the ones occurring in the formula before the CNF conversion) and the "dependent" variables (i.e., the ones introduced during the CNF conversion) can be extremely useful in driving the solver [14,15,23,12].

SIM SAT Solver: SIM is an efficient SAT solver based on the Davis-Logemann-Loveland procedure. Two are the distinguishing features of SIM. First, it can limit the branching to a subset of the variables, assuming that the others can be assigned by unit propagation. Second, it allows for relevance learning, and branching heuristics based on boolean constraint propagation which analyze the whole set of (relevant) variables. As [23,12] show, these features can produce dramatic speed-ups in the overall performances of the SAT checker, and thus of the whole system. SIM also features many other branching heuristics, and size learning (see [16]).

Simulation/Trace Manipulation: The simulation package allows for the interactive and random simulation of the behaviour of the model being processed.

It is compatible both with the BDD-based and the SAT-based representation, and encapsulates a uniform trace handling mechanism through which the stored traces can be inspected and rerun.

5 Conclusions

NuSMV is a robust, well structured and flexible platform for symbolic model checking, designed to be applicable in technology transfer projects. In this paper, we have shown how BDD-based and SAT-based model checking are integrated in the new version of NuSMV, that significantly extends the previous version. In particular, we have discussed the functionalities and the architecture of Nu-SMV2, that integrates SAT-based state of the art verification techniques, is able to working as a problem flattener in DIMACS format, and tackles the state explosion with cone of influence reduction.

NuSMV2 is currently being used as the verification kernel of a CAD tool developed in a technology transfer project, where an imperative style programming language is used to describe embedded controllers. The integration of decomposition techniques (e.g., abstraction and compositional verification) is under development. In the future, we plan to investigate a tighter integration between BDD-based and SAT-based technologies. The new internal architecture also opens up the possibility to integrate different boolean encodings [10] and different (e.g., non boolean) verification engines.

References

1. Parosh Aziz Abdulla, Per Bjesse, and Niklas Eén. Symbolic reachability analysis based on SAT-solvers. In Susanne Graf and Michael Schwartzbach, editors, *Proc. Tools and Algorithms for the Construction and Analysis of Systems TACAS, Berlin, Germany*, volume 1785 of *LNCS*. Springer-Verlag, 2000.
2. S. Berezin, S. Campos, and E. M. Clarke. Compositional reasoning in model checking. In *Proc. COMPOS*, 1997.
3. A. Biere, A. Cimatti, E. Clarke, M. Fujita, and Y. Zhu. Symbolic Model Checking Using SAT Procedures instead of BDDs. In *Proc. 36th Conference on Design Automation*, 1999.
4. A. Biere, A. Cimatti, E. Clarke, and Y. Zhu. Symbolic model checking without BDDs. In *Proceedings of the Fifth International Conference on Tools and Algorithms for the Construction and Analysis of Systems (TACAS '99)*, 1999.
5. A. Borälv. A Fully Automated Approach for Proving Safety Properties in Interlocking Software Using Automatic Theorem-Proving. In S. Gnesi and D. Latella, editors, *Proceedings of the Second International ERCIM Workshop on Formal Methods for Industrial Critical Systems*, Pisa, Italy, July 1997.
6. R. E. Bryant. Symbolic Boolean manipulation with ordered binary-decision diagrams. *ACM Computing Surveys*, 24(3):293–318, September 1992.
7. J. R. Burch, E. M. Clarke, K. L. McMillan, D. L. Dill, and L. J. Hwang. Symbolic Model Checking: 10^{20} States and Beyond. *Information and Computation*, 98(2):142–170, June 1992.

8. A. Cimatti, E.M. Clarke, F. Giunchiglia, and M. Roveri. NuSMV: a new Symbolic Model Verifier. In N. Halbwachs and D. Peled, editors, *Proceedings Eleventh Conference on Computer-Aided Verification (CAV'99)*, number 1633 in Lecture Notes in Computer Science, pages 495–499, Trento, Italy, July 1999. Springer-Verlag.

9. E. Clarke, O. Grumberg, and K. Hamaguchi. Another Look at LTL Model Checking. *Formal Methods in System Design*, 10(1):57–71, February 1997.

10. E. Clarke and X. Zhao. Word Level Symbolic Model Checking: A New Approach for Verifying Arithmetic Circuits. Technical Report CMU-CS-95-161, School of Computer Science, Carnegie Mellon University, Pittsburgh, PA 15213-3891, USA, May 1995.

11. E. M. Clarke and E. A. Emerson. Synthesis of synchronization skeletons for branching time tem poral logic. In *Logic of Programs: Workshop*. Springer Verlag, May 1981. Lecture Notes in Computer Science No. 131.

12. Fady Copty, Limor Fix, Enrico Giunchiglia, Gila Kamhi, Armando Tacchella, and Moshe Vardi. Benefits of bounded model checking at an industrial setting. In *Proceedings of CAV 2001*, pages 436–453, 2001.

13. Ranan Fraer, Gila Kamhi, Barukh Ziv, Moshe Y. Vardi, and Limor Fix. Prioritized traversal: Efficient reachability analysis for verification and falsification. In *Proceedings of the 12th International Conference on Computer Aided Verification*, pages 389–402. Springer, July 2000.

14. E. Giunchiglia, A. Massarotto, and R. Sebastiani. Act, and the rest will follow: Exploiting determinism in planning as satisfiability. In *Proc. AAAI*, 1998.

15. E. Giunchiglia and R. Sebastiani. Applying the Davis-Putnam procedure to non-clausal formulas. In Evelina Lamma and Paola Mello, editors, *Proceedings of AI*IA'99: Advances in Artificial Intelligence*, pages 84–94. Springer Verlag, 1999.

16. Enrico Giunchiglia, Marco Maratea, Armando Tacchella, and Davide Zambonin. Evaluating search heuristics and optimization techniques in propositional satisfiability. In Rajeev Goré, Alexander Leitsch, and Tobias Nipkow, editors, *Proceedings of IJCAR 2001*, volume 2083 of *Lecture Notes in Computer Science*, pages 347–363. Springer, 2001.

17. G. J. Holzmann. The model checker Spin. *IEEE Trans. on Software Engineering*, 23(5):279–295, May 1997. Special issue on Formal Methods in Software Practice.

18. K.L. McMillan. *Symbolic Model Checking*. Kluwer Academic Publ., 1993.

19. Matthew W. Moskewicz, Conor F. Madigan, Ying Zhao, Lintao Zhang, and Sharad Malik. Chaff: Engineering an efficient sat solver. In *Proceedings of the 38th Design Automation Conference*, pages 530–535. ACM, 2001.

20. J.P. Quielle and J. Sifakis. Specification and verification of concurrent systems in CESAR. In *Proceedings of the Fifth International Symposium in Programming*, 1981.

21. R. K. Ranjan, A. Aziz, B. Plessier, C. Pixley, and R. K. Brayton. Efficient BDD algorithms for FSM synthesis and verification. In *IEEE/ACM Proceedings International Workshop on Logic Synthesis*, Lake Tahoe (NV), May 1995.

22. K. Ravi and F. Somenzi. High-density reachability analysis. In *International Conference on Computer Aided Design*, pages 154–158, Los Alamitos, Ca., USA, November 1995. IEEE Computer Society Press.

23. O. Shtrichman. Tuning SAT checkers for bounded model-checking. In *Proc. 12th International Computer Aided Verification Conference (CAV)*, 2000.

24. F. Somenzi. CUDD: CU Decision Diagram package — release 2.1.2. Department of Electrical and Computer Engineering — University of Colorado at Boulder, April 1997.

$PreUnion(S,R, isSubset)$: composite formula

1	S_{res}, S, R: composite formula
2	$isSubset$:boolean
3	$isSubset \leftarrow true$
4	$S_{res} \leftarrow S$
5	for each composite atom s in S do
6	for each composite atom r in R do
7	$s_k = \text{PRE}(s, r)$
8	if $s_k \not\subseteq S$ then
9	$isSubset \leftarrow false$
10	$S_{res} \leftarrow S_{res} \cup s_k$
110	return S_{res}

$EfficientEF(S, R)$: composite formula

1	S, R: composite formula
2	$isSubset$: boolean
3	$S_{new} \leftarrow S$
4	do
5	$S_{old} \leftarrow S_{new}$
6	$S_{new} \leftarrow PreUnion(S_{old}, R, isSubset)$
7	$S_{new} \leftarrow Simplify(S_{new})$
8	while $(\neg isSubset)$
9	return S_{new}

(a)   (b)

Fig. 4. (a)A pre-condition algorithm with subset check and union (b) A more efficient algorithm for computing the least fixed point for EF

S_{new} that satisfy (3) during the subset check at line 6 of the algorithm. An additional improvement can be achieved by taking union of s_k with S_{res} only if s_k is not subset of S and prevent the unnecessary increase in the number of composite atoms in S_{res}. Figure 4(a) and 4(b) show the algorithms $preUnion$, which computes pre-condition along with subset check and union, and $EfficientEF$, which computes least fixed point for EF using $preUnion$ algorithm, respectively.

8   Experiments

We have experimented the heuristics explained in the previous sections using a set of specifications. Some of the specifications are well known concurrency problems such as Bakery (BAKERY*) and Ticket (TICKET*) algorithms for mutual exclusion problem, Sleeping Barber (BARBER*), Readers Writers (RW*), and Bounded Buffer Producer Consumer (PC*) problems [4]. We also included specifications of a cache coherence protocol (COHERENCE*) [13], insertion sort (INSERTIONSORT) algorithm [14], an office light control system (LIGHTCONTROL) [8] and a safety injection system for a nuclear reactor (SIS*) [12]. The "*"character indicates that the specification has several versions each with different temporal property or with different number of concurrent components. For Readers Writers and Sleeping Barber problems we have also used the parameterized versions meaning that the specification models the system with arbitrary number of processes. We obtained the experimental results on a SUN ULTRA 10 workstation with 768 Mbytes of memory, running SunOs 5.7.

Experimental results for the verifier with different versions of the simplification algorithm and without simplification is given in Table 1. The label $S2$-$S3$-$S4$ indicates that at each simplification point the simplification algorithm with $S2$, $S3$, and $S4$ are called in this order. So a multi-level simplification is achieved starting with the least aggressive version and continuing by increasing the degree real variables as linear arithmetic constraints. As a result, BDDs are restricted to finite domains and polyhedral representation becomes inefficient when it is used for a large set of boolean variables. However, it is very likely that a large software specification would use more than one data type. Motivated with this observation, we have designed and implemented the Composite Symbolic Library [19] that combines several symbolic representations. Our current implementation uses BDDs for boolean and enumerated variables and polyhedra for (unbounded) integers. However, Composite Symbolic Library can be easily extended with new symbolic representations since we have adopted an object-oriented approach in its design.

In this paper, we present several heuristics for efficient manipulation of this composite representation. Our heuristics make use of the following observations: 1) efficient operations on BDDs can be used to mask expensive operations on polyhedra, 2) our disjunctive representation can be exploited by computing pre and post-conditions and subset checks incrementally, and 3) size of a composite representation can be minimized by iteratively merging matching constraints and removing redundant ones. We have implemented the above ideas and experimented with a large set of examples. Experimental results indicate effectiveness of our heuristics.

Techniques that are similar to our heuristics have been used in the literature. In [14], local subsumption test is used during the fixpoint computations to remove the redundant constrained facts. This is similar to our approach for preventing the increase in the size of the disjunctive composite representation during fixpoint computation by removing redundant disjuncts. However, we use full subsumption test. Local subsumption test can also be used as a heuristic to test the convergence of fixpoint computations [14]. However, there can be cases where fixpoint computation that uses the local subsumption test does not converge whereas the fixpoint computation that uses the full subsumption test converges.

Hytech, a tool for verification of hybrid systems, simplifies formulas using rewrite rules [3]. The approach used in [3] is for simplification of linear arithmetic formulas on real variables. Our work is different in two respects: 1) We use linear arithmetic formulas on integer variables. 2) Our heuristics are not for simplification of linear arithmetic formulas, this is handled by the constraint manipulator we use [2]. Rather, our heuristics are for simplification of composite formulas which contain a mixture of boolean and integer variables. In Hytech tool boolean or enumerated variables (for example control states) are eliminated by partitioning the state space [3].

In [18], a linear partitioning algorithm for convex polyhedra is used to efficiently test if a single convex polyhedron is subsumed by a union of convex polyhedra. This approach is analogous to our subset check heuristic where the union of convex polyhedra corresponds to our disjunctive composite representation and the single convex polyhedron corresponds to a single disjunct of composite representation.

The rest of the paper is organized as follows. In Section 2 and Section 3, we explain Composite Symbolic Library and our model checker that uses the composite symbolic representation, respectively. In Section 4, we present heuristics that masks expensive polyhedral operations with BDD operations. We introduce an efficient subset check algorithm for composite symbolic representation in Section 5. In Section 6, we propose several algorithms with different aggressiveness levels for minimization of composite symbolic representation. We explain how we can improve a fixpoint algorithm in Section 7. In Section 8, we present the experimental results of the heuristics that we propose in Sections 3-7. Finally, in Section 9, we give our conclusions.

2   Composite Symbolic Library

Composite Symbolic Library is a symbolic manipulator for model checking systems with heterogeneous data types. In Composite Symbolic Library different symbolic representations are combined using the *composite model checking* approach [6]. Our current implementation of the Composite Symbolic Library uses two symbolic representations: BDDs for boolean logic formulas and polyhedral representation for Presburger arithmetic formulas. We call these representations *basic symbolic representations*.

Each variable type in the system to be verified is assigned to the most efficient basic symbolic representation for that variable type. Boolean and enumerated variables are mapped to BDD representation, and integers are mapped to arithmetic constraint representation. We encode the sets of system states and the transition relation of the system in Disjunctive Normal Form (DNF), as a disjunction of conjunctions of basic symbolic representations (e.g., a disjunct consists of conjunction of a boolean formula stored as a BDD representing the states of boolean and enumerated variables, and a Presburger arithmetic constraint representing the states of integer variables). We call this DNF representation a *composite symbolic representation* since it combines different basic symbolic representations.

We used an object-oriented design for the Composite Symbolic Library. An abstract class called Symbolic serves as an interface to all symbolic representations in the Composite Symbolic Library including the composite representation. A class called BoolSym serves as a wrapper for the BDD library CUDD [1] and derived from abstract class Symbolic. Similarly, IntSym class is also derived from abstract class Symbolic and serves as a wrapper for the Omega Library [2]. A class called CompSym is the class for composite representations. It is derived from Symbolic and uses IntSym and BoolSym (through the Symbolic interface) to manipulate composite representations.

The object-oriented design for the Composite Symbolic Library has several advantages: 1) The manipulation of the composite representations is independent of the manipulation of the basic symbolic representations and number of basic symbolic representations. CompSym accesses basic symbolic representations using only the Symbolic interface and it uses the number of basic symbolic representations as a parameter. 2) It is easy to replace the Omega Library and CUDD Library with other symbolic manipulators as long as one writes a wrapper around the new symbolic manipulator which conforms to the `Symbolic` interface. 3) Verification is polymorphic. Since the verification procedures use the `Symbolic` interface they work both for composite symbolic representations and basic symbolic representations. I.e., based on the input specification our current implementation can be used as a BDD-based model checker, a polyhedra-based model checker or a composite model checker.

To analyze a system using Composite Symbolic Library, one has to specify its initial condition, transition relation, and state space using a set of *composite formulas*. A composite formula is obtained by combining boolean and integer formulas with logical connectives. A boolean formula consists of boolean variables or constants joined with logical connectives. An integer formula consists of integer variables or constants joined with arithmetic operators $+$ and $-$, arithmetic predicates $<, >, =, \leq, \geq$, logical connectives, and quantifiers $\exists$ and $\forall$. Since symbolic representations in the Composite Symbolic Library currently support only Presburger arithmetic formulas, we restrict arithmetic operators to $+$ and $-$. However, we allow multiplication with a constant and quantification.

In `CompSym`, a composite formula, P, is represented in DNF as

$$P = \bigvee_{i=1}^{n} \bigwedge_{j=1}^{t} p_{ij}$$

where p_{ij} denotes the formula of basic symbolic representation type j in the ith disjunct, and n and t denote the number of disjuncts and the number of basic symbolic representation types, respectively. We call each disjunct $\wedge_{j=1}^{t} p_{ij}$ a *composite atom*. Each composite atom is implemented as an instance of a class called `compAtom`. The `compAtom` class has a field called `representation`. `representation` field is an array of class `Symbolic` and the size of the array is the number of basic symbolic representations. Semantically, each `compAtom` object represents a conjunction of formulas each of which is either a boolean or an integer formula (which are represented as `BoolSym` and `IntSym` objects, respectively). A composite formula stored in a `CompSym` object is implemented as a list of `compAtom` objects, which corresponds to the disjunction in the DNF above.

The `CompSym` class includes methods (such as intersection, union, complement, satisfiability check, equivalence check, etc.) which manipulate composite representations in the above form. These methods in turn call the related method of basic symbolic methods (which are implemented in `IntSym` and `BoolSym` classes). Note that all these operations can be effectively computed both for boolean logic formulas and Presburger arithmetic formulas.

3   Symbolic Verifier

Given a set of states S and a transition relation R, pre-condition PRE(S, R) are all the states that can reach a state in S with a single transition in R

(i.e., the set of predecessors of all the states in S). Post-condition $\text{POST}(S, R)$ is defined similarly. Given a set S and a transition relation R both represented using composite symbolic representation as $S \equiv \bigvee_{i=1}^{n_S} \bigwedge_{j=1}^{t} s_{ij}$ and $R \equiv \bigvee_{i=1}^{n_R} \bigwedge_{j=1}^{t} r_{ij}$ the pre-condition can be computed as

$$\text{PRE}(S, R) \equiv \bigvee_{i=1}^{n_R} \bigvee_{k=1}^{n_S} \bigwedge_{j=1}^{t} \text{PRE}(s_{kj}, r_{ij})$$

The above property holds because the existential variable elimination in the $\text{PRE}(S, R)$ computation distributes over the disjunctions, and due to the partitioning of the variables based on the basic symbolic types, the existential variable elimination also distributes over the conjunction above.

Our symbolic model checker computes fixpoints for CTL temporal operators using the function $\text{PRE}(S, R)$ and fixpoint computations [8]. In the experiments reported in this paper we use the basis $\{\text{EX}, \text{EG}, \text{EU}\}$ for CTL formulas [11].

4   Masking Integer Operations

Composite Symbolic Library currently supports two basic symbolic representations: BDDs to represent boolean and enumerated variables and polyhedral representation of linear arithmetic constraints to represent integer variables. Existential variable elimination for linear integer arithmetic constraints is NP-complete and it is used in satisfiability check and pre and post condition computations. However, since BDD representation is canonical, satisfiability check for BDDs can be performed in constant time by comparing the root node to the unique BDD that corresponds to *false*. This discrepancy in the performances of BDDs and polyhedral representation in checking satisfiability can be exploited to speed up pre and post condition computation on the composite symbolic representation.

A composite atom $s = b \wedge i$, where b and i denote the BDD part and polyhedral part, respectively, is satisfiable iff both b and i are satisfiable. Since satisfiability check for polyhedral representation is expensive, by checking the satisfiability of the BDD part first we can avoid checking satisfiability for the polyhedral part whenever the BDD part is not satisfiable. If we find out that the BDD part is not satisfiable we can conclude that the composite atom is not satisfiable.

Given two composite formulas $S = \bigvee_{j=1}^{n_S} b_{sj} \wedge i_{sj}$ and $R = \bigvee_{k=1}^{n_R} b_{rk} \wedge i_{rk}$, where S represents a set and R represents the transition relation, b_{sj} and b_{rk} correspond to boolean formulas, and i_{sj} and i_{rk} correspond to integer formulas, pre-condition of S with respect to R can be written as

$$\text{PRE}(S, R) = \bigvee_{j=1}^{n_S} \bigvee_{k=1}^{n_R} \text{PRE}(b_{sj}, b_{rk}) \wedge \text{PRE}(i_{sj}, i_{rk})$$

Instead of computing $\text{PRE}(b_{sj}, b_{rk})$ and $\text{PRE}(i_{sj}, i_{rk})$ and then taking the intersection of the two, we can first compute $\text{PRE}(b_{sj}, b_{rk})$ and then check it for satisfiability. Since $\text{PRE}(b_{sj}, b_{rk})$ is a boolean formula and represented by BDDs, checking satisfiability of $\text{PRE}(b_{sj}, b_{rk})$ is cheaper than checking satisfiability of $\text{PRE}(i_{sj}, i_{rk})$, which is represented by polyhedra. We should compute $\text{PRE}(i_{sj}, i_{rk})$ that involves manipulation of polyhedral representation only if $\text{PRE}(b_{sj}, b_{rk})$ is satisfiable. If it is not satisfiable then we will not compute $\text{PRE}(i_{sj}, i_{rk})$ since we can deduce that $\text{PRE}(b_{sj}, b_{rk}) \wedge \text{PRE}(i_{sj}, i_{rk})$ evaluates to *false*. As a result expensive integer manipulation is masked by cheaper boolean manipulation.

5   Subset Check

A composite formula $A = \bigvee_{i=1}^{n} a_i$ is subset of a composite formula $B = \bigvee_{k=1}^{m} b_k$ iff $\forall i$ s.t. $1 \leq i \leq n$, $a_i \subseteq B$. So the most straightforward way of checking subset relation between composite formulas A and B is to iterate through the composite atoms in A and check subset relation between each composite atom a_i in A and B. If there exists a composite atom a_i in A such that a_i is not subset of B we can conclude that A is not subset of B. On the other hand, if there exists no such composite atom in A then we can conclude that A is subset of B.

Figure 1(a) shows the algorithm for checking subset relation between two composite formulas A and B. For each composite atom a_i in A, first the algorithm checks if a_i is subset of any composite atom in B (lines 4-8). A composite atom $a = \bigwedge_{i=1}^{t} a_i$ is subset of composite atom $b = \bigwedge_{i=1}^{t} b_i$ iff $\forall i$ s.t. $1 \leq i \leq t$, $a_i \subseteq b_i$, where t is the number of basic types. If there exists no composite atom b in B such that a is subset of b then this does not mean that a is not subset of B. Next, the algorithm computes $a \cap \neg B$ and assigns the result to composite formula C. If C is satisfiable then it means a is not subset of B and the algorithm exits by returning false (lines 9-12). Otherwise the algorithm continues until either it finds out that there exists a composite atom a that is not subset of B or it has checked all the composite atoms in A in which case it returns true (line 13).

Time complexity of the algorithm in Figure 1(a) is

$$O(n_A \times n_B \times \sum_{j=1}^{t} T_{IsSubset}^{j} + n_A \times (\sum_{i=1}^{n_B} \sum_{j=1}^{t} T_{Complement}^{j} + t^{n_B} \times \sum_{j=1,1 \leq t_j \leq t}^{n_B} T_{Intersection}^{t_j} + n_B \times \sum_{j=1}^{t} T_{IsEmpty}^{j})).$$

where n_A, n_B, t, and T_{Op}^{i} are number of composite atoms in A, number of composite atoms in B, number of basic symbolic representations and time complexity of operation Op for ith basic symbolic representation, respectively. Expensive part of the algorithm is computing the complement of composite formula B (line 10) since time complexity of complement operation on a composite formula B is exponential in the number of composite atoms in B. For the subset check algorithm, computing complement of B means that all the composite atoms in B are taken into consideration to decide if a composite atom a is subset of B. However, deciding if a composite atom a is subset of a composite formula B does not always require to consider all the composite atoms in B. For instance, let composite atom a and composite formula B be,

$$a = (x \wedge y \wedge (z > 0 \vee z < -4)), \; B = (x \wedge z \geq 0) \vee (x \wedge z \leq -1) \vee (\neg x \wedge z < 0)$$

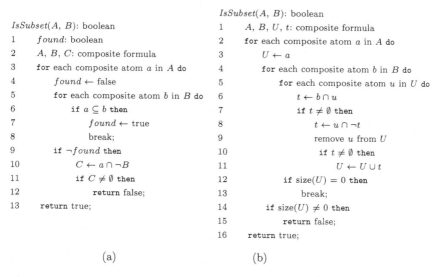

IsSubset(A, B): boolean

	IsSubset(A, B): boolean
1	A, B, U, t: composite formula
2	for each composite atom a in A do
3	U ← a
4	for each composite atom b in B do
5	for each composite atom u in U do
6	t ← b ∩ u
7	if t ≠ ∅ then
8	t ← u ∩ ¬t
9	remove u from U
10	if t ≠ ∅ then
11	U ← U ∪ t
12	if size(U) = 0 then
13	break;
14	if size(U) ≠ 0 then
15	return false;
16	return true;

(a)   (b)

Fig. 1. Subset check algorithms performing negation at (a) composite formula level
and at (b) composite atom level

where x and y are boolean variables and z is an integer variable. Since each
composite atom in a composite formula corresponds to a disjunct of the composite formula, B has three composite atoms b_1, b_2, and b_3 that correspond to
$(x \wedge z \geq 0)$, $(x \wedge z \leq -1)$, and $(\neg x \wedge z < 0)$, respectively. In order to decide if a
is subset of B we do not need to consider all the composite atoms in B. For this
example, it is sufficient to compare a against b_1 and b_2 (note that a is subset of
$b_1 \vee b_2$) only to conclude that a is subset of B. However, the algorithm given in
Figure 1(a) will process b_1, b_2, and b_3 by computing complement of B.

In the light of this observation we propose a more efficient solution to subset
check problem for composite formulas. Given two composite formulas A and B,
for each composite atom a in A, our solution iteratively computes uncovered
subset of a, U, that is not covered by the composite atoms in B that have been
examined so far. U is initialized to a and for each k s.t. $1 \leq k \leq n_B$, U is
updated as $U \cap \neg b_k$. After U is updated using b_k it is checked for emptiness.
If it becomes empty then the algorithm skips checking the remaining composite
atoms in B and concludes that a is subset of B. Otherwise, it continues with b_{k+1}.
After checking all composite atoms in B if U is not empty then the algorithm
concludes that a is not subset of B. The algorithm is given in Figure 1(b).
Note that in this algorithm there is no complement operation on the composite
formula level. Instead complement is computed for composite atoms in B as
needed. Time complexity of subset check algorithm in Figure 1(b) is $O(n_A \times$
$(t-1)^{n_B} \times \sum_{i=1}^{t}(T_{Satisfiability}^{i} + T_{Intersection}^{i})$. Even though this algorithm has
also an exponential worst case time complexity, in the average case we expect it
to perform better than the algorithm in Figure 1(a).

6   Simplification Algorithm

The number of composite atoms in a composite formula which results from the intersection operation is linear in the product of the number of composite atoms of the input composite formulas. The number of composite atoms in a composite formula which results from the negation operation is exponential in the number of composite atoms of the input composite formula. Most of the time these resulting composite formulas are not minimal in terms of the number of composite atoms they have. For instance, composite formula A that represents the formula $(x \wedge y = z + 1) \vee (t \wedge y = z + 1) \vee ((x \vee t) \wedge y > z)$, where x and t are boolean variables and y and z are integer variables, has three composite atoms that correspond to the three disjuncts $(x \wedge y = z+1)$, $(t \wedge y = z+1)$, and $((x \vee t) \wedge y > z)$. However, A can be equivalently composed of a single composite atom that represents the formula $((x \vee t) \wedge y > z)$. Since time complexity of manipulating composite formulas is dependent on the number of composite atoms we need to reduce the number of composite atoms in a composite formula as much as possible to make the verification feasible in terms of both time and memory. We present a simplification algorithm that can be tuned for 4 different degrees of aggressiveness. First we would like to present the most aggressive version of the algorithm and then explain how aggressiveness can be traded for efficiency in a reasonable way.

A composite formula having two composite atoms, a and b, can be simplified and represented by a single composite atom c if one of the following holds: 1) a is subset of b. In this case $c = b$. 2) a is superset of b. In this case $c = a$. 3) There exists a basic type j s.t. for all basic types i s.t. $i \neq j$, $a_i = b_i$. In this case for all i s.t. $i \neq j$, $c_i = a_i$ and $c_j = a_j \vee b_j$.

Figure 2 shows the simplification algorithm. The algorithm takes each pair of composite atoms a and b in a composite formula and checks if union of the formula represented by a and b can be represented by a single composite atom r based on the above rules. The algorithm stops when there exists no two composite atoms in the composite formula that can be replaced by a single composite atom. The steps that make the algorithm aggressive are at lines 22 and 23. At line 22 the composite atom r that can replace a and b is inserted to the head of the list of composite atoms and a is set to the head of the list at line 23. This ensures that composite atom r can be compared against all other composite atoms in the list.

We can loosen the post condition of the simplification algorithm and make the algorithm less aggressive and more efficient in three ways. The first way exploits the fact that equivalence check on BDDs is cheaper than equivalence check on polyhedral representation. At line 14 of the *Simplification* algorithm in Figure 2, a_t and b_t, where t is a basic type, are checked for equivalence. Instead of checking equivalence of a_t and b_t for each basic type t, we can check it for only boolean type. This makes the *Simplification* algorithm less expensive and less aggressive meaning that given two composite atoms a and b, the *Simplification* algorithm will be able to combine a and b into a single composite atom r if a

```
Simplify(composite formula A)
1      a, b, r: composite atom
2      success: boolean
3      list_A: list of composite atoms
4      let list_A be the list of composite atoms in A
5      a ← head(list_A)
6      while a ≠ NULL do
7          b ← next(a)
8          while b ≠ NULL do
9              if a ⊆ b then remove a from list_A; break
10             else if b ⊆ a then temp ← b ; b ← next(b) ; remove temp from list_A
11             else
12                 success ← false
13                 for each basic type t do
14                     if a_t ≠ b_t then
15                         if ¬success then index ← t ; success ← true
16                         else success ← false ; break
17                     if success then
18                         remove a and b from list_A
19                         for each basic type t do
20                             if index = t then r_t ← a_t ∨ b_t
21                             else r_t ← a_t
22                         insert r to head of list_A
23                         a ← head(list_A) ; break
24                     else b ← next(b)
25         a ← next(a)
```

Fig. 2. An algorithm for simplifying a given composite formula

(b) is subset of b (a) or $a_{boolean}$ is equal to $b_{boolean}$. If $a_{boolean}$ is not equal to $b_{boolean}$ the algorithm will conclude that a and b cannot be combined.

The second way is to avoid subset check. At lines 9 and 10 *Simplification* algorithm in Figure 2 checks if a is subset of b or vice versa, respectively. By eliminating subset check between a and b the algorithm will combine two composite formula a and b only if $a_{boolean}$ is equal to $b_{boolean}$.

The third way is to consider only a subset of composite atom pairs in a given composite formula. At line 22 of the *Simplify* algorithm in Figure 2, composite atom r, which is combination of composite atoms a and b, is inserted at the head of $list_A$ and a is set to the head of $list_A$ at line 23. These two steps ensure that composite formula A is minimal by forcing analysis of every pair of composite atoms in A. However, if r is inserted at the end of $list_A$ without making a point to head of $list_A$ r is not compared with other composite atoms and the resulting composite formula A is no longer minimal (i.e., there may be pairs of composite atoms in A which can be merged).

By using the three ways of aggressiveness reduction we obtain 4 different versions of *Simplification* algorithm which we represent by $S1$, $S2$, $S3$, and $S4$

ComputeEF(composite formula P, composite formula R): composite formula

1      $S_{new} \leftarrow P$

2   do

3          $S_{old} \leftarrow S_{new}$

4          $S_{new} \leftarrow \text{PRE}(S_{old}, R) \cup S_{old}$

5          $S_{new} \leftarrow Simplify(S_{new})$

6   while $\neg isSubset(S_{new}, S_{old})$

7   return S_{new}

Fig. 3. An algorithm for computing the least fixed point for EF

in increasing aggressiveness order. Let n denote the number of composite atoms in the input composite formula:

- S1: Number of executions of the inner while loop is $O(n^2)$ and checks equivalence relation only on boolean type and eliminates subset check.
- S2: Number of executions of the inner while loop is $O(n^3)$ and checks equivalence relation only on boolean type and eliminates subset check.
- S3: Number of executions of the inner while loop is $O(n^3)$ and checks equivalence relation only on boolean type. However, it performs subset check.
- S4: Number of executions of the inner while loop is $O(n^3)$, checks equivalence relation on all types and performs subset check.

7 Combining Pre-condition, Subset Check, and Union Computations

All CTL operators can be defined in terms of a least or a greatest fixpoint. EF is defined as a least fixpoint as EF $p \equiv \mu x \,.\, p \;\vee\; EX\; x$. Figure 3 shows the algorithm for computing the least fixpoint for EF. Given two composite formulas $P = \bigvee_{i=1}^{n_P} p_i$ and $R = \bigvee_{j=1}^{n_R} r_j$, where P represents a set of states and R represents the transition relation, the algorithm computes the set of states that satisfy $EF(P)$ iteratively. S_{new} represents the largest subset of the fixed point computed so far. At line 4 of *ComputeEF* algorithm $S_{new} = \bigvee_{k=1}^{n_S} s_k$ where one of the following holds for s_k:

1. $s_k = \text{PRE}(p_i, r_j)$, where $1 \leq i \leq n_P$ and $1 \leq j \leq n_R$, and $s_k \not\subseteq S_{old}$,

2. $s_k = \text{PRE}(p_i, r_j)$, where $1 \leq i \leq n_P$ and $1 \leq j \leq n_R$, and $s_k \subseteq S_{old}$,

3. $s_k \subseteq S_{old}$ and there exists no i, j, where $1 \leq i \leq n_P$ and $1 \leq j \leq n_R$, s.t $s_k = \text{PRE}(p_i, r_j)$.

Note that composite atoms that satisfy (1) can be used to decide if S_{new} is subset of S_{old} earlier during the computation of pre-condition and eliminate subset check at line 6 of the algorithm. This may serve as an improvement over the algorithm in Figure 3 since we can eliminate processing composite atoms in

PreUnion(*S*,*R*, *isSubset*): composite formula

1	S_{res}, S, R: composite formula
2	$isSubset$:boolean
3	$isSubset \leftarrow true$
4	$S_{res} \leftarrow S$
5	**for** each composite atom s in S **do**
6	**for** each composite atom r in R **do**
7	$s_k = \text{PRE}(s, r)$
8	**if** $s_k \not\subseteq S$ **then**
9	$isSubset \leftarrow false$
10	$S_{res} \leftarrow S_{res} \cup s_k$
110	**return** S_{res}

EfficientEF(*S*, *R*): composite formula

1	S, R: composite formula
2	$isSubset$: boolean
3	$S_{new} \leftarrow S$
4	**do**
5	$S_{old} \leftarrow S_{new}$
6	$S_{new} \leftarrow PreUnion(S_{old}, R, isSubset)$
7	$S_{new} \leftarrow Simplify(S_{new})$
8	**while** ($\neg isSubset$)
9	**return** S_{new}

(a)   (b)

Fig. 4. (a)A pre-condition algorithm with subset check and union (b) A more efficient algorithm for computing the least fixed point for EF

S_{new} that satisfy (3) during the subset check at line 6 of the algorithm. An additional improvement can be achieved by taking union of s_k with S_{res} only if s_k is not subset of S and prevent the unnecessary increase in the number of composite atoms in S_{res}. Figure 4(a) and 4(b) show the algorithms *preUnion*, which computes pre-condition along with subset check and union, and *EfficientEF*, which computes least fixed point for *EF* using *preUnion* algorithm, respectively.

8   Experiments

We have experimented the heuristics explained in the previous sections using a set of specifications. Some of the specifications are well known concurrency problems such as Bakery (BAKERY*) and Ticket (TICKET*) algorithms for mutual exclusion problem, Sleeping Barber (BARBER*), Readers Writers (RW*), and Bounded Buffer Producer Consumer (PC*) problems [4]. We also included specifications of a cache coherence protocol (COHERENCE*) [13], insertion sort (IN-SERTIONSORT) algorithm [14], an office light control system (LIGHTCONTROL) [8] and a safety injection system for a nuclear reactor (SIS*) [12]. The "*"character indicates that the specification has several versions each with different temporal property or with different number of concurrent components. For Readers Writers and Sleeping Barber problems we have also used the parameterized versions meaning that the specification models the system with arbitrary number of processes. We obtained the experimental results on a SUN ULTRA 10 workstation with 768 Mbytes of memory, running SunOs 5.7.

Experimental results for the verifier with different versions of the simplification algorithm and without simplification is given in Table 1. The label S2-S3-S4 indicates that at each simplification point the simplification algorithm with $S2$, $S3$, and $S4$ are called in this order. So a multi-level simplification is achieved starting with the least aggressive version and continuing by increasing the degree

Table 1. Verification Time (T, in seconds) and Memory (M, in Mbytes) Results for Different Versions of Simplification vs No Simplification. (↑ means the program ran out of memory, $> x$ means execution did not terminate in x seconds, and (L) indicates that the specification has been verified for a liveness property)

Problem Instance	S2-S3-S4 T	M	S1 T	M	S2 T	M	S3 T	M	S4 T	M	None T	M
BAKERY2-1	0.21	7.8	0.08	7.7	0.09	7.8	0.10	7.7	0.2	7.7	0.1	80
(L)BAKERY2-2	0.26	0.9	0.34	8.8	0.53	8.8	0.31	8.5	0.35	7.8	↑	↑
BAKERY3-1	8.26	19.6	3.61	21.2	3.44	21.5	3.48	20.3	8.85	19.5	5.71	30
(L)BAKERY3-2	51.32	34.7	255.45	324	370	323	109.7	77.5	81.23	34.9	↑	↑
TICKET2-1	1.07	10.2	0.56	10.4	0.59	10.3	0.60	10.4	0.87	10.2	1.81	17.4
(L)TICKET2-2	3.13	13.8	1.3	13.8	1.31	13.8	1.30	13.5	2.19	13.4	↑	↑
TICKET3-1	14.71	28	15.39	58	15.49	58	13.56	43.3	21.42	35.2	↑	↑
(L)TICKET3-2	29.73	29	61.28	173	75.48	173	28.2	62	119.95	60	↑	↑
BARBER2-1	4.62	17.7	4.8	21.5	4.52	21	3.59	17.6	4.52	17.6	59.3	197
BARBER2-2	0.27	8.8	0.21	9	0.25	9	0.23	9	0.27	8.8	0.28	9.3
BARBER2-3	1.58	12.8	1.2	13.7	1.49	13.8	1.51	13.8	1.55	12.8	2.93	20
BARBER3-1	10.93	26.6	13.68	35.2	13.22	34.5	9.14	26.4	10.59	26.4	↑	↑
BARBER3-2	0.35	9.5	0.35	9.8	0.32	9.7	0.33	9.8	0.30	9.5	0.5	10
BARBER3-3	4.12	18.1	2.79	20.5	4.39	21	4.31	21	3.93	18	66.89	205
BARBER4-1	21.98	38.5	26.86	53.7	29.92	52.7	18.85	38.1	21.05	38.1	↑	↑
BARBER4-2	0.43	10.1	0.43	10.5	0.46	10.5	0.43	10.5	0.39	10.1	0.83	13.3
BARBER4-3	8.76	25.9	5.31	30.7	10.09	32.2	9.93	32	8.61	25.8	↑	↑
BARBERP-1	6.69	24	5.17	21.1	5.64	24	6.53	24	7.8	24	173	228
BARBERP-2	0.21	9.3	0.13	9.3	0.16	9.3	0.19	9.3	0.20	9.3	0.38	10.3
BARBERP-3	1.19	13.4	0.72	12.4	0.78	13.4	0.89	13.4	1.14	13.4	3.77	19.5
COHERENCE-1	0.34	11.3	0.24	11.2	0.25	11.2	0.29	11.2	0.30	11.3	0.23	11.5
(L)COHERENCE-2	2.74	14.8	0.78	13.7	0.74	13.6	0.82	13.1	4.03	15.6	2.1	24.8
(L)COHERENCE-3	11.97	29.8	2.09	22.8	2.11	22.2	2.42	21.1	18.8	32.8	21.97	161
(L)COHERENCE-4	13.14	27.7	1.98	19.3	1.93	19.3	2.03	19.3	27.09	36.9	↑	↑
COHERENCE-REF-1	0.27	11	0.27	11	0.19	11	0.22	11	0.25	11	0.16	11.1
(L)COHERENCE-REF-2	0.97	11.4	>83	>60	>83	>60	>83	>60	>83	>60	↑	↑
(L)COHERENCE-REF-3	5.52	20.8	>139	>181	>139	>181	>139	>181	>139	>181	↑	↑
(L)COHERENCE-REF-4	23.25	27.7	>109	>118	>109	>118	>109	>118	>109	>118	↑	↑
INSERTIONSORT	0.2	8.5	0.12	8.5	0.11	8.5	0.11	8.4	0.23	8.4	0.21	8.7
PC5	0.07	7.7	0.05	7.7	0.06	7.7	0.06	7.7	0.05	7.7	0.05	8.1
PC10	0.09	8.5	0.09	8.5	0.08	8.5	0.10	8.5	0.09	8.5	0.09	9.5
PC30	0.25	11.8	0.24	11.8	0.25	11.8	0.25	11.8	0.23	11.8	0.23	28.3
RW16	0.02	8.1	0.02	8.1	0.02	8.1	0.02	8.1	0.02	8.1	↑	↑
RW32	0.03	10.8	0.03	10.8	0.03	10.8	0.03	10.8	0.03	10.8	↑	↑
RW64	0.05	20.6	0.05	20.6	0.05	20.6	0.05	20.6	0.05	20.6	↑	↑
RWP	0.01	9	0.01	9	0.01	9	0.01	9	0.01	9	0.01	9
SIS-1	0.01	7.5	0.01	7.5	0.01	7.5	0.01	7.5	0.01	7.5	0.01	7.7
SIS-2	0.07	19.4	0.02	19.4	0.02	19.4	0.03	19.4	0.06	19.4	0.02	23.8
LIGHTCONTROL	0.12	7.9	0.08	8	0.10	8	0.09	8	0.09	7.9	0.09	8.4

of aggressiveness. Results show that multi-level simplification performs better than single level simplification. It also indicates that the speedup obtained by simplifying the composite representation is significant. When there is no simplification for most of the examples the verifier could not even complete due to memory blow up.

The results in Table 2 show that combining subset check and union with pre-condition computation speedups the verification. There are two reasons for the speedup: 1) Since disjuncts that are computed as the result of the pre-condition computation are not included in the resulting composite formula if they are subset of the result from the previous iteration, the resulting composite formula has a smaller size. 2) Only the disjuncts, which are results of the pre-condition

Table 2. Verification Time (T, in seconds) and Memory (M, in Mbytes) Results for Inefficient vs Efficient Subset Check, Pre-Condition Computation Without Union vs With Union, and Without Integer Masking vs With Integer Masking. (L) indicates that the specification has been verified for a liveness property. + and - denote inclusion and exclusion of the heuristic, respectively.

Problem Instance	−Subset T	M	+Subset T	M	−PreUnion T	M	+PreUnion T	M	−Mask T	M	+Mask T	M
BAKERY2-1	0.26	10.9	0.21	7.8	0.32	7.8	0.21	7.8	0.24	8.7	0.21	7.8
(L)BAKERY2-2	0.34	9.4	0.26	7.9	0.3	7.9	0.26	7.9	0.41	8	0.26	7.9
BAKERY3-1	20.99	268	8.26	19.6	20.37	16.1	8.26	19.6	8.34	28.8	8.26	19.6
(L)BAKERY3-2	54	69	51.32	34.7	50.04	34.7	49.47	34.7	57.34	36.6	51.32	34.7
TICKET2-1	1.16	18.3	1.07	10.2	1.22	9.6	1.07	10.2	1.14	13.2	1.07	10.2
(L)TICKET2-2	3.31	23.2	3.13	13.8	3.26	12.3	3.13	13.8	3.35	19.7	3.13	13.8
TICKET3-1	18.87	159	14.71	28	29.14	20.1	14.71	28	14.76	37.4	14.71	28
(L)TICKET3-2	36.47	204	29.73	29	66.53	34.2	29.73	29	32.67	49.9	29.73	29
BARBER2-1	8.03	122	4.62	17.7	6.32	15.7	4.62	17.7	4.65	21.4	4.62	17.7
BARBER2-2	0.2	10.1	0.27	8.8	0.37	8.3	0.27	8.8	0.24	9	0.2	8.8
BARBER2-3	1.69	34.4	1.58	12.8	2	11.1	1.58	12.8	1.63	14.5	1.58	12.8
BARBER3-1	21.75	299	10.93	26.6	11.53	18.8	10.93	26.6	11.07	31.1	10.93	26.6
BARBER3-2	0.21	11.2	0.35	9.5	0.46	8.6	0.35	9.5	0.36	9.7	0.35	9.5
BARBER3-3	6.03	105	4.12	18.1	4.15	13.7	4.12	18.1	4.12	20.5	4.12	18.1
BARBER4-1	43.77	554	21.98	38.5	20.62	22.8	21.98	38.5	22.21	44.4	21.98	38.5
BARBER4-2	0.27	12.3	0.43	10.1	0.59	8.9	0.43	10.1	0.44	10.4	0.43	10.1
BARBER4-3	16.94	264	8.76	25.9	8.38	16.7	8.76	25.9	8.87	29.1	8.76	25.9
BARBERP-1	3	23.1	2.83	12.9	4.49	12.9	2.83	12.9	2.9	14.9	2.83	12.9
BARBERP-2	0.3	10.4	0.29	9.2	0.6	9.7	0.29	9.2	0.32	9.5	0.29	9.2
BARBERP-3	3.04	37.4	2.62	14.5	4.13	13.8	2.62	14.5	2.72	17.6	2.62	14.5
COHERENCE-1	0.37	13.4	0.34	11.3	0.86	10	0.34	11.3	0.38	13	0.34	11.3
(L)COHERENCE-2	4.92	53.9	2.74	14.8	4.88	15.4	2.74	14.8	3.43	29.3	2.74	14.8
(L)COHERENCE-3	21.61	169	11.97	29.8	26.45	35.4	11.97	29.8	13.93	91.1	11.97	29.8
(L)COHERENCE-4	15.65	96.2	13.14	24.6	13.38	22.1	13.14	24.6	25.64	49.7	13.14	24.6
COHERENCE-REF-1	0.28	11.9	0.27	11	0.56	10.1	0.27	11	0.33	12.7	0.27	11
(L)COHERENCE-REF-2	1.17	21.2	0.97	11.4	1.93	11.2	0.97	11.4	1.26	14.3	0.97	11.4
(L)COHERENCE-REF-3	6.47	67.5	5.5	20.8	5.62	15.4	5.52	20.8	6.79	42.4	5.52	20.8
(L)COHERENCE-REF-4	27.45	125	23.25	27.7	26.52	29.5	23.25	27.7	49.38	49.4	23.25	27.7
INSERTIONSORT	0.2	9.1	0.2	8.5	0.26	8.6	0.2	8.5	0.3	10.8	0.2	8.5
PC5	0.07	7.6	0.07	7.7	0.12	7.7	0.07	7.7	0.07	7.8	0.07	7.7
PC10	0.09	8.4	0.09	8.5	0.22	8.5	0.09	8.5	0.09	8.6	0.09	8.5
PC30	0.25	11.6	0.25	11.8	0.62	11.7	0.25	11.8	0.26	11.8	0.25	11.8
RW16	0.02	8.1	0.02	8.1	0.03	8.1	0.02	8.1	0.02	8.1	0.02	8.1
RW32	0.03	10.8	0.03	10.8	0.05	10.8	0.03	10.8	0.04	10.8	0.03	10.8
RW64	0.04	20.6	0.05	20.6	0.1	20.6	0.05	20.6	0.08	20.6	0.05	20.6
RWP	0.01	9	0.01	9	0.01	9	0.01	9	0.01	9	0.01	9
SIS-1	0.01	7.5	0.01	7.5	0.01	7.5	0.01	7.5	0.01	7.5	0.01	7.5
SIS-2	0.07	19.4	0.07	19.4	0.08	19.4	0.07	19.4	0.38	27.2	0.07	19.4
LIGHTCONTROL	0.13	8.8	0.12	7.9	0.17	7.6	0.12	7.9	0.12	8.5	0.12	7.9

computation in the *current iteration*, are checked for subset relation against the resulting composite formula from the previous step. Average speedup for combining pre-condition computation with union and subset check heuristic is %24.

Verification times of the specifications with and without masking the integer pre-condition computation, if possible, by boolean satisfiability check are given in Table 2. Results show that masking integer pre-condition computation speeds up the verification and the speedup becomes higher for the specifications where the temporal property to be checked is a liveness property. The reason may be that liveness properties involve two fixpoint computations: one for EG and one for EF^1. Additionally, a fixpoint iteration for EG involves a pre-condition computation followed by an intersection operation whereas a fixpoint iteration for EF involves a pre-condition computation followed by a union operation. Since intersection causes a quadratic increase (whereas union causes a linear increase) in the composite formula size, EG fixpoint iterates are likely to grow faster. Average speedup for masking heuristic is %13.

Verification times of the specifications for inefficient and efficient subset check algorithms are given in Table 2. In most of the experiments the efficient subset check algorithm shown in Figure 1(b) performs better than the subset check algorithm shown in Figure 1(a) that computes negation operation on composite formula level. As a result it supports the idea behind the efficient subset check algorithm: Process composite atoms as needed and perform negation on composite atom level instead of composite formula level which has an exponential time complexity. Average speedup for efficient subset check heuristic is %11.

9   Conclusion

We presented several heuristics for efficient manipulation of composite symbolic representation that combines several constraint representations that are specialized to different domains. We have implemented these heuristics and used them in Composite Symbolic Library which is a symbolic manipulator for model checking systems with heterogeneous data.

Our experiments indicate that verification times are reduced significantly by using our simplification heuristic for composite formulas. When simplification was not used approximately %50 of the examples could not even complete since they ran out memory. Heuristics for combining the pre-condition computation with subset check and union, avoiding the negation at composite formula level and performing it at composite atom level, and masking expensive integer manipulation with boolean manipulation also improve the verification times significantly. Composite Symbolic Library is available at:

http://www.cs.ucsb.edu/~bultan/composite/

References

1. CUDD: CU decision diagram package, http://vlsi.colorado.edu/~fabio/CUDD/.
2. The Omega project, http://www.cs.umd.edu/projects/omega/.
3. R. Alur, T. A. Henzinger, and P. Ho. Automatic symbolic verification of embedded systems. *IEEE Transactions on Software Engineering*, 22(3):181–201, March 1996.
4. G. R. Andrews. *Concurrent Programming: Principles and Practice*. The Benjamin/Cummings Publishing Company, Redwood City, California, 1991.

---

[1] Note that the verifier computes the negation of a liveness property $AGAFp$ and computes the fixpoint for $EFEG(\neg p)$. Then it checks satisfiability of $I \wedge EFEG(\neg p)$. Similarly, for an invariant property AGp it computes the fixpoint for the negation of AGp and checks satisfiability of $I \wedge EF(\neg p)$

5. R. E. Bryant. Graph-based algorithms for boolean function manipulation. *IEEE Transactions on Computers*, 35(8):677–691, 1986.

6. T. Bultan, R. Gerber, and C. League. Composite model checking: Verification with type-specific symbolic representations. *ACM Transactions on Software Engineering and Methodology*, 9(1):3–50, January 2000.

7. T. Bultan, R. Gerber, and W. Pugh. Model-checking concurrent systems with unbounded integer variables: Symbolic representations, approximations, and experimental results. *ACM Transactions on Programming Languages and Systems*, 21(4):747–789, July 1999.

8. T. Bultan and T. Yavuz-Kahveci. Action language verifier. In *Proceedings of the 6th IEEE Intl. Conference on Automated Software Engineering (ASE 2001)*, 2001.

9. J. R. Burch, E. M. Clarke, K. L. McMillan, D. L. Dill, and L. H. Hwang. Symbolic model checking: 10^{20} states and beyond. In *Proceedings of the 5th Annual IEEE Symposium on Logic in Computer Science*, pages 428–439, January 1990.

10. W. Chan, R. J. Anderson, P. Beame, S. Burns, F. Modugno, D. Notkin, and J. D. Reese. Model checking large software specifications. *IEEE Transactions on Software Engineering*, 24(7):498–520, July 1998.

11. E.M. Clarke, O. Grumberg, and D.A. Peled. *Model checking*. The MIT Press, Massachusetts, Cambridge, 1999.

12. P. J. Courtois and D. L. Parnas. Documentation for safety critical software. In *Proc. of the 15th Intl. Conf. on Software Engineering*, pages 315–323, May 1993.

13. G. Delzanno and T. Bultan. Constraint-based verification of client server protocols. In *Proceedings of the Seventh Intl. Conference on Principles and Practice of Constraint Programming (CP 2001)*.

14. Giorgio Delzanno and Andreas Podelski. Constraint-based deductive model checking. *Journal of Software and Tools for Techn. Transfer*, 3(3):250–270, 2001.

15. N. Halbwachs. Delay analysis in synchronous programs. In C. Courcoubetis, editor, *Proceedings of computer aided verification*, volume 697 of *Lecture Notes in Computer Science*, pages 333–346. Springer-Verlag, 1993.

16. N. Halbwachs, P. Raymond, and Y. Proy. Verification of linear hybrid systems by means of convex approximations. In B. LeCharlier, editor, *Proceedings of Intl. Symposium on Static Analysis*, volume 864 of *LNCS*. Springer-Verlag, Sept. 1994.

17. K. L. McMillan. *Symbolic model checking*. Kluwer, Massachusetts, 1993.

18. D. Srivastava. Subsumption and indexing in constraint query languages with linear arithmetic constraints. *Annals of Math. and Artificial Intelligence*, 8:315–343, 1993.

19. T. Yavuz-Kahveci, M. Tuncer, and T. Bultan. Composite symbolic library. In *Proceedings of the 7th Intl. Conference on Tools and Algorithms for the Construction and Analysis of Systems*, volume 2031 of *LNCS*, April 2001.

Constraint-Based Model Checking
for Parameterized Synchronous Systems

Giorgio Delzanno

Dipartimento di Informatica e Scienze dell'Informazione
Università di Genova, via Dodecaneso 35, 16146 Italy
giorgio@disi.unige.it

Abstract. We present a fully-automatic method for checking *safety properties* of parameterized synchronous systems based on a *backward reachability* procedure working over *real arithmetics*. We consider here concurrent systems consisting of many identical (finite-state) processes and one monitor where processes may react *non-deterministically* to the messages sent by the monitor. This type of non-determinism allows us to model abstractions of situations in which processes are re-allocated according to individual properties. We represent concisely collections of global states *counting* the number of processes in a given state during a run of the global system, i.e., we reason modulo *symmetries*. We use a special class of *linear arithmetic constraints* to represent collections of *global* system states. We define a *decision procedure* for checking safety properties for parameterized systems using *efficient* constraints operations defined over *real arithmetics*. The procedure can be implemented using existing *constraint-based symbolic model checkers* or tools for *program analysis* defined over *real-arithmetics*.

1 Introduction

The verification of concurrent systems with an arbitrary number of processes is an important and challenging research goal. Concurrent systems composed by many similar finite-state processes arise in several contexts like hardware designs, communication protocols, and cache coherence policies. When applied to the verification of instances with a large number of processes, traditional finite-state verification techniques suffer from the state-explosion problem. Alternative techniques are necessary in order to reason on (possibly infinite) families of processes. *Network invariants* [30,31], *bisimulation relations* [5], *network grammars* [12], *abstract interpretation* [32], *search procedures* [23,20], *well-structured systems* [1,22] are examples of techniques used to attack different instances of the problem.

Though in general the verification problem for parameterized concurrent systems is *undecidable* [3], decision procedures have been discovered for the verification of subclasses where systems consist of many *identical, finite-state* processes. Specifically, German and Sisla [23] have defined a procedure to verify temporal properties for families of CCS-like processes and one monitor with point-to-point

A. Armando (Ed.): FroCoS 2002, LNAI 2309, pp. 72–86, 2002.

communication. In [20], Emerson and Namjoshi have extended the model with a global operation of *synchronization* achieved through broadcast messages. In this setting, all processes react *deterministically* to the broadcast and move to a special state. In [21], Esparza, Finkel and Mayr have shown that verification of a special class of safety properties is decidable for the systems of [20]. This result is obtained for the model checking problem called *control state reachability* that consists of deciding whether a state from a given *upward-closed* set of (unsafe) states is reachable from one initial states. The algorithm that decides the problem is based on *backward reachability* [1].

In this paper we present a fully automatic method based on *constraint-based symbolic model checking* (see e.g. [1,10,9,16]) for the verification of *safety properties* of a class of parameterized synchronous systems that extends the models proposed in [23,20,21]. Specifically, we consider here concurrent systems with many identical (finite-state) processes and one monitor where processes may react *non-deterministically* to the 'broadcast' messages sent by the monitor. This type of non-determinism allows us to model 'abstractions' of situations in which processes are re-allocated according to individual properties. Safety checking for this class of parameterized systems can be reduced to *control state reachability* problems for a special class of *infinite-state* systems with data variables of integer type. The reduction works as follows. We use a set of *counters* (one for each process state) to keep track of the number of processes in a given state during a run of the original concurrent system. This way, we represent sets of global states modulo *symmetries*. The resulting integer systems, we named *reallocation machines*, are an extension of Vector Addition Systems and Broadcast Protocols (the models underlying the systems of [23,20,21]) where we add reset and *non-deterministic* transfer operations in the style of P/T nets with marking-dependent arcs [11].

In our previous work [16,14], we have proposed to use technology and results from *constraint programming* in order to devise model checking procedure for *integer systems*. The methodology suggested in [16,14] consists of the following steps. We use *linear constraints* to represent collection of infinite set of states. We lift the *backward reachability* algorithm of [1] (we know it guarantees termination for the systems of [23,20]) to the constraint-level using operations like variable elimination, satisfiability, and entailment. Finally, we apply the following *relaxation* to the constraint operations. Everytime we need to solve an *integer* constraint problem we relax the condition that the solutions must be integral and we solve the corresponding problem over the *reals*. The advantage is that solving constraint over the reals is computationally much easier than over the integers (in the worst case, polynomial vs exponential [34]). It is important to note that we apply this 'abstraction' *during* the analysis and not at the semantic-level of our machines (i.e. we do not change the semantic domain of our systems; instead we make the operations that handle constraints more efficient). The relaxation integer-reals is a well-established technique used in integer programming and program analysis (see e.g [6,34,13,25,26]). Though in general the relaxation gives us approximated results, we have shown in [14] that the symbolic backward reachability over reals is still a *decision procedure* for the control state reachability problem of the broadcast protocols of [20].

The main technical contribution of this paper is the extension of the result in [14]: we show that symbolic backward reachability over reals is a *decision procedure* for the control reachability problem of the new class of re-allocation machines. Our results show that existing symbolic model checkers (e.g. [16,25,26,28]) and tools for program analysis working on *real arithmetics* (e.g. [13]) can be applied with the guarantee of *termination* and *accuracy in the results* to check safety properties of synchronous parameterized systems that can be represented via re-allocation machines. In practical experiments, we are currently using two of such tools, namely, DMC [16] (based on a constraint solver over reals) and HyTech [28] (based on the efficient *polyhedra* library of Halbwachs [25]), to verify safety properties of examples taken from the literature (e.g. abstractions of cache-coherence protocols and control systems).

2   One Monitor, Many Processes

Following [23,20], we consider a concurrent system composed by many identical *finite-state* processes and by one *monitor*. In this paper we limit ourselves to specify the *communication layer* of a system. Without loss of generality, we assume that processes can communicate only with the monitor. This assumption will simplify the technical aspects of our presentation. A parameterized system $\mathcal{S}$ consists of the following components. The set Σ_P denotes the messages that processes send to the monitor. The indexed set $\Sigma_i = \Sigma_P \times \{i\}$ denotes the messages σ_i sent by process i. All processes have the same set of states Q_P. The set Σ_M denotes the messages that the monitor sends to the processes. The monitor is represented as a *deterministic* finite-state machine $\mathcal{M} = \langle Q_M, \Sigma_M \cup (\Sigma_P \times \mathbb{N}), \delta_M \rangle$, where $\delta_M : Q_M \times (\Sigma_M \cup (\Sigma_P \times \mathbb{N})) \to Q_M$ (the monitor receives messages from any process). Process i is represented as a *non-deterministic* finite state machine $\mathcal{P}_i = \langle Q_P, \Sigma_M \cup \Sigma_i, \delta_i \rangle$, where $\delta_i : Q_P \times (\Sigma_M \cup \Sigma_i) \times Q_P$. To enforce the condition that all processes behave in the same way, we require that $\delta_i(q, \sigma_m) = \delta_j(q, \sigma_m)$ and that $\delta_i(q, \sigma_i) = \delta_j(q, \sigma_j)$ for any message $\sigma_m \in \Sigma_M$, $\sigma \in \Sigma_P$, $q \in Q_P$ and any process i, j. For simplicity, we limit the *non-determinitism* of a process to the *reactions* to a monitor message $\sigma_m \in \Sigma_M$ as follows: upon reception of σ_m, the target state q' for process i may be picked up non-deterministically from a set $\Pi(\sigma_m)$ that does not depend on the current state q. More precisely, given $\sigma_m \in \Sigma_M$, let us fix the set $\Pi(\sigma_m) \subseteq Q_P$. If $q \in \Pi(\sigma_m)$ then $\delta_i(q, \sigma_m) = \{q\}$; otherwise, if $q \notin \Pi(\sigma_m)$, then either $\delta_i(q, \sigma_m) = \{q\}$ or $\delta_i(q, \sigma_m) = \Pi(\sigma_m)$. We also allow *deterministic reactions*. In this case $\delta_i(q, \sigma_m)$ is a singleton for all q (with no further restrictions). By hypothesis, we cannot distinguish one process from another. However, we can use non-deterministic reactions to model *abstractions* of situations in which processes are re-allocated according to individual properties (e.g. priorities). We will clarify this point in Example 1. We describe a system with n processes as a *global*, finite-state machine $\mathcal{M}_G = \langle Q_G, \Sigma_G, \delta_G \rangle$, where $Q_G = Q_M \times Q^n$, $\Sigma_G = \Sigma_M \cup (\Sigma \times \{1, \ldots, n\})$, and $\delta_G : Q_G \times \Sigma_G \times Q_G$.

The global transition relation is defined as follows. If a *process sends a message to the monitor*, i.e., $\sigma_i \in \Sigma_i$, $\langle q_i, \sigma_i, q_i' \rangle \in \delta_i$, and $\langle q, \sigma_i, q' \rangle \in \delta_M$, then $\langle\langle q, q_1, \ldots, q_n \rangle, \sigma_i, \langle q', q_1', \ldots, q_n' \rangle\rangle \in \delta_G$ and $q_j' = q_j$ for every $j \neq i$. If the *monitor sends a message* to all processes, i.e., $\sigma \in \Sigma_M$, $\langle q, \sigma_M, q' \rangle \in \delta_M$ and $\langle q_i, \sigma_M, q_i' \rangle \in \delta_i$ for $i : 1, \ldots, n$, then $\langle\langle q, q_1, \ldots q_n \rangle, \sigma, \langle q', q_1', \ldots, q_n' \rangle\rangle \in \delta_G$. An element of Q_G is called a *global state* (denoted as $G, G_1, \ldots$ etc). A *run* of $\mathcal{M}_G$ is a sequence of global states $G_1, G_2, \ldots, G_i, \ldots$ where $\langle G_i, \sigma, G_{i+1} \rangle \in \delta_G$ for some $\sigma \in \Sigma_G$. We write $G_1 \rightarrow^* G_2$ to denote that there exists a run starting from G_1 and reaching G_2.

Example 1. In Fig. 1, we show an abstraction of a multiprocess system with a *load balancing* monitor. Here $Q = \{req, use, high, low\}$, $\Sigma_P = \{req, release\}$, $Q_M = \{idle, busy\}$, and $\Sigma_M = \{swap\_in, swap\_out\}$. In the initial configuration of the system the processes are in state *req*, whereas the monitor is in state *idle*. When the monitor broadcasts the message *swap_out* (and moves to *busy*) all processes in the CPU are suspended. Two different priorities are assigned to the suspended processes. This is simulated through the non-deterministic reaction to *swap-out* with target states $\Pi(swap\_out) = \{high, low\}$. When the CPU is released by the monitor (through the broadcast *release*), it is assigned to processes with *high* priority. Processes with *low*-priority go back to the *request* state. This behaviour is simulated through the *deterministic* reaction to the broadcast *swap_in*.

Our definition of parameterized systems extends the model of German and Sisla [23] and the Broadcast Protocols of Emerson and Namjoshi [20] with a global *non-deterministic* synchronization operation. In this paper we are interested in automatic verification methods for *safety* properties, i.e., to check that during a run of the system it is not possible to reach *inconsistent* states. In Example 1, when the monitor is busy no process can be in state *use*. Thus, all global state where *use* and *busy* occur simultaneously must be considered as unsafe states. Actually, given a parameterized system we would like to check this type of safety properties independently from the parameter n=number of processes. This problem can be reduced to the following *parameterized* reachability problem.

Definition 1 (Parameterized Reachability). *Given a parameterized system $\mathcal{S}$ with n processes, let $I(n)$ and $U(n)$ be the set of initial and unsafe global states of the corresponding global machine $\mathcal{M}_G$. The parameterized reachability problem is defined as: $\exists n \geq 1$ s.t. $G_1 \rightarrow^* G_2$ for $G_1 \in I(n)$, $G_2 \in U(n)$?*

If the reachability problem is satisfied for a given m, then the safety property (whose complement is represented as $U(m)$) is violated for an instance of the system with m processes.

From Parameterized Systems to Re-allocation Machines. We show next that a parameterized system $\mathcal{S}$ can be described in terms of extensions of Vector Addition Systems similar to P/T nets with transfer and reset arcs [11]. We will call these integer systems *re-allocation machines*. Intuitively, the idea is to use tuples of positive integers to count the number of processes in each state $q \in Q_G$

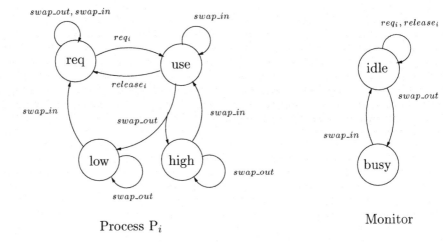

Process P_i Monitor

Fig. 1. Load balancing monitor.

at any time during a run of the global machine $\mathcal{M}_G$ associated to $\mathcal{S}$. This way, we exploit the *symmetries* in the global states and reduce the state-space we need to visit. In Example 1, for $n = 3$ we use the tuple $\langle c_{req}, c_{use}, c_{high}, c_{low}, c_{idle}, c_{busy} \rangle$ with $c_{req} = 2$, $c_{use} = 1$, $c_{idle} = 1$ and all other components $= 0$, to represent all global states where one process is in state *use*. In the following we will use **c** to denote a vector of constants $\langle c_1, \ldots, c_K \rangle$ and **x** to denote the vector of variables $\langle x_1, \ldots, x_K \rangle$. $\mathbf{x} \geq \mathbf{c}$ denotes the constraint $x_1 \geq c_1 \wedge \ldots \wedge x_K \geq c_K$ (similarly for $=, \leq$ etc). Given a $K \times K$-matrix A with elements $\{a_{i,j}\}_{i,j:1,\ldots,K}$, $A \cdot \mathbf{x} \geq \mathbf{c}$ denotes the constraint $a_{1,1}x_1 + \ldots + a_{1,n}x_n \geq c_1 \wedge \ldots \wedge a_{n,1}x_1 + \ldots + a_{n,n}x_n \geq c_n$.

Definition 2 (Re-allocation machine). *A re-allocation machine $\mathcal{R}$ is a tuple $\langle K, C_0, \tau \rangle$, where $K \geq 1$ is a natural number, $C_0 \subseteq \mathcal{P}(\mathbb{N}^K)$ is the initial configuration, $\tau \subseteq \mathbb{N}^K \times \mathbb{N}^K$ is a transition relation defined via a set of guarded commands*[1] $G(\mathbf{x}, \mathbf{x}') \rightarrow T(\mathbf{x}, \mathbf{x}')$ *with the following features. A guard is defined as*

$$G(\mathbf{x}, \mathbf{x}') \equiv D_1 \cdot \mathbf{x}' \geq D_2 \cdot \mathbf{x} \wedge \mathbf{x} \geq \mathbf{d},$$

where D_1, D_2 are $K \times K$ diagonal matrices with 0 and 1 coefficients[2], *and $\mathbf{d}$ is a vector of positive integers. A transformation is defined as*

$$T(\mathbf{x}, \mathbf{x}') \equiv A \cdot \mathbf{x}' = B \cdot \mathbf{x} + \mathbf{c},$$

where A and B are $K \times K$-matrices with unite vectors as columns, and $\mathbf{c}$ is a vector of K integers. We also assume that for each guard of the form $x_i' \geq x_i$ in $D_1 \cdot \mathbf{x}' \geq D_2 \cdot \mathbf{x}$ there exists an assignment of the form $x_i' + \ldots = x_i + \ldots$ in the corresponding row of the transition equation $A \cdot \mathbf{x}' = B \cdot \mathbf{x} + \mathbf{c}$.

A run of $\mathcal{R}$ is a (possibly infinite) sequence of states $\mathbf{c}_1, \ldots, \mathbf{c}_i, \ldots$ where, at step i, $G_r(\mathbf{c}_i, \mathbf{c}_{i+1}) \wedge T_r(\mathbf{c}_i, \mathbf{c}_{i+1})$ evaluates to *true* for some rule r. The predecessor operator $pre : \mathcal{P}(\mathbb{N}^K) \rightsquigarrow \mathcal{P}(\mathbb{N}^K)$ associated to $\mathcal{R}$ is defined as

$$pre(S) = \{\mathbf{c} \mid \mathbf{c} \ \tau \ \mathbf{c}', \ \mathbf{c}' \in S\}.$$

We use $pre_{|r}$ to indicate the restriction of pre to a given transition rule r in $\mathcal{R}$. Re-allocation machines are extensions of Vector Addition Systems and Broadcast Protocols. In Vector Addition Systems $G(\mathbf{x}) \equiv \mathbf{x} \geq \mathbf{c}$ and $T(\mathbf{x}, \mathbf{x}') \equiv \mathbf{x}' = I \cdot \mathbf{x} + \mathbf{d}$, whereas in Broadcast Protocols $G(\mathbf{x}) \equiv \mathbf{x} \geq \mathbf{c}$ and $T(\mathbf{x}, \mathbf{x}') \equiv \mathbf{x}' = A \cdot \mathbf{x} + \mathbf{d}$, and A is a matrix with unit vectors as colunmns. The re-allocation machine $\mathcal{R}_S$ associated to a parameterized system S with n processes is defined as follows. Let $\mathcal{M}_G$ be the global machine $\langle Q_G, \Sigma_G, \delta_G \rangle$ with $Q_G = \{q_1, \ldots, q_K\}$. $\mathcal{R}_S$-states are tuples $\langle c_1, \ldots, c_K \rangle$ where $c_i \in \mathbb{N}$ keeps track of how many processes are in state q_i during a run of $\mathcal{M}_G$. An $\mathcal{R}_S$-transition is defined over the tuple of variables $\langle x_1, \ldots, x_K \rangle$ (x_i is the counter for q_i) ranging over positive integers. We define them by cases depending on the type of messages. (Notes: since all processes are indentical, we consider an arbitrary process i with transition relation δ_i. Furthermore, we will omit all equalities of the form $x' = x$.)

A process sends a message to the monitor, i.e., $\langle q_p, \sigma_i, q_l \rangle \in \delta_i$ and $\langle q_r, \sigma_i, q_s \rangle \in \delta_M$ for some $q_p, q_l \in Q_P$, $q_r, q_s \in Q_M$ and $\sigma_i \in \Sigma_i$. In this case, we simply keep track of the local *synchronization* between the process and the monitor by decrementing and incrementing the counters for the corresponding starting and target states:

$$G(\mathbf{x}, \mathbf{x}') \equiv x_p \geq 1 \land x_r \geq 1,$$
$$T(\mathbf{x}, \mathbf{x}') \equiv x'_p = x_p - 1 \land x'_l = x_l + 1 \land x'_r = x_r - 1 \land x'_s = x_s + 1.$$

The monitor sends a broadcast, i.e., $\langle q_r, \sigma_m, q_s \rangle \in \delta_M$ for some $q_r, q_s \in Q_M$ and $\sigma_m \in \Sigma_M$. It is important to note that in the semantics of S we have assumed that *all processes* react simultaneously to the monitor message. We have two subcases.

(1) If the reaction of process i to σ_m is *deterministic*, then we simply re-allocate the counters of all processes as follows. Let $\Theta(\sigma_m, q_p) = \{ q_j \mid \langle q_j, \sigma_m, q_p \rangle \in \delta_i \}$, and $\Xi(\sigma_m) = \{q_i \mid \Theta(\sigma_m, q_i) = \emptyset \}$. (Note: if $\langle q_j, \sigma_m, q_p \rangle \in \delta_i$, then all processes in q_j must move to q_p, namely $x'_j = 0, x_p = x_j + \ldots$ etc.)

$$G(\mathbf{x}, \mathbf{x}') \equiv x_r \geq 1,$$
$$T(\mathbf{x}, \mathbf{x}') \equiv x'_r = x_r - 1 \land x'_s = x_s + 1 \land \Theta$$
$$\text{where } \Theta \equiv \bigwedge_{q_p \in Q_P} x'_p = \Sigma_{q_k \in \Theta(\sigma_m, \sigma_p) \neq \emptyset} \ x_k \ \land \ \bigwedge_{q_p \in \Xi(\sigma_m)} x'_p = 0.$$

(2) If the reaction is *non-deterministic*, the set of states $\Pi(\sigma_m) \subseteq Q_P$ in which all processes move when they receive σ_m is fixed a priori (by definition of S). Before we give the $\mathcal{R}_S$ rule, we define the set $\Omega(\sigma_m) = \{q_p \notin \Pi(\sigma_m) \mid \delta_i(q_p, \sigma_m) = \Pi(\sigma_m)\}$. The corresponding $\mathcal{R}$-transition is as follows. (Note: if $\delta_i(q_j, \sigma_m) = \{q_p, q_l, \ldots\}$ then all processes in q_j will move to one of $q_p, q_l, \ldots$, i.e., $x'_p + x'_l + \ldots = x_j + \ldots$).

$$G(\mathbf{x}, \mathbf{x}') \equiv x_r \geq 1 \land \bigwedge_{q_j \in \Pi(\sigma_m)} x'_j \geq x_j,$$
$$T(\mathbf{x}, \mathbf{x}') \equiv x'_r = x_r - 1 \land x'_s = x_s + 1 \land \Theta$$
$$\text{where } \Theta \equiv \Sigma_{q_p \in \Pi(\sigma_M)} x'_p = \Sigma_{q_j \in \Omega(\sigma_m)} x_j \ \land \ \bigwedge_{q_j \in \Omega(\sigma_m)} x'_j = 0.$$

(1) $x_{req} \geq 1, \; x_{idle} \geq 1 \; \longrightarrow \; x'_{req} = x_{req} - 1, \; x'_{use} = x_{use} + 1.$

(2) $x_{use} \geq 1, \; x_{idle} \geq 1 \; \longrightarrow \; x'_{use} = x_{use} - 1, \; x'_{req} = x_{req} + 1.$

(3) $x_{idle} \geq 1, \; x'_{high} \geq x_{high}, \; x'_{low} \geq x_{low} \; \longrightarrow$
$x'_{idle} = x_{idle} - 1, \; x'_{busy} = x_{busy} + 1,$
$x'_{high} + x'_{low} = x_{high} + x_{low} + x_{use}, \; x'_{use} = 0.$

(4) $x_{busy} \geq 1 \; \longrightarrow$
$x'_{busy} = x_{busy} - 1, \; x'_{idle} = x_{idle} + 1, \; x'_{high} = 0, \; x'_{low} = 0,$
$x'_{use} = x_{use} + x_{high}, \; x'_{req} = x_{req} + x_{low}.$

Fig. 2. Re-allocation machine for the Example 1: (1)=req_i, (2)=$release_i$, (3)=$swap\_out$, (4)=$swap\_in$.

The constraint in $T(\mathbf{x}, \mathbf{x'})$ in point (a) and (b) perform the necessary re-allocations of tokens. A sum in the left hand side of = denotes a non-deterministic re-allocation. The guards $x'_p \geq x_p$ in (b) ensure that at least all processes with state $q_p \in \Pi(\sigma_M)$ will not change state.

Remark 1. The basic model we defined in Section 2 can be enriched easily with *internal actions* ($\langle q_r, \sigma_i, q_s \rangle \in \delta_i$ modeled as $x_r \geq 1 \wedge x'_r = x_r - 1 \wedge x'_s = x_s + 1$) and *inter-process communication* (as in the case of process-monitor communication).

Example 2. The re-allocation machine associated to the example 1 is defined in Fig. 2 (where x_s is the number of processes in state s). The guards $x'_{high} \geq x_{high}$ and $x'_{low} \geq x_{low}$ in the *swap_out* rule ensure that only the processes in x_{use} are redistributed between x_{high} and x_{low} (i.e. there is no migration of processes from state *low* to *high* or vice versa from state *high* to state *low*).

2.1 From Parameterized Reachability in $\mathcal{S}$ to Reachability in $\mathcal{R}_{\mathcal{S}}$.

Given a global state G of a parameterized system $\mathcal{S}$, let us define the mapping $\# : Q_G \to \mathbb{N}^k$ such that $\#G$ is the tuple $\langle c_1, \ldots, c_K \rangle$ where c_i=number of processes of G in state q_i. The following property relates the runs in $\mathcal{S}$ with the runs of the corresponding re-allocation machine $\mathcal{R}_{\mathcal{S}}$.

Proposition 1. For every run $G_1 G_2 \ldots$ in $\mathcal{S}$, $\#G_1 \#G_2 \ldots$ is a run in $\mathcal{R}_{\mathcal{S}}$. Viceversa, for every run $\mathbf{c}_1 \mathbf{c}_2 \ldots$ in $\mathcal{R}_{\mathcal{S}}$, there exists a run $G_1 G_2 \ldots$ in $\mathcal{S}$ with $\#G_i = \mathbf{c}_i$ for $i \geq 1$.

As a consequence, if there exist two global states G, G' such that $G \to^* G'$ in $\mathcal{S}$, then $\#G \to^* \#G'$ in $\mathcal{R}_{\mathcal{S}}$. Viceversa, given two $\mathcal{R}_{\mathcal{S}}$-state $\mathbf{c}, \mathbf{c'}$, if $\mathbf{c} \to \mathbf{c'}$ in $\mathcal{R}_{\mathcal{S}}$ then there exist two global states G, G' such that $\#G = \mathbf{c}$ and $\#G' = \mathbf{c'}$ and $G \to^* G'$ in $\mathcal{S}$. It is important to note that $\mathcal{R}_{\mathcal{S}}$ gives us a description of a parameterized system $\mathcal{S}$ *independently* from the parameter n=number of processes (states in $\mathcal{R}_{\mathcal{S}}$ are tuples of length K=number of states in $\mathcal{S}$). Thus, Prop. 1 allows us to reduce the parameterized reachability problem for $\mathcal{S}$ to a reachability problem for $\mathcal{R}_S$. We proceed as follows. We first express the parameterized initial and unsafe global states $S_o(n)$ and $S_f(n)$ via the mapping $\#$. We obtain two set of tuples $C_0(n)$ and $C_f(n)$ that depend on n. Now, we define $C_0 = \bigcup_{n \geq 1} C_0(n)$ and $C_f = \bigcup_{n \geq 1} C_f(n)$, and try to solve the reachability problem: exist $\mathbf{c} \in C_0$, $\mathbf{c}' \in C_f$ s.t. $\mathbf{c} \rightarrow^* \mathbf{c}'$? in $\mathcal{R}_S$.

Example 3. For a fixed n, the initial state $S_o(n)$ of the system of Example 1 is the global states with n processes in state *req* and one (the monitor) in state *idle*. Thus, $C_0(n)$ is the set of tuples with $c_{req} = n$, $c_{idle} = 1$ and $c_q = 0$ for all other states q. The system should satisfy the following invariant: when the monitor is in state *busy* there no processes can be in state *use*. In other words, $S_f(n)$ (the set of unsafe states) is the set of global states G with at least one process in *busy* and one in *use*, i.e., $C_f(n)$ is the set of tuples with $c_{use} \geq 1$, $c_{busy} \geq 1$, and arbitrary values for the remaining counters. C_0 is the set of tuples with $c_{req} \geq 1$, $c_{idle} = 1$ and $c_q = 0$ for all other states q, whereas C_f is the set of tuples with $c_{use} \geq 1$, $c_{busy} \geq 1$ and $c_q \geq 0$ for any other state q.

The counters $x_1, \ldots, x_K$ assume potentially *unbounded* values during a run of $\mathcal{R}_S$. Thus, the set of (backward or forward) reachable states of $\mathcal{R}_S$ is potentially *infinite*, even if the initial (unsafe) set of states is finite, i.e., $\mathcal{R}_S$ is an *infinite-state* machine. We show next that the reachability problem for re-allocation machines can always be decided when C_f is an *upward-closed* set of tuples over $\mathbb{N}^K$. Following [1,22], we call this instance of the reachability problem *control state reachability*. Note that $S \subseteq \mathbb{N}^K$ is upward-closed if for all $\mathbf{c} \in S$ if $\mathbf{c}' \geq \mathbf{c}$ then $\mathbf{c}' \in S$ (where $\geq$ is the pointwise ordering of tuples of natural numbers). As for C_f in Example 3, set of unsafe states can often be represented as upward-closed sets. This result is obtained using the general methodology to prove well-structuredness of systems given in [1,22] and applied to subclass of re-allocation machines like Vector Addition Systems and broadcast protocols, e.g., in [8,22,21]

Theorem 1. The control state reachability problem is decidable for re-allocation machines.

3 Data Structures for Symbolic Model Checking

The decidabilty result for the control reachability problem allows us to consider re-allocation machines as a sort of *finite-state systems*. An abstract algorithm for backwards reachability has been given in [1,22]. Given a upward-closed set C_f of states, the algorithm repeatedly applies the predecessor operator until a fixpoint is reached, corresponding to the set of all predecessors of C_f. If this set contains some of the initial configurations, then C_f is reachable. Upward-closed sets equipped with the subset relation form a well-quasi ordering. This property ensures the theoretical termination of the algorithm. In order to turn the abstract algorithm into a practical method, it is necessary to find efficient and compact representation of upward-closed sets. In previous works integer constraint systems (for Petri Nets [15] and Broadcast Protocols [15]) and graph-based data structures (for Petri Nets [17]) have been proposed as symbolic representation for upward-closed sets. Integer constraint systems (e.g. linear arithmetic constraints interpreted over the integers) provide a natural representation of the semantics of parameterized systems, whereas graph-based structures like the Sharing Trees used in [17] provide for a compact representation of collections of minimal points. In this paper, as an alternative to the previous methods we apply the following *relaxation* of the constraint operations: we solve linear problems over the domain of *reals* instead that over the domain of *integers*. This way, we can exploit efficient (polynomial-time) operations to handle symbolic representation of upward-closed sets (in contrast to the exponential-time operations required by integer constraints [15]). The algorithm of [1] turns out to be robust under the new interpretation of constraints. Furthermore, similarly to the approach in [17], the subclass of linear constraints we introduce below provides a compact representation of collections of upward-closed sets.

Towards Compact Data Structures. The class $\mathcal{AD}$ of constraints we are interested is that of *additive constraints* [15], i.e., linear arithmetic constraints of the following form:

$$\varphi ::= \varphi \wedge \varphi \mid x_{i_1} + \ldots + x_{i_k} \geq c,$$

where $x_1, \ldots, x_K$ are variables (ranging over positive integers or reals) and c is a positive integer. We give next the properties of additive constraints when interpreted over *integers* and then consider the case in which they are interpreted over the *reals*. In the rest of the paper we will use the lower-case letters $\varphi, \psi, \ldots$ to denote constraints and the upper-case letters $\Psi, \Phi, \ldots$ to denote *sets* (disjunctions) of constraints.

The *denotation* of a constraint φ is defined as $[\![\varphi]\!] = \{\mathbf{t} \mid \mathbf{t} \in \mathbb{N}^K \text{ satisfies } \varphi\}$. The definition is extended to sets in the natural way. Furthermore, we say that a constraint $\varphi = \varphi_1 \wedge \ldots \wedge \varphi_k$ (φ_i atomic) is *minimal* if there are no φ_j such that $[\![\varphi_j]\!] \subseteq [\![\varphi \setminus \varphi_j]\!]$ (e.g. $x + y \geq 4 \wedge x \geq 2 \wedge y \geq 2$ is not minimal). In the rest of the paper we will mainly consider minimal constraints. A constraint ψ *entails* a constraint φ, written $\varphi \sqsubseteq \psi$, if and only if $[\![\psi]\!] \subseteq [\![\varphi]\!]$. *Full entailment* bewteen two sets of $\mathcal{AD}$-constraints Φ and Ψ is defined as follows: $\Phi \sqsubseteq \Psi$ if and only if $[\![\Psi]\!] \subseteq [\![\Phi]\!]$. We give sufficient conditions for the full test via the *pairwise entailment* test defined as follows: $\Phi \preccurlyeq \Psi$ if and only if for all $\psi \in \Psi$ there exists $\varphi \in \Phi$ such that $\varphi \sqsubseteq \psi$. It is important to note that, while $\Phi \preccurlyeq \Psi$ implies $\Phi \sqsubseteq \Psi$, the reverse implication does not hold. As a counterexample, take $\Phi = \{x \geq 1, y \geq 1\}$ and $\Psi = \{x + y \geq 1\}$. Then, $\Phi \sqsubseteq \Psi$ holds but neither $x \geq 1 \sqsubseteq x + y \geq 1$ nor $y \geq 1 \sqsubseteq x + y \geq 1$ holds. An $\mathcal{AD}$-constraint is equivalent to a disjunction of constraints built up from atomic constraints without additions, i.e., having form $x_1 \geq c_1 \wedge \ldots \wedge x_n \geq c_n$, $c_i \in \mathbb{N}$. We will call this class $\mathcal{WA}$. Formally, let $dec : \mathcal{AD} \rightsquigarrow \mathcal{P}(\mathcal{WA})$ be the following map: $dec(x_1 + \ldots + x_n \geq c) = \{x_1 \geq c_1 \wedge \ldots \wedge x_n \geq c_n \mid c_1 + \ldots + c_n = c, \ c_i \in \mathbb{N}\}$, $dec(\varphi_1 \wedge \varphi_2) = \{\gamma_1 \wedge \gamma_2 \mid \gamma_1 \in dec(\varphi_1), \ \gamma_2 \in dec(\varphi_2)\}$. Given an $\mathcal{AD}$-constraint φ, $dec(\varphi)$ is a set of $\mathcal{WA}$-constraints such that $[\![\varphi]\!] = [\![dec(\varphi)]\!]$. The cardinality of

$dec(\varphi)$ may be exponential in the size of φ (constants and number of conjuncts). As an example, note that $dec(x_1 + x_2 \geq 1 \wedge \ldots \wedge x_n + x_{n+1} \geq 1)$ for an odd natural number n, is a set of $\mathcal{WA}$-constraints of size 2^n. The constraints of this set correspond to the paths of a complete binary tree with two outcoming edges per node labeled, respectively, $x_i \geq 1$ and $x_{i+1} \geq 1$, for $i : 1, 3, 5 \ldots, n$. The constraint obtained conjoining the labels on one path is not comparable (w.r.t. $\sqsubseteq$) with the constraints associated to the other paths. Note that disjunctions of $\mathcal{WA}$-constraints are in one-to-one relation (modulo logical equivalences) with the *minimal points of upward-closed sets*. This property makes $\mathcal{AD}$-constraints good candidates to concisely represent finite unions of upward-closed sets.

Example 4. The additive constraint $x_{busy} \geq 1 \wedge x_{use} \geq 1$ represents the set C_f of Example 3. With constraints, we compact further the representation of $\mathcal{S}$ global state: an additive constraints like $x_{high} + x_{low} \geq 2$ represents the set of $\mathcal{R}_{\mathcal{S}}$-states consisting of tuples where either $c_{high} = 2$ and $c_{low} = 0$, $c_{high} = 1$ and $c_{low} = 1$ or $c_{high} = 0$ and $c_{low} = 2$. In turn, each of these states represents sets of $\mathcal{S}$ global states (2 processes are in state *high*, or in state *low*, etc).

Towards Efficient Operations. Following techniques from *integer linear programming*, we reduce the complexity of the manipulation of $\mathcal{AD}$-constraints as follows. Everytime we need to solve a system of inequalities $A \cdot \mathbf{x} \leq \mathbf{b}$ we relax the condition that $\mathbf{x}$ is a vector of positive *integers* and look instead for a *real* solution of the corresponding linear problem. This way, we obtain an *approximation* of the original set of integer solutions that, however, can be computed in polynomial time [34]. Formally, the relaxation is defined as follows. Given a constraint φ, we define $[\![\varphi]\!]_{\mathbb{R}}$ as the set of real solutions $\{\mathbf{c} \in \mathbb{R}_+ \mid \mathbf{c} \ satisfies \ \varphi \}$. The entailment relation over $\mathbb{R}_+$ is defined then as $\varphi \sqsubseteq_{\mathbb{R}} \psi$ if and only if $[\![\psi]\!]_{\mathbb{R}} \subseteq [\![\varphi]\!]_{\mathbb{R}}$. Full entailment over $\mathbb{R}_+$ is defined as $\Phi \sqsubseteq_{\mathbb{R}} \Psi$ if and only if $[\![\Psi]\!]_{\mathbb{R}} \subseteq [\![\Phi]\!]_{\mathbb{R}}$; pairwise entailment as $\Phi \preccurlyeq_{\mathbb{R}} \Psi$ if and only if for all $\psi \in \Psi$ there exist $\phi \in \Phi$ s.t. $\phi \sqsubseteq_{\mathbb{R}} \psi$. Following [10,16,28], we can define a symbolic predecessor operator using constraint-operations to handle set of states via linear constraints. When applying the above relaxation to the symbolic predecessor operator (restricted to one transition) we obtain:

$$\mathbf{sym\_pre}_{\mathbb{R}}(\bigvee_{i \in I} M_i \cdot \mathbf{x}' \geq \mathbf{e_i}) \equiv \bigvee_{i \in I} \exists_{\mathbb{R}} \mathbf{x}'. \ G(\mathbf{x}, \mathbf{x}') \wedge T(\mathbf{x}', \mathbf{x}) \wedge M_i \cdot \mathbf{x}' \geq \mathbf{e_i},$$

where $\mathbf{x}$ and $\mathbf{x}'$ range over *positive real numbers*, and $\exists_{\mathbb{R}}$ indicates that elimination of the variables in $\mathbf{x}'$ must be performed over $\mathbb{R}_+$. It is interesting to note that, whenever we consider sets of $\mathcal{AD}$-constraints, an application of $\mathbf{sym\_pre}_{\mathbb{R}}$ does not lose precision w.r.t. $\mathbf{sym\_pre}$. In fact, the following property holds.

Proposition 2. The class $\mathcal{AD}$ of additive constraints is closed under application of $\mathbf{sym\_pre}_{\mathbb{R}}$. Furthermore, $pre([\![\Phi]\!]) = [\![\mathbf{sym\_pre}_{\mathbb{R}}(\Phi)]\!]$. (note: $[\![\Phi]\!]$ denotes the set *integer* solutions of Φ).

On the basis of the newly defined operators we obtain the implementation of the algorithm of [1] shown in Fig. 3.

Proc Symb-Reach-over-$\mathbb{R}(\Phi_o, \Phi_f$: set of additive constraints)
$\quad \Phi := \Phi_f; \ \Psi := \emptyset;$
$\quad$ **while** $\Phi \neq \emptyset$ **do**
$\quad\quad$ **choose** $\varphi \in \Phi; \quad \Phi := \Phi \setminus \{\varphi\};$
$\quad\quad$ **if** $sat_{\mathbb{R}}(\varphi \wedge \Phi_o)$ **then return** *reachable*
$\quad\quad$ **else if** $\nexists \psi \in \Psi. \ \psi \sqsubseteq_{\mathbb{R}} \varphi$ **then** $\Psi := \Psi \cup \{\varphi\}; \quad \Phi := \Phi \cup \mathbf{sym\_pre}_{\mathbb{R}}(\varphi);$
$\quad$ **end_while**;
$\quad$ **return** *unreachable*;
end.

Fig. 3. Symbolic reachability.

To prove that the algorithm of [1] is *robust* when lifting the interpretation of $\mathcal{AD}$-constraint from $\mathbb{N}$ to $\mathbb{R}_+$, we have to show that Symb-Reach-over-$\mathbb{R}$ terminates on input formed by additive constraints. This is a consequence of the following proposition.

Proposition 3. $\langle \mathcal{AD}, \sqsubseteq_{\mathbb{R}} \rangle$ is a well-quasi-ordering.

Let us now study the complexity of the algorithm. Specifically, (1) we study the complexity of $\mathbf{sym\_pre}_{\mathbb{R}}$; (2) we define a class of initial conditions that allows us to obtain an exact implementation of the algorithm [1]; (3) we study the complexity of the fixpoint test. Prop. 2 shows that, in our setting, *variable elimination* can be equivalently computed over the reals and over the integers. Thus, in both cases the size of intermediate results will remain polynomial in the size of the set of constraints compute at the previous steps. Let us consider now the 'reachability' test $sat_{\mathbb{R}}(\varphi \wedge \Phi_0)$. As mentioned in the previous sections, in our model the initial set of states is not necessarily an upward-closed sets of states. In order to ensure that the algorithm $\mathbf{sym\_pre}_{\mathbb{R}}$ gives only accurate answers for the control reachability problem we must find a class of constraints that (a) is powerful enough to express interesting *initial sets of states* for parameterized systems; (b) when conjoined with $\mathcal{AD}$-constraints the resulting constraint is satisfiable over $\mathbb{N}$ iff it is satisfiable over $\mathbb{R}_+$. For the sake of this paper, we consider the class of $\mathcal{IC}$-onstraints (*initial condition*) defined as follows.

$$\varphi ::= \varphi \wedge \varphi \mid x_i = c_i \mid \psi,$$

where c_i is a positive integer, and ψ is an $\mathcal{AD}$-constraint. It is easy to check that an $\mathcal{IC}$-constraint φ is satisfiable in $\mathbb{N}$ if and only it is satisfiable in $\mathbb{R}_+$. Furthermore, we can use $\mathcal{IC}$-constraints to express parameterized initial configuration as in the example of Section 2. Let us consider now the termination test. The main advantage of the procedure $\mathbf{sym\_pre}_{\mathbb{R}}$ is that the entailment test can be performed in *polynomial* time, whereas the termination test over the integers would have exponential cost (checking $\psi_1 \sqsubseteq \psi_2$ for additive constraints is co-NP hard [15]). In fact, note that $\phi \sqsubseteq_{\mathbb{R}} (\psi_1 \wedge \psi_2)$ holds if and only if $\phi \wedge \neg\psi_1$ and $\phi \wedge \neg\psi_2$ are not satisfiable. Thus, the entailment test can be reduced to a (polynomial) number of linear problems. Following from the previous observations, we have the following proposition.

Theorem 2. Symb-Reach-over-$\mathbb{R}(\Phi_o, \Phi_f)$ solves the control reachability problem for a given re-allocation machine $\mathcal{R}$ wrt. the set Φ_o of $\mathcal{IC}$-constraints (initial conditions), and the set Φ_f of $\mathcal{AD}$-constraints (unsafe states). Furthermore, each step of the procedure is polynomial in the size of the set of constraints computed in the previous steps.

A last remark on the termination test. As in the integer case, pairwise entailment $\Phi \preceq_\mathbb{R} \Psi$ (used in the procedure Symb-Reach-over-$\mathbb{R}$) gives only sufficient conditions for the corresponding full test $\Phi \sqsubseteq_\mathbb{R} \Psi$ (take the same example used for $\sqsubseteq$ and $\preceq$). Thus, if polynomial, $\Phi \sqsubseteq_\mathbb{R} \Psi$ would give better sufficient conditions to test $\Phi \sqsubseteq \Psi$ than $\Phi \preceq_\mathbb{R} \Psi$. (Note that, $\Phi \sqsubseteq \Psi$ does not imply $\Phi \sqsubseteq_\mathbb{R} \Psi$, as it can be seen by taking $\Phi = \{x \geq 1, y \geq 1\}$ and $\Psi = \{x + y \geq 1\}$). Unfortunately, the following proposition shows that the full test over $\mathbb{R}_+$ is exponential.

Proposition 4. Checking $\Phi \sqsubseteq_\mathbb{R} \Psi$ is co-NP hard in the size of the sets of $\mathcal{AD}$-constraints Φ and Ψ.

4   Experimental Results

The verification algorithm based on real arithmetics of Fig. 3 is basically the *backward reachability* procedure implemented in existing symbolic model checkers like e.g. [16,25,26,28], and methods for program analysis like e.g.[13]. We have applied DMC [16], based on the real constraint solver, and HyTech [28], based on Halbwachs' polyhedra library [25], on several examples of parameterized systems and integer-valued systems that belong to the classes of systems we have defined in this paper (see Section 2 and Def. 2). For instance, we automatically check safety properties for parameterized versions of the *Load Balancing Monitor* of Example 1, the *Write-once* and the *Synapse N+1* cache coherence protocols [27], and the *Central Server System* of [2]. The method works well for examples where the intermediate results contain many additive constraints (e.g., when the transformations are more complicated than simple increments/decrements of variables). For 'pathologic' examples like Petri Nets it is necessary to go one step further and represent 'constraints' using techniques like the one discussed in [17,18]. We have also applied the same method (i.e. real-based tools) for a different class of integer systems that extend Broadcast Protocols with more powerful guards (but with the same transformations as Broadcast Protocols) for which the decidability of the control state reachability problem does not hold any more. These experiments are treated in detail in [14].

5   Related Works

The decision procedure for families of asynchronous processes of [23] is based on that for forward reachability of Vector Addition Systems (with state). The verification technique proposed by Emerson and Namjoshi in [20] is an extension of the *covering graph construction* of [29]. For broadcast protocols (a subclass of re-allocation machines), this construction is not guaranteed to terminate [21].

In [15], Delzanno, Esparza and Podelski propose to use additive constraints as a symbolic representation of upward-closed sets. However, they interpret the constraints over *integers* and prove that operations like *entailment* may be exponential in this case. In [14], we have studied a different extensions of broadcast protocols in which guards are allowed to contain *tests for zero*. Though when considering zero-tests verification becomes undecidable in general, we managed to verify *cache-coherence protocols* by using constraint-model checking as push-button technology. In [4], Petri Nets have been used as abstract model for *multi-threaded C programs*. Forward exploration has been used to verufy safety properties for abstraction of programs of an existing C library. In [18], extensions of Petri Nets that provide deterministic broadcast and asynchronous rendez-vous have been proposed as abstract models for multithreaded Java programs. Verification is tackled by using a symbolic representation of upward closed sets of markings called Covering Sharing Trees [17,18]. Apart from the differences in the abstract models of parameterized system, in this paper we focus our attention on the representation of integer system via real arithmetics. The experiment in [17,18] show however that specialized data structures can outperforms general purpose tools like HyTech on particular classes of verification problems (e.g. covering for Petri Nets).

Relaxation methods (abstractions with polyhedra) for integer or hybrid systems have been studied in [6,13,16,25,26,28]. Several other approaches exist to attack the verification problem of parameterized *concurrent systems*. In [32], Lesens and Saïdi compute *abstract networks* using *counters* to keep track of the number of processes in a given state. Differently from our approach, they consider only linear transformations (as in Broadcast Protocols); they do not give decision procedures for subclasses of the resulting systems. Among other semi-automatic methods we mention [5,12,30,33], while automated generation of invariants has been studied, e.g., in [12,31].

6   Conclusions

We have proposed a methodology to verify safety properties for parameterized system with many identical processes based on the following points. We first reduce the state-space of the original system by representing *global states* modulo *symmetries*. The system we obtain can be represented via infinite-state machines whose states are tuples of (potentially unbounded) integers; each tuple represents a collection of global states. We reduce further the state-space by representing collection of tuples via linear arithmetic constraints whose 'natural' (i.e. induced by the semantics of re-allocation machines) interpretation is the domain of positive integers. At this point, we obtain efficient verification procedures by executing the analysis over the reals, i.e., by means of the relaxation integer-reals applied to the constraint operations. Relaxation of integer problems into linear problems is typical of integer programming and program analysis [13,34]. For the class of systems we consider in this paper, we obtain the following nice property: the procedure working over the reals is a decision procedure for the problem originally formulated over the integers, i.e., the relaxation preserves the termination and the accuracy of the method. We are currently working on application of this methodology (even for more general classes where termination is no more guaranteed [14]) for the verification of practical examples of parameterized systems like communication and cache coherence protocols. It would be important to a make further step in the direction of efficient and compact manipulation of constraints, e.g., to handle examples like Petri Nets where, due to the dimension of the disjunctions generated during the analysis, even efficient constraint libraries like [25] (used by HyTech) may get into troubles. Recent works like [17,18] indicate possible BDD-like structures for the representation of subclasses of linear constraints.

References

1. P. A. Abdulla, K. Cerāns, B. Jonsson and Y.-K. Tsay. General Decidability Theorems for Infinite-State Systems. In *Proc. of LICS 96*, pp. 313–321, 1996.
2. M. Ajmone Marsan, G. Balbo, G. Conte, S. Donatelli, and G. Franceschinis. *Modelling with Generalized Stochastic Petri Nets*. Series in Parallel Computing. John Wiley & Sons, 1995.
3. K. Apt and D. Kozen. Limits for Automatic Verification of Finite-state Concurrent Systems. Information Processing Letters 15, pp. 307-309, 1986.
4. T. Ball, S. Chaki, S. K. Rajamani. Parameterized Verification of Multithreaded Software Libraries. In *Proc. TACAS '01*, LNAI 2031, pages 158-173, 2001.
5. M. C. Browne, E. M. Clarke, O. Grumberg. Reasoning about Networks with Many Identical Finite State Processes. Information and Computation 81(1): 13–31, 1989.
6. B. Bérard, and L. Fribourg. Reachability analysis of (timed) Petri nets using real arithmetic. In *Proc. of CONCUR 99*, LNAI 1664, pp. 178-193.
7. B. Boigelot and P. Wolper. Verifying Systems with Infinite but Regular State Space. In *Proc. of CAV 98*, *LNAI* 1427, pp. 88–97. Springer, 1998.
8. A. Bouajjani and R. Mayr. Model Checking Lossy Vector Addition Systems. In *Proc. of STACS 99*, LNAI 1563, pp. 323–333. 1999.
9. T. Bultan. BDD vs. Constraint-Based Model Checking: An Experimental Evaluation for Asynchronous Concurrent Systems. *Proc. of TACAS 2000*, LNAI 1785, pp. 441–455, 2000.
10. T. Bultan, R. Gerber, and W. Pugh. Symbolic Model Checking of Infinite-state Systems using Presburger Arithmetics. In *Proc. of CAV 97* , LNAI 1254, pp. 400–411, 1997.
11. G. Ciardo. Petri nets with marking-dependent arc multiplicity: properties and analysis. In *Proc. of ICATPN*, LNAI 815, pp. 179-198, 1994.
12. E. Clarke, O. Grumberg, S. Jha. Verifying Parameterized Networks. TOPLAS 19(5): 726-750 (1997).
13. P. Cousot and N. Halbwachs. Automatic Discovery of Linear Restraints among Variables of a Program. In *Proc. of POPL 78*, pp. 84–96, 1978.
14. G. Delzanno. Automated Verification of Parameterized Cache Coherence Protocols. In *Proc. CAV'00*, LNAI 1855, pp. 53–68, 2000.
15. G. Delzanno, J. Esparza, and A. Podelski. Constraint-based Analysis of Broadcast Protocols. In *Proc. of CSL 99*, LNAI 1683, pp. 50–66, 1999.
16. G. Delzanno and A. Podelski, Model Checking in CLP. In *Proc. of TACAS 99*, LNAI 1579, pp. 223–239, 1999.

17. G. Delzanno, J.-F. Raskin, and L. Van Begin. Attacking Symbolic State Explosion. In *Proc. CAV 2001*, LNAI 2102, pages 298–310, Springer, 2001.

18. G. Delzanno, J.-F. Raskin, and L. Van Begin. Towards the Automated Verification of Multithreaded Java Programs. To appear in *TACAS 2002*, April 2001.

19. E. A. Emerson and K. S. Namjoshi. Automatic Verification of Parameterized Synchronous Systems. In *Proc. CAV 96, LNAI* 1102, pp. 87–98, 1996.

20. E. A. Emerson and K. S. Namjoshi. On Model Checking for Non-deterministic Infinite-state Systems. In *Proc. LICS 98*, pp. 70–80, 1998.

21. J. Esparza, A. Finkel, and R. Mayr. On the Verification of Broadcast Protocols. In *Proc. LICS 99*, pp. 352–359, 1999.

22. A. Finkel and Ph. Schnoebelen. Well-structured transition systems everywhere! *Theoretical Computer Science*, 256(1-2):63–92, 2001.

23. S. M. German, A. P. Sistla. Reasoning about Systems with Many Processes. JACM 39(3): 675-735 (1992).

24. S. Graf and H. Saïdi. Construction of Abstract State Graphs with PVS. In *Proc. of CAV 97*, LNAI 1254, pp. 72-83, 1997.

25. N. Halbwachs. Delay analysis in synchronous programs. In *Proc. CAV 93*, LNAI 697, pp. 333-346, 1993.

26. N. Halbwachs and Y.-E. Proy and P. Raymond. Verification of Linear Hybrid Systems by Means of Convex Approximations. In *Proc. SAS 94*, LNAI 864, pp. 223-237, 1994

27. J. Handy. The Cache Memory Book. Academic Press, 1993.

28. T. A. Henzinger, P.-H. Ho, and H. Wong-Toi. HyTech: a Model Checker for Hybrid Systems. In *Proc. CAV 97*, LNAI 1254, pp. 460-463, 1997.

29. R. M. Karp and R. E. Miller. Parallel Program Schemata. *Journal of Computer and System Sciences*, 3, pp. 147-195, 1969.

30. R. P. Kurshan and K. McMillan. A Structural Induction Theorem for Processes. In *Proc. 8th ACM Symp. on Principles of Distributed Computing*, pp. 239-247, 1989.

31. D. Lesens and N. Halbwachs and P. Raymond. Automatic Verification of Parameterized Linear Networks of Processes. In *Proc. of POPL 97*, pp. 346-357, 1997.

32. D. Lesens and H. Saidi. Automatic Verification of Parameterized Networks of Processes by Abstraction. In *Proc. INFINITY 97*, 1997.

33. K. L. McMillan. Verification of Infinite State Systems by Compositional Model Checking. In *Proc. CHARME 99*, LNAI 1703, pp. 219–234, 1999.

34. A. Schrijver. Theory of Linear and Integer Programming. Wiley and Sons, 1998.

35. D. Srivistava. Subsumption and Indexing in Constraint Query Languages with Linear Arithmetic Constraints. Annals of Mathematics and Artificial Intelligence, 8(3-4): 315-343, 1993.

A Rewrite Rule Based Framework for Combining Decision Procedures *

Preliminary Draft

Deepak Kapur

Department of Computer Science, University of New Mexico
Albuquerque, NM 87131, U.S.A.
kapur@cs.unm.edu

Abstract. A rewrite rule based framework for combining decision procedures for universally quantified theories is proposed. It builds on the key ideas of Shostak's combination approach. A distinctive feature of the proposed framework is that its soundness and completeness can be easily established. Furthermore, the framework has the desired property of being efficient (by avoiding duplication of equality reasoning in all decision procedures) as well as generating canonical forms as in Shostak's combination framework. It thus enables tight integration of decision procedures with equational and inductive reasoning based on rewriting.

1 Introduction

A framework for combining decision procedures for universally quantified theories that satisfy certain constraints is proposed. The framework is influenced by Shostak's approach presented in [25,26] for such theories for which canonical forms of terms can be computed and equations can be solved. The proposed approach is based on the concepts of ground rewriting and completion, and generalizes our earlier formulation of a completion based view of Shostak's congruence closure algorithm as discussed in [8]. The focus here is on universally quantified theories with equality as the only predicate. However, as briefly discussed near the end of the paper, the proposed framework is also useful for considering universally quantified theories with predicate symbols (such as $\leq, \subseteq$) whose semantics are related to the equality predicate.

The proposed approach offers key advantages: the framework is simple, easy to understand, prove correct as well as implement. It is based on building a canonizer function for generating canonical forms for arbitrary (mixed) terms as well as a solver function for solving arbitrary (mixed) equations in the combination of theories from the corresponding functions for the component theories. Most importantly, it nicely integrates rewriting based reasoning with decision procedures in a tight fashion [12,13,9,10]. As a result, it becomes possible to effectively

---

* Partially supported by National Science Foundation Grant Nos. CCR-0113611, CCR-0098114 and CDA-9503064.

A. Armando (Ed.): FroCoS 2002, LNAI 2309, pp. 87–102, 2002.

use decision procedures for equational and inductive reasoning as demonstrated in our rewrite-rule based theorem prover *Rewrite Rule Laboratory (RRL)* [16]. This theorem prover has been successfully used in many applications, particularly mechanical verification of number-theoretic properties of arbitrary width and generic arithmetic circuits; for details, the reader can see [15]. More recently [14,7], we have been interested in extending the power of decision procedures by integrating induction schemes suggested by recursively defined functions with the objective of automatically deciding the validity of a large class of universally quantified formulas about such functions whose proofs need inductive reasoning. Our main objective has been to develop methods and heuristics so that "obvious" properties about commonly used data structures arising while reasoning about computations can be proved automatically. For a rewrite-based approach for building decision procedure, see also [1].

In the rest of the introduction, we discuss the significance of the proposed approach in the context of the recent surge of interest in the use of decision procedures as well as their combinations. Particularly, there have been several attempts to fix Shostak's original proposal for combining decision procedures as outlined in [26], as well as develop an amalgamation of Shostak's approach and Nelson and Oppen's combination framework [19,20] with the hope of exploiting advantages of both the approaches. This work is of interest not only from a theoretical stand point but also because after nearly 20 years, there has once again been a revival of interest in the use of decision procedures for verification (hardware and software), type inference, extended static analysis of computation descriptions, generating proofs for proof-carrying code, etc.

It is well-known that Shostak's original paper contained numerous errors some of which are quite subtle. Implementations of the algorithms proposed in Shostak's two papers [25,26] were buggy (see comments in [5,24] about SRI's implementation of Shostak's approach, as well as comments in [4,18] about implementations at Stanford). Consequently, a paper by Cyrluk, Lincoln and Shankar [5] claimed to have fixed these bugs and even give a completeness proof. In Ph.D. dissertations by Levitt [18] and Bjorner [4] from Stanford, these bugs were supposedly fixed albeit in a different way. Other papers from Dill's group [2,3] claimed to give simple proofs of modified Shostak's combination procedure. A recent paper from SRI entitled *Deconstructing Shostak* [24] briefly reviewed problems with all the previous approaches including those in [5] in its introduction[1]. This paper finally claims to fix Shostak's approach and even gives a soundness, termination and completeness proof. It is unclear to us whether even this most recent paper from SRI [24] has been able to fix the bugs since the presentation of the algorithm is quite involved and most of the proofs are sketchy and hard

---

[1] Most of the errors appear to have to do with computing canonical forms of mixed terms using canonizers and solutions of equations. We think this is partly because Shostak's approach [25,26] allows replacing the left side of an equation by its right side even when the left side is properly embedded in the right side; see [8] for examples. Attempted fixes do not work because either the canonical form computation does not terminate or two congruent terms do not have the same canonical form.

to follow.[2] It is difficult to feel confident about these modifications/extensions because they introduce more subtle data structures and functions to fix the bugs.

We are however of the opinion that the key ideas in Shostak's original paper are basically correct. The approach developed in this paper builds on these key ideas, and develops a method which we submit, is the closest in spirit to Shostak's original combination algorithm (even though the proposed algorithm avoids some of the complicated data structures needed for book-keeping). Proofs have been omitted from this version because of space limitations; a longer version with proofs will be available as a technical report.

2   Preliminaries and Definitions

We assume a family of languages characterizing different domains and data structures, and their associated universally quantified theories. Except for Section 7, for theories under consideration, the only predicate in each $\mathcal{L}_i$ is =. It is assumed that each language has its own set of variable symbols which is disjoint from each other. The only shared symbols among languages are the equality symbol =, which is assumed to have the standard interpretation, and constant symbols (introduced for reasons discussed below.) We will reserve $\mathcal{L}_0$ for the language of uninterpreted function symbols and equality; let $\mathcal{T}_0$ be the associated universally quantified theory. Let $\mathcal{L}_i$ be the language of an i-th theory, and $\mathcal{T}_i$ be the associated universally quantified theory for $i > 0$. Any function symbol in $\mathcal{L}_i$, $i \neq 0$, is called an i-interpreted symbol (or simply an interpreted symbol).

Subterms within a given term t are identified by their respective *positions*, which are sequences of nonnegative integers. Given a position p, let $t[p]$ be the subterm of t at position p. Similarly, let $t(p)$ be the function symbol at position p in t. They are defined in the standard way as follows: if $p = \epsilon$, the empty position, then $t[\epsilon] = t$ itself. If t is a variable, then $t(\epsilon)$ is t itself; otherwise, if $t = f(t_1, \cdots, t_k)$, then $t(\epsilon)$ is f, the outermost function symbol of t. If $p = ip'$, where i is a nonzero number and p' is a sequence, then $t[p] = t[ip']$ and $t(p) = t(ip')$ are defined only if $t = f(t_1, \cdots, t_k)$ and $i \leq k$; in that case, $t[ip'] = t_i[p']$, and $t(ip') = t_i(p')$, where t_i is the i-th argument of the outermost symbol f of t.

Let $s[t]$ indicate that t appears as a subterm in s, where s is a term; we will abuse the notation and let s stand for a literal as well. Similarly, let $S[t]$ indicate that t appears in a finite set S of terms (or literals). Similarly, $s[t/c]$ stands for replacing t appearing in s by c. Given a term s, a position p in s, let $s[p] \leftarrow t$ stand for the term obtained by replacing the subterm at position p in s by t.

2.1   Pure Terms, Mixed Terms and Types

The type of a term t is i, where $t(\epsilon) \in \mathcal{L}_i$; then s is called an i-term. (If s is a constant shared among many languages, then there is some deliberate ambiguity

---

[2] On a simple example, $\{x+1 = f(x-1)-1\}$, we were told in private communication by Harald Ruess (April 21, 2001), one of the coauthors, that their method will not be able to deduce $f(-1+x) = f(-3+f(-1+x))$ from it even though the unsatisfiability of $\{x + 1 = f(x - 1) - 1, f(-1 + x) \neq f(-3 + f(-1 + x))\}$ can be detected!!!

about its type. An appropriate index is chosen in that case to serve as the type of a shared constant to assign the proper type to equations.) If s_1, s_2 are i-terms in an equation $s_1 = s_2$, the type of $s_1 = s_2$ is also i. For $i > 0$, a *pure i-term* consists only of variables, constants, and interpreted function symbols in $\mathcal{L}_i$.

A nonvariable *mixed i-term*, in contrast, includes symbols from at least two different languages; often we will be considering mixed terms which include both uninterpreted symbols and interpreted symbols. A nonvariable term whose outermost symbol is uninterpreted, will be called *uninterpreted* even though it is mixed and may include some interpreted symbols.[3] A term in which all function symbols are uninterpreted is called *purely* uninterpreted (also a pure 0-term).

Given a mixed term, it can be *purified* by introducing new symbols to stand for its *alien* subterms. A nonvariable subterm $s' = s[p]$ at position p in a mixed i-term s is i-*alien* if the type of s' is different from the type of s. Further, an i-alien subterm s' of s at position p is a maximal i-alien subterm if for all all $p' < p$, the type of $s[p']$ is i.

Given an i-term t, let $s_1, \cdots, s_m$ be all the (maximal) i-alien subterms of t at positions $p_1, \cdots, p_m$, respectively. The term $t[s_1/u_1, \cdots, s_m/u_m] = (((t[p_1] \leftarrow u_1)[p_2] \leftarrow u_2) \cdots [p_m] \leftarrow u_m)$ is a pure i-term if each u_k is a new symbol belonging to $\mathcal{L}_i$ as well as $\mathcal{L}_j$, where the type of s_k is j. For each $\mathcal{L}_i$, we introduce an operator π_i such that $\pi_i(t)$ gives the pure i-term obtained by replacing in t, all maximal i-alien subterms in t by introducing new symbols $u_1, \cdots, u_m$. If t is pure, then $\pi_i(t) = t$. $\pi_i(t)$ purifies only i-terms, and is the identity function on non-i terms. Since $\pi_i^{-1} = \{u_1 \rightarrow s_1, \cdots, u_m \rightarrow s_m\}$ is a substitution, we further abuse the notation and write the **reverse** substitution π_i as $\{s_1 \rightarrow u_1, \cdots, s_m \rightarrow u_m\}$; . Similarly, given a finite set T of mixed i-terms, $\pi_i(T) = \{\pi_i(t) \mid t \in T\}$ stand for the pure i-terms obtained by *consistently* replacing maximal i-alien subterms in terms in T by new symbols (meaning that common maximal i-alien subterms in terms in T are replaced by the same new symbol).

Given a term t, its *impurity depth* is defined as follows: For every constant or variable position $p = p_1 p_2 \cdots p_k, k \geq 0$ in t, the *impurity depth* of a position p in t is the number of changes in the types of function symbols along the path from the root of t to the leaf node $t(p)$: $\langle t(\epsilon), t(p_1), t(p_1 p_2), \cdots, t(p_1 p_2 \cdots p_k) \rangle$. The *impurity depth* of a term is then the maximum over the impurity depths of each leaf position p in t. Many proofs are done by performing induction on the impurity depths of terms appearing in an equation.

3   Properties of Theories Being Combined

The following assumptions are made about each consistent universal theory $\mathcal{T}_i, i > 0$, over interpreted symbols. The universal theory of equality over uninterpreted symbols $\mathcal{T}_0$ is handled differently as discussed in Section 4.

---

[3] If the outermost symbol of a nonvariable term is uninterpreted, then it can be given any interpretation, irrespective of interpreted symbols in the term.

1. There exists a function σ_i, called *canonizer* following Shostak [26], which when given any term (atom, formula) in $\mathcal{L}_i$, returns its *canonical* form. σ_i satisfies the following properties:
   (a) $\mathcal{T}_i \models t = \sigma_i(t)$ (soundness),
   (b) for any $s_1, s_2 \in \mathcal{L}_i$, $\mathcal{T}_i \models s_1 = s_2$ iff $\sigma_i(s_1) \equiv \sigma_i(s_2)$ (completeness), and
   (c) $\sigma_i(\sigma_i(t)) \equiv \sigma_i(t)$.
   No other properties of σ_i need to be assumed.
2. There exists a function $solve_i$, again following Shostak, such that for any equation $s_1 = s_2$ in $\mathcal{T}_i$, $solve_i(\{s_1 = s_2\})$ returns[4]
   (a) **no solution**, represented by $\emptyset$, if and only if $s_1 = s_2$ is unsatisfiable with $\mathcal{T}_i$, i.e., $\mathcal{T}_i \cup \{s_1 = s_2\}$ is inconsistent,
   (b) ϵ, the identity substitution, to imply that any substitution for constant symbols is a solution for $s_1 = s_2$, which is the case if and only if $\mathcal{T}_i \models s_1 = s_2$, and
   (c) the most general solution written as rewrite rules $\theta = \{x_k \to t_k \mid 1 \leq k \leq n\}$ such that $\mathcal{T}_i \models (s_1 = s_2) \Leftrightarrow (x_1 = t_1 \wedge \cdots \wedge x_n = t_n)$, where (i) $x_k \neq x_j$ for $k \neq j$, (ii) x_k does not appear in any t_j, and (ii) $\sigma_i(t_k) \equiv t_k$, i.e., t_k is in canonical form with respect to the canonizer σ_i of $\mathcal{T}_i$. Symbols x_k's appear in s_1, s_2; t_k's could, however, include new symbols not in s_1, s_2.

Remark: Many papers and theses in the literature attribute the above conditions on equational theories to Shostak [26]. A careful study of that paper reveals that Shostak advocated a related but different set of conditions. Firstly, Shostak's σ-theory has both uninterpreted and interpreted symbols (p. 2). Secondly, Shostak required that for purely interpreted terms t, u, the canonizer produces identical canonical forms for t and u if and only $t = u$ is valid in the theory, which is the same as the condition above; further, the canonizer must act as an identity on uninterpreted terms. It is unclear what behavior Shostak required of the canonizer on mixed terms, i.e., terms containing both uninterpreted and interpreted symbols (e.g. $f(x) - f(x), f(y + x - x) - f(y)$). Thirdly, σ-theory is required to be *algebraically solvable* to mean that only for a pure interpreted equation, there is a function which returns either true, or false or a conjunction of equations, such that if the interpreted equation has no variables, then the answer is true or false; otherwise, the conjunction of equations must be in the solved form in the above sense, and must be equivalent to the input equation. Once again, nothing is said about how the solver should behave on equations which have both interpreted and uninterpreted symbols. On

---

[4] It is not necessary for $solve_i$ to assume that the two sides of an equation given as input are in canonical form. Also, it is not necessary for $solve_i$ to produce an output in which the substitutions are in canonical form. $solve_i$ can also take a finite set of equations as input, in which case, it produces a simultaneous solution for all the equations in the input. In certain cases, $solve_i$ may return a finite set of most general solutions (as in the case of associative-commutative theories), instead of a single most general solution. Such theories are not convex in the sense of [22]. The proposed framework generalizes to nonconvex theories as well, but for simplifying the presentation, we will assume at most a single solution for each equation.

p. 5, Shostak, however, did remark that the solver can be extended in a natural way to deal with equations with uninterpreted symbols by treating maximally uninterpreted subterms of an equation as distinct variables.

We will not mix uninterpreted and interpreted symbols in any theory, since in our view, the universally quantified theory of equations with uninterpreted symbols plays a different role than other universally quantified theories. As will be discussed later, the $solve_0$ function for $\mathcal{T}_0$ is the identity function (Shostak remarked that also on p. 5); so unlike the above requirement on the solve function for other theories, it does not produce a solution of the form $x = t_i$, where x is a constant symbol.

The following universal theories are considered below. (i) Presburger arithmetic involving interpreted symbols $0, 1, \cdots, +, -$; its index is p; (ii) the theory of finite lists as an example of recursive data structure proposed in [26,21]; its index is l; (iii) the theory of equality over uninterpreted symbols; its index is 0. Shostak discussed some other theories as well, for which the proposed combination framework works. Other candidate theories we have considered elsewhere include the universal theories of free constructors and equality as well as over the data structure of bit vectors.

The canonical form of a term in the universal theory of Presburger arithmetic is a simplified sum of linear terms in ascending order, starting with a nonzero constant followed by variables with nonzero coefficients in lexicographic order; the canonizer is denoted by σ_p. $solve_p$ on an equation in Presburger arithmetic returns a solution in terms of one of the variables in the equation.

The canonical form for a term in the theory of finite lists with interpreted symbols $cons, car, cdr$ can be obtained by applying the following rewrite rules:

$$
\begin{aligned}
&1.\ cons(car(x),\ cdr(x)) \to x,\\
&2.\ car(cons(x,y)) \qquad \to x,\\
&3.\ cdr(cons(x,y)) \qquad \to y.
\end{aligned}
$$

A solver for the theory based on eliminating car, cdr and introducing new variables is discussed in [26].

3.1   Extended Canonizer

Because of the conditions imposed on σ_i and $solve_i$, the solution, δ_i, of a finite set of equations in $\mathcal{T}_i$ can be used as a canonical rewrite system. Symbols in a pure i-term t for which there is a solution, can be eliminated from t. The canonical form of t after substituting for δ_i is thus $\sigma_i(\delta_i(t))$. For instance, given a pure term t, say $x + 1 + y - 2 + x$ in Presburger arithmetic and a solution $\{x \to 2 * y - 3\}$, the canonical form of t is $-1 + 2 * x + y$; the extended canonical form (after applying the solution as well) is $-7 + 5 * y$.

3.2   A Decision Procedure for a Universally Quantified Theory

For a theory $\mathcal{T}_i, i > 0$, with σ_i and $solve_i$, a universally quantified formula α can be checked for validity as follows. Negate α, Skolemize it (by introducing new constant symbols for variables), obtain a disjunctive normal form, and check whether each disjunct in the disjunctive normal form, which is a conjunction of equations and disequations (negated equations), is unsatisfiable as follows.

For each equality literal $l = r$,

1. solve $l = r$ using the solver $solve_i$.
   (a) If the solver returns true, then discard it;
   (b) if the solver returns false, then the conjunction itself is unsatisfiable;
2. otherwise, take the solution and apply it on the equations not yet processed as well as on all the disequations.

Once all the equations are processed, then for any disequation $u \neq v$, check whether $solve_i$ returns true on $u = v$. If so, then the original conjunction is unsatisfiable. If the solver does not return true, then the original conjunction is satisfiable. In every step, after a solution is found, each of the disequations can be checked for unsatisfiability, instead of performing the check at the end.

If the conjunction is satisfiable, the algorithm can be modified to get a solution by incrementally composing the solution of each equation.

4 Universal Theory of Equality over Uninterpreted Symbols

There exist many algorithms for deciding the universally quantified theory of equality over uninterpreted symbols. A popular and common way is to decide the unsatisfiability of a conjunction of ground equations and disequations by computing the congruence closure of ground equations. Given a finite set of ground equations $\{s_1 = t_1, \cdots, s_k = t_k\}$, where each s_i, t_j is ground, its congruence closure is the equivalence closure preserved by every function symbol appearing in the equations. To decide whether another ground equation $u = v$ follows from $\{s_1 = t_1, \cdots, s_k = t_k\}$, it is checked whether u and v are in the same congruence class in the congruence closure.

There are many different algorithms for computing congruence closure (cc) proposed in the literature [25,20,6]. In [8], we proposed a reformulation of Shostak's algorithm as completion in a rewrite-based framework; in practice also, the algorithm has been shown to be highly competitive in comparison to other algorithms [27]. In the proposed combination framework, any of the congruence closure algorithms can be used for combining it with a decision procedure of another theory. However, we use our algorithm for the discussion below, because in our opinion, it is closest in spirit to Shostak's combination framework for decision procedures. Below, we briefly review the main ideas of the algorithm discussed in [8].

Given a finite set of ground equations $\{s_1 = t_1, \cdots, s_k = t_k\}$,

1. introduce new symbols for all nonconstant subterms in s_i, t_j's. For each subterm, introduce a unique symbol; this relationship is expressed as a rewrite rule from the subterm to the symbol. The above equations then become equations on constant symbols standing for nodes in the dag representation of s_j, t_j's.

2. Choose a total ordering on new symbols and constants, depending upon the nature of canonical forms desired, with nonconstant symbols always greater than constant symbols in the ordering. The selected ordering is used to orient equations into terminating rewrite rules. Thus, a rule is either of the form $f(c_1, \cdots, c_j) \to d$ or $c_j \to d$, where $c_1, \cdots, c_j, d$ are constant symbols, and f is an uninterpreted nonconstant symbol.

3. Use the rewrite rules on constant symbols for interreduction as well as for normalizing nonconstant left sides, which may result in two left sides becoming equal, leading to new equalities among constant symbols (completion).

This process eventually terminates, generating canonical forms with respect to the congruence relation. Rewrite rules can be expressed in the original signature, if needed, by replacing new constant symbols by subterms they stand for.

4.1   Canonizer and Solver

For $\mathcal{T}_0$, σ_0 is the identity function since there are no relations on function symbols, and thus, every term is in canonical form. $solve_0$ on an equation is the identity function (unless the equation is of the form $s = s$, in which it returns $true$). In this sense, $\mathcal{T}_0$ does not appear to satisfy the requirement on theories discussed in Section 3. $\mathcal{T}_0$ should be viewed as consisting of infinitely many constant symbols where there is a distinct symbol for each term, and a quantifier-free formula is a formula on these constant symbols.[5] An equation thus relates two constant symbols, and $solve_0(c_i = c_j)$ produces the solution by orienting the equation into a rewrite rule when c_i, c_j do not have the same canonical form. Rewrite rules over constant symbols expressing the congruence closure above specify the solution δ_0 for the equations. The extended canonizer $\sigma_0(\delta_0(t)) = \delta_0(t)$ gives the canonical form of t with respect to the congruence relation.

5   Combination Framework

Given two theories $\mathcal{T}_i, \mathcal{T}_j$, each admitting $\sigma_i, \sigma_j, solve_i, solve_j$, it is shown below how σ and $solve$ can be constructed for the combined theory in which formulas have symbols from both $\mathcal{L}_i, \mathcal{L}_j$. If both $\mathcal{T}_i$ and $\mathcal{T}_j$ involve only interpreted symbols, σ and $solve$ are easier to construct as shown below. In case $\mathcal{T}_i$ is the universal theory of equality over uninterpreted symbols (i.e., $i = 0$), then some caution is required, as $solve$ has to be constructed in a special way using the congruence closure algorithm discussed in Section 4.

5.1   Combining Canonizers

There are many ways to define σ, much like computing a normal form of a term with respect to a terminating rewrite system; two obvious ones are bottom-up (innermost-out) and top-down (outermost-in). Below, we give a bottom-up

---

[5] That is the view taken in [8] of Shostak's congruence closure algorithm.

method. The following definition works irrespective of whether one of i, j is 0; as stated above, σ_0 is assumed to be the identity function.

Definition 1. *Without any loss of generality, let t be a term of type i.*

$$\sigma(t) = \sigma_i(t), \qquad\qquad\qquad\qquad \text{if } t \text{ is a pure } i\text{-term,}$$
$$\pi_i^{-1}(\sigma_i(g(\cdots, t_{i_1}, \cdots, u_{j_1}, \cdots))) \qquad \text{otherwise,}$$

where g is an i-symbol, t_{i_k}'s are pure i-terms serving as arguments of g, s_{j_k}'s are maximal i-alien terms (of type j) at positions p_k's in t, and $\pi_i(\sigma(s_{j_k})) = u_{j_k}$, a new symbol introduced to stand for s_{j_k}.

The termination of the above algorithm is obvious, as the number of steps is bounded by the impurity-depth of t.

Theorem 1. (a) $\sigma(\sigma(t)) \equiv \sigma(t)$.
(b) *If $\sigma(s) \equiv \sigma(t)$, then $\mathcal{T}_i \cup \mathcal{T}_j \models s = t$.*
(c) *If $\mathcal{T}_i \cup \mathcal{T}_j \models s = t$, then $\sigma(s) \equiv \sigma(t)$.*

5.2 Combining Solvers

Combining solvers for $\mathcal{T}_i$ and $\mathcal{T}_j, i, j \neq 0$, is somewhat different from combining a solver for $\mathcal{T}_0$ with $\mathcal{T}_i, i \neq 0$. Because of space limitations, we discuss them together with the hope of not causing confusion.

Consider an equation of $s = t$ of type i[6]. We consider two cases:

(i) $i > 0$: Apply $solve_i$ on $s' = t'$, where $s' = \pi_i(s), t' = \pi_i(t)$ obtained by replacing maximal i-alien subterms in s and t by new constant symbols using π_i. If $solve_i$ declares unsatisfiability, then $s = t$ is unsatisfiable. Otherwise, π_i^{-1} is applied on the solution $\delta_i' = \{x_1 \rightarrow r_1, \cdots, x_n \rightarrow r_n\}$ returned by $solve_i$, since $x_k's$ could be new symbols as well as r_k's can have occurrences of new symbols introduced by π_i[7]. Let $\delta_i = \pi_i^{-1}(\delta_i') = \{\pi_i^{-1}(x_1) = \pi_i^{-1}(r_1), \cdots, \pi_i^{-1}(x_n) = \pi_i^{-1}(r_n)\}$.

Consider an equation $\pi_i^{-1}(x_l) = \pi_i^{-1}(r_l)$ in δ_i. There are following subcases:

- Both $\pi_i^{-1}(x_l)$ and $\pi_i^{-1}(r_l)$ are pure i-terms; this is a solved form so it is included in the solution Θ collected so far. This substitution can be applied to eliminate $\pi_i^{-1}(x_l)$ from other solutions in Θ.
- Both $\pi_i^{-1}(x_l)$ and $\pi_i^{-1}(r_l)$ are j-terms $(j \neq i)$: Do $solve(\pi_i^{-1}(x_l) = \pi_i^{-1}(r_l))$.
- $\pi_i^{-1}(r_l)$ is a mixed i-term: Include $x_l \rightarrow r_l$ as a solution in Θ; x_l can be eliminated from other solutions in Θ. Also recursively invoke $solve(\pi_i^{-1}(u_{j_k}) = u_{j_k})$ for each new constant symbol u_{j_k} introduced for a maximal i-alien subterm in $\pi_i^{-1}(r_l)$; in case $\pi_i^{-1}(x_l) \neq x_l$, also $solve(\pi_i^{-1}(x_l) = x_l)$.

---

[6] It is not necessary for s and t to be in canonical form. The analysis and proofs become easier if s and t are assumed to be in canonical form, as then, a single new symbol is introduced for equivalent maximal i-alien subterms in s and t having the same canonical form. Henceforth, s and t are assumed to be in canonical forms.
[7] Recall that π_i^{-1} is a substitution.

(ii) $i = 0$: If both s and t are pure 0-terms, apply the congruence closure algorithm (Section 4) on $s = t$. If s (or t, resp.) is a term of the form $f(s_1, \cdots, s_n)$, where f is uninterpreted, each s_l is either a constant or a purely interpreted term, then include in Θ the solution $f(\sigma(s_1), \cdots, \sigma(s_n)) \rightarrow u$; $u = \sigma(t)$ if t is purely interpreted or a constant, and otherwise, u is a new symbol to stand for t; further, do $solve(t = u)$. In all other cases, apply the algorithm on $s' = t'$, where $s' = \pi_0(s)$, $t' = \pi_0(t)$; also recursively do $solve(\pi_0^{-1}(u_k) = u_k)$ for each maximal 0-alien subterm $\pi_0^{-1}(u_k)$ in s and t for which the new symbol u_k is introduced.

Only substitutions for symbols and uninterpreted terms in which the outermost uninterpreted symbol has interpreted terms as arguments are kept as solutions in Θ. If two identical uninterpreted terms are assigned two different substitutions, this results in a new equation relating the two substitutions which must be solved; for this, it is important to keep interpreted subterms appearing in the left side of a substitution in their canonical forms. Since in each step, either a pure equation is being solved, or the impurity depth of each new equation being solved is lower than the impurity depth of the original equation, the recursive procedure terminates. The algorithm terminates either detecting unsatisfiability or the result is a substitution for constant symbols and uninterpreted terms of the form $f(e_1, \cdots, e_k)$, where f is an uninterpreted symbol, and each e_l is an interpreted term.

For example, consider the equation $2 * car(x) - 2 * cdr(y) = 0$ in the combination of theories of Presburger arithmetic and finite lists. $solve_p(2 * car(x) - 2 * cdr(y) = 0)$ will give either $\{car(x) \rightarrow cdr(y)\}$ or $\{cdr(y) \rightarrow car(x)\}$ as follows: alien subterms $car(x)$ and $cdr(y)$ are replaced by new symbols u_1 and u_2, respectively, giving the pure equation $2 * u_1 - 2 * u_2 = 0$ to be solved; the solution can be either $u_1 \rightarrow u_2$ or $u_2 \rightarrow u_1$. Consider the first solution: $\{car(x) \rightarrow cdr(y)\}$; this gives a new equation $\{car(x) = cdr(y)\}$ which must be solved in the theory of lists. (The second solution will also give the same equation to be solved in the theory of lists.) The first equation $car(x) = cdr(y)$ can be solved as: $x \rightarrow cons(cdr(y), z)$, or $y \rightarrow cons(z, car(x))$. Each of these solutions can be easily verified by substituting for the respective symbol.

Theorem 2. (a) *If $solve_i(s' = t')$ is unsatisfiable, then $s = t$ has no solution and $solve(s = t)$ returns no solution.*

(b) *If $solve_i(s' = t')$ produces the identity substitution as the solution (implying $s' = t'$ is valid in $\mathcal{T}_i$), then $s = t$ is valid in $\bigcup \mathcal{T}_i$ and $solve(s = t)$ returns the identity solution as well.*

(c) *If $solve_i(s' = t')$ produces δ'_i as the solution, then $(s = t) \Leftrightarrow \delta_i$ is valid in $\bigcup \mathcal{T}_i$, where $\pi_i(s) = s'$, $\pi_i(t) = t'$, and $\delta_i = \pi_i^{-1}(\delta'_i)$, and the impurity depth of each equation in δ_i is lower than the impurity depth of $s = t$.*

5.3   Combination Algorithm

The combination algorithm is the algorithm implementing a decision procedure for a universally quantified theory discussed in subsection 3.2. Given a conjunction α of equations and disequations, equations are solved one by one and the solution obtained so far is collected as $\Theta = \{x_1 \to r_1, \cdots, x_n \to r_n\}$, where each x_k is either a constant symbol or $f(t_1, \cdots, t_l)$, where f is an uninterpreted symbol, $l > 0$, each t_m is either a constant or a pure interpreted term (consisting only of interpreted symbols) in canonical form; each r_k is also either a constant or a pure interpreted term in canonical form. Before inputting an equation to *solve*, Θ is applied on it. If in the process of solving equations, some equation is found to be unsatisfiable by *solve*, then α is unsatisfiable. After all the equations have been processed without detecting unsatisfiability, Θ is applied on each disequation and the result is brought to canonical form using σ. α is unsatisfiable if for some disequation $s \neq t$ (which is the result of applying the solutions obtained so far), $\sigma(s) \equiv \sigma(t)$. Otherwise, α is satisfiable.

We illustrate the algorithm using an example found difficult by various fixes of Shostak's combination procedure [5,24]. More examples are discussed in [11].

Example 1: $\{f(y-1) - 1 = y + 1, f(x) + 1 = x - 1, x + 1 = y\}$.

First, $f(y-1) - 1 = y + 1$ is processed; $\sigma(f(y-1) - 1)$ gives $-1 + f(-1+y)$; $\sigma(y+1) = 1 + y$. $solve(-1 + f(-1 + y) = 1 + y)$ replaces the maximal alien subterm $f(-1+y)$ by u_1, invokes $solve_p(-1+u_1 = 1+y)$. The result can give any of the two solutions: (i) $u_1 = 2+y$, (ii) $y = -2+u_1$ with $\delta_p = \{u_1 = f(-1+y)\}$.

The equation $f(x) + 1 = x - 1$ is similarly processed; its canonical form is $1 + f(x) = -1 + x$. A new symbol u_2 is introduced to stand for $f(x)$. *solve* can again give two possible solution (i) $u_2 = -2 + x$, (ii) $x = 2 + u_2$, with $\delta_p = \{u_2 = f(x)\}$. These nonoverlapping solutions from two equations can be combined in four different ways. We choose $\Theta = \{y \to -2 + u_1, x \to 2 + u_2\}$ and $\delta_p = \{f(-1+y) = u_1, f(x) = u_2\}$ since it is most interesting as the left side in each case is embedded in the right side; other possibilities will work as well. Eliminating y, x from δ_p extends $\Theta = \{y \to -2 + u_1, x \to 2 + u_2, f(-3 + u_1) \to u_1, f(2 + u_2) \to u_2\}$.

To process $x + 1 = y$, Θ is applied on both sides and canonical forms are computed: $3 + u_2 = -2 + u_1$. $solve_p$ can give two possible solutions: (i) $\{u_1 \to 5 + u_2\}$, and (ii) $\{u_2 \to -5 + u_1\}$. Let us consider the first solution for illustration; it is used to eliminate u_1 from Θ and the extended Θ is: $\{y \to 3 + u_2, x \to 2 + u_2, f(2 + u_2) \to 5 + u_2, f(2 + u_2) \to u_2, u_1 \to 5 + u_2\}$. Using the congruence closure, the left sides of two substitutions are equal, giving a new equation: $5 + u_2 = u_2$. $solve_p$ on this equation detects unsatisfiability. Hence the original formula is unsatisfiable.

6   A Calculus for Combining Decision Procedures

We present the above combination framework as a calculus generalizing our approach proposed in [8] for Shostak's congruence closure algorithm; the calculus is inspired by the presentation in [27] of our algorithm in [8]. Below, we give the calculus for the combination of three theories: $\mathcal{T}_0, \mathcal{T}_i, \mathcal{T}_j, i, j \neq 0$, to avoid repetition; by disregarding literals in $\mathcal{T}_0$, we get a combination of $\mathcal{T}_i, \mathcal{T}_j$, whereas by disregarding literals in $\mathcal{T}_j$, we have a combination of $\mathcal{T}_0$ with $\mathcal{T}_j$.

As in [8], there are still two kinds of rules expressing a solution but they are more complex: $f(e_1, \cdots, e_k) \to d$ and $c_i \to d$, where each of $e_1, \cdots, e_k, d$ is either a pure term (including constant) or a mixed term with i- and j-symbols, c_i is a constant symbol, and f is an uninterpreted function symbol.[8] By an i, j-term below, we mean a term only with interpreted symbols from $\mathcal{L}_i, \mathcal{L}_j$. It includes pure i-terms as well as pure j-terms (including constants).

A computation is a pair consisting of a finite set of literals, denoted by L, which remain to be processed, and a finite set of rules, denoted by Θ, representing the solution obtained so far. The initial state is $L, \{\}$, where L is the set of literals in a conjunction α of literals. If α is unsatisfiable, the algorithm terminates with a contradiction. For a satisfiable formula α, the result is a substitution Θ specifying the solution of all equations implied by α, along with disequations in L.

Below, a total well-founded ordering on function symbols is used with the restriction that (i) an uninterpreted nonconstant function symbol is bigger than constant symbols and interpreted symbols and (ii) a new constant symbol introduced to stand for a term is smaller than all the symbols in the term.

1. constant introduction: $\dfrac{(L[t],\Theta)}{(L[t/c]\cup\{t=c\},\Theta)}$,

where t is a nonconstant pure k-term $(k = 0, i, j)$ appearing as an argument to a function symbol not in $\mathcal{L}_k$, and c is a new constant symbol introduced of type k as well as of the type of the function symbol to which t is an argument.

2. solution extension-1: $\dfrac{(L[t],\Theta)}{(L[t/c],\Theta\cup\{t\to c\})}$,

t is $f(e_1, \cdots, e_k)$, where f is an uninterpreted function symbol, each e_l is either a constant or an i, j-term in canonical form (i.e., $\sigma(e_l) \equiv e_l$), and c is a new constant symbol of type 0.

3. solution extension-2: $\dfrac{(L\cup\{t=c\},\Theta)}{(L,\Theta\cup\{t\to c\})}$,

where t is either (a) a constant, or (b) $f(e_1, \cdots, e_k)$, where f is an uninterpreted symbol, each e_l is either a constant or an i, j-term in canonical form, and c is a constant symbol with $t > c$ in the well-founded ordering.

4. solve: $\dfrac{(L\cup\{s=t\},\Theta)}{(L,\Theta\cup\delta)}$,

where s, t are pure i-terms (j-terms), and $solve_i(\sigma(\Theta(s)) = \sigma(\Theta(t)))$ $(solve_j(\sigma(\Theta(s)) = \sigma(\Theta(t)))$, resp.) generates the solution δ (different from $valid$ or $unsatisfiable$), expressed as $\{c_1 \to t_1, \cdots, c_k \to t_k\}$.

---

[8] For the combination of $\mathcal{T}_0, \mathcal{T}_i$, each of $e_1, \cdots, e_k, d$ is either a constant or a pure i-term in the calculus below. For the combination of $\mathcal{T}_i, \mathcal{T}_j$ (implying there are no uninterpreted symbols), the left side of each rule in Θ below is a constant symbol. In earlier presentations of this work, the requirements on the left side of rules expressing a solution were even stricter, namely each left side was required to be either a constant symbol or an uninterpreted terms whose arguments are constant symbols as in [8]. This resulted in a technical conditions on solvers for $\mathcal{T}_i, i > 0$, which is, strictly speaking, unnecessary.

5. contradiction (solve): $\dfrac{(L\cup\{s=t\},\Theta)}{(\{\},\square)}$,

where s and t are the same as in 4 above except that the solver detects *unsatis fiability*.

6. contradiction: $\dfrac{(L\cup\{t\neq t\},\Theta)}{(\{\},\square)}$.

7. equality propagation: $\dfrac{(L,\Theta\cup\{t\rightarrow c,t\rightarrow d\})}{(L\cup\{c=d\},\Theta\cup\{t\rightarrow c\})}$.

The following three steps use a rule in Θ to reduce L and Θ. As a result, the left and right sides of rules in Θ need not remain in canonical forms.

8. simplification-1: $\dfrac{(L[t],\Theta\cup\{t\rightarrow c\})}{(L[t/c],\Theta\cup\{t\rightarrow c\})}$,

9. simplification-2: $\dfrac{(L,\Theta\cup\{s[c]\rightarrow t,c\rightarrow d\})}{(L,\Theta\cup\{s[c/d]\rightarrow t,c\rightarrow d\})}$,

10. simplification-3: $\dfrac{(L,\Theta\cup\{t\rightarrow e[c],c\rightarrow d\})}{(L,\Theta\cup\{t\rightarrow e[c/d],c\rightarrow d\})}$,

where c is a constant, each of d,e is either a constant or an i,j-term (with e containing c), and $s[c]$ is an uninterpreted term properly containing c.

The following inference steps compute the canonical forms of i,j-terms in L and Θ. (These steps can be integrated into the other inference rules. For efficiency, it is better to keep arguments to uninterpreted symbols in the left side of a rule in Θ as well as the right side of each rule in Θ in canonical form.)

11. canonization-1: $\dfrac{(L[t],\Theta)}{(L[t/s],\Theta)}$,   **12. canonization-2:** $\dfrac{(L,\Theta[t])}{(L,\Theta[t/s])}$,

where t, a pure i-term (j-term) not in canonical form, appears as an argument to a function symbol not in $\mathcal{L}_i$ ($\mathcal{L}_j$, resp.), and $s \equiv \sigma_i(t)$ ($s \equiv \sigma_j(t)$, resp.).

13. tautology deletion: $\dfrac{(L\cup\{t=t\},\Theta)}{(L,\Theta)}$.

The soundness of each inference rule can be easily established. Many terminating algorithms can be developed by combining these inference rules. One particularly useful algorithm can be formulated as the regular expression $((11+12)^* \circ 13^* \circ (1+2+3)^* \circ (4^*+7^*)^* \circ (8+9+10)^*)^*$.

The following table illustrates the use of the inference system on Example 1 discussed in the previous section.

7   Predicate Symbols with Semantics Related to Equality

The discussion so far assumed that a formula under consideration is a conjunction of equations and disequations. We now briefly discuss an approach for combining decision procedures for universal theories which include predicate symbols other than $=$ but whose semantics is related to $=$. Examples of such theories include Presburger arithmetic, finite set theory, lattices, boolean algebras, etc.

L	Θ	Inference Rule
$\{f(y-1)-1=y+1,$ $f(x)+1=x-1, x+1=y\}$	$\{\}$	
$\{f(-1+y)-1=y+1,$ $f(x)+1=x-1, x+1=y\}$	$\{\}$	11, canonization-1
$\{c_1-1=y+1,$ $f(x)+1=x-1, x+1=y\}$	$\{f(-1+y)\to c_1\}$	2, solution extn-1
$\{f(x)+1=x-1, x+1=y\}$	$\{f(-1+y)\to c_1, y\to -2+c_1\}$	4, solve
$\{c_2+1=x-1, x+1=y\}$	$\{f(-1+y)\to c_1, y\to -2+c_1,$ $f(x)\to c_2\}$	2, solution extn-1
$\{x+1=y\}$	$\{f(-1+y)\to c_1, y\to -2+c_1,$ $f(x)\to c_2, x\to 2+c_2\}$	4, solve
$\{\}$	$\{f(-1+y)\to c_1, y\to -2+c_1,$ $f(x)\to c_2, x\to 2+c_2, c_1\to 5+c_2\}$	4, solve
$\{\}$	$\{f(-1+(-2+c_1))\to c_1, y\to -2+c_1,$ $f(x)\to c_2, x\to 2+c_2, c_1\to 5+c_2\}$	9, simplification-2
$\{\}$	$\{f(-3+c_1))\to c_1, y\to -2+c_1,$ $f(x)\to c_2, x\to 2+c_2, c_1\to 5+c_2\}$	12, canonization-2
$\{\}$	$\{f(-3+(5+c_2))\to c_1, y\to -2+c_1,$ $f(x)\to c_2, x\to 2+c_2, c_1\to 5+c_2\}$	9, simplification-2
$\{\}$	$\{f(2+c_2)\to c_1, y\to -2+c_1,$ $f(x)\to c_2, x\to 2+c_2, c_1\to 5+c_2\}$	12, canonization-2
$\{\}$	$\{f(2+c_2)\to c_1, y\to -2+c_1,$ $f(2+c_2)\to c_2, x\to 2+c_2, c_1\to 5+c_2\}$	9, simplification-2
$\{\}$	$\{f(2+c_2)\to 5+c_2, y\to -2+c_1,$ $f(2+c_2)\to c_2, x\to 2+c_2, c_1\to 5+c_2\}$	10, simplification-3
$\{5+c_2=c_2\}$	$\{f(2+c_2)\to 5+c_2, y\to -2+c_1,$ $x\to 2+c_2, c_1\to 5+c_2\}$	5, equality prop.
$\{\}$	$\square$	6, contradiction

For instance, from a formula $s\le t\wedge t\le s$ in Presburger arithmetic, where s,t are terms, $s=t$ can be deduced; similarly from a formula $s\subseteq t\wedge t\subseteq s$ in set theory, $s=t$ can be deduced. In general, equality literals may be implicitly present in a formula without having any explicit occurrence of $=$. The approach discussed below was implemented in our theorem prover RRL in 1990 [12] using Fourier-Motzkin's method for deducing equalities from inequalities in a quantifier-free formula in Presburger arithmetic over the rationals as observed in [17].

Given a finite set (conjunction) M of literals which do not involve the equality symbol, there must exist a sound and complete algorithm for deducing all equalities from M, i.e., the algorithm outputs one of the followings:

- a finite set of literals M' and an nonempty set of equalities E' such that
  - $\mathcal{T}_i \models \bigwedge M \Leftrightarrow (\bigwedge M' \wedge \bigwedge E')$, and
  - $\mathcal{T}_i \wedge M \models s=t$ iff $\mathcal{T}_i \wedge E' \models s=t$.
- a finite set of literals $M' \le M$, including $M'=M$, and no equality iff there does not exist any s,t such that $\mathcal{T}_i \wedge M \models s=t$.

For Presburger arithmetic over rationals (or reals), the Fourier-Motzkin's procedure precisely does that [17]. In the process of checking the unsatisfiability of a given set of inequalities, the method also determines what inequalities become equalities, which are used to eliminate the inequalities. In the case of integers, the procedure is more complex as illustrated by the simple example: $2x \leq 5$ and $2x \geq 3$ leads to the equality $2x = 4$, which cannot be determined easily. In [12,23], these issues are discussed in more detail.

The following inference step is added to the calculus in Section 6:

14. deducing equalities: $\dfrac{(L,\Theta)}{(L'\cup E',\Theta)}$,

where E' is the nonempty complete set of implicit equalities deduced from L (i.e. $E' \cap L$ is empty) using the decision procedure, and L' is the simplification of L using E'. This rule can be applied after equality propagation in the regular expression specifying the algorithm in Section 6.

Rules for tautology deletion and contradiction based on the semantics of the new predicate symbols are also added. For examples, in the case of the ordering relation $\leq$, the literal $t \leq t$ can be deleted since it is a tautology; similarly, $t < t$ is a contradiction since it is equivalent to $t \leq t \wedge t \neq t$.

More details will be given in a technical report [11].

References

1. A. Armando, S. Ranise, and M. Rusinowitch, "Uniform derivation of superposition based decision procedures," Proc. *Computer Science in Logic (CSL'01)*, 2001.
2. C.W. Barrett, D.L. Dill and J. Levitt, "Validity checking for combinations of theories with equality," Proc. *Formal Methods in Computer-Aided Design* (eds. Srivas and Camilleri), LNAI, Nov. 1996, 187-201.
3. C.W. Barrett, D.L. Dill and A. Stump, "A framework for cooperating decision procedures," Proc. *CADE-17* (ed. Mcallester), LNAI 1831, Pittsburgh, June 2000.
4. N.S. Bjorner, *Integrating Decision Procedures for Temporal Verification.* Ph.D. Dissertation, Dept. of Computer Science, Stanford University, CA, Nov. 1998.
5. D. Cyrluk, P. Lincoln, and N. Shankar, "On Shostak's decision procedures for combination of theories," Proc. *Automated Deduction - CADE 13,* LNAI 1104 (eds. McRobbie and Slaney), Springer Verlag (1996), 463-477.
6. P.J. Downey, R. Sethi, and R.E. Tarjan, "Variations on the common subexpression problem," *JACM*, 27(4) (1980), 758-771,
7. J. Giesl and D. Kapur, "Decidable classes of inductive theormes," Proc. *Intl. Joint Conf. Automated Reasoning, IJCAR-2001,* Siena, Italy, LNAI , June 2001.
8. D. Kapur, "Shostak's congruence closure as completion," Proc. *RTA'97* (ed. Comon), LNAI 1232, May 1997, Spain.
9. D. Kapur, "Rewriting, decision procedures and lemma speculation for automated hardware verification," Proc. *Theorem Provers in Higher-order Logics, TPHOL* New Jersey (ed. Gunter and Felty), Springer LNAI 1275, August 1997, 171-182.
10. D. Kapur, "Rewriting, Induction and Decision Procedures: A Case Study of Presburger Arithmetic," *Symbolic-algebraic methods and verification methods-Theory and Applications*, (eds. G. Alefeld, J. Rohn, S. Rump, T. Yamamato), Springer Mathematics, Wien-NY, 2001, 129-144.

11. D. Kapur, *A Rewrite Rule based Framework for Combining Decision Procedures.* Tech. Report, Dept. of Computer Science, Univ. of New Mexico, 2002.

12. D. Kapur and X. Nie, "Reasoning about numbers in Tecton," Proc. *8th International Symposium on Methodologies for Intelligent Systems, (ISMIS'94)*, Charlotte, North Carolina, October 1994, 57-70.

13. D. Kapur and M. Subramaniam, "New uses of linear arithmetic in automated theorem proving for induction," *J. Automated Reasoning,* 16(1-2) (1996), 39-78

14. D. Kapur and M. Subramaniam, "Extending decision procedures with induction schemes," Proc. *CADE-17,* LNAI 1831, Pittsburgh, June 2000, 324-345.

15. D. Kapur and M. Subramaniam, "Using an induction prover for verifying arithmetic circuits," *Intl. J. of Software Tools for Technology Transfer,* Springer Verlag, Vol. 3(1), Sep. 2000, 32-65.

16. D. Kapur and H. Zhang, "An overview of Rewrite Rule Laboratory (RRL), " *Computers and Math. with Applications,* 29(2) (1995), 91-114.

17. J.-L. Lassez and M.J. Maher, On Fourier's algorithm for linear arithmetic constraints, *J. of Automated Reasoning,* 9, 1992, 373-379.

18. J. R. Levitt, *Formal Verification Techniques for Digital Systems.* Ph.D. Dissertation, Dept. of Electrical Engineering, Stanford University, CA, Dec. 1998.

19. G. Nelson, and D.C. Oppen, "Simplification by cooperating decision procedures," *ACM Tran. on Programming Languages and Systems* 1 (2) (1979) 245-257.

20. G. Nelson, and D.C. Oppen, "Fast decision procedures based on congruence closure," *JACM,* 27(2) (1980), 356-364.

21. D. Oppen, "Reasoning about recursively defined data structures," Proc. *5th Annual Symposium on Principles of Prog. Langs.* (1979), 151-157.

22. D. Oppen, "Complexity, convexity and combination of theories," *Theoretical Computer Science,* 12, 1980.

23. W. Pugh, "The Omega test: A fast practical integer programming algorithm for dependence analysis," *CACM,* 35(8), Aug 1992, 102-114.

24. H. Ruess and N. Shankar, "Deconstructing Shostak," Proc. *LICS 2001,* Boston, June 2001.

25. R.E. Shostak, "An algorithm for reasoning about equality," *Communications of ACM,* 21(7) (1978), 583-585.

26. R.E. Shostak, "Deciding combination of theories," *JACM* 31(1), (1984) 1-12.

27. A. Tiwari, *Decision Procedures in Automated Deduction.* Ph.D. Dissertation, Dept. of Computer Science, State University of New York, Stony Brook, August 2000.

28. H. Zhang, D. Kapur, and M.S. Krishnamoorthy, "A mechanizable induction principle for equational Specifications," Proc. *CADE-9,* Argonne, IL (eds. Lusk& Overbeek), Springer LNAI 310, May 1988, 162-181.

Combining Sets with Integers

Calogero G. Zarba

Stanford University and University of Catania

Abstract. We present a decision procedure for a constraint language combining stratified sets of ur-elements with integers in the presence of a cardinality operator. Our decision procedure is an extension of the Nelson-Oppen combination method specifically tailored to the combination domain of sets, integers, and ur-elements.

1   Introduction

The cardinality of a set is the number of its elements. Thus, in order to reason about set-theoretic formulae involving the cardinality operator, a set-theoretic theorem prover needs the ability to reason about numbers. Such ability can be basically provided in two ways: either by representing numbers directly as sets by means of the set-theoretic identities $0 = \emptyset$ and $n+1 = n \cup \{n\}$, or by employing specialized decision procedures for arithmetic. We argue that, although the former solution is very elegant, the latter is more practical and more amenable to modularization.

In this paper we introduce a constraint language involving the cardinality operator and combining:

1. finite sets of ur-elements;
2. the integers;
3. an arbitrary first order theory T of the ur-elements.

We use a decision procedure for T and a decision procedure for integer linear arithmetic as black boxes to provide in a modular fashion a decision procedure for the satisfiability of constraints in the combined language.

Our decision procedure can be seen as:

- an *augmentation* method which takes a decision procedure for integer linear arithmetic and turns it into a decision procedure for a conservative extension of integer linear arithmetic to a theory of sets with a cardinality operator;
- a *combination* method for the union of an arbitrary theory T of the ur-elements with the theory of finite sets with integers.

Our decision procedure is an extension of the Nelson-Oppen combination method specifically tailored to the combination domain of sets, integers, and ur-elements.

A. Armando (Ed.): FroCoS 2002, LNAI 2309, pp. 103–116, 2002.

The Nelson-Oppen combination method [5,6] combines satisfiability checkers for stably infinite[1] first-order theories over disjoint signatures into a single satisfiability checker for the union theory by means of propagating equalities.

It should be noted, however, that although the Nelson-Oppen combination method requires the stable infiniteness of the combined theories, our decision procedure remains correct even if the underlying theory T of the ur-elements is not stably infinite.

1.1 Related Work

Several decidability results concerning the cardinality operator have been obtained in computable set theory. In their seminal paper, Ferro, Omodeo and Schwartz [4] prove the decidability of the fragment of set theory known as **MLS** (*multi-level syllogistic*), which contains the basic set theoretic constructs of membership, set equality, union, intersection, and set difference. They also prove the decidability of the extension of **MLS** with the singleton operator and the finite cardinality operator together with arithmetic addition, subtraction and comparison. Cantone and Cutello [1] prove the decidability of the extension of **MLS** with the singleton operator and rank and cardinality comparisons.

It should be noted, however, that the above results deal with pure Zermelo-Fraenkel set theory and do not address the problem of combining in a modular way sets with integers and ur-elements.

The combination of sets with integers and of sets with reals was addressed by Cantone, Cutello and Schwartz [2], who prove the decidability of an unquantified theory of sets of integers and of an unquantified theory of sets of reals, but without the cardinality operator. The combination of sets with ur-elements was addressed by Cantone and Zarba [3], who give a tableau calculus for combining set reasoning with first-order reasoning.

The decision procedure presented in this paper is inspired by the satisfiability procedure presented in [8], where we combine flat lists of ur-elements with integers in the presence of a length function.

1.2 Organization of the Paper

The paper is organized as follows. In Section 2 we define the constraint language **F2LSC** (*finite two-level syllogistic with cardinality*) for combining finite sets with integers and ur-elements in the presence of a cardinality operator. In Section 3 we present our decision procedure, and in Section 4 we prove its correctness. Finally, in Section 5 we conclude the paper by pointing at directions for future research.

---

[1] A first-order theory T is stably infinite if every unquantified formula φ which is satisfiable in T is also satisfiable in an infinite model of T.

2   The Constraint Language F2LSC

In this section we introduce the constraint language **F2LSC** (*finite two-level syllogistic with cardinality*) for expressing constraints over finite sets, integers, and ur-elements.[2]

2.1   Syntax

The language **F2LSC** is an unquantified many-sorted language with three sorts ur, int and set, plus the following symbols:

- the constants:
  - 0 and 1, both of sort int (*zero* and *one*);
  - $\emptyset$, of sort set (*empty set*);
  - arbitrarily many constants of sort ur;
- the function symbols:
  - $+$ and $-$, both of sort int $\times$ int $\to$ int (*addition* and *subtraction*);
  - $\{\cdot\}$, of sort ur $\to$ set (*singleton set*);
  - $\cup, \cap, \setminus$, of sort set $\times$ set $\to$ set (*union, intersection* and *set difference*);
  - $|\cdot|$, of sort set $\to$ int (*cardinality*);
  - arbitrarily many function symbols of sort $\underbrace{\text{ur} \times \ldots \times \text{ur}}_{n} \to \text{ur}$, for each $n \geq 1$;
- the predicate symbols:
  - $<$, of sort int $\times$ int (*less-than*);
  - $\in$, of sort ur $\times$ set (*membership*);
  - arbitrarily many predicate symbols of sort $\underbrace{\text{ur} \times \ldots \times \text{ur}}_{n}$, for each $n \geq 1$;
- an equality symbol $=_{\tau}$, for each $\tau \in \{\text{ur}, \text{int}, \text{set}\}$;[3]
- variables of sort τ, for each $\tau \in \{\text{ur}, \text{int}, \text{set}\}$.

Definition 1. *F2LSC-terms (resp. F2LSC-formulae) are well sorted terms (resp. formulae) constructed using the symbols of the language F2LSC.*

Definition 2. *A set-term[4] is* PURE *if all symbols in it are ur-variables or set-variables, or one of* $\emptyset, \{\cdot\}, \cup, \cap, \setminus$. *Pure ur-terms and pure int-terms are defined similarly.*

A PURE set-PREDICATE *is a predicate of the form* $u \in t$ *or* $s = t$, *where* u *is an ur-variable and* s, t *are pure set-terms. Similarly one can define pure ur-predicates, pure int-predicates and, in general, pure τ-formulae, for $\tau \in \{\text{ur}, \text{int}, \text{set}\}$.*

---

[2] Ur-elements (also known as *atoms* or *individuals*) are objects which contain no elements but are distinct from the empty set. "Ur" is a German prefix meaning "primitive" or "original".

[3] We will write $=$ in place of $=_{\tau}$ when τ is clear from the context.

[4] For a sort τ, a τ-term is a term of sort τ.

2.2   Semantics

Definition 3. *An* INTERPRETATION $\mathcal{A}$ *of* **F2LSC** *is a many-sorted interpretation of the sorts, variables and symbols in the language* **F2LSC** *satisfying the following conditions:*

- *each sort* $\tau \in \{\mathsf{ur}, \mathsf{int}, \mathsf{set}\}$ *is mapped to a non-empty set* A_τ *such that:*
  - A_{ur} *is a non-empty set;*
  - A_{int} *is the set of all integers* $\mathbb{Z} = \{0, \pm 1, \pm 2, \ldots\}$;
  - $A_{\mathsf{set}} = \{a \in 2^{A_{\mathsf{ur}}} : a \text{ is finite}\}$;
- *for each sort* τ, *each variable* x *of sort* τ *is mapped to an element* $x^{\mathcal{A}}$ *in* A_τ;
- *the symbols* $0, 1, \emptyset, +, -, \{\cdot\}, \cap, \cup, \setminus, <, \in$ *are interpreted as in their intuitive meaning;*
- $=_\tau$ *is interpreted as the identity in* A_τ, *for* $\tau \in \{\mathsf{ur}, \mathsf{int}, \mathsf{set}\}$.

In the rest of the paper the calligraphic letters $\mathcal{A}$, $\mathcal{B}$, ... will denote interpretations, and the corresponding Roman letters, properly subscripted, will denote the domains of the interpretations.

Definition 4. *A* **F2LSC**-*formula* φ *is*

- VALID, *if it evaluates to true in all interpretations;*
- SATISFIABLE, *if it evaluates to true in some interpretation;*
- UNSATISFIABLE, *if it evaluates to false in all interpretations.*

2.3   Theories

In **F2LSC** the elements of sort ur can be modeled by means of ur-*theories*.

Definition 5. *An* ur-*theory is any collection of universally quantified pure* ur-*formulae.*

Given an ur-theory T, a T-interpretation is an interpretation of **F2LSC** in which all formulae in T evaluate to true.

Definition 6. *Given an* ur-*theory* T, *a* **F2LSC** *formula* φ *is*

- T-VALID, *if it evaluates to true in all* T-*interpretations;*
- T-SATISFIABLE, *if it evaluates to true in some* T-*interpretation;*
- T-UNSATISFIABLE, *if it evaluates to false in all* T-*interpretations.*

2.4   Venn Diagrams and Places

Venn diagrams [7] are a visual representations of relationships among sets using overlapping ovals that divide the plane into regions. Some basic set-theoretic identities like

$$(x \cup y) \cup z = x \cup (y \cup z)$$

or

$$x \setminus (y \cap z) = (x \setminus y) \cup (x \setminus z)$$

can be nicely shown on a blackboard using Venn diagrams. For more complex identities, however, writing on a blackboard is not anymore a feasible way to proceed: we need the help of digital computers. Indeed, using computers we can conveniently represent the Venn regions in a Venn diagram by means of *places*.

Places are one of the most important and successful tool of computable set theory. The following is a formal definition.

Definition 7. *Let V be a collection of* set-variables. *A* PLACE *of V is a map $\pi : V \to \{0, 1\}$ such that $\pi(x) = 1$, for at least one variable $x \in V$. Given an interpretation $\mathcal{M}$ of* **F2LSC** *and a place π of V, the notation $venn_{\mathcal{M}}(\pi)$ stands for the set $\bigcap_{\pi(x)=1} x^{\mathcal{M}} \setminus \bigcup_{\pi(y)=0} y^{\mathcal{M}}$.*

It should be noted, however, that places were not invented to represent just *any* Venn region. The real intuition is that places are meant to represent the *non-empty* Venn regions.

In the computable set theory literature, the idea of places as syntactic place holders of non-empty Venn regions is permeated in all proofs which use places as a device for proving decidability results for extensions of **MLS**. In particular, this idea is at the base of the decision procedure described in the next section.

3   A Decision Procedure for F2LSC

Let T be an ur-theory for which a decision procedure for unquantified pure ur-formulae is available. We now describe a decision procedure for checking the T-satisfiability of any unquantified **F2LSC**-formula φ. Note that, by converting φ into a disjunctive normal form, without loss of generality we may restrict ourselves to consider only conjunctions of **F2LSC**-literals.

The decision procedure consists of four phases, which we systematically describe in the next four subsections.

3.1   First Phase: Variable Abstraction

The first phase of our decision procedure takes as input a conjunction φ of mixed **F2LSC**-literals, and converts it into a conjunction of pure **F2LSC**-literals. More specifically, the output of the variable abstraction phase is a pair $\langle \varphi', \varphi'' \rangle$ of conjunctions of **F2LSC**-literals with the following properties:

(a) $\varphi' \cup \varphi''$ is T-satisfiable if and only if so is φ;
(b) each literal in φ' is pure;
(c) each pure set-literal in φ' is of the form $x = y, x \neq y, x = \{u\}, x = y \cup z$, $x = y \cap z$, or $x = y \setminus z$, where x, y, z are set-variables and u is an ur-variable;
(d) each literal in φ'' is of the form $v = |x|$, where v is an int-variable and x is a set-variable.

In order to ensure properties (a), (b) and (d), we first let $\varphi' := \varphi$ and $\varphi'' := \emptyset$, and then we repeatedly apply the following transformations until nothing more can be done:

1. pick a literal of the form $s \in t$ (resp. $s \notin t$) in φ' where s is not an ur-variable, replace it with the literal $u_s \in t$ (resp. $u_s \notin t$), where u_s is a newly generated ur-variable, and add the literal $u_s = s$ to φ';
2. pick a term of the form $\{t\}$ in φ' where t is not an ur-variable, replace it with $\{u_t\}$, where u_t is a newly generated ur-variable, and add the literal $u_t = t$ to φ';
3. pick a term of the form $|t|$ in φ', and replace it with a newly generated int-variable v_t; in addition:
   - if t is a **set**-variable, add the literal $v_t = |t|$ to φ'';
   - if t is not a **set**-variable, generate a new **set**-variable x_t, and add the literals $x_t = t$ and $v_t = |x_t|$ to φ' and φ'', respectively.

It can be seen by standard ranking arguments that the above process eventually terminates, and that at its end properties (a), (b) and (d) hold. In order to enforce also property (c), we then repeatedly apply to φ' the following additional transformations until nothing more can be done:

1' replace each literal of the form $u \in t$ (resp. $u \notin t$) with the literal $t = t \cup \{u\}$ (resp. $t \neq t \cup \{u\}$);
2' replace every occurrence of the symbol $\emptyset$ with a newly generated **set**-variable w, and add the literal $w = w \setminus w$ to φ';
3' pick a term of the form $\{u\}$, where u is an ur-variable, replace every occurrence of it with a newly introduced **set**-variable w; and add the literal $w = \{u\}$ to φ';
4' pick a term of the form $x \cup y$ (resp. $x \cap y$, $x \setminus y$) where x, y are **set**-variables; replace every occurrence of it with a newly introduced **set**-variable z; and add the literal $z = x \cup y$ to φ' (resp. $z = x \cap y$, $z = x \setminus y$).

Note however that, in order to ensure termination, transformations 3' and 4' must be applied using the restriction that any given term cannot be picked more than once.

3.2 Second Phase: Partition

In the second phase we partition $\varphi' \cup \varphi''$ into four disjoint sets of literals φ_{ur}, φ_{int}, φ_{set}, and φ_{size} where

   - φ_{ur} contains all pure ur-literals in φ';
   - φ_{int} contains all pure int-literals in φ';
   - φ_{set} contains all pure set-literals in φ';
   - $\varphi_{size} = \varphi''$.

We call $\varphi_{ur} \cup \varphi_{int} \cup \varphi_{set} \cup \varphi_{size}$ a conjunction of **F2LSC**-literals in *separate* form. Moreover, in the rest of the paper we will denote with U_φ the collection of ur-variables occurring in both φ_{ur} and φ_{set}, and with V_φ the collection of set-variables occurring in $\varphi_{set} \cup \varphi_{size}$.

3.3   Third Phase: Decomposition

Let $\varphi = \varphi_{\text{ur}} \cup \varphi_{\text{int}} \cup \varphi_{\text{set}} \cup \varphi_{\text{size}}$ be a conjunction of **F2LSC**-literals in separate form. In the third phase of our decision procedure we nondeterministically guess an *arrangement* of φ. Intuitively, an arrangement of φ specifies:

- which ur-variables in U_φ are to be modeled as equals and which not;
- which Venn regions in the Venn diagram relative to V_φ are empty and which are not;
- for each ur-variable u, which Venn region should contain u.

More formally, we have the following definition.

Definition 8. *Let* $\varphi = \varphi_{\text{ur}} \cup \varphi_{\text{int}} \cup \varphi_{\text{set}} \cup \varphi_{\text{size}}$ *be a conjunction of* **F2LSC***-literals in separate form. An* ARRANGEMENT *of* φ *is a triple* $\langle R, \Pi, at \rangle$ *where:*

- $R \subseteq U_\varphi \times U_\varphi$ *is an equivalence relation;*
- Π *is a (finite) collection of places of* V_φ;
- at *is a map from* U_φ *into* Π.

Note that guessing an arrangement $\rho = \langle R, \Pi, at \rangle$ of φ is equivalent to guess that φ is satisfied by a T-interpretation $\mathcal{M}$ of **F2LSC** such that:

- if uRv then $u^{\mathcal{M}} = v^{\mathcal{M}}$, and if not uRv then $u^{\mathcal{M}} \neq v^{\mathcal{M}}$;
- if $\pi \in \Pi$ then $venn_{\mathcal{M}}(\pi) \neq \emptyset$, and if $\pi \notin \Pi$ then $venn_{\mathcal{M}}(\pi) = \emptyset$;
- if $at(u) = \pi$ then $u \in venn_{\mathcal{M}}(\pi)$.

For an arrangement $\rho = \langle R, \Pi, at \rangle$ we define the following collection of literals:

$$res_{\text{ur}}(\rho) = \{u = v : u, v \in U_\varphi \text{ and } uRv\} \cup$$
$$\{u \neq v : u, v \in U_\varphi \text{ and not } uRv\}$$

and

$$res_{\text{int}}(\rho) = \{0 < v_\pi : \pi \in \Pi\} \cup$$
$$\{v_\pi = 1 : \pi \in range(at)\} \cup$$
$$\{v = \sum_{\pi(x)=1} v_\pi : \text{ the literal } v = |x| \text{ is in } V_{\text{size}}\}$$

where, for each place $\pi \in \Pi$, v_π is a newly generated variable whose intuitive meaning is the cardinality of the Venn region $\bigcap_{\pi(x)=1} x \setminus \bigcup_{\pi(y)=0} y$.

In order to better understand the intuitive meaning of $res_{\text{ur}}(\rho)$ and $res_{\text{int}}(\rho)$, assume that there exists a T-interpretation $\mathcal{M}$ of **F2LSC** satisfying φ and such that:

- $u^{\mathcal{M}} = v^{\mathcal{M}}$ iff uRv, for each ur-variable $u, v \in U_\varphi$;
- $venn_{\mathcal{M}}(\pi) \neq \emptyset$, for each $\pi \in \Pi$;
- if $at(u) = \pi$ then $u^{\mathcal{M}} \in venn_{\mathcal{M}}(\pi)$, for each $u \in U_\varphi$ and for each $\pi \in \Pi$.

- $v_\pi^M = |venn_M(\pi)|$, for each $\pi \in \Pi$.

Then, the following must be true.

- $u^M = v^M$ if and only if uRv.
- If $\pi \in \Pi$ then $venn_M(\pi) \neq \emptyset$ and therefore $v_\pi^M > 0$.
- If $\pi \in range(at)$ then there exists an ur-variable u such that $at(u) = \pi$. But then a literal of the form $x = \{u\}$ must occur in φ_{set}. Since $u^M \in venn_M(\pi)$, we have that $venn_M(\pi) \cap x^M \neq \emptyset$, and therefore $v_\pi^M = 1$.
- If the literal $v = |x|$ is in V_{size} then the cardinality of x^M is the sum of the cardinality of the Venn regions contained in x^M.

Before describing the fourth and last phase of our decision procedure, we need to introduce the notation $|ur| \geq n$, which intuitively stands for stands for a formula forcing the domain of ur-elements to have cardinality at least n. Formally, we use the notation $\psi \cup \{|ur| \geq n\}$, for every conjunction ψ of pure ur-literals and every $n > 0$, to denote a conjunction of literals obtained by using the following process:

- generate n new ur-variables $u_1, \ldots, u_n$ not occurring in ψ;
- let $|ur| \geq n$ be the conjunction $\bigwedge_{i<j} u_i \neq u_j$.

3.4   Fourth Phase: Check

Let $\varphi = \varphi_{ur} \cup \varphi_{int} \cup \varphi_{set} \cup \varphi_{size}$ be a conjunction of **F2LSC**-literals in separate form, and let $\rho = \langle R, \Pi, at \rangle$ be an arrangement of φ.

The fourth phase of our decision procedure consists of three steps.

Step 1: Check that ρ satisfies the following conditions:
   (C1) $at(u) = at(v)$ if and only if uRv, for each two ur-variables $u, v \in U_\varphi$;
   (C2) if $x = y$ is in φ_{set} then $\pi(x) = \pi(y)$, for each place $\pi \in \Pi$;
   (C3) if $x \neq y$ is in φ_{set} then $\pi(x) \neq \pi(y)$, for some place $\pi \in \Pi$;
   (C4) if $x = \{u\}$ is in φ_{set} then $\pi(x) = 1$ if and only if $at(u) = \pi$, for each place $\pi \in \Pi$;
   (C5) if $x = y \cup z$ is in φ_{set} then $\pi(x) = 1$ if and only if $\pi(y) = 1$ or $\pi(z) = 1$, for each place $\pi \in \Pi$;
   (C6) if $x = y \cap z$ is in φ_{set} then $\pi(x) = 1$ if and only if $\pi(y) = 1$ and $\pi(z) = 1$, for each place $\pi \in \Pi$;
   (C7) if $x = y \setminus z$ is in φ_{set} then $\pi(x) = 1$ if and only if $\pi(y) = 1$ and $\pi(z) = 0$, for each place $\pi \in \Pi$.

If the arrangement ρ does not satisfy conditions (C1)–(C7) output `fail`, otherwise proceed to step 2.

Step 2: If $\varphi_{int} \cup res_{int}(\rho)$ is unsatisfiable (in $\mathbb{Z}$) output `fail`; otherwise compute the minimal value of $\sum_{\pi \in \Pi} v_\pi$ in a solution of $\varphi_{int} \cup res_{int}(\rho)$. Note that this can be effectively done in a naïve way by opportunely iterating over all possible assignments over the variables in $\varphi_{int} \cup res_{int}(\rho)$. Denote with $minsol(\varphi, \rho)$ this value, and proceed to step 3.

Step 3: If $\varphi_{ur} \cup res_{ur}(\rho) \cup \{|ur| \geq minsol(\varphi, \rho)\}$ is T-unsatisfiable output `fail`; otherwise output `succeed`.

Note that all the above steps can be effectively executed. In particular, Step 2 can be performed by using any decision procedure for integer linear arithmetic (since integer linear arithmetic is a decidable and complete theory), whereas Step 3 can be performed by using the available decision procedure for T.

3.5   An Example

As an example of how our decision procedure works, let us consider the following T-valid **F2LSC**-formula, where T is the empty ur-theory:

$$x = \{u\} \cup x \;\to\; |x \cup \{u\}| < |x| + |\{u\}|. \tag{1}$$

Clearly, in order to prove that (1) is T-valid, it suffices to prove that the following conjunction

$$\varphi = \left\{ \begin{array}{l} x = \{u\} \cup x, \\ \neg\,(|x \cup \{u\}| < |x| + |\{u\}|) \end{array} \right\}$$

is T-unsatisfiable. After applying the variable abstraction phase we obtain the following conjunction $\varphi' \cup \varphi''$:

$$\varphi' = \left\{ \begin{array}{l} x = y \cup x, \\ y = \{u\}, \\ z = x \cup y, \\ \neg(v_1 < v_2 + v_3) \end{array} \right\}, \qquad \varphi'' = \left\{ \begin{array}{l} v_1 = |z|, \\ v_2 = |x|, \\ v_3 = |y| \end{array} \right\},$$

which is partitioned in:

$$\varphi_{ur} = \emptyset, \qquad\qquad \varphi_{int} = \{\neg(v_1 < v_2 + v_3)\},$$

$$\varphi_{set} = \left\{ \begin{array}{l} x = y \cup x, \\ y = \{u\}, \\ z = x \cup y \end{array} \right\}, \qquad \varphi_{size} = \left\{ \begin{array}{l} v_1 = |z|, \\ v_2 = |x|, \\ v_3 = |y| \end{array} \right\}.$$

We now need to guess an arrangement $\rho = \langle R, \Pi, at \rangle$. Since $U_\varphi = \emptyset$, the only possible choice for R is $R = \emptyset$. On the other hand, since $V_\varphi = \{x, y, z\}$, there are 2^{2^3-1} possible choices for Π, and for each of them there are many choices for at. Nevertheless, there are only two arrangements, depicted in Figures 1 and 2, which satisfy all properties (C1)–(C7).

Let us consider the arrangement $\rho = \langle R, \Pi, at \rangle$ depicted in Figure 1 and formally defined by:

$$R = \emptyset, \qquad\qquad \pi_1(x) = \pi_1(y) = \pi_1(z) = 1,$$
$$\Pi = \{\pi_1, \pi_2\}, \qquad\qquad \pi_2(x) = \pi_2(z) = 1,$$
$$at(u) = \pi_1, \qquad\qquad \pi_2(y) = 0.$$

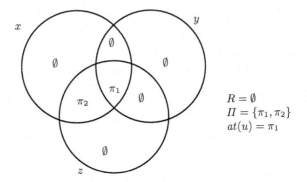

$R = \emptyset$
$\Pi = \{\pi_1, \pi_2\}$
$at(u) = \pi_1$

Fig. 1. An arrangement.

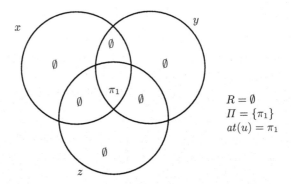

$R = \emptyset$
$\Pi = \{\pi_1\}$
$at(u) = \pi_1$

Fig. 2. An arrangement.

We have

$$res_{\text{int}}(\rho) = \left\{ \begin{array}{l} v_{\pi_1} = 1\,, \\ 0 < v_{\pi_2}\,, \\ v_1 = v_{\pi_1} + v_{\pi_2}\,, \\ v_2 = v_{\pi_1}\,, \\ v_3 = v_{\pi_1} + v_{\pi_2} \end{array} \right\}\,,$$

and therefore Step 2 of the check phase fails, since $\varphi_{\text{int}} \cup res_{\text{int}}(\rho)$ is unsatisfiable (in $\mathbb{Z}$).

Similarly, it can be verified that Step 2 of the check phase also fails with the arrangement depicted in Figure 2. Thus, the check phase fails with all possible arrangements, and therefore we conclude that φ is T-unsatisfiable, and consequently that (1) is T-valid.

4   Soundness, Completeness and Decidability

In this section we prove that our decision procedure is sound and complete for the T-satisfiability of conjunctions of **F2LSC**-literals. Let us start with soundness.

Theorem 1 (soundness). *Let* $\varphi = \varphi_{ur} \cup \varphi_{int} \cup \varphi_{set} \cup \varphi_{size}$ *be a conjunction of* **F2LSC***-literals in separate form, and let T be an* ur*-theory. Assume that there exists an arrangement* $\rho = \langle R, \Pi, at \rangle$ *of φ such that:*

(i) ρ satisfies conditions (C1)–(C7) of page 110;
(ii) $\varphi_{int} \cup res_{int}(\rho)$ is satisfiable (in $\mathbb{Z}$);
(iii) $\varphi_{ur} \cup res_{ur}(\rho) \cup \{|ur| \geq minsol(\varphi, \rho)\}$ is T-satisfiable.

Then φ is T-satisfiable.

Proof. Let $\mathcal{A}$ be a T-interpretation satisfying $\varphi_{ur} \cup res_{ur}(\varphi)$, and let $\mathcal{B}$ be a solution of $\varphi_{int} \cup res_{int}(\varphi)$ such that $\sum_{\pi \in \Pi} v_{\pi}^{\mathcal{B}} = minsol(\varphi, \rho)$.

We now start to define an interpretation $\mathcal{M}$. First, we specify the domains by putting $M_{ur} = A_{ur}$, $M_{int} = \mathbb{Z}$, and $M_{set} = \{a \in 2^{A_{ur}} : a \text{ is finite}\}$. Then, we put $u^{\mathcal{M}} = u^{\mathcal{A}}$, for every ur-variable u, and $v^{\mathcal{M}} = u^{\mathcal{B}}$, for every int-variable v.

In order to define $\mathcal{M}$ over the set-variables, we first define $\mathcal{M}$ over the places in Π by means of the following construction:

- If $\pi \in range(at)$ then there exists an ur-variable $u \in U_{\varphi}$ such that $at(u) = \pi$, and we put $\pi^{\mathcal{M}} = \{u^{\mathcal{M}}\}$. Note that this definition is sound. In fact, if there are two ur-variables $u, v \in U_{\varphi}$ such that $at(u) = \pi$ and $at(v) = \pi$ then, by property (C1), uRv follows, and therefore the literal $u = v$ is in $res_{ur}(\rho)$, which implies that $u^{\mathcal{M}} = v^{\mathcal{M}}$.
- If instead $\pi \notin range(at)$ then we pick $v_{\pi}^{\mathcal{B}}$ elements in A_{ur} and we put $\pi^{\mathcal{M}}$ to be the set of such picked elements.

It is important that the above construction satisfy the property that the sets $\pi^{\mathcal{M}}$'s be pairwise disjoint, that is, $\pi_0^{\mathcal{M}} \cap \pi_1^{\mathcal{M}} = \emptyset$, for every two distinct places $\pi_0, \pi_1 \in \Pi$. This property can certainly be forced, provided that A_{ur} contains at least $\sum_{\pi \in \Pi} v_{\pi}^{\mathcal{B}}$ elements. Indeed, $\sum_{\pi \in \Pi} v_{\pi}^{\mathcal{B}} = minsol(\varphi, \rho)$ and A_{ur} has at least $minsol(\varphi, \rho)$ elements.

We can now define $\mathcal{M}$ over the set-variables, by putting $x^{\mathcal{M}} = \bigcup_{\pi(x)=1} \pi^{\mathcal{M}}$, for every set-variable x.

We claim that $\mathcal{M}$ is a T-interpretation satisfying φ. Clearly, $\mathcal{M}$ satisfies $T \cup \varphi_{ur} \cup \varphi_{int}$. Moreover, it is easy to verify that, in virtue of properties (C2)–(C7), $\mathcal{M}$ also satisfies all the literals in φ_{set}. Finally, consider a literal of the form $v = |x|$ in φ_{size}. We have $|x^{\mathcal{M}}| = \left|\bigcup_{\pi(x)=1} \pi^{\mathcal{M}}\right| = \sum_{\pi(x)=1} |\pi^{\mathcal{M}}| = \sum_{\pi(x)=1} v_{\pi}^{\mathcal{B}}$, and since the literal $\sum_{\pi(x)=1} v_{\pi} = v$ is in $res_{int}(\rho)$, we infer that $|x^{\mathcal{M}}| = v^{\mathcal{B}} = v^{\mathcal{M}}$. This concludes the proof. $\square$

Our decision procedure is also complete, as proved by the following theorem.

Theorem 2 (completeness). *Let* $\varphi = \varphi_{\mathsf{ur}} \cup \varphi_{\mathsf{int}} \cup \varphi_{\mathsf{set}} \cup \varphi_{\mathsf{size}}$ *be a* T-*satisfiable conjunction of* **F2LSC**-*literals in separate form.*
Then there exists an arrangement $\rho = \langle R, \Pi, at \rangle$ *of* φ *such that:*

(a) ρ *satisfies conditions (C1)–(C7) of page 110;*
(b) $\varphi_{\mathsf{int}} \cup res_{\mathsf{int}}(\rho)$ *is satisfiable (in* $\mathbb{Z}$*);*
(c) $\varphi_{\mathsf{ur}} \cup res_{\mathsf{ur}}(\rho) \cup \{|\mathsf{ur}| \geq minsol(\varphi, \rho)\}$ *is* T-*satisfiable.*

Proof. Let $\mathcal{M}$ be a T-interpretation satisfying φ. Let us define an arrangement $\rho = \langle R, \Pi, at \rangle$ of φ as follows:

- for each two variables $u, v \in U_\varphi$, we let uRv if and only if $u^{\mathcal{M}} = v^{\mathcal{M}}$;
- $\Pi = \{\pi : venn_{\mathcal{M}}(\pi) \neq \emptyset\}$;
- for each $u \in U_\varphi$, we let $at(u)$ be the unique place π such that $venn_{\mathcal{M}}(\pi) = \{u\}$.[5]

Note that, by construction, we have that

(i) $\pi(x) = 1$ if and only if $venn_{\mathcal{M}}(\pi) \subseteq x^{\mathcal{M}}$, for each $\pi \in \Pi$ and $x \in V_\varphi$;
(ii) $x^{\mathcal{M}} = \bigcup_{\pi(x)=1} venn_{\mathcal{M}}(\pi)$.

We can now verify that ρ satisfies conditions (C1)–(C7) of page 110.

(C1) By construction.
(C2) Let the literal $x = y$ be in φ_{set} and assume, for a contradiction, that $\pi(x) \neq \pi(y)$, for some place $\pi \in \Pi$. Without loss of generality, let $\pi(x) = 1$ and $\pi(y) = 0$. Since $x^{\mathcal{M}} = y^{\mathcal{M}}$, we have that $venn_{\mathcal{M}}(\pi) \subseteq x^{\mathcal{M}}$ and $venn_{\mathcal{M}}(\pi) \not\subseteq y^{\mathcal{M}} = x^{\mathcal{M}}$, a contradiction.
(C3) Let the literal $x \neq y$ be in φ_{set}. Then $x^{\mathcal{M}} \neq y^{\mathcal{M}}$. If it were $\pi(x) = \pi(y)$, for each place $\pi \in \Pi$, then by (ii) above we would have $x^{\mathcal{M}} = y^{\mathcal{M}}$, a contradiction.
(C4) Let the literal $x = \{u\}$ be in φ_{set}. Then $at(u) = \pi$ iff $venn_{\mathcal{M}}(\pi) = \{u^{\mathcal{M}}\}$ iff $venn_{\mathcal{M}}(\pi) \subseteq \{u^{\mathcal{M}}\}$ iff $venn_{\mathcal{M}} \subseteq x^{\mathcal{M}}$ iff $\pi(x) = 1$.
(C5) Let the literal $x = y \cup z$ be in φ_{set}. Then $\pi(x) = 1$ iff $venn_{\mathcal{M}}(\pi) \subseteq x^{\mathcal{M}}$ iff $venn_{\mathcal{M}}(\pi) \subseteq y^{\mathcal{M}} \cup z^{\mathcal{M}}$ iff $venn_{\mathcal{M}}(\pi) \subseteq y^{\mathcal{M}} \vee venn_{\mathcal{M}}(\pi) \subseteq z^{\mathcal{M}}$ iff $\pi(y) = 1 \vee \pi(z) = 1$.
(C6) Analogously to condition (C5).
(C7) Analogously to condition (C5).

Next, in order to verify property (b), notice that by assumption $\mathcal{M}$ satisfies φ_{int}. In addition, since the variables v_π's do not occur in φ, we can safely extend $\mathcal{M}$ by letting $v_\pi^{\mathcal{M}} = |venn_{\mathcal{M}}(\pi)|$, for each place $\pi \in \Pi$. We claim that now $\mathcal{M}$ also satisfies $res_{\mathsf{int}}(\rho)$. In fact:

- Let the literal $v_\pi > 0$ be in $res_{\mathsf{int}}(\rho)$. Since $venn_{\mathcal{M}}(\pi) \neq \emptyset$ it follows that $v_\pi^{\mathcal{M}} > 0$.

---

[5] Such place exists because for each $u \in U_\varphi$ there must be a literal of the form $x = \{u\}$ in φ_{set}.

- Let the literal $v_\pi = 1$ be in $res_{int}(\rho)$, for some $\pi \in range(at)$. Then $at(u) = x$, for some variable $u \in U_\varphi$. It follows that $venn_\mathcal{M}(\pi) = \{u^\mathcal{M}\}$ which implies $v_\pi^\mathcal{M} = 1$.

- Let the literal $v = \sum_{\pi(x)=1} v_\pi$ be in $res_{int}(\rho)$. Then the literal $v = |x|$ is in φ_{size}, and therefore $v^\mathcal{M} = |x^\mathcal{M}|$. By property (ii) we have $v^\mathcal{M} = |x^\mathcal{M}| = \sum_{\pi(x)=1} |venn_\mathcal{M}(\pi)| = \sum_{\pi(x)=1} v_\pi^\mathcal{M}$.

It remains to verify that property (c) also holds. To do this, note that by assumption $\mathcal{M}$ satisfies φ_{ur}, and that by construction $\mathcal{M}$ satisfies $res_{ur}(\rho)$. In addition, we claim that M_{ur} has at least $minsol(\varphi, \rho)$ elements. In fact M_{ur} as at least $\sum_{\pi \in \Pi} v_\pi^\mathcal{M}$ elements and $\sum_{\pi \in \Pi} v_\pi^\mathcal{M} \geq minsol(\varphi, \rho)$. Therefore $\mathcal{M}$ satisfies $|ur| \geq n$, which completes the proof. $\qquad\square$

Combining Theorems 1 and 2 with the observation that there is only a finite number of arrangements of any collection φ of **F2LSC**-literals in separate form, we obtain the following decidability result.

Theorem 3 (decidability). *Let T be an* ur-*theory for which a decision procedure for unquantified pure* ur-*formulae is available. Then the T-satisfiability problem of unquantified formulae in the language* **F2LSC** *is decidable.*

5   Conclusion

We defined the constraint language **F2LSC** for combining finite sets with integers and ur-elements in the presence of a cardinality operator. We then presented a decision procedure for **F2LSC** and we proved its correctness. In particular, our decision procedure remains correct even if the underlying theory T of the ur-elements is not stably infinite.

Although not shown in this paper, it is easy to verify that our decision procedure can be easily adapted to the case of sets of integers, thus allowing the expression of constraints of the form $|x| \in x$, which are forbidden by the syntax of **F2LSC**.

Regarding future research, we plan to develop smart heuristics for exploring the space of all possible arrangements. We also plan to extend the results of this paper to the general case in which sets may be infinite.

Acknowledgments

Henny B. Sipma gave useful comments on an earlier draft. Bernd Finkbeiner explained me the meaning of the German prefix "ur". Three anonymous referees gave very helpful comments and suggested several improvements.

This research was supported in part by NSF(ITR) grant CCR-01-21403, by NSF grant CCR-99-00984-001, by ARO grant DAAD19-01-1-0723, and by ARPA/AF contracts F33615-00-C-1693 and F33615-99-C-3014.

References

1. Domenico Cantone and Vincenzo Cutello. A decision procedure for set-theoretic formulae involving rank and cardinality comparison. In A. Bertoni, C. Böhm, and P. Miglioli, editors, *Proceedings of the 3rd Italian Conference on Theoretical Computer Science*, pages 150–163. World Scientific, 1989.
2. Domenico Cantone, Vincenzo Cutello, and Jacob T. Schwartz. Decision problems for Tarski's and Presburger arithmetics extended with sets. In *Proceedings of the fourth Computer Science Logic Workshop*, volume 533 of *Lecture Notes in Computer Science*, pages 95–109. Springer, 1990.
3. Domenico Cantone and Calogero G. Zarba. A tableau calculus for integrating first-order reasoning with elementary set theory reasoning. In Roy Dyckhoff, editor, *Automated Reasoning with Analytic Tableaux and Related Methods*, volume 1847 of *Lecture Notes in Artificial Intelligence*, pages 143–159. Springer, 2000.
4. Alfredo Ferro, Eugenio G. Omodeo, and Jacob T. Scwhartz. Decision procedures for elementary sublanguages of set theory. I. Multi-level syllogistic and some extensions. *Communications on Pure and Applied Mathematics*, 33(5):599–608, 1980.
5. Greg Nelson and Derek C. Oppen. Simplification by cooperating decision procedures. *ACM Transactions on Programming Languages and Systems*, 1(2):245–257, 1979.
6. Cesare Tinelli and Mehdi T. Harandi. A new correctness proof of the Nelson-Oppen combination procedure. In Franz Baader and Klaus U. Schulz, editors, *Frontiers of Combining Systems*, volume 3 of *Applied Logic Series*, pages 103–120. Kluwer Academic Publishers, 1996.
7. John Venn. On the diagrammatic and mechanical representation of propositions and reasonings. *The London, Edinburgh, and Dublin Philosophical Magazine and Journal of Science*, 9(59):1–18, 1880.
8. Calogero G. Zarba. Combining lists with integers. In Rajeev Gorè, Alexander Leitsch, and Tobias Nipkow, editors, *International Joint Conference on Automated Reasoning (Short Papers)*, Technical Report DII 11/01, pages 170–179. University of Siena, Italy, 2001.

Solving Nonlinear Equations by Abstraction, Gaussian Elimination, and Interval Methods

Martine Ceberio and Laurent Granvilliers

IRIN – University of Nantes – France
2, rue de la Houssinière – B.P. 92208 – F-44322 Nantes Cedex 3
{ceberio,granvilliers}@irin.univ-nantes.fr

Abstract. The solving engines of most of constraint programming systems use interval-based consistency techniques to process nonlinear systems over the reals. However, few symbolic-interval cooperative solvers are implemented. The challenge is twofold: control of the amount of symbolic computations, and prediction of the accuracy of interval computations over transformed systems.

In this paper, we introduce a new symbolic pre-processing for interval branch-and-prune algorithms based on box consistency. The symbolic algorithm computes a linear relaxation by abstraction of the nonlinear terms. The resulting rectangular linear system is processed by Gaussian elimination. Control strategies of the densification of systems during elimination are devised. Three scalable problems known to be hard for box consistency are efficiently solved.

1 Introduction

Except in CLP($\Re$) [11] and RISC-CLP(Real) [10], real constraint solving is implemented in most recent constraint programming platforms and systems by hybrid methods that combine interval methods and local consistency techniques: In CLP systems like CLIP [9], CLP(BNR) [3], DeclIC [6], ECL^{i}PS^e [19] and PrologIV [1]; in libraries like ILOG Solver [14]; and in specific systems like Numerica [18]. However, only a few platforms, e.g., Unicalc [15] and the system of [12], integrate a symbolic-interval cooperative solver (see [8] for a survey of the symbolic-interval cooperation in constraint programming). The goal is to improve the precision of numerically computed solutions by changing constraint representation. The first problem is to control the amount of symbolic computations. For instance, in [12], Gröbner bases are computed for systems of polynomial equations, but the algorithms are exponential in time and memory. The second problem is to predict the precision of interval computations over the transformed systems. In general, as proposed in [16], redundant constraints are added to the constraint store, to ensure that the precision is equivalent in the worst case. Nevertheless, the whole process can be slower. Actually, the control of symbolic computations is crucial for efficiency.

In this paper, we are interested in symbolic pre-processings for box consistency [2], an adaptation of arc consistency over intervals. This technique has

A. Armando (Ed.): FroCoS 2002, LNAI 2309, pp. 117–131, 2002.

been implemented in Numerica [18], a modeling language which solving engine
has been shown to be efficient for a wide class of problems. Nevertheless, box
consistency can be weak. This is due to the locality of reasonings inherited from
arc consistency, and to the dependency problem of interval arithmetic. Several
attempts have been made to handle these problems: in [12,7], use of computer
algebra methods to combine constraints; in [4], factorization of constraint expressions to eliminate occurrences of variables; in [18,16], computation of linear
relaxations using Taylor series. Note that interval-based expansions in Taylor
series are precise for tight variable domains.

The first contribution of this paper is a new symbolic pre-processing for box
consistency over systems of nonlinear equations. The core algorithm performs
a Gaussian elimination over a linear relaxation of the user system obtained by
abstraction of nonlinear terms. Note that a similar idea is expressed in [20] for
systems of inequations and the simplex algorithm (the abstraction process is
slightly different). The main motivation is to eliminate occurrences of patterns
occurring in the user system. Control strategies of elimination steps are devised
since in general, the linear systems to be processed are $(n \times m)$ systems where
$m >> n$. The aim is to keep the density of linear systems in reasonable bounds.
With respect to related works, our algorithm handles both problems inherent
in box consistency; it is polynomial in time and memory (e.g., with respect to
Gröbner bases computations); and it is efficient for large domains (e.g., with
respect to expansions in Taylor series).

The second contribution of this paper concerns the solving of three scalable
problems (two are quasi-linear) known to be hard for box consistency: the problems of Bratu, Brown, and Yamamura that can be found in [20,7]. The lack of
precision of box consistency computations induces the generation of a huge number of quasi-solutions. The symbolic pre-processing generates quasi triangular or
diagonal forms for which box consistency is efficient.

The rest of the paper is organized as follows. Interval techniques are presented
in Section 2. The new symbolic pre-processing is introduced in Section 3. In
Section 4, a set of experiments are discussed. We conclude in Section 5.

2   Interval Constraints

2.1   Real-Based Structure

Consider a structure $\Sigma = (\mathbb{R}, \mathcal{O}, \{=\})$ and a set of variables $\mathcal{X}$ over $\mathbb{R}$.

Definition 1 (Σ-term). *A Σ-term is defined by structural induction as follows:*

- *Every constant $r \in \mathbb{R}$ is a Σ-term.*
- *Every variable $x \in \mathcal{X}$ is a Σ-term.*
- *Given an operation symbol $\Diamond \in \mathcal{O}$ of arity n, and n Σ-terms $t_1, \ldots, t_n$,*
  $\Diamond(t_1, \ldots, t_n)$ is a Σ-term.

Σ-terms are commonly called expressions. *Given a Σ-term t, let V_t denote the
set of variables occurring in t.*

In the following, Σ-terms are interpreted as real functions, as follows: $\mathbb{R}$ corresponds to the set of real numbers, and $\mathcal{O} = \{+, -, \times, \div, \dots\}$ is the set of usual operations over $\mathbb{R}$. Given a Σ-term t with $n = V_t$, the corresponding function is defined by

$$f : \mathbb{R}^n \to \mathbb{R}, \quad (x_1, \dots, x_n) \mapsto t(x_1, \dots, x_n).$$

Note that a real function can be defined by infinitely many Σ-terms. In the following, we will describe symbolic algorithms on Σ-terms preserving the equivalence of the corresponding functions.

2.2   Interval Arithmetic

Real Interval Arithmetic. Interval Arithmetic (IA) is an arithmetic over sets of real numbers called *intervals*. IA has been proposed by Ramon E. Moore [13] in the late sixties in order to model uncertainty, and to tackle rounding errors of numerical computations.

Definition 2 (interval). *A* closed real interval *is a closed and connected set of real numbers. The set of closed real intervals is denoted by* $\mathbb{IR}$*. Every* $\boldsymbol{x} \in \mathbb{IR}$ *is denoted by* $[\underline{x}, \overline{x}]$*, where its bounds are defined by* $\underline{x} = \inf \boldsymbol{x}$ *and* $\overline{x} = \sup \boldsymbol{x}$*. In the following, elements of* $\mathbb{IR}$ *are simply called* real intervals*.*

In order to represent the real line with closed sets, $\mathbb{R}$ is compactified in the obvious way with the infinities $\{-\infty, +\infty\}$. The set $\mathbb{IR}$ is then augmented, for every $r \in \mathbb{R}$, with the following intervals:

$$
\begin{aligned}
[-\infty, r] &= \{x \in \mathbb{R} \mid x \leqslant r\} \\
[r, +\infty] &= \{x \in \mathbb{R} \mid x \geqslant r\} \\
[-\infty, +\infty] &= \mathbb{R}
\end{aligned}
$$

The usual conventions apply: $(+\infty) + (+\infty) = +\infty$, *etc.* Given a subset ρ of $\mathbb{R}$, the *convex hull* of ρ is the real interval

$$\mathsf{Hull}\,(\rho) = [\inf \rho, \sup \rho].$$

The *width* of a real interval $\boldsymbol{x}$ is the real number $w(\boldsymbol{x}) = \overline{x} - \underline{x}$.

Elements of $\mathbb{IR}^n$ also define boxes. Given $(\boldsymbol{x_1}, \dots, \boldsymbol{x_n})^T \in \mathbb{IR}^n$, the corresponding *box* is the Cartesian product of intervals $\boldsymbol{X} = \boldsymbol{x_1} \times \cdots \times \boldsymbol{x_n}$. By misuse of notation, the same symbol is used for vectors and boxes. The *width* of a box is defined as follows:

$$w(\boldsymbol{x_1} \times \cdots \times \boldsymbol{x_n}) = \max_{1 \leqslant i \leqslant n} w(\boldsymbol{x_i})$$

IA operations are set theoretic extensions of the corresponding real operations. Given $\boldsymbol{x}, \boldsymbol{y} \in \mathbb{IR}$ and an operation $\diamond \in \{+, -, \times, \div\}$, we have:

$$\boldsymbol{x} \diamond \boldsymbol{y} = \mathsf{Hull}\,(\{x \diamond y \mid (x, y) \in \boldsymbol{x} \times \boldsymbol{y}\}).$$

They can be implemented by real computations over the bounds of intervals. Note that the following formulas for multiplication and division are valid only for non-infinite intervals. Given two intervals $x = [a, b]$ and $y = [c, d]$, we have:

$$\begin{cases} x & + & y & = & [a + c, b + d] \\ x & - & y & = & [a - d, b - c] \\ x & \times & y & = & [\min\{ac, ad, bc, bd\}, \max\{ac, ad, bc, bd\}] \\ x & \div & y & = & [\min\{a/c, a/d, b/c, b/d\}, \max\{a/c, a/d, b/c, b/d\}] \text{ if } 0 \notin [c, d] \\ & & x^n & = & \begin{cases} [a^n, b^n] & \text{if } n \text{ is an odd natural number} \\ [0, \max\{|a|, |b|\}^n] & \text{if } n \text{ is even} \end{cases} \end{cases}$$

The associative and commutative laws are preserved over $\mathbb{R}$. However, the distributive law does not always hold. Only the so-called sub-distributive law holds. For all $x, y, z \in \mathbb{R}$, we have:

associativity:	$(x + y) + z = x + (y + z)$	$(xy)z = x(yz)$
commutativity:	$(x + y) = (y + x)$	$xy = yx$
sub-distributivity:	$x \times (y + z) \subseteq x \times y + x \times z$	

An immediate consequence of sub-distributivity is that factorized interval expressions give tighter interval computations. For instance, we have

$$\forall x \in \mathbb{R}, \ x \times (x^3 + 1) \subseteq x \times x^3 + x.$$

But if $x \times x^3$ is replaced with x^4, the sub-distributive law is not verified. For instance, given $x = [-2, 1]$, we have:

$$[-7, 14] = x \times (x^3 + 1) \nsubseteq x^4 + x = [-2, 17].$$

A fundamental problem in Interval Arithmetic consists in finding expressions that lead to tight interval computations.

Floating-Point Interval Arithmetic. Let $\mathbb{F}$ be the set of machine-representable IEEE floating-point numbers, that is a finite subset of rational numbers. Given a floating-point number a, let a^+ denote $\min\{x \in \mathbb{F} \mid x > a\}$ and let a^- denote $\max\{x \in \mathbb{F} \mid x < a\}$.

In practice, the set of real intervals $\mathbb{R}$ is replaced with the set of floating-point intervals $\mathbb{F}$. A *floating-point interval* is a real interval bounded by floating-point numbers. The main difference between $\mathbb{R}$ and $\mathbb{F}$ is that computations over $\mathbb{F}$ need to be rounded. Given a real number $r \in \mathbb{R}$, we define:

$$\text{downward rounding:} \quad \lfloor r \rfloor = \max\{x \in \mathbb{F} \mid x \leqslant r\}$$
$$\text{upward rounding:} \quad \lceil r \rceil = \min\{x \in \mathbb{F} \mid x \geqslant r\}$$

Real intervals are mapped on $\mathbb{F}$ by outward rounding, as follows: Each $[a, b] \in \mathbb{R}$ is replaced with $[\lfloor a \rfloor, \lceil b \rceil] \in \mathbb{F}$. Actually, Floating-Point IA corresponds to Real IA where all intermediate results of interval computations are outward rounded. This way, some properties of $\mathbb{R}$ are preserved: commutativity, sub-distributivity, fundamental theorem of IA, monotonicity of natural extensions for inclusion. Nevertheless, two important properties are lost: associativity and Moore's theorem described in the next section.

In the following, we will consider Floating-Point IA. Note that the results also hold for $\mathbb{R}$. The set $\mathbb{F}$ will be simply denoted by $\mathbb{I}$. Elements of $\mathbb{F}$ will be called *intervals*. Σ-terms will be referred to as *terms* or *expressions*.

2.3 Interval Extensions

IA is able to represent outer approximations of real quantities. The range of a real function f over a domain D, denoted by $\boldsymbol{f}^u(D)$, can be computed by interval extensions.

Definition 3 (interval extension). *An* interval extension *of a real function* $f : D_f \subset \mathbb{R}^n \to \mathbb{R}$ *is a function* $\varphi : \mathbb{I}^n \to \mathbb{I}$ *such that*

$$\forall \boldsymbol{X} \in \mathbb{I}^n, \ (\boldsymbol{X} \in D_f \ \Rightarrow \ \boldsymbol{f}^u(\boldsymbol{X}) = \{f(X) \mid X \in \boldsymbol{X}\} \subseteq \varphi(\boldsymbol{X})).$$

This inclusion formula is called Fundamental Theorem of IA. *Interval extensions are also called* interval forms *or* inclusion functions.

This definition implies the existence of infinitely many interval extensions of a given real function. *Natural extensions* are obtained from expressions of real functions. As for Σ-terms, consider an interval structure $\Sigma' = (\mathbb{I}, \mathcal{O}', \{\dot{=}\})$, a set of variables $\mathcal{X}'$ over $\mathbb{I}$, and the set of Σ'-terms interpreted as interval functions.

Definition 4 (natural extension). *Let* t *be a* Σ-term *and let* $n = V_t$. *Let* $\boldsymbol{t} = \sigma(t)$ *be the* Σ'-term *obtained from* t *by structural induction as follows:*

- *if* $t = r \in \mathbb{R}$ *then* $\boldsymbol{t} = \sigma(t) = \mathsf{Hull}(\{r\})$;
- *if* $t = x_i \in \mathcal{X}$ *then* $\boldsymbol{t} = \sigma(t) = \boldsymbol{x_i} \in \mathcal{X}'$;
- *if* $t = \Diamond(t_1, \ldots, t_m)$ *then* $\boldsymbol{t} = \sigma(t) = \Diamond'(\sigma(t_1), \ldots, \sigma(t_m))$, *where* $\Diamond' \in \mathcal{O}'$ *is the corresponding operation to* $\Diamond \in \mathcal{O}$.

Let the real function $f : (x_1, \ldots, x_n) \mapsto t(x_1, \ldots, x_n)$ *be the interpretation of* t, *and let* $\boldsymbol{f} : (\boldsymbol{x_1}, \ldots, \boldsymbol{x_n}) \mapsto \boldsymbol{t}(\boldsymbol{x_1}, \ldots, \boldsymbol{x_n})$ *be the interpretation of* $\boldsymbol{t}$. *The interval function* $\boldsymbol{f} : \mathbb{I}^n \to \mathbb{I}$ *is called the* natural extension *of* f *w.r.t.* t. *The evaluation of* $\boldsymbol{f}$ *is called* natural interval evaluation *of* f *w.r.t.* t.

Natural extensions are *inclusion monotonic*, that follows from the monotonicity of interval operations.

In Def. 4, natural extensions are defined by the syntax of real expressions. In particular, two expressions of a given real function f generally lead to different natural interval extensions. The overestimation problem, known as *dependency problem of IA*, is due to the decorrelation of the occurrences of a variable during interval evaluation. For instance, given $\boldsymbol{x} = [a, b]$ with $a \neq b$, we have:

$$\boldsymbol{x} - \boldsymbol{x} = [a - b, b - a] \supsetneq 0.$$

An important result is Moore's theorem known as *Theorem of single occurrences*.

Theorem 1 (Moore [13]). *Let t be a Σ-term and let the real function f :* $D_f \subset \mathbb{R}^n \to \mathbb{R}$, $(x_1, \ldots, x_n) \mapsto t(x_1, \ldots, x_n)$ *be the interpretation of t. If x_i occurs only once in t, $1 \leqslant i \leqslant n$, then*

$$\forall \boldsymbol{X} \in \mathbb{IR}^n, (\boldsymbol{X} \subseteq D_f \Rightarrow \boldsymbol{f}^u(\boldsymbol{X}) = \boldsymbol{f}(\boldsymbol{X})).$$

In other words, there is no overestimation over $\mathbb{IR}$ if all variables occur only once in the given expression.

2.4 Constraints

We consider the duality expression-relation of constraints. A real constraint is either a subset of $\mathbb{R}^n$ or a formula made from a relation symbol and Σ-terms. An interval constraint is defined in the same way from Σ'. In this paper, we only consider equations. Moreover, we consider that an interval domain is associated with each variable. A constraint c is said to be satisfied/verified by an element if this element belongs to the relation defined by c.

Definition 5 (natural extension). *Consider two terms t and u such that $V_t = \{x_1, \ldots, x_k, \ldots, x_n\}$ and $V_u = \{x_k, \ldots, x_n, \ldots, x_m\}$. Let f be the function defined by t, and let g be the function defined by u. Let $c : t = u$ be a real constraint. The natural extension of c is the interval constraint defined by*

$$C : \begin{cases} t \doteq u \\ \{(\boldsymbol{x}_1, \ldots, \boldsymbol{x}_m) \in \mathbb{I}^m \mid \boldsymbol{f}(\boldsymbol{x}_1, \ldots, \boldsymbol{x}_n) \cap \boldsymbol{g}(\boldsymbol{x}_k, \ldots, \boldsymbol{x}_m)\} \neq \varnothing \} \end{cases}$$

The main property guaranteed by IA is the following: if C is empty, then c has no solution.

Example 1 (rejection of a box). Consider the natural extension of a constraint $c : x^2 - x = y + 3$. Then c has no solution in the box $[0, 1] \times [-1, 1]$ since

$$([0, 1]^2 - [0, 1]) \cap ([-1, 1] + [3, 3]) = \varnothing.$$

Unfortunately, interval evaluation alone is often too weak. For instance, a very large domain that contains only one solution of the real constraint cannot be reduced. There is a need for domain pruning (narrowing) operators. The so-called *box consistency* pruning method will be introduced in the next section.

2.5 Box Consistency

Box consistency [2] is a consistency property of variable domains. Given a variable x occurring in a constraint c, conditions on the domain of x guarantee the satisfaction of c.

We introduce a preliminary definition. Consider a n-ary constraint c, a box $\boldsymbol{x}_1 \times \cdots \times \boldsymbol{x}_n \in \mathbb{I}^n$, and a natural $1 \leqslant i \leqslant n$. The i-th projection of c is the set

$$\pi_i(c) = \{x_i \mid \exists x_1 \in \boldsymbol{x}_1, \ldots, \exists x_{i-1} \in \boldsymbol{x}_{i-1},$$
$$\exists x_{i+1} \in \boldsymbol{x}_{i+1}, \ldots, \exists x_n \in \boldsymbol{x}_n, (x_1, \ldots, x_n) \in c\}.$$

Definition 6 (box consistency). *Consider a constraint $c(x_1, \ldots, x_n)$ and a box X. Let C denote the natural extension of c. Let $1 \leqslant i \leqslant n$ be a natural. We say that x_i is box consistent w.r.t. the i-th projection of c if*

$$x_i = \mathsf{Hull}\left(\{a_i \in x_i \mid (x_1, \ldots, x_{i-1}, \mathsf{Hull}\left(\{a_i\}\right), x_{i+1}, \ldots, x_n) \in C\}\right)$$

Interval evaluation alone just checks if X belongs to C. Box consistency defines a search procedure on x_i. The external convex hull is used to limit the search at bounds of x_i. The associated pruning operator computes the greatest box consistent interval that is included in x_i. This operator is classically implemented by a dichotomous search combined with an interval Newton method. Interval evaluation is used to reject the sub-domains.

A more surprising effect is that the dependency problem of IA on x_i vanishes. For instance, the interval evaluation of $x - x$ over $\mathbb{R}$ is replaced with $\{x - x \mid x \in x\} = \{0\}$.

In practice, we are interested in solving a set of constraints given a box (initial variable domains). The solution set contains the elements of the box satisfying all constraints. Box consistency has to be combined with a bisection method in a more general branch-and-prune algorithm [17]. A set of boxes is maintained, each box being processed by two operations: domain pruning to contract it, and domain bisection to generate more precise sub-boxes. The result is a set of boxes of a given width (precision). Furthermore, the method is complete: the union of computed boxes is a superset of the solution set.

2.6 Box Consistency Can Be Weak

Box consistency can be weak for two reasons: the dependency problem of IA and the locality of reasonings.

Example 2 (dependency problem). Consider constraint $c : x_1 + x_2 - x_2 = 0$ and box $[-1, 1] \times [0, 2]$. Then x_1 is box consistent w.r.t. c. The satisfaction process is in two steps: x_2 is replaced with $[0, 2]$ in c, that leads to $x_1 + [-2, 2] = 0$. Each bound of x_1 verifies the natural extension $x_1 + [-2, 2] \doteq 0$. For instance we compute for the left bound:

$$[-1, -1] + [-2, 2] = [-3, 1] \qquad [-3, 1] \cap [0, 0] \neq \varnothing$$

Example 3 (locality of reasonings). Consider constraints $c_1 : x_1 + x_2 = 0$ and $c_2 : x_1 - x_2 = 0$, and box $[-1, 1]^2$. There is only one solution $(0, 0)$ shared by c_1 and c_2. However, box consistency cannot prune the domains. The reason is that box consistency does not tackle the conjunction $c_1 \wedge c_2$ as a whole, but c_1 and c_2 independently. Actually, a reduction of the box would necessarily discard solutions of each constraint (that is not allowed). The geometric interpretation can be useful: c_1 and c_2 are the diagonals of the square defined by the box.

Both problems can be handled by symbolic computations: constraint simplification for the first one, e.g., factorization, to eliminate occurrences of variables, and combination of constraints before interval reasonings for the problem of locality. In the next section, a new symbolic algorithm that aims at handling both problems is presented.

3   Symbolic Computations

The dilemma of symbolic-interval cooperations is to improve constraint representation for accelerating the whole process (not only the interval process). This can be achieved by fast, but possibly weak, symbolic computations and precise interval contractions at low cost.

In this section, we describe a symbolic algorithm for systems of nonlinear equations over the real numbers that can be used as a pre-processing for interval branch-and-prune computations. The algorithm first applies an abstraction over the initial system of equations (see Section 3.1). The result is a linear system of equations and a set of nonlinear equations. The second part combines Gaussian elimination over the linear system and the linearization of nonlinear equations if some variables are fixed during elimination (see Section 3.2). This idea comes from [5]. The resulting system is a combination of the linear and nonlinear equations (see Section 3.3). We expect that some nonlinearities have vanished and that the system is in partial triangular form. A strategy that controls the symbolic computation steps is proposed in Section 3.4.

Note that for systems of linear equations, our algorithm just performs a Gaussian elimination.

3.1   Abstraction Phase

Consider a set of nonlinear equations c_i, $1 \leqslant i \leqslant m$, over n variables $x_1, \ldots, x_n$. Each equation is rewritten as a sum of linear and nonlinear terms, as follows:

$$c_i : \sum_{j \in J_i} a_j x_j + \sum_{k \in K_i} b_k g_k(x_1, \ldots, x_n) = d_i \quad a_j, b_k \in \mathbb{R}$$

The abstraction consists in replacing in all constraints each nonlinear term g_k with a fresh variable u_k. Constraint c_i is transformed into

$$lc_i : \sum_{j \in J_i} a_j x_j + \sum_{k \in K_i} b_k u_k = d_i$$

We obtain a linear system $Lc = \{lc_1, \ldots, lc_m\}$.

A fresh variable u_k is considered for replacing a nonlinear term $g_k(x_1, \ldots, x_n)$ only if g_k has not already been abstracted by a variable u_l, $l < k$. Such a mechanism uses a dictionary of already parsed nonlinear terms. The effect is the sharing of equivalent nonlinear terms in the whole system. As a consequence, the occurrences of a nonlinear term can be eliminated from the linear system. A second system of nonlinear equations is obtained: $Ac = \{ac_1, \ldots, ac_p\}$, called the abstract system, where ac_k is the equation $u_k = g_k(x_1, \ldots, x_n)$, $1 \leqslant k \leqslant p$.

The worst case complexity corresponds to a dense system with no linear term such that the nonlinear terms are not much different (worst case of dictionary management). In this case, the form of c_i is

$$c_i : \sum_{h \in H_i} b_h g_h(x_1, \ldots, x_n) = d_i$$

Let N be an upper bound of the cardinals of the H_i. Each g_h is compared with each g_l appearing in Ac. Since there are at most mN nonlinear terms in the initial system, the number of comparisons is bounded by $\frac{1}{2}mN(mN - 1)$. Let F be an upper bound of the number of operations symbols in the g_h. Then, $\frac{1}{2}mN(mN - 1)F$ is an upper bound of the number of comparisons of operations symbols in the worst case. The worst case complexity in time is $\mathcal{O}(m^2 N^2 F)$.

In practice, we observe a worst case complexity for dense nonlinear systems in $\mathcal{O}(m^4)$ since F is generally $\mathcal{O}(1)$ and N is $\mathcal{O}(m)$. For sparse nonlinear systems, N is generally $\mathcal{O}(1)$. The complexity becomes $\mathcal{O}(m^2 F)$. For dense square linear systems, the process is $\mathcal{O}(m^2)$.

3.2 Elimination Phase

We consider both aforementioned linear and abstract systems:

$$Lc = \begin{cases} lc_1 : \sum_{j \in J_1} a_j x_j + \sum_{k \in K_1} b_k u_k = d_1 \\ \quad \vdots \\ lc_m : \sum_{j \in J_m} a_j x_j + \sum_{k \in K_m} b_k u_k = d_m \end{cases}$$

$$Ac = \begin{cases} ac_1 : u_1 = g_1(x_1, \ldots, x_n) \\ \quad \vdots \\ ac_p : u_p = g_p(x_1, \ldots, x_n) \end{cases}$$

Lc is a $(m, n' + p)$-rectangular linear system, where n' is the number of original variables appearing in a linear term ($n' \leqslant n$). In general, $(n' + p)$ is much greater than n if few nonlinearities are shared by constraints of the initial system: the linear system Lc is sparse.

We propose a new algorithm combining Gaussian elimination over Lc, and elimination in Ac of the variables that have been fixed in Lc. This algorithm is described in Table 1. The output is a set of abstract and linear constraints, that will be transformed by a "concretization" process (see Section 3.3).

This algorithm is parameterized by two components: a function that chooses the next pivot; a criterion $ControlCriterion$ that determines if the last elimination step has been sufficiently efficient. Control strategies are discussed in Section 3.4.

3.3 Concretization Phase

After elimination, the systems Lc and Ac have to be merged. The result is a new (m, n) system that is equivalent to the initial system: they have the same real solutions. The concretization phase is a two-step process:

1. **Elimination of abstract variables**: each constraint $u = g$ from Ac is considered, and u is replaced with g in Lc. After this phase, Lc is a (m, n) system that is equivalent to the initial system.
2. **Post-processing**: each constraint $x_i = f$ from Lc is considered. For each constraint c in Lc such that x_i and the variables of f occur in c, then x_i is replaced with f in c. These constraints are chosen in increasing order of numbers of variables, occurrences of variables, and operation symbols. An

Example (post-processing). Consider the set $S = \{x + y^2 = 0, y + x^2 = 0\}$. After the first concretization phase, we obtain $S' = \{x = -y^2, y = -x^2\}$. No elimination has happened since no term is shared among constraints. Nevertheless, x can be replaced with $-y^2$ in the second constraint. The resulting system is $S'' = \{x = -y^2, y = -(-y^2)^2\}$. In general, such a process is very efficient for box consistency computations. There are two reasons:

- one variable is eliminated from c_2 (reduction of locality effects);
- the new occurrences of variables from c_1 do not increase the dependency problem of IA on y in c_2 (this is a feature of box consistency).

Note that this last reason can be violated in the case of multivariate constraints (see Section 2.6). However, we have observed a good average behavior.

3.4 Strategies

The elimination algorithm is parameterized by two components implementing the choice of pivots, and a stopping criterion. The main problem that may arise during elimination is a too important densification of the linear system, in particular if the initial system Lc is much sparse. We have to define a strategy of choice of pivots in order to control the densification process. Moreover, we propose to implement a stopping criterion that determines whether an elimination step does not increase too much the density.

Choice of Pivot. Denote the set of non-marked equations from Lc at elimination step i by $Lc^{(i)}$. The strategy of choice of the i-th pivot (c, x) is as follows, where the conditions are given in decreasing order of importance:

1. x necessarily occurs in $Lc^{(i)} \setminus \{c\}$; c, x and (c, x) are said to be *eligible*;
2. there is no other eligible constraint with less variables;
3. the number of non-eligible variables in c is minimum (w.r.t. $c' \in Lc^{(i)}$);
4. x is the variable of c that occurs the least in $Lc^{(i)} \setminus \{c\}$;
5. x is the variable of c that occurs the most in $Lc^{(i)} \setminus \{c\}$ with the same coefficient.

Stopping Criterion. We propose an implementation χ of the *ControlCriterion* component. Consider the set $Lc^{(i)}$ of non-marked equations from Lc at the i-th elimination step. Let (c, x) be the chosen pivot. Denote $Lc^{(i)} \setminus \{c\}$ by L, and let l be the cardinal of L. For each constraint $c_j \in L$, denote the number of variables

Table 1. Combination of Gaussian Elimination and Linearization.

Symbolic processing of $Ac \cup Lc$

Input
    Linear system $Lc = \{lc_1, \ldots, lc_m\}$ over the set of variables Lx.
    Abstract system $Ac = \{ac_1, \ldots, ac_p\}$ over the set of variables Ax.
    Sets of variables $X = \{x_1, \ldots, x_n\}$ and $U = \{u_1, \ldots, u_p\}$.
Output
    Set of constraints

do
    $save \leftarrow Lc$
  • *Gaussian elimination step*
    Choose a pivot (lc, y) from Lc such that lc is not marked
    Eliminate y in the rest of Lc
    Mark lc for further elimination steps
    $Lx \leftarrow Lx \setminus \{y\}$
  • *Linearization of abstract constraints in the case of fixed variables*
    for each univariate equation $lc' : az = b$ in Lc **do**
      Mark lc' for further elimination steps
      for each equation $u = g$ with $z \in g$ in Ac **do**
        Replace z with b/a in g
        if g is linear in x and $u, x \in Lx$
        then
          Replace u with x in Lc
          $Lx \leftarrow Lx \setminus \{u\}$
          Remove $u = g$ from Ac
        fi
      od
    od
while $Lx \neq \emptyset$ **and** *ControlCriterion(save,Lc)* is verified

if *ControlCriterion(save,Lc)* is not verified
then
  return $save \cup Ac$ // *State before the last elimination*
else
  return $Lc \cup Ac$ // *Final state after complete elimination*
fi

from $\{x_1, \ldots, x_n\}$ occurring in c_j by n_j, and denote the number of abstract variables by p_j. Let n'_j and p'_j be the values of n_j and p_j after the elimination step. We define χ as follows:

$$\chi : \left\{ \frac{1}{l} \cdot \sum_{c_j \in L} \left(\left(\frac{1}{n-1} \cdot \frac{n'_j - n_j}{\max(1, n_j)} \right) + \left(\frac{4}{3} \cdot \frac{p'_j - p_j}{\max(1, p_j)} \right)^2 \right) \leq 1 \right\}$$

Criterion χ is implemented as the mean value for all the constraints from L of an estimation of the densification of c_j. A failure of χ means that the elimination process has to be stopped on $Lc^{(i)}$. The densification formula is a sum of two terms associated to the user and abstract variables. Intuitively, the densification due to the user variables is considered as a gentle effect (coefficient $(n-1)^{-1}$). Nevertheless, the densification due to abstract variables is penalized. From a threshold of 3/4 (resulting from coefficient 4/3), the growth of the number of abstract variables is quadratically increased. Finally, note that χ always succeeds if the input system (before abstraction) is linear.

4   Experimental Results

A set of experimental results from a symbolic-interval branch-and-prune algorithm are discussed. The symbolic algorithm is described in the previous section. The domain pruning algorithm implements box consistency (in its early version). The branching procedure uses a round-robin strategy. Each bisection stage generates 3 sub-domains. The width of the output boxes is smaller than 10^{-8}.

4.1   Description of Benchmarks

We use as benchmarks three scalable quasi-linear problems and the problem of Solotarev [7,20]. These problems are intractable for box consistency: a huge number of quasi-solutions are generated.

Bratu. The user system is square, sparse and quasi-linear:

$$x_{k-1} - 2x_k + x_{k+1} + h\exp(x_k) = 0, \quad 1 \leqslant k \leqslant n$$

with $x_0 = x_{n+1} = 0$ and $h = 1/(n+1)^2$. The initial box is $[-10^8, +10^8]^n$. The transformed system is dense and lower triangular:

$$-(k+1)x_k + (k+2)x_{k+1} + h\sum_{i=1}^{k} i\exp(x_i) = 0, \quad 1 \leqslant k \leqslant n$$

Brown. The user system and the transformed system are given by:

$$\begin{cases} x_k + \sum_{i=1}^{n} x_i = n+1, \ 1 \leqslant k \leqslant n-1 \\ \prod_{i=1}^{n} x_i = 1 \end{cases} \qquad \begin{cases} x_k = x_{k+1}, \quad 1 \leqslant k \leqslant n-2 \\ nx_{n-1} + x_n = n+1, \\ x_{n-1}^{n-1}(n+1-nx_{n-1}) = 1 \end{cases}$$

The initial box is $[-10^8, +10^8]^n$. Gaussian elimination processes the $n-1$ user linear equations. The key strategy consists in choosing x_n as the first pivot since it occurs with the same coefficient in all equations.

Yamamura. Yamamura's system is described by:

$$x_k - \frac{1}{2n} \sum_{i=1}^{n} (x_i^3 + k) = 0, \quad 1 \leqslant k \leqslant n$$

The initial box is $[-10^8, +10^8]^n$. The main feature is that each nonlinear term x_i^3 is abstracted by only one variable. The transformed system is as follows:

$$\begin{cases} x_1 - \frac{1}{2n} \sum_{i=1}^{n} \left((x_1 + \frac{i-1}{2n})^3 + k \right) = 0, \\ x_{k+1} = x_1 + \frac{k}{2n}, \quad 1 \leqslant k \leqslant n - 1 \end{cases}$$

4.2   Result Analysis

The results on a PC Pentium-III/933MHz are reported in Table 2. For each couple of systems (user, tranformed) we give: the number of variables v, the solving time in seconds, the number of computed solutions (output boxes), and the number of bisection stages. Blank cases indicate problems that cannot be solved in less than one hour.

We easily conclude that our symbolic pre-processing is efficient for the set of benchmarks. A more detailed analysis is described now.

Brown, Yamamura. For both user systems, the abstraction process generates square linear systems. Gaussian elimination then derives triangular systems. As a consequence, box consistency is very efficient over the transformed systems.

Bratu. We observe a regular behavior from the problem with 9 variables. The solving time and the number of bisections double between two consecutive systems. Box consistency is exponential for the user systems. The efficiency of box consistency for the transformed systems is more surprising since each constraint contains a sum of exponentials. However, the result is obtained: Bratu's problem is now a gentle benchmark.

Solotarev. The number of quasi-solutions is decreased with 3 orders of magnitude, while the solving is 4 times slower. The reason is that a variable has been eliminated from a particular constraint during the symbolic process. Note that the transformed system is triangular, and that several quasi-solutions remain. A solution to this phenomena is probably to increase the precision of interval arithmetic (e.g., using a multi-precision library).

5   Conclusion

We have proposed a new symbolic pre-processing for box consistency. Both of our objectives have been reached: control of symbolic computations since the symbolic algorithm is polynomial in time and memory, and improvement of the precision of interval computations. Solutions for both weaknesses of box consistency are proposed: linear combination of constraints for the locality of reasonings, and elimination of nonlinear patterns for the dependency problem of interval arithmetic. The experimental results from a prototype are promising.

Three directions for further research are identified. First of all, the combination of our algorithm with linear relaxations from expansions in Taylor series is promising. Their complementarity lies in the handling of tight and large domains. Experimental work will be conducted.

In order to improve the simplification of constraint expressions, elementary functions could be replaced with polynomial expressions resulting from expansions in Taylor series. However, the loss of precision induced by relaxations has to be determined.

Table 2. Experimental results (computation times in seconds).

Problem	v	Solving of initial system			Solving of transformed system		
		Time	Solutions	Bisections	Time	Solutions	Bisections
Bratu	5	0.30	2	15	0.30	2	34
	6	1.40	6	181	1.30	9	301
	7	1.10	3	69	0.60	4	289
	8	19.80	60	4012	12.90	95	2014
	9	1.20	2	31	0.20	1	10
	10	2.30	2	64	0.10	1	0
	11	4.40	6	125	0.10	1	0
	12	9.40	4	281	0.10	1	0
	13	20.50	6	594	0.10	1	0
	14	46.40	11	1382	0.20	1	0
	15	94.40	12	2765	0.20	1	0
Brown	5	67.70	1228	56282	0.10	2	1
	6	1596.00	20713	1139205	0.10	2	1
	7				0.10	2	1
	8				0.10	2	1
	9				0.10	2	1
	10				0.10	2	1
Yamamura	5				0.10	3	55
	6				0.10	3	55
	7				0.10	3	57
	8				0.20	3	56
	9				0.20	3	57
	10				0.20	3	55
Solotarev	4	280.00	254971	439227	916.00	187	103

For polynomial systems, a comparison with computer algebra techniques like Gröbner bases has to be done. Is our algorithm more efficient for some problems? For instance, the system of Brown can be a good candidate for this study.

Acknowledgements

This work has been partly supported by the COCONUT IST project from the European Community.

References

1. Prolog IV: constraints inside, 1996. Prolog IV reference manual.
2. F. Benhamou, D. McAllester, and P. Van Hentenryck. CLP(Intervals) Revisited. In *Procs. of ILPS'94, Intl. Logic Prog. Symp.*, pages 124–138, Ithaca, USA, 1994. MIT Press.
3. F. Benhamou and W. J. Older. Applying Interval Arithmetic to Real, Integer and Boolean Constraints. *J. of Logic Programming*, 32(1):1–24, 1997.
4. M. Ceberio and L. Granvilliers. Solving Nonlinear Systems by Constraint Inversion and Interval Arithmetic. In *Procs. of AISC'2000, 5th Intl. Conf. on Artificial Intelligence and Symbolic Computation*, volume 1930 of *LNAI*, Madrid, Spain, 2000. Springer-Verlag.
5. A. Colmerauer. Naive Solving of Non-linear Constraints. In F. Benhamou and A. Colmerauer, editors, *Constraint Logic Programming: Selected Research*, pages 89–112. MIT Press, 1993.
6. F. Goualard, F. Benhamou, and L. Granvilliers. An Extension of the WAM for Hybrid Interval Solvers. *J. of Functional and Logic Programming*, 5(4):1–31, 1999.
7. L. Granvilliers. A Symbolic-Numerical Branch and Prune Algorithm for Solving Non-linear Polynomial Systems. *J. of Universal Comp. Sci.*, 4(2):125–146, 1998.
8. L. Granvilliers, E. Monfroy, and F. Benhamou. Symbolic-Interval Cooperation in Constraint Programming. In *Procs. of ISSAC'2001, 26th Intl. Symp. on Symbolic and Algebraic Computation*, pages 150–166, Univ. of Western Ontario, London, Ontario, Canada, 2001. ACM Press.
9. T. J. Hickey. CLIP: a CLP(Intervals) Dialect for Metalevel Constraint Solving. In *Procs. of PADL'2000, Intl. Workshop on Practical Aspects of Declarative Languages*, volume 1753 of *LNCS*, pages 200–214, Boston, USA, 2000. Springer-Verlag.
10. H. Hong. RISC-CLP(Real): Constraint Logic Programming over Real Numbers. In F. Benhamou and A. Colmerauer, editors, *Constraint Logic Programming: Selected Research*. MIT Press, 1993.
11. J. Jaffar, S. Michaylov, P. Stuckey, and R. Yap. The CLP($\Re$) Language and System. *ACM Trans. on Programming Languages and Systems*, 14(3):339–395, 1992.
12. P. Marti and M. Rueher. A Distributed Cooperating Constraints Solving System. *Intl. J. on Artificial Intelligence Tools*, 4(1–2):93–113, 1995.
13. R. E. Moore. *Interval Analysis*. Prentice-Hall, Englewood Cliffs, NJ, 1966.
14. J.-F. Puget and M. Leconte. Beyond the Glass Box: Constraints as Objects. In *Procs. of ILPS'95, Intl. Logic Programming Symposium*, pages 513–527, Portland, USA, 1995. MIT Press.
15. A. Semenov and A. Leshchenko. Interval and Symbolic Computations in the Unicalc Solver. In *Procs. of INTERVAL'94*, pages 206–208, St-Petersburg, Russia, 1994.
16. M. H. Van Emden. Algorithmic Power from Declarative Use of Redundant Constraints. *Constraints*, 4(4):363–381, 1999.
17. P. Van Hentenryck, D. McAllester, and D. Kapur. Solving Polynomial Systems Using a Branch and Prune Approach. *SIAM J. on Numerical Analysis*, 34(2):797–827, 1997.
18. P. Van Hentenryck, L. Michel, and Y. Deville. *Numerica: a Modeling Language for Global Optimization*. MIT Press, 1997.
19. M. Wallace, S. Novello, and J. Schimpf. ECLiPSe : A Platform for Constraint Logic Programming. Technical report, IC-Parc, London, 1997.
20. K. Yamamura, H. Kawata, and A. Tokue. Interval Analysis using Linear Programming. *BIT*, 38:188–201, 1998.

A Generalization of Shostak's Method
for Combining Decision Procedures

Clark W. Barrett, David L. Dill, and Aaron Stump

Stanford University, Stanford, CA 94305, USA
http://verify.stanford.edu

Abstract. Consider the problem of determining whether a quantifier-free formula ϕ is satisfiable in some first-order theory $\mathcal{T}$. Shostak's algorithm decides this problem for a certain class of theories with both interpreted and uninterpreted function symbols. We present two new algorithms based on Shostak's method. The first is a simple subset of Shostak's algorithm for the same class of theories but without uninterpreted function symbols. This simplified algorithm is easy to understand and prove correct, providing insight into how and why Shostak's algorithm works. The simplified algorithm is then used as the foundation for a generalization of Shostak's method based on a variation of the Nelson-Oppen method for combining theories.

1 Introduction

In 1984, Shostak introduced a clever and subtle algorithm which decides the satisfiability of quantifier-free formulas in a combined theory which includes a first-order theory (or combination of first-order theories) with certain properties and the theory of equality with uninterpreted function symbols [12]. But despite the fact that Shostak's method is less general than its predecessor, the Nelson-Oppen method [8,9], it has generated considerable interest and is the basis for decision procedures found in several tools, including PVS [10], STeP [4,6], and SVC [1,2,7].

There are several good reasons for this. First of all, it is easier to implement: the Nelson-Oppen method provides a framework for combining decision procedures, but gives no help on how to construct the individual decision procedures. But as we show in the next section, at the core of Shostak's procedure is a simple method for generating decision procedures for a large class of theories. A second reason for the success of Shostak's method is that despite requiring more restrictive conditions in order to accommodate a theory, a wide variety of useful theories have been shown to satisfy these conditions [4,12]. Finally, empirical studies have shown that Shostak's method is an order of magnitude more efficient than the Nelson-Oppen method [5].

Unfortunately, the original paper is difficult to follow, due in part to the fact that it contains several errors, and despite an ongoing effort to understand and clarify the method [5,11,14], it remains difficult to understand.

A. Armando (Ed.): FroCoS 2002, LNAI 2309, pp. 132–146, 2002.

In this paper, we take a new approach to explaining Shostak's algorithm. We first present a subset of the original algorithm, in particular, the subset which decides formulas *without* uninterpreted function symbols. This algorithm is surprisingly simple and straightforward, and gives considerable insight into how Shostak's algorithm works.

This algorithm then forms the basis for a more general algorithm that lies at an abstraction level somewhere between the general Nelson-Oppen framework and the highly-specialized Shostak procedure. The purpose is to describe an algorithm which is abstract enough that it can be understood and proved correct, but specific enough that it is not hard to see how to specialize it further to recover Shostak's original algorithm. The correctness proof of this algorithm relies on a new variation of the Nelson-Oppen procedure and new theorem which relates *convexity* (a requirement for Shostak) and *stable-infiniteness* (a requirement for Nelson-Oppen).

It is our hope that this exercise will not only shed light on how Shostak's method can be seen as an efficient refinement of the Nelson-Oppen method, but also provide a generalization which can be used to achieve other efficient refinements. Indeed, one such possible refinement is described in the first author's dissertation [3].

In Section 2, below, some preliminary definitions and notation are given. The simple algorithm without uninterpreted function symbols is presented in Section 3. Section 4 reviews the Nelson-Oppen method in preparation for the generalized algorithm which is presented in Section 5. Finally, Section 6 compares our approach to other work on Shostak's algorithm and describes the refinements necessary to recover Shostak's original algorithm.

2   Preliminary Concepts

2.1   Some Notions from Logic

A *theory* is a set of closed formulas. For the purposes of this paper, all theories are assumed to be first-order and to include the axioms of equality. The *signature* of a theory is the set of function, predicate (other than equality), and constant symbols appearing in those sentences. A *literal* is an atomic formula or its negation. To avoid confusion with the logical equality symbol $=$, we use the symbol $\equiv$ to indicate that two logical expressions are syntactically identical.

For a given model, M, a *variable assignment* ρ is a function which assigns to each variable an element of the domain of M. We write $M \models_\rho \phi$ if ϕ is true in the model M with variable assignment ρ. If Φ is a set of formulas, then $M \models_\rho \Phi$ indicates that $M \models_\rho \phi$ for each $\phi \in \Phi$. In general, whenever sets of formulas are used as logical formulas, the intended meaning is the conjunction of the formulas in the set. A formula ϕ is satisfiable if there exists some model M and variable assignment ρ such that $M \models_\rho \phi$. If Γ is a set of formulas and ϕ is a formula, then $\Gamma \models \phi$ means that whenever a model and variable assignment satisfy Γ, they also satisfy ϕ. A set S of literals is *convex* in a theory $\mathcal{T}$ if $\mathcal{T} \cup S$ does not entail any disjunction of equalities between variables without entailing one of the equalities itself. A theory $\mathcal{T}$ is convex if every set of literals in the language of the theory is convex in $\mathcal{T}$.

2.2 Equations in Solved Form

Definition 1. *A set $\mathcal{S}$ of equations is said to be in* solved form *iff the left-hand side of each equation in $\mathcal{S}$ is a variable which appears only once in $\mathcal{S}$. We refer to the variables which appear only on the left-hand sides as* solitary *variables.*

A set $\mathcal{S}$ of equations in solved form defines an idempotent substitution: the one which replaces each solitary variable with its corresponding right-hand side. If $\mathcal{S}$ is an expression or set of expressions, we denote the result of applying this substitution to $\mathcal{S}$ by $\mathcal{S}(\mathcal{S})$. Another interesting property of equations in solved form is that the question of whether such a set $\mathcal{S}$ entails some formula ϕ in a theory $\mathcal{T}$ can be answered simply by determining the validity of $\mathcal{S}(\phi)$ in $\mathcal{T}$:

Proposition 1. *If $\mathcal{T}$ is a theory with signature Σ and $\mathcal{S}$ is a set of Σ-equations in solved form, then $\mathcal{T} \cup \mathcal{S} \models \phi$ iff $\mathcal{T} \models \mathcal{S}(\phi)$.*

Proof. Clearly, $\mathcal{T} \cup \mathcal{S} \models \phi$ iff $\mathcal{T} \cup \mathcal{S} \models \mathcal{S}(\phi)$. Thus we need only show that $\mathcal{T} \cup \mathcal{S} \models \mathcal{S}(\phi)$ iff $\mathcal{T} \models \mathcal{S}(\phi)$. The "if" direction is trivial. To show the other direction, assume that $\mathcal{T} \cup \mathcal{S} \models \mathcal{S}(\phi)$. Any model of $\mathcal{T}$ can be made to satisfy $\mathcal{T} \cup \mathcal{S}$ by assigning any value to the non-solitary variables of $\mathcal{S}$, and then choosing the value of each solitary variable to match the value of its corresponding right-hand side. Since none of the solitary variables occur anywhere else in $\mathcal{S}$, this assignment is well-defined and satisfies $\mathcal{S}$. By assumption then, this model and assignment also satisfy $\mathcal{S}(\phi)$, but none of the solitary variables appear in $\mathcal{S}(\phi)$, so the initial arbitrary assignment to non-solitary variables must be sufficient to satisfy $\mathcal{S}(\phi)$. Thus it must be the case that every model of $\mathcal{T}$ satisfies $\mathcal{S}(\phi)$ with every variable assignment. □

Corollary 1. *If $\mathcal{T}$ is a satisfiable theory with signature Σ and $\mathcal{S}$ is a set of Σ-equations in solved form, then $\mathcal{T} \cup \mathcal{S}$ is satisfiable.*

3   Algorithm S1

In this section we present an algorithm, based on a subset of Shostak's algorithm, for deciding satisfiability of quantifier-free formulas in a theory $\mathcal{T}$ which meets certain conditions. We call such a theory a *Shostak* theory.

Definition 2. *A satisfiable theory $\mathcal{T}$ with signature Σ is a* Shostak *theory if the following conditions hold.*

1. *Σ does not contain any predicate symbols.*
2. *$\mathcal{T}$ is convex.*

3. *There exists a* canonizer *canon, a computable function from Σ-terms to Σ-terms, with the property that $\mathcal{T} \models a = b$ iff $canon(a) \equiv canon(b)$.*
4. *There exists a* solver *solve, a computable function from Σ-equations to sets of formulas defined as follows:*
   (a) *If $\mathcal{T} \models a \neq b$, then $solve(a = b) = \{false\}$.*
   (b) *Otherwise, $solve(a = b)$ returns a set $\mathcal{S}$ of equations in solved form such that $\mathcal{T} \models [(a = b) \leftrightarrow \exists \overline{x}.\mathcal{S}]$, where $\overline{x}$ is the set of variables which appear in $\mathcal{S}$ but not in a or b. Each of these variables must be fresh.*

These requirements are slightly different from those given by Shostak and others. These differences are discussed in Section 6 below. In the rest of this section, $\mathcal{T}$ is assumed to be a Shostak theory with signature Σ, canonizer *canon*, and solver *solve*. As we will show, the solver can be used to convert an arbitrary set of equations into a set of equations in solved form. The canonizer is used to determine whether a specific equality is entailed by a set of equations in solved form, as shown by the following proposition.

Proposition 2. *If $\mathcal{S}$ is a set of Σ-equations in solved form, then $\mathcal{T} \cup \mathcal{S} \models a = b$ iff $canon(\mathcal{S}(a)) \equiv canon(\mathcal{S}(b))$.*

Proof. By Proposition 1, $\mathcal{T} \cup \mathcal{S} \models a = b$ iff $\mathcal{T} \models \mathcal{S}(a) = \mathcal{S}(b)$. But $\mathcal{T} \models \mathcal{S}(a) = \mathcal{S}(b)$ iff $canon(\mathcal{S}(a)) \equiv canon(\mathcal{S}(b))$ by the definition of *canon*. $\qquad\square$

```
S1(Γ, Δ, canon, solve)
1.   S := ∅;
2.   WHILE Γ ≠ ∅ DO BEGIN
3.      Remove some equality a = b from Γ;
4.      a* := S(a);  b* := S(b);
5.      S* := solve(a* = b*);
6.      IF S* = {false} THEN RETURN FALSE;
7.      S := S*(S) ∪ S*;
8.   END
9.   IF canon(S(a)) ≡ canon(S(b)) for some a ≠ b ∈ Δ THEN RETURN FALSE;
10.  RETURN TRUE;
```

Fig. 1. Algorithm S1: based on a simple subset of Shostak's algorithm

Algorithm *S1* (shown in Fig. 1) makes use of the properties of a Shostak theory to check the joint satisfiability of an arbitrary set of equalities, Γ, and an arbitrary set of disequalities, Δ, in a Shostak theory with canonizer *canon* and solver *solve*. Since the satisfiability of any quantifier-free formula can be determined by first converting it to disjunctive normal form, it suffices to have a satisfiability procedure for a conjunction of literals. Since Σ contains no predicate symbols, all Σ-literals are either equalities or disequalities. Thus, Algorithm *S1* is sufficient for deciding the satisfiability of quantifier-free Σ-formulas. Termination of the algorithm is trivial since each step terminates and each time line 3 is executed the size of Γ is reduced. The following lemmas are needed before proving correctness.

Lemma 1. *If T' is a theory, Γ and Θ are sets of formulas, and S is a set of equations in solved form, then for any formula ϕ, $T' \cup \Gamma \cup \Theta \cup S \models \phi$ iff $T' \cup \Gamma \cup S(\Theta) \cup S \models \phi$.*

Proof. Follows trivially from the fact that $\Theta \cup S$ and $S(\Theta) \cup S$ are satisfied by exactly the same models and variable assignments. $\square$

Lemma 2. *If Γ is any set of formulas, then for any formula ϕ, and Σ-terms a and b,*

$$T \cup \Gamma \cup \{a = b\} \models \phi \text{ iff } T \cup \Gamma \cup solve(a = b) \models \phi.$$

Proof.
$\Rightarrow$: Given that $T \cup \Gamma \cup \{a = b\} \models \phi$, suppose that $M \models_\rho T \cup \Gamma \cup solve(a = b)$. It is easy to see from the definition of *solve* that $M \models_\rho a = b$ and hence by the hypothesis, $M \models_\rho \phi$.
$\Leftarrow$: Given that $T \cup \Gamma \cup solve(a = b) \models \phi$, suppose that $M \models_\rho T \cup \Gamma \cup \{a = b\}$. Then, since $T \models (a = b) \leftrightarrow \exists \overline{x}.solve(a = b)$, there exists a modified assignment ρ^* which assigns values to all the variables in $\overline{x}$ and satisfies $solve(a = b)$ but is otherwise equivalent to ρ. Then, by the hypothesis, $M \models_{\rho^*} \phi$. But the variables in $\overline{x}$ are *new* variables, so they do not appear in ϕ, meaning that changing their values cannot affect whether ϕ is true. Thus, $M \models_\rho \phi$. $\square$

Lemma 3. *If Γ, $\{a = b\}$, and S are sets of Σ-formulas, with S in solved form, and if $S^* = solve(S(a = b))$ then if $S^* \neq \{false\}$, then for every formula ϕ, $T \cup \Gamma \cup \{a = b\} \cup S \models \phi$ iff $T \cup \Gamma \cup S^* \cup S^*(S) \models \phi$.*

Proof.
$$
\begin{array}{lll}
T \cup \Gamma \cup \{a = b\} \cup S \models \phi & \Leftrightarrow & T \cup \Gamma \cup \{S(a = b)\} \cup S \models \phi \quad \text{Lemma 1} \\
& \Leftrightarrow & T \cup \Gamma \cup S^* \cup S \models \phi \quad\quad\quad \text{Lemma 2} \\
& \Leftrightarrow & T \cup \Gamma \cup S^* \cup S^*(S) \models \phi \quad \text{Lemma 1}
\end{array}
$$
    $\square$

Lemma 4. *During the execution of Algorithm S1, S is always in solved form.*

Proof. Clearly, S is in solved form initially. Consider one iteration. By construction, a^* and b^* do not contain any of the solitary variables of S, and thus by the definition of *solve*, S^* doesn't either. Furthermore, if $S^* = \{false\}$ then the algorithm terminates at line 6. Thus, at line 7, S^* must be in solved form. Applying S^* to S guarantees that none of the solitary variables of S^* appear in S, so the new value of S is also in solved form. $\square$

Lemma 5. *Let Γ_n and S_n be the values of Γ and S after the while loop in Algorithm S1 has been executed n times. Then for each n, and any formula ϕ, the following invariant holds: $T \cup \Gamma_0 \models \phi$ iff $T \cup \Gamma_n \cup S_n \models \phi$.*

Proof. The proof is by induction on n. For $n = 0$, the invariant holds trivially. Now suppose the invariant holds for some $k \geq 0$. Consider the next iteration.

$$
\begin{aligned}
\mathcal{T} \cup \Gamma_0 \models \phi \quad &\Leftrightarrow \quad \mathcal{T} \cup \Gamma_k \cup \mathcal{S}_k \models \phi && \text{Induction Hypothesis} \\
&\Leftrightarrow \quad \mathcal{T} \cup \Gamma_{k+1} \cup \{a = b\} \cup \mathcal{S}_k \models \phi && \text{Line 3} \\
&\Leftrightarrow \quad \mathcal{T} \cup \Gamma_{k+1} \cup \mathcal{S}^* \cup \mathcal{S}^*(\mathcal{S}_k) \models \phi && \text{Lemmas 3 and 4} \\
&\Leftrightarrow \quad \mathcal{T} \cup \Gamma_{k+1} \cup \mathcal{S}_{k+1} \models \phi && \text{Line 7}
\end{aligned}
$$

$\square$

Now we can show the correctness of Algorithm *S1*.

Theorem 1. *Suppose $\mathcal{T}$ is a Shostak theory with signature Σ, canonizer canon, and solver solve. If Γ is a set of Σ-equalities and Δ is a set of Σ-disequalities, then $\mathcal{T} \cup \Gamma \cup \Delta$ is satisfiable iff* S1$(\Gamma, \Delta, canon, solve) =$ TRUE.

Proof. Suppose S1$(\Gamma, \Delta, canon, solve) =$ FALSE. If the algorithm terminates at line 9, then, $canon(\mathcal{S}(a)) \equiv canon(\mathcal{S}(b))$ for some $a \neq b \in \Delta$. It follows from Proposition 2 and Lemma 5 that $\mathcal{T} \cup \Gamma \models a = b$, so clearly $\mathcal{T} \cup \Gamma \cup \Delta$ is not satisfiable. The other possibility is that the algorithm terminates at line 6. Suppose the loop has been executed n times and that Γ_n and $\mathcal{S}_n$ are the values of Γ and $\mathcal{S}$ at the end of the last loop. It must be the case that $\mathcal{T} \models a^* \neq b^*$, so $\mathcal{T} \cup \{a^* = b^*\}$ is unsatisfiable. Clearly then, $\mathcal{T} \cup \{a^* = b^*\} \cup \mathcal{S}_n$ is unsatisfiable, so by Lemma 1, $\mathcal{T} \cup \{a = b\} \cup \mathcal{S}_n$ is unsatisfiable. But $\{a = b\}$ is a subset of Γ_n, so $\mathcal{T} \cup \Gamma_n \cup \mathcal{S}_n$ must be unsatisfiable, and thus by Lemma 5, $\mathcal{T} \cup \Gamma$ is unsatisfiable.

Suppose on the other hand that S1$(\Gamma, \Delta, canon, solve) =$ TRUE. Then the algorithm terminates at line 10. By Lemma 4, $\mathcal{S}$ is in solved form. Let $\overline{\Delta}$ be the disjunction of equalities equivalent to $\neg(\Delta)$. Since the algorithm does not terminate at line 9, $\mathcal{T} \cup \mathcal{S}$ does not entail any equality in $\overline{\Delta}$. Because $\mathcal{T}$ is convex, it follows that $\mathcal{T} \cup \mathcal{S} \not\models \overline{\Delta}$. Now, since $\mathcal{T} \cup \mathcal{S}$ is satisfiable by Corollary 1, it follows that $\mathcal{T} \cup \mathcal{S} \cup \Delta$ is satisfiable. But by Lemma 5, $\mathcal{T} \cup \Gamma \models \phi$ iff $\mathcal{T} \cup \mathcal{S} \models \phi$, so in particular $\mathcal{T} \cup \mathcal{S} \models \Gamma$. Thus $\mathcal{T} \cup \mathcal{S} \cup \Delta \cup \Gamma$ is satisfiable, and hence $\mathcal{T} \cup \Gamma \cup \Delta$ is satisfiable. $\square$

3.1   An Example

Perhaps the most obvious example of a Shostak theory is the theory of linear rational arithmetic. A simple canonizer for this theory can be obtained by imposing an order on all variables (lexicographic or otherwise), and combining like terms. For example, $canon(z + 3y - x - 5z) \equiv -x + 3y + (-4z)$. Similarly, a solver can be obtained simply by solving for one of the variables in an equation. Consider the following system of equations:

$$
\begin{aligned}
x + 3y - 2z &= 1 \\
x - y - 6z &= 1 \\
2x + 8y - 2z &= 3
\end{aligned}
$$

The following table shows values for Γ, $\mathcal{S}$, $\mathcal{S}(a = b)$, and $\mathcal{S}^*$ at each iteration of Algorithm *S1* starting with $\Gamma = \{x+3y-2z = 1, x-y-6z = 1, 2x+8y-2z = 3\}$:

Γ	S	$S(a = b)$	S^*
$x + 3y - 2z = 1$ $x - y - 6z = 1$ $2x + 8y - 2z = 3$	$\emptyset$	$x + 3y - 2z = 1$	$x = 1 - 3y + 2z$
$x - y - 6z = 1$ $2x + 8y - 2z = 3$	$x = 1 - 3y + 2z$	$1 - 3y + 2z - y - 6z = 1$	$y = -z$
$2x + 8y - 2z = 3$	$x = 1 + 5z$ $y = -z$	$2(1 + 5z) + 8(-z) - 2z = 3$	false

The solver detects an inconsistency when it tries to solve the equation obtained after applying the substitution from S. The solver indicates this by returning {false}, which results in the algorithm returning **FALSE**.

3.2   Combining Shostak Theories

In [12], Shostak claims that two Shostak theories can always be combined to form a new Shostak theory. A canonizer for the combined theory is obtained simply by composing the canonizers from each individual theory. A solver for the combined theory is ostensibly obtained by repeatedly applying the solver for each theory (treating terms in other theories as variables) until a true variable is on the left-hand side of each equation in the solved form. This does in fact work for many theories, providing a simple and efficient method for combining Shostak theories. However, as pointed out in [7] and [11], the construction of the solver as described is not always possible. We do not address this issue here, but mention it as a question which warrants further investigation.

4   The Nelson-Oppen Combination Method

Nelson and Oppen [8,9] described a method for combining decision procedures for theories which are stably-infinite and have disjoint signatures. A theory $\mathcal{T}$ is stably-infinite if any quantifier-free formula is satisfiable in some model of $\mathcal{T}$ iff it is satisfiable in an infinite model of $\mathcal{T}$. In this section, we assume $\mathcal{T}_1$ and $\mathcal{T}_2$ are two such theories with signatures Σ_1 and Σ_2 respectively (the generalization to more than two theories is straightforward). Furthermore, we let $\mathcal{T} = \mathcal{T}_1 \cup \mathcal{T}_2$ and $\Sigma = \Sigma_1 \cup \Sigma_2$. The Nelson-Oppen procedure decides the satisfiability in $\mathcal{T}$ of a set Φ of Σ-literals.

4.1   Tinelli and Harandi's Approach

There have been many detailed presentations of the Nelson-Oppen method. Tinelli and Harandi's approach is particularly appealing because it is rigorous and conceptually simple [13]. Here we give a brief review of the method based on their approach. First, a few more definitions are required.

Members of Σ_i, for $i = 1, 2$ are called i-symbols. In order to associate all terms with some theory, each variable is also arbitrarily associated with either $\mathcal{T}_1$ or $\mathcal{T}_2$.

A variable is called an i-variable if it is associated with $\mathcal{T}_i$ (note that an i-variable is *not* an i-symbol, as it is not a member of Σ_i). A Σ-term t is an i-term if it is an i-variable, a constant i-symbol, or an application of a functional i-symbol. An i-predicate is an application of a predicate i-symbol. An atomic i-formula is an an i-predicate or an equality whose left term is an i-term. An i-literal is an atomic i-formula or the negation of an atomic i-formula. An occurrence of a j-term t in either a term or a literal is i-alien if $i \neq j$ and all super-terms (if any) of t are i-terms. An i-term or i-literal is *pure* if it contains only i-symbols (i.e. its i-alien sub-terms are all variables).

Given an equivalence relation $\sim$, let $dom_\sim$ be the domain of the relation. We define the following sets of formulas induced by $\sim$:

$$E_\sim = \{x = y \mid x, y \in dom_\sim \text{ and } x \sim y\}$$
$$D_\sim = \{x \neq y \mid x, y \in dom_\sim \text{ and } x \not\sim y\}$$
$$A_\sim = E_\sim \cup D_\sim.$$

Let Ar be a set of equalities and disequalities. If $Ar = A_\sim$ for some equivalence relation $\sim$ with domain $\mathcal{V}$, we call Ar an *arrangement* of $\mathcal{V}$.

The first step in determining the satisfiability of Φ is to transform Φ into an equisatisfiable formula $\Phi_1 \wedge \Phi_2$ where Φ_i consists only of pure i-literals as follows. Let ψ be some i-literal in Φ containing a non-variable i-alien j-term t. Replace all occurrences of t in ψ with a new j-variable z and add the equation $z = t$ to Φ. Repeat until every literal in Φ is pure. The literals can then easily be partitioned into Φ_1 and Φ_2. It is easy to see that Φ is satisfiable if and only if $\Phi_1 \wedge \Phi_2$ is satisfiable.

Now, let $\mathcal{V}$ be the set of all variables which appear in both Φ_1 and Φ_2. A simple version of the Nelson-Oppen procedure simply guesses an equivalence relation $\sim$ on $\mathcal{V}$ nondeterministically, and then checks whether $\mathcal{T}_i \cup \Phi_i \cup A_\sim$ is satisfiable. The correctness of the procedure is based on the following theorem from [13].

Theorem 2. *Let $\mathcal{T}_1$ and $\mathcal{T}_2$ be two stably-infinite, signature-disjoint theories and let Φ_i be a set of pure i-literals for $i = 1, 2$. Let $\mathcal{V}$ be the set of variables which appear in both Φ_1 and Φ_2. Then $\mathcal{T}_1 \cup \mathcal{T}_2 \cup \Phi_1 \cup \Phi_2$ is satisfiable iff there exists an arrangement Ar of $\mathcal{V}$ such that $\mathcal{T}_i \cup \Phi_i \cup Ar$ is satisfiable for $i = 1, 2$.*

4.2   A Variation of the Nelson-Oppen Procedure

The first step in the version of the Nelson-Oppen procedure described above changes the structure and number of literals in Φ. However, it is possible to give a version of the procedure which does not change the literals in Φ by instead treating alien terms as variables. This simplifies the algorithm by eliminating the need for the purification step. But more importantly, this variation is required for the combination of Shostak and Nelson-Oppen described next.

First, we introduce a *purifying* operator which formalizes the notion of treating alien terms as variables. Let v be a mapping from Σ-terms to variables such that for $i = 1, 2$, each i-term t is mapped to a *fresh* i-variable $v(t)$. Then, for some Σ-formula or Σ-term α, define $\gamma_i(\alpha)$ to be the result of replacing all i-alien occurrences of terms t by $v(t)$. It is easy to see that as a result, $\gamma_i(\alpha)$ is i-pure. Since γ_i simply replaces terms with unique place-holders, it is injective. We will denote its inverse by γ_i^{-1}. We will also denote by $\gamma_0(\alpha)$ the result of replacing each maximal term (i.e. terms without any super-terms) t in α by $v(t)$. Thus, the only terms in $\gamma_0(\alpha)$ are variables.

Our variation on the Nelson-Oppen procedure works as follows. Given a set of literals, Φ, first partition Φ into two sets Φ_1 and Φ_2, where Φ_i is exactly the set of i-literals in Φ. Let $\mathcal{V}$ be the set of all terms which are i-alien (for some i) in some literal in Φ or in some sub-term of some literal in Φ. $\mathcal{V}$ consists of exactly those terms that would end up being replaced by variables in the original Nelson-Oppen method. $\mathcal{V}$ will also be referred to as the set of *shared* terms. As before, an equivalence relation $\sim$ on $\mathcal{V}$ is guessed. If $\mathcal{T}_i \cup \gamma_i(\Phi_i \cup A_\sim)$ is satisfiable for each i, then $\mathcal{T} \cup \Phi$ is satisfiable, as shown by the following theorem.

Theorem 3. *Let $\mathcal{T}_1$ and $\mathcal{T}_2$ be two stably-infinite, signature-disjoint theories and let Φ be a set of literals in the combined signature Σ. If Φ_i is the set of all i-literals in Φ and $\mathcal{V}$ is the set of shared terms in Φ, then $\mathcal{T}_1 \cup \mathcal{T}_2 \cup \Phi$ is satisfiable iff there exists an equivalence relation $\sim$ on $\mathcal{V}$ such that for $i = 1, 2$, $\mathcal{T}_i \cup \gamma_i(\Phi_i \cup A_\sim)$ is satisfiable.*

Proof.

$\Rightarrow$: Suppose $M \models_\rho \mathcal{T} \cup \Phi$. Let $a \sim b$ iff $a, b \in \mathcal{V}$ and $M \models_\rho a = b$. Then clearly for $i = 1, 2$, $M \models_\rho \mathcal{T}_i \cup \Phi_i \cup A_\sim$. It is then easy to see that $\mathcal{T}_i \cup \gamma_i(\Phi_i \cup A_\sim)$ is satisfiable by choosing a variable assignment which assigns to each variable $v(t)$ the corresponding value of the term t which it replaces.

$\Leftarrow$: Suppose that for each i, $T_i \cup \gamma_i(\Phi_i \cup A_\sim)$ is satisfiable. Consider $i = 1$. Let Θ_1 be the set of all equations $v(t) = t$, where $t \in \mathcal{V}$ is a 1-term. Consider $\gamma_1(\Theta_1)$. Since γ_1 never replaces 1-terms and each $v(t)$ is a new variable, it follows that $\gamma_1(\Theta_1)$ is in solved form, and its solitary variables are exactly the variables which are used to replace 1-terms. Thus, by Corollary 1, $\mathcal{T}_1 \cup \gamma_1(\Theta_1)$ is satisfiable. Furthermore, since none of the solitary variables of $\gamma_1(\Theta_1)$ appear in $\gamma_1(\Phi_1 \cup A_\sim)$, a satisfiable assignment for $\mathcal{T}_1 \cup \gamma_1(\Theta_1)$ can be constructed from the satisfying assignment for $\mathcal{T}_1 \cup \gamma_1(\Phi_1 \cup A_\sim)$ (which exists by hypothesis) so that the resulting assignment satisfies $\mathcal{T}_1 \cup \gamma_1(\Phi_1 \cup A_\sim \cup \Theta_1)$. Now, each term in $\gamma_1(A_\sim)$ is the right-hand side of some equation in $\gamma_1(\Theta_1)$, so by repeatedly applying equations from $\gamma_1(\Theta_1)$ as substitutions, $\gamma_1(A_\sim)$ can be transformed into $\gamma_0(A_\sim)$, and thus $\mathcal{T}_1 \cup \gamma_1(\Phi_1 \cup \Theta_1) \cup \gamma_0(A_\sim)$ must also be satisfiable. Applying the same argument with $i=2$, we conclude that $\mathcal{T}_2 \cup \gamma_2(\Phi_2 \cup \Theta_2) \cup \gamma_0(A_\sim)$ is satisfiable. But for each i, $\gamma_i(\Phi_i \cup \Theta_i)$ is a set of i-literals. Furthermore, $\gamma_0(A_\sim)$ is an arrangement of the variables shared by these two sets, so Theorem 2 can be applied to conclude that $\mathcal{T} \cup \Phi \cup \Theta_1 \cup \Theta_2$, and thus $\mathcal{T} \cup \Phi$, is satisfiable. $\qquad\square$

5   Combining the Methods

Let $\mathcal{T}_1, \mathcal{T}_2, \Sigma_1, \Sigma_2, \mathcal{T}$, and Σ be defined as in the previous section, with the additional assumptions that $\mathcal{T}_1$ is a Shostak theory and that neither $\mathcal{T}_1$ nor $\mathcal{T}_2$

admits trivial models (typically, theories of interest do not admit trivial models, or can be easily modified so that this is the case). The following theorem shows that both theories are also stably-infinite.

Theorem 4. *Every convex first-order theory with no trivial models is stably-infinite.*

Proof. Suppose $\mathcal{U}$ is a first-order theory which is not stably-infinite. Then there exists some quantifier-free set of literals Φ which is satisfiable in a finite model of $\mathcal{U}$, but not in an infinite model of $\mathcal{U}$. Let $\exists \overline{x} \Phi$ be the existential closure of Φ. Then $\exists \overline{x}.\Phi$ is true in some finite model, but not in any infinite model, of $\mathcal{U}$. It follows that $\mathcal{U} \cup \{\exists \overline{x}.\Phi\}$ is a theory with no infinite models. By first-order compactness, there must be some finite cardinality n such that there is a model of $\mathcal{U} \cup \{\exists \overline{x}.\Phi\}$ of cardinality n, but none of cardinality larger than n. Clearly, $\mathcal{U} \cup \Phi$ is satisfiable in some model of size n, but not in any models larger than n. It follows by the pigeonhole principle that if $y_i, 0 \leq i \leq n$ are fresh variables, then $\mathcal{U} \cup \Phi \models \bigvee_{i \neq j} y_i = y_j$, but because $\mathcal{U}$ has no trivial models (i.e. models of size 1), $\mathcal{U} \cup \Phi \not\models y_i = y_j$ for any i, j with $i \neq j$. Thus, $\mathcal{U}$ is not convex. □

5.1   The Combined Algorithm

Suppose Φ is a set of Σ-literals. As in Section 4.2, divide Φ into Φ_1 and Φ_2 where Φ_i contains exactly the i-literals of Φ. Let $\mathcal{V}$ be the set of shared terms. By Theorem 3, $\mathcal{T} \cup \Phi_1 \cup \Phi_2$ is satisfiable iff there exists an equivalence relation $\sim$ such that for $i = 1, 2$, $\mathcal{T}_i \cup \gamma_i(\Phi_i \cup A_\sim)$ is satisfiable.

In order for the approach in Algorithm *S1* to function in a multiple-theory environment, it is necessary to generalize the definition of equations in solved form to accommodate the notion of treating alien terms as variables. A set $\mathcal{S}$ of equations is said to be in *i-solved form* if $\gamma_i(\mathcal{S})$ is in solved form. If $\mathcal{S}$ is a set of equations in i-solved form and $\mathcal{V}$ is an expression or set of expressions in a mixed language including Σ_i, then we define $\mathcal{S}(\mathcal{V})$ to be the result of replacing each left-hand side in $\mathcal{S}$ which occurs as an i-alien in $\mathcal{V}$ with the corresponding right-hand side. Formally, $\mathcal{S}(\mathcal{V})$ is redefined to be $\gamma_i^{-1}(\gamma_i(\mathcal{S})(\gamma_i(\mathcal{V})))$, i.e. the application of $\mathcal{S}$ to $\mathcal{V}$ should be equivalent to first replacing all i-alien terms with variables in both $\mathcal{S}$ and $\mathcal{V}$, then doing the substitution, and then finally restoring the i-alien terms to their places. We similarly need to extend the definitions of *canon* and *solve*. Let $canon(\alpha)$ denote $\gamma_1^{-1}(canon(\gamma_1(\alpha)))$ and $solve(\beta)$ denote $\gamma_1^{-1}(solve(\gamma_1(\beta)))$.

Now, let Γ be the set of equalities in Φ_1 and Δ the set of disequalities in Φ_1. Furthermore, let Sat_2 be a decision procedure for satisfiability of literals in $\mathcal{T}_2$:

$$Sat_2(\Phi) = \texttt{TRUE} \quad iff \quad \mathcal{T}_2 \cup \gamma_2(\Phi) \not\models \text{false}.$$

Algorithm *S2* is a modification of Algorithm *S1* which accommodates the additional theory $\mathcal{T}_2$. Essentially, the algorithm is identical except for the addition of lines 3 through 5 which check whether Φ_2 is consistent in theory $\mathcal{T}_2$ with an arrangement $A_\sim$. The equivalence relation $\sim$ on $\mathcal{V}$ is derived from $\mathcal{S}$ as follows:

$$a \sim b \quad iff \quad a, b \in \mathcal{V} \text{ and } canon(\mathcal{S}(a)) \equiv canon(\mathcal{S}(b))$$

```
S2(Γ, Δ, canon, solve, Φ₂, Sat₂)
 1.  S := ∅;
 2.  WHILE Γ = ∅ OR ¬Sat₂(Φ₂ ∪ A∼) DO BEGIN
 3.      IF ¬Sat₂(Φ₂ ∪ A∼) THEN BEGIN
 4.          IF ¬Sat₂(Φ₂ ∪ E∼) THEN RETURN FALSE;
 5.          ELSE Choose a ≠ b ∈ D∼ such that ¬Sat₂(Φ₂ ∪ E∼ ∪ {a ≠ b});
 6.      END ELSE Remove some equality a = b from Γ;
 7.      a* := S(a); b* := S(b);
 8.      S* := solve(a* = b*);
 9.      IF S* = {false} THEN RETURN FALSE;
10.      S := S*(S) ∪ S*;
11. END
12. IF a∼b for some a ≠ b ∈ Δ THEN RETURN FALSE;
13. RETURN TRUE;
```

Fig. 2. Algorithm S2: a generalization of Shostak's algorithm

In each iteration of the while loop, an equation is processed and integrated with S. This equation is either the result of the current arrangement being inconsistent in $\mathcal{T}_2$ (lines 3 through 5) or simply an equation from Γ (line 6). As shown below, the definition of $\sim$ ensures that S is consistent with $A_\sim$. Similarly, equations are added to S until $A_\sim$ is also consistent with Φ_2. Thus, when the algorithm returns TRUE, both Φ_1 and Φ_2 are known to be consistent with the arrangement $A_\sim$. Line 5 requires a little explanation. If the algorithm reaches line 5, it means that $\Phi_2 \cup E_\sim \cup D_\sim$ is not satisfiable in $\mathcal{T}_2$, but $\Phi_2 \cup E_\sim$ is. It follows from convexity of $\mathcal{T}_2$ that there must be a disequality $a \neq b$ in $D_\sim$ such that $\Phi_2 \cup E_\sim \cup \{a \neq b\}$ is not satisfiable in $\mathcal{T}_2$.

Algorithm $S2$ terminates because each step terminates and in each iteration either the size of Γ is reduced by one or two equivalence classes in $\sim$ are merged. As before, the correctness proof requires a couple of preparatory lemmas.

Lemma 6. *Suppose S is a set of Σ-formulas in 1-solved form, $\mathcal{V}$ is a set of Σ-terms, and $\sim$ is defined as above. If $\approx$ is an equivalence relation on $\mathcal{V}$ such that $\mathcal{T}_1 \cup \gamma_1(A_\approx \cup S)$ is satisfiable, then $E_\sim \subseteq A_\approx$. In other words, every arrangement of $\mathcal{V}$ consistent with S must include $E_\sim$.*

Proof. Consider an arbitrary equation $a = b$ between terms in $\mathcal{V}$. $a = b \in E_\sim$ iff $canon(S(a)) \equiv canon(S(b))$ iff (by Proposition 2) $\mathcal{T}_1 \cup \gamma_1(S) \models \gamma_1(a = b)$. So $\gamma_1(a = b)$ must be true in every model and assignment satisfying $\mathcal{T}_1 \cup \gamma_1(S)$. In particular, if $\mathcal{T}_1 \cup \gamma_1(A_\approx \cup S)$ is satisfiable, the corresponding model and assignment must also satisfy $\gamma_1(a = b)$. Since either the equation $a = b$ or the disequation $a \neq b$ must be in $A_\approx$, it must be the case that $a = b \in A_\approx$. Thus, $E_\sim \subseteq A_\approx$. □

Lemma 7. *Let Γ_n and S_n be the values of Γ and S after the loop in Algorithm S2 has been executed n times. Then for each n, the following invariant holds: $\mathcal{T} \cup \Phi$ is satisfiable iff there exists an equivalence relation $\approx$ on $\mathcal{V}$ such that*

(1) $\mathcal{T}_1 \cup \gamma_1(\Gamma_n \cup \Delta \cup A_\approx \cup \mathcal{S}_n)$ *is satisfiable, and*
(2) $\mathcal{T}_2 \cup \gamma_2(\Phi_2 \cup A_\approx)$ *is satisfiable.*

Proof. The proof is by induction on n. For the base case, notice that by Theorem 3, $\mathcal{T} \cup \Phi$ is satisfiable iff there exists an equivalence relation $\approx$ such that (1) and (2) hold with $n = 0$.

Before doing the induction case, we first show that for some fixed equivalence relation $\approx$, (1) and (2) hold when $n = k$ iff (1) and (2) hold when $n = k + 1$. Notice that (2) is independent of n, so it is only necessary to consider (1). There are two cases to consider.

First, suppose that the condition of line 3 is true and line 5 is executed. We first show that (1) holds when $n = k$ iff the following holds:

(3) $\mathcal{T}_1 \cup \gamma_1(\Gamma_{k+1} \cup \Delta \cup A_\approx \cup \{a = b\} \cup \mathcal{S}_k)$ *is satisfiable.*

Since line 6 is not executed, $\Gamma_{k+1} = \Gamma_k$. The if direction is then trivial since the formula in (1) is a subset of the formula in (3). To show the only if direction, first note that it follows from line 5 that $\mathcal{T}_2 \cup \gamma_2(\Phi_2 \cup E_\sim) \models \gamma_2(a = b)$. But by Lemma 6, $E_\sim \subseteq A_\approx$, so it follows that $\mathcal{T}_2 \cup \gamma_2(\Phi_2 \cup A_\approx) \models \gamma_2(a = b)$. Since either $a = b \in A_\approx$ or $a \neq b \in A_\approx$, it must be the case that $a = b \in A_\approx$ and thus (3) follows trivially from (1). Now, by Lemma 3 (where ϕ is false), if line 10 is reached, then (3) holds iff

(4) $\mathcal{T}_1 \cup \gamma_1(\Gamma_{k+1} \cup \Delta \cup A_\approx \cup \mathcal{S}^*(\mathcal{S}_k) \cup \mathcal{S}^*)$ *is satisfiable,*

where $\mathcal{S}^* = solve(\mathcal{S}(a = b))$. But $\mathcal{S}_{k+1} = \mathcal{S}^*(\mathcal{S}_k) \cup \mathcal{S}^*$, so (4) is equivalent to (1) with $n = k + 1$.

In the other case, line 6 is executed (so that $\Gamma_{k+1} = \Gamma_k - \{a = b\}$). Thus, (1) holds with $n = k$ iff $\mathcal{T}_1 \cup \gamma_1(\Gamma_{k+1} \cup \Delta \cup \{a = b\} \cup A_\approx \cup \mathcal{S}_k)$ is satisfiable, which is equivalent to (3). As in the previous case, it then follows from Lemma 3 that (1) holds at k iff (1) holds at $k + 1$.

Thus, given an equivalence relation, (1) and (2) hold at $k + 1$ exactly when they hold at k. It follows easily that if an equivalence relation exists which satisfies (1) and (2) at k, then there exists an equivalence relation satisfying (1) and (2) at $k + 1$ and vice-versa. Finally, the induction case assumes that that $\mathcal{T} \cup \Phi$ is satisfiable iff there exists an equivalence relation $\approx$ such that (1) and (2) hold at k. It follows from the above argument that $\mathcal{T} \cup \Phi$ is satisfiable iff there exists an equivalence relation $\approx$ such that (1) and (2) hold at $k + 1$.   □

Theorem 5. *Suppose that $\mathcal{T}_1$ is a Shostak theory with signature Σ_1, canonizer canon, and solver solve, and that $\mathcal{T}_2$ is a convex theory with signature Σ_2 disjoint from Σ_1 and satisfiability procedure Sat_2. Suppose also that neither $\mathcal{T}_1$ nor $\mathcal{T}_2$ admit trivial models, and let $\mathcal{T} = \mathcal{T}_1 \cup \mathcal{T}_2$ and $\Sigma = \Sigma_1 \cup \Sigma_2$. Suppose Φ is a set of Σ-literals. Let Γ be the subset of Φ which consists of 1-equalities, Δ the subset of Φ which consists of 1-disequalities, and Φ_2 the remainder of the literals in Φ. $\mathcal{T} \cup \Phi$ is satisfiable iff $S2(\Gamma, \Delta, canon, solve, \Phi_2, Sat_2) = \text{TRUE}$.*

Proof. First note that by the same argument used in Lemma 4, $\mathcal{S}$ is always in 1-solved form.

Suppose $\text{S2}(\Gamma, \Delta, canon, solve, \Phi_2, Sat_2) = \textsf{FALSE}$. If the algorithm terminates at line 9 or 12, then the proof that Φ is unsatisfiable is the same as that for Algorithm *S1* above. If it stops at line 4, then suppose there is an equivalence relation $\approx$ satisfying condition (1) of Lemma 7. It follows from Lemma 6 that $E_\sim \subseteq A_\approx$. But since the algorithm terminates at line 4, $\mathcal{T}_2 \cup \gamma_2(\Phi_2 \cup A_\approx)$ must be unsatisfiable. Thus condition (2) of Lemma 7 cannot hold. Thus, by Lemma 7, $\mathcal{T} \cup \Phi$ is unsatisfiable.

Suppose on the other hand that $\text{S2}(\Gamma, \Delta, canon, solve, \Phi_2, Sat_2) = \textsf{TRUE}$. By the definition of $\sim$ and Proposition 2, $a = b \in A_\sim$ iff $\mathcal{T}_1 \cup \gamma_1(\mathcal{S}) \models \gamma_1(a = b)$. It follows from the convexity of $\mathcal{T}_1$ and Corollary 1 that $\mathcal{T}_1 \cup \gamma_1(\mathcal{S} \cup A_\sim)$ is satisfiable. It then follows from the fact that *S2* does not terminate at line 12 (as well as convexity again) that $\mathcal{T}_1 \cup \gamma_1(\mathcal{S} \cup \Delta \cup A_\sim)$ is satisfiable. This is condition (1) of Lemma 7. Condition (2) must hold because the while loop terminates. Thus, by Lemma 7, $\mathcal{T} \cup \Phi$ is satisfiable. □

6   A Comparison with Shostak's Original Method

There are two main ways in which this work differs from Shostak's original method, which is best represented by Ruess and Shankar in [11]. The first is in the set of requirements a theory must fulfill. The second is in the level of abstraction at which the algorithm is presented.

6.1   Requirements on the Theory

Of the four requirements given in our definition of a Shostak theory, the first two are clarifications which are either assumed or not addressed in other work, and the last two are similar to, but slightly less restrictive, than the requirements listed by others. The first requirement is simply that the theory contain no predicate symbols. This is a minor point that is included simply to be explicit about an assumption which is implicit in other work. Shostak's method does not give any guidance on what to do if a theory includes predicate symbols. One possible approach is to encode predicates as functions, but this only works if the resulting encoding admits a canonizer and solver.

The second requirement is that the theory be convex. This may seem overly restrictive since Shostak claims that non-convex theories can be handled [12]. Consider, however, the following simple non-convex theory with signature $\{a, b\}$: $\{a \neq b, \forall x.(x = a \vee x = b)\}$. It is easy to see that this theory admits a (trivial) canonizer and a solver. However, for the unsatisfiable set of formulas $\{x \neq y, y \neq z, x \neq z\}$, any version of Shostak's algorithm will fail to detect the inconsistency. Ruess and Shankar avoid this difficulty by restricting their attention to the problem of whether $\mathcal{T} \cup \Gamma \models a = b$ for some set of equalities Γ. However, the ability to solve this problem does not lead to a self-contained decision procedure unless the theory is convex.

The third requirement on the theory is that a canonizer exist. Shostak gave several additional properties that must be satisfied by the canonizer. These are not needed at the level of abstraction of our algorithms, though some efficient implementations may require the additional properties.

A similar situation arises with the requirements on the solver: only a subset of the original requirements are needed. Note that although we require the set of equalities returned by the solver to be equisatisfiable with the input set in *every* model of $\mathcal{T}$, whereas Ruess and Shankar require only that it be equisatisfiable with the input set in every σ-model[1], it is not difficult to show that their requirements on the canonizer imply that every model of $\mathcal{T}$ must be a σ-model.

6.2   Level of Abstraction

Algorithm *S2* looks very different from Shostak's original published algorithm as well as most other published versions, though these are, in fact, closely related. An algorithm equivalent to that found in [11] can be obtained by making a number of refinements. We do not have the space to describe these in detail, but we outline them briefly below. We also describe some general principles they exemplify which could be used in other refinements.

The most obvious refinement is to replace $\mathcal{T}_2$ by the theory of equality with uninterpreted function symbols. The data structure for $\mathcal{S}$ can be expanded to include all equations (not just the 1-equations), obviating the need to track Φ_2 separately. The check for satisfiability in $\mathcal{T}_2$ is replaced by a simple check for congruence closure over the terms in $\mathcal{S}$. The general principle here is that if $\mathcal{S}$ can be expanded to track the equalities in another theory, then equality information only needs to be maintained in one place, which is more efficient.

Another refinement is that a more sophisticated substitution can be applied at line 7 of Algorithm *S2*. The more sophisticated substitution considers each sub-term t, and if it is known to be equivalent to a term u already appearing in $\mathcal{S}$, then all instances of t are replaced with u. For terms in the Shostak theory, this is essentially accomplished by applying the canonizer. For uninterpreted function terms, it is a bit more subtle. For example, if $x = y \in \mathcal{S}$ and $f(x)$ appears in $\mathcal{S}$, then if $f(y)$ is encountered, it can be replaced by $f(x)$. As a result, fewer total terms are generated and thus fewer terms need to be considered when updating $\mathcal{S}$ or when performing congruence closure. The general principle is that simplifications and substitutions which reduce the total number of terms can improve efficiency. This is especially important in a natural generalization of Algorithm *S2* to accommodate non-convex theories in which the search for an appropriate arrangement of the shared terms can take time which is more than exponential in the number of shared terms [9].

---

[1] In the notation of Ruess and Shankar, the canonizer is denoted by σ, and a σ-*model* M is one where $M \models a = \sigma(a)$ for any term a.

Acknowledgments

We are especially grateful to Natarajan Shankar for many helpful and productive conversations regarding Shostak's method. We would also like to thank Cesare Tinelli and the anonymous referees who provided important corrections and valuable feedback. This work was partially supported by the National Science Foundation Grant CCR-9806889, and the DARPA PCES program (DARPA/AirForce contract number F33615-00-C-1693).

References

1. C. Barrett, D. Dill, and J. Levitt. Validity Checking for Combinations of Theories with Equality. In M. Srivas and A. Camilleri, editors, *Formal Methods in Computer-Aided Design*, volume 1166 of *Lecture Notes in Computer Science*, pages 187–201. Springer-Verlag, 1996.
2. C. Barrett, D. Dill, and A. Stump. A Framework for Cooperating Decision Procedures. In *17th International Conference on Automated Deduction*, Lecture Notes in Computer Science. Springer-Verlag, 2000.
3. Clark W. Barrett. *Checking Validity of Quantifier-Free Formulas in Combinations of First-Order Theories*. PhD thesis, Stanford University, 2002.
4. Nikolaj S. Bjørner. *Integrating Decision Procedures for Temporal Verification*. PhD thesis, Stanford University, 1999.
5. D. Cyrluk, P. Lincoln, and N. Shankar. On Shostak's Decision Procedure for Combinations of Theories. In M. McRobbie and J. Slaney, editors, *13th International Conference on Computer Aided Deduction*, volume 1104 of *Lecture Notes in Computer Science*, pages 463–477. Springer-Verlag, 1996.
6. Z. Manna et al. STeP: Deductive-Algorithmic Verification of Reactive and Real-time Systems. In *8th International Conference on Computer-Aided Verification*, volume 1102 of *Lecture Notes in Computer Science*, pages 415–418. Springer-Verlag, 1996.
7. Jeremy R. Levitt. *Formal Verification Techniques for Digital Systems*. PhD thesis, Stanford University, 1999.
8. G. Nelson and D. Oppen. Simplification by Cooperating Decision Procedures. *ACM Transactions on Programming Languages and Systems*, 1(2):245–57, 1979.
9. Derek C. Oppen. Complexity, Convexity and Combinations of Theories. *Theoretical Computer Science*, 12:291–302, 1980.
10. S. Owre, J. Rushby, and N. Shankar. PVS: A Prototype Verification System. In D. Kapur, editor, *11th International Conference on Automated Deduction*, volume 607 of *Lecture Notes in Artificial Intelligence*, pages 748–752. Springer-Verlag, 1992.
11. H. Ruess and N. Shankar. Deconstructing Shostak. In *16th Annual IEEE Symposium on Logic in Computer Science*, pages 19–28, June 2001.
12. Robert E. Shostak. Deciding Combinations of Theories. *Journal of the Association for Computing Machinery*, 31(1):1–12, 1984.
13. C. Tinelli and M. Harandi. A New Correctness Proof of the Nelson-Oppen Combination Procedure. In F. Baader and K. Schulz, editors, *1st International Workshop on Frontiers of Combining Systems (FroCoS'96)*, volume 3 of *Applied Logic Series*. Kluwer Academic Publishers, 1996.
14. Ashish Tiwari. *Decision Procedures in Automated Deduction*. PhD thesis, State University of New York at Stony Brook, 2000.

Combining Relational Algebra, SQL, and Constraint Programming

Marco Cadoli and Toni Mancini

Dipartimento di Informatica e Sistemistica
Università di Roma "La Sapienza"
Via Salaria 113, 00198 Roma, ITALY
cadoli|tmancini@dis.uniroma1.it

Abstract. The goal of this paper is to provide a strong interaction between constraint programming and relational DBMSs. To this end we propose extensions of standard query languages such as relational algebra (RA) and SQL, by adding constraint solving capabilities to them. In particular, we propose non-deterministic extensions of both languages, which are specially suited for combinatorial problems. Non-determinism is introduced by means of a *guessing* operator, which declares a set of relations to have an arbitrary extension. This new operator results in languages with higher expressive power, able to express all problems in the complexity class NP. Some syntactical restrictions which make data complexity polynomial are shown. The effectiveness of both languages is demonstrated by means of several examples.

1 Introduction

The efficient solution of NP-hard combinatorial problems, such as resource allocation, scheduling, planning, etc. is crucial for many industrial applications, and it is often achieved by means of ad-hoc hand-written programs. Specialized programming languages [7,15] or libraries [10] for expressing constraints are commercially available. Data encoding the instance are either in text files in an ad-hoc format, or in standard relational DBs accessed through libraries callable from programming languages such as C++ (cf., e.g., [11]). In other words, there is not a strong integration between the data definition and the constraint programming languages.

The goal of this paper is to integrate constraint programming into relational database management systems (R-DBMSs): to this end we propose extensions of standard query languages such as relational algebra (RA) and SQL, by adding constraint solving capabilities to them.

In principle RA can be used as a language for testing constraints. As an example, given relations A and B, testing whether all tuples in A are contained in B can be done by computing the relation $A - B$, and then checking its emptiness. Anyway, it must be noted that RA is unfeasible as a language for expressing NP-hard problems, since it is capable of expressing just a strict subset of the

A. Armando (Ed.): FroCoS 2002, LNAI 2309, pp. 147–161, 2002.

polynomial-time queries (cf., e.g., [1]). As a consequence, an extension is indeed needed.

The proposed generalization of RA is named *NP-Alg*, and it is proven to be capable of expressing all problems in the complexity class NP. We focus on NP because this class contains the decisional version of most combinatorial problems of industrial relevance [8]. *NP-Alg* is RA plus a simple *guessing* operator, which declares a set of relations to have an arbitrary extension. Algebraic expressions are used to express constraints. Several interesting properties of *NP-Alg* are provided: its data complexity is shown to be NP-complete, and for each problem ξ in NP we prove that there is a fixed query that, when evaluated on a database representing the instance of ξ, solves it. Combined complexity is also addressed.

Since *NP-Alg* expresses all problems in NP, an interesting question is whether a query corresponds to an NP-complete or to a polynomial problem. We give a partial answer to it, by exhibiting some syntactical restrictions of *NP-Alg* with polynomial-time data complexity.

In the same way, NP-SQL is the proposed non-deterministic extension of SQL, the well-known language for querying relational databases [14], having the same expressive power of *NP-Alg*. We believe that writing an NP-SQL query for the solution of a combinatorial problem is only moderately more difficult than writing SQL queries for a standard database application. The advantage of using NP-SQL is twofold: it is not necessary to learn a completely new language or methodology, and integration of the problem solver with the information system of the enterprise can be done very smoothly. The effectiveness of both *NP-Alg* and NP-SQL as constraint modeling languages is demonstrated by showing several queries which specify combinatorial problems.

2   *NP-Alg*: Syntax and Semantics

We refer to a standard definition of RA with the five operators $\{\sigma, \pi, \times, -, \cup\}$ [1]. Other operators such as "$\bowtie$" and "$/$" can be defined as usual. Temporary relations such as $T = algexpr(\ldots)$ will be used to make expressions easier to read. As usual queries are defined as mappings which are partial recursive and generic, i.e., constants are uninterpreted.

Let D denote a finite relational database, $edb(D)$ the set of its relations, and DOM the unary relation representing the set of all constants occurring in D.

Definition 1 (Syntax of *NP-Alg*). *An NP-Alg expression has two parts:*

1. *A set $\mathbf{Q} = \{Q_1^{(a_1)}, \ldots, Q_n^{(a_n)}\}$ of new relations of arbitrary arity, denoted as Guess $Q_1^{(a_1)}, \ldots, Q_n^{(a_n)}$. Sets $edb(D)$ and $\mathbf{Q}$ must be disjoint.*
2. *An ordinary expression exp of RA on the new database schema $[edb(D), \mathbf{Q}]$.*

For simplicity, in this paper we focus on *boolean* queries. For this reason we restrict *exp* to be a relation which we call $FAIL$.

Definition 2 (Semantics of *NP-Alg*). *The semantics of an NP-Alg expression is as follows:*

1. *For each possible extension ext of the relations in* **Q** *with elements in DOM, the relation FAIL is evaluated, using ordinary rules of RA.*
2. *If there is an extension ext such that FAIL = ∅, the* answer *to the boolean query is "yes" (denoted as FAIL◇∅). Otherwise the* answer *is "no".*
   When the answer is "yes", the extension of relations in **Q** *is a solution for the problem instance.*

A trivial implementation of the above semantics obviously requires exponential time, since there are exponentially many possible extensions of the relations in **Q**. Anyway, as we will show in Section 4.3, some polynomial-time cases indeed exist.

The reason why we focus on a relation named $FAIL$ is that, typically, it is easy to specify a decision problem as a set of constraints (cf. forthcoming Sections 3 and 5). As a consequence, an instance of the problem has a solution iff there is an arbitrary choice of the guessed relations such that all constraints are satisfied, i.e., $FAIL = ∅$. A $FOUND^{(1)}$ query can be anyway defined as $FOUND = DOM - \pi_{\$1}(DOM \times FAIL)$. In this case, the answer is "yes" iff there is an extension ext such that $FOUND \neq ∅$.

3   Examples of *NP-Alg* Queries

In this section we show the specifications of some NP-complete problems, as queries in *NP-Alg*. All examples are on uninterpreted structures, i.e., on unlabeled directed graphs, because we adopt a pure RA with uninterpreted constants. As a side-effect, the examples show that, even in this limited setting, we are able to emulate integers and ordering. This is very important, because the specification of very simple combinatorial problems requires integers and ordering.

In Section 5 we use the full power of NP-SQL to specify some real-world problems.

3.1   *k*-Colorability

We assume a directed graph is represented as a pair of relations $NODES^{(1)}$ and $EDGES^{(2)}(from, to)$ $(DOM = NODES)$. A graph is *k-colorable* if there is a k-partition $Q_1^{(1)}, \ldots, Q_k^{(1)}$ of its nodes, i.e., a set of k sets such that:

- $\forall i \in [1, k], \forall j \in [1, k], j \neq i \rightarrow Q_i \cap Q_j = ∅$,
- $\bigcup_{i=1}^{k} Q_i = NODES$,

and each set Q_i has no pair of nodes linked by an edge. The problem is well-known to be NP-complete (cf., e.g., [8]), and it can be specified in *NP-Alg* as follows:

$$Guess \; Q_1^{(1)}, \ldots, Q_k^{(1)}; \tag{1a}$$

$$FAIL\_DISJOINT = \bigcup_{\substack{i=1,\ldots,k \\ j \neq i}} Q_i \bowtie Q_j; \tag{1b}$$

$$FAIL\_COVER = NODES \; \Delta \; \bigcup_{i=1}^{k} Q_i; \tag{1c}$$

$$FAIL\_PARTITION = FAIL\_DISJOINT \; \cup \; FAIL\_COVER; \tag{1d}$$

$$FAIL\_COLORING = \pi_{\$1} \left[\bigcup_{i=1}^{k} \left(\left(\sigma_{\$1 \neq \$2}(Q_i \times Q_i) \right)_{\substack{\$1=EDGES.from \\ \$2=EDGES.to}}^{\bowtie} EDGES \right) \right]; \tag{1e}$$

$$FAIL = FAIL\_PARTITION \; \cup \; FAIL\_COLORING. \tag{1f}$$

Expression (1a) declares k new relations of arity 1. Expression (1f) collects all constraints a candidate coloring must obey to:

- (1b) and (1c) make sure that Q is a partition of $NODES$ ("Δ" is the symmetric difference operator, i.e., $A \; \Delta \; B = (A - B) \cup (B - A)$, useful for testing equality since $A \; \Delta \; B = \emptyset \Longleftrightarrow A = B$).
- (1e) checks that each set Q_i has no pair of nodes linked by an edge.

We observe that in the specification above the $FAIL\_PARTITION$ relation (1d) makes sure that an extension of $Q_1^{(1)}, \ldots, Q_k^{(1)}$ is a *k-partition* of $NODES$. Such an expression can be very useful for the specification of problems, so we introduce a *metaexpression*:

$$failPartition^{(1)}(N^{(k)}, P_1^{(k)}, \ldots, P_n^{(k)}),$$

which returns an empty relation iff $\{P_1^{(k)}, \ldots, P_n^{(k)}\}$ is a partition of $N^{(k)}$. The prefix $fail$ in the name of the metaexpression reminds that it should be used in checking constraints. Other metaexpressions will be introduced in the following examples, and are summarized in Section 3.4.

3.2   Independent Set

Let a (directed) graph be defined, as usual, with the two relations $NODES^{(1)}$ and $EDGES^{(2)}$, and let $k \leq |NODES|$ be an integer, which is specified by a relation $K^{(1)}$ containing exactly k tuples. A subset N of $NODES$, with $|N| \geq k$ is said to be an *independent set of size at least k* of the graph if N contains no pair of nodes linked by an edge.

The problem of determining whether an input graph has an independent set of size at least k is NP-complete (cf., e.g., [8]), and it can be easily specified in *NP-Alg*. However, since we have to "count" the elements of N, before presenting the *NP-Alg* query for the independent set problem, we show a method to determine whether two relations $N^{(1)}$ and $K^{(1)}$ have the same cardinality or not. Consider the following *NP-Alg* query:

$$Guess\ NK^{(2)};$$

$$FAIL = \left(\underset{\$1}{\pi}(NK) \mathbin{\Delta} N\right) \cup \left(\underset{\$2}{\pi}(NK) \mathbin{\Delta} K\right) \cup$$

$$\underset{\$1}{\pi}\left(NK \underset{\substack{\$1 \neq \$1 \\ \wedge \\ \$2 = \$2}}{\bowtie} NK\right) \cup \underset{\$1}{\pi}\left(NK \underset{\substack{\$1 = \$1 \\ \wedge \\ \$2 \neq \$2}}{\bowtie} NK\right).$$

The idea is to guess a binary relation NK which is a bijection between N and K. The first (resp. second) subexpression discards all candidates such that the first (resp. second) column is not the same as N (resp. K). The two joins ($\bowtie$) make sure that exactly one N value is paired to exactly one K value (and vice versa). As a consequence, $FAIL \diamond \emptyset$ iff N and K have the same cardinality. Obviously, deleting the first (resp. second) join, $FAIL \diamond \emptyset$ iff $|N| \geq |K|$ (resp. $|N| \leq |K|$).

Given the reusability of the previous expression, we define the metaexpressions $failSameSize^{(1)}(N, K)$, $failGeqSize^{(1)}(N, K)$, $failLeqSize^{(1)}(N, K)$ as shortcuts for the respective definitions. So, an *NP-Alg* query that specifies the independent set problem is the following:

$$Guess\ N^{(1)};$$

$$FAIL = failGeqSize^{(1)}(N, K) \cup \underset{\$1}{\pi}\left[(N \times N) \underset{\substack{\$1 = EDGES.from \\ \wedge \\ \$2 = EDGES.to}}{\bowtie} EDGES\right].$$

The former subexpression of $FAIL$ specifies the constraint $|N| \geq k$ (to enhance readability, the guessing of the NK relation, used only by the metaexpression, is omitted). The latter one returns an empty relation iff no pair of nodes in N is linked by an edge. An extension of N is an independent set (with size at least k) of the input graph iff the corresponding $FAIL$ relation is empty.

3.3   More Examples

We can specify in *NP-Alg* other famous problems over graphs like *dominating set*, *transitive closure* (TC), and *Hamiltonian path* (HP). We remind that TC, indeed a polynomial-time problem, is not expressible in RA (cf., e.g., [1]), because it intrinsically requires a form of recursion. In *NP-Alg* recursion can be simulated by means of guessing.

HP is the problem of finding a traversal of a graph which touches each node exactly once. The possibility to specify HP in *NP-Alg* has some consequences which deserve some comments. Consider a unary relation DOM, with $|DOM| = M \neq 0$ and the complete graph C defined by the relations $NODES = DOM$ and $EDGES = DOM \times DOM$. An HP H of C is a total ordering of the M

elements in DOM: in fact it is a *successor* relation. The transitive closure of H is the corresponding *less-than* relation.

As a consequence, considering a bijection between the M elements in DOM and the subset $[1, M]$ of the integers, we actually have the possibility to "count" between 1 and M. Furthermore, the Hamiltonian paths of C correspond to the *permutations* of $[1, M]$. Once the elements in DOM have been ordered (so we can consider them as integers), we can introduce arithmetic operations.

Permutations are very useful for the specification of several problems. As an example, in the *n-queens* problem (in which the goal is to place n non-attacking queens on an $n \times n$ chessboard) a candidate solution is a permutation of order n, representing the assignment of a pair ⟨row, column⟩ to each queen. Interestingly, to check the attacks of queens on diagonals, in *NP-Alg* we can guess a relation encoding the subtraction of elements in DOM.

Finally, in the full paper we show the specification of other problems not involving graphs, such as *satisfiability of a propositional formula* and *evenness of the cardinality of a relation*.

3.4   Useful Syntactic Sugar

Previous examples show that guessing relations as subsets of DOM^k (for integer k) is enough to express many NP-complete problems. Forthcoming Theorem 3 shows that this is indeed enough to express all problems in NP.

Nevertheless, metaexpressions such as $failPartition$ can make queries more readable. In this section we briefly summarize the main metaexpressions we designed.

- $empty^{(1)}(R) = DOM - \pi_{\$1}(DOM \times R^{(k)})$, returns an empty relation if R is a non-empty one (and vice versa).
- $complement^{(k)}(R^{(k)})$ returns the active complement (wrt DOM^k) of R.
- $failPartition^{(1)}(N^{(k)}, P_1^{(k)}, \ldots, P_n^{(k)})$ (cf. Subsection 3.1) returns an empty relation iff $\{P_1^{(k)}, \ldots, P_n^{(k)}\}$ is a partition of N.
- $failSuccessor^{(1)}(SUCC^{(2k)}, N^{(k)})$ returns an empty relation iff $SUCC$ encodes a correct successor relation on elements in N, i.e., a 1-1 correspondence with the interval $[1, |N|]$.
- $failSameSize^{(1)}(N, K)$, $failGeqSize^{(1)}(N, K)$, $failLeqSize^{(1)}(N, K)$ (cf. Subsection 3.2) return an empty relation iff $|N|$ is, respectively, $=$, $\geq$, $\leq$ $|K|$. We remark that a relation NK satisfying $failGeqSize^{(1)}(N, K)$ is actually a *function* with domain N and range K. Since elements in K can be ordered (cf. Subsection 3.3), NK is also an *integer function* from elements of N to the interval $[1, |K|]$. Integer functions are very useful for the specification of *resource allocation* problems, such as *integer knapsack* (see also examples in Section 5.2). In the full paper we show that we can guess general functions (total, partial, injective, surjective) from a given domain to a given range.

– $failPermutation^{(1)}(PERM^{(2k)}, N^{(k)})$ returns an empty relation iff $PERM$ is a permutation of the elements in N. The ordering sequence is given by the first k columns of $PERM$.

4   Computational Aspects of NP-Alg

In this section we focus on the main computational aspects of *NP-Alg*: data and combined complexity, expressive power, and polynomial fragments.

4.1   Data and Combined Complexity

The *data complexity*, i.e., the complexity of query answering assuming the database as input and a fixed query (cf. [1]), is one of the most important computational aspects of a language, since queries are typically small compared to the database.

Since we can express NP-complete problems in *NP-Alg* (cf. Section 3), the problem of deciding whether $FAIL \diamond \emptyset$ is NP-hard. Since the upper bound is clearly NP, we have the first computational result on *NP-Alg*.

Theorem 1. *The data complexity of deciding whether $FAIL \diamond \emptyset$ for an NP-Alg query, where the input is the database, is NP-complete.*

Another interesting measure is *combined complexity*, where both the database and the query are part of the input. It is possible to show that, in this case, to determine whether $FAIL \diamond \emptyset$ is hard for the complexity class NE defined as $\bigcup_{c>1} NTIME\,(2^{cn})$ (cf. [13]), i.e., the class of all problems solvable by a non-deterministic machine in time bounded by 2^{cn}, where n is the size of the input and c is an arbitrary constant.

Theorem 2. *The combined complexity of deciding whether $FAIL \diamond \emptyset$ for an NP-Alg query, where the input is both the database and the query, is NE-hard.*

In the full paper the theorem is proved by reducing the NE-complete problem of the *succinct 3-colorability* of a graph [12] into the problem of deciding if an *NP-Alg* query has a solution.

4.2   Expressive Power

The *expressiveness* of a query language characterizes the problems that can be expressed as fixed, i.e., instance independent, queries. In this section we prove the main result about the expressiveness of *NP-Alg*, by showing that it captures exactly NP, or equivalently (cf. [6]) queries in the existential fragment of second-order logic (SO$_\exists$).

Of course it is very important to be assured that we can express *all* problems in the complexity class NP. In fact, Theorem 1 says that we are able to express *some* problems in NP. We remind that the expressive power of a language is in general less than or equal to its data complexity. In other words, there exist languages whose data complexity is hard for class C in which not every query in C can be expressed; several such languages are known, cf., e.g., [1].

In the following, σ denotes a fixed set of relational symbols not including equality "$=$", and $\mathbf{S}$ denotes a list of variables ranging over relational symbols distinct from those in σ. By Fagin's theorem [6] any NP-recognizable collection $\mathbf{D}$ of finite databases over σ is defined by a second-order existential formula. In particular, we deal with second-order formulae of the following kind:

$$(\exists \mathbf{S})(\forall \mathbf{X})(\exists \mathbf{Y}) \; \varphi(\mathbf{X}, \mathbf{Y}), \tag{2}$$

where φ is a first-order formula containing variables among $\mathbf{X}, \mathbf{Y}$ and involving relational symbols in $\sigma \cup \mathbf{S} \cup \{=\}$. The reason why we can restrict our attention to second-order formulae in the above normal form is explained in [12]. As usual, "$=$" is always interpreted as "identity".

We illustrate a method that transforms a formula of the kind (2) into an NP-Alg expression ψ. The transformation works in two steps:

1. the first-order formula $\varphi(\mathbf{X}, \mathbf{Y})$ obtained by eliminating all quantifiers from (2) is translated into an expression PHI of plain RA;
2. the expression ψ is defined as:

$$Guess \; Q_1^{(a_1)}, \ldots, Q_n^{(a_n)}; \; FAIL = DOM^{|\mathbf{X}|} - \pi_{\mathbf{X}}(PHI), \tag{3}$$

where $a_1, \ldots, a_n$ are the arities of the n predicates in $\mathbf{S}$, and $|\mathbf{X}|$ is the number of variables occurring in $\mathbf{X}$.

The first step is rather standard, and is briefly sketched here just for future reference. A relation R (with the same arity) is introduced for each predicate symbol $r \in \sigma \cup \mathbf{S}$. An atomic formula of first-order logic is translated as the corresponding relation, possibly prefixed by a selection that accounts for constant symbols and/or repeated variables, and by a renaming of attributes mapping the arguments. Selection can be used also for dealing with atoms involving equality. Inductively, the relation corresponding to a complex first-order formula is built as follows:

- $f \wedge g$ translates into $F \bowtie G$, where F and G are the translations of f and g, respectively;
- $f \vee g$ translates into $F' \cup G'$, where F' and G' are derived from the translations F and G to account for the (possibly) different schemata of f and g;
- $\neg f(\mathbf{Z})$ translates into $\underset{\substack{\$1 \to F.\$1 \\ \vdots \\ \$|\mathbf{Z}| \to F.\$|\mathbf{Z}|}}{\rho} (DOM^{|\mathbf{Z}|} - F)$.

Relations obtained through such a translation will be called q-free.

The following theorem claims that the above translation is correct.

Theorem 3. *For any NP-recognizable collection $\mathbf{D}$ of finite databases over σ –characterized by a formula of the kind (2)– a database D is in $\mathbf{D}$, i.e., $D \models (\exists \mathbf{S})(\forall \mathbf{X})(\exists \mathbf{Y}) \; \varphi(\mathbf{X}, \mathbf{Y})$, if and only if $FAIL \diamond \emptyset$, when ψ (cf. formula (3)) is evaluated on D.*

4.3   Polynomial Fragments

Polynomial fragments of second-order logic have been presented in, e.g., [9]. In this section we use some of those results to show that it is possible to isolate polynomial fragments of *NP-Alg*.

Theorem 4. *Let s be a positive integer, PHI a q-free expression of RA on a relational vocabulary $edb(D) \cup \{Q^{(s)}\}$, and Y_1, Y_2 the names of two attributes of PHI. An NP-Alg query of the form:*

$$Guess\ Q^{(s)}; \quad FAIL\ = (DOM \times DOM) - \pi_{Y_1,Y_2}\ (PHI).$$

can be evaluated in polynomial time.

Some interesting queries obeying the above restriction can indeed be formulated. As an example, *2-colorability* can be specified as follows (when $k = 2$, k-colorability, cf. Section 3.1, becomes polynomial):

Guess $C^{(1)}$;

$$FAIL = DOM \times DOM - \begin{bmatrix} complement(EDGES) \cup \\ C \times complement(C)\ \cup\ complement(C) \times C \end{bmatrix}.$$

C and its complement denote the 2-partition. The constraint states that each edge must go from one subset to the other one.

Another polynomial problem of this class is *2-partition into cliques* (cf., e.g., [8]), which amounts to decide whether there is a 2-partition of the nodes of a graph such that the two induced subgraphs are complete. An *NP-Alg* expression which specifies the problem is:

Guess $P^{(1)}$;

$FAIL = DOM \times DOM-$

$\qquad [complement(P) \times P\ \cup\ P \times complement(P)\ \cup\ EDGES].$

A second polynomial class (in which, e.g., the *disconnectivity* problem, i.e., to check whether a graph is not connected, can be expressed) is defined by the following theorem.

Theorem 5. *Let $PHI(X_1,\ldots,X_k,Y_1,Y_2)$ $(k > 0)$ be a q-free expression of RA on a relational vocabulary $edb(D) \cup \{Q^{(1)}\}$. An NP-Alg query of the form:*

Guess $Q^{(1)}$;

$$X(X_1,\ldots,X_k) = PHI(X_1,\ldots,X_k,Y_1,Y_2) \ / \ \rho_{\substack{\$1 \to Y_1 \\ \$2 \to Y_2}} (DOM \times DOM);$$

$FAIL\ = empty(X).$

can be evaluated in polynomial time.

The classes identified by the above theorems correspond respectively to the Eaa and E_1e^*aa classes of [9], which are proved to be polynomial by a mapping into instances of 2SAT.

5   The NP-SQL Language

In this section we describe the NP-SQL language, a non-deterministic extension of SQL having the same expressive power as *NP-Alg*, and present some specifications written in this language.

5.1   Syntax of NP-SQL

NP-SQL is a strict superset of SQL. The problem instance is described as a set of ordinary tables, using the data definition language of SQL. The novel construct CREATE PROBLEM is used to specify a problem. It has two parts, which correspond to the two parts of Definition 1:

1. definition of the guessed tables, by means of the new keyword GUESS;
2. specification of the constraints that must be satisfied by guessed tables, by means of the standard SQL keyword CHECK.

Furthermore, the user can specify the desired output by means of the new keyword RETURN. In particular, the output is computed when an extension of the guessed tables satisfying all constraints is found. Of course, it is possible to specify many guessed tables, constraints and return tables. The syntax is as follows (terminals are either capitalized or quoted):

```
CREATE PROBLEM problem_name '('
        (GUESS TABLE table_name ['('('aliases')'] AS guessed_table_spec)+
        (CHECK '(' condition ')')+
        (RETURN TABLE return_table_name AS query)*
')'
```

The guessed table table_name gets its schema from its definition guessed_table_spec. The latter expression is similar to a standard SELECT-FROM-WHERE SQL query, except for the FROM clause which can contain also expressions such as:

```
SUBSET OF SQL_from_clause |
[TOTAL | PARTIAL] FUNCTION_TO '(' (range_table | min '..' max) ')'
        AS field_name_list OF SQL_from_clause |
(PARTITION '(' n ')' | PERMUTATION) AS field_name OF SQL_from_clause
```

with SQL_from_clause being the content of an ordinary SQL FROM clause (e.g., a list of tables). The schema of such expressions consists in the attributes of SQL_from_clause, plus the extra field_name (or field_name_list), if present.

In the FROM clause the user is supposed to specify the shape of the search space, either as a plain subset (like in *NP-Alg*), or as a mapping (i.e., partition, permutation, or function) from the domain defined by SQL_from_clause. Mappings require the specification of the range and the name of the extra field(s) containing range values. As for PERMUTATION, the range is implicitly defined to be a subset of integers. As for FUNCTION_TO the range can be either an interval min..max of a SQL enumerable type, (e.g., integers) or the set of values of the primary key of a table denoted by `range_table`. The optional keyword `PARTIAL` means that the function can be defined over a subset of the domain (the default is `TOTAL`). We remind that using partitions, permutations or functions does not add any expressive power to the language (cf. Section 3.4.)

Finally, the `query` that defines a return table is an ordinary SQL query on the tables defining the problem instance plus the guessed ones, and it is evaluated for an extension of the guessed tables satisfying all constraints.

Once a problem has been specified, its solution can be obtained with an ordinary SQL query on the return tables:

```
SELECT field_name_list FROM problem_name.return_table_name WHERE cond
```

The table `ANSWER(n INTEGER)` is implicitly defined locally to the `CREATE PROBLEM` construct, and it is empty iff the problem has no solution.

5.2   Examples

In this section we exhibit the specification of some problems in NP-SQL. In particular, to highlight its similarity with *NP-Alg*, we show the specification of the graph coloring problem of Section 3.1. Afterwards, we exploit the full power of the language and show how some real-world problems can be easily specified.

k-Colorability. We assume an input database containing relations `NODES(n)`, `EDGES(f,t)` (encoding the graph), and `COLORS(id,name)` (listing the *k* colors).

```
CREATE PROBLEM Graph_Coloring (  // COLORING contains tuples of
                                 // the kind <NODES.n, COLORS.id>,
                                 // with COLORS.id arbitrarily chosen.
  GUESS TABLE COLORING AS
    SELECT n, color FROM TOTAL FUNCTION_TO(COLORS) AS color OF NODES
    CHECK ( NOT EXISTS (
      SELECT * FROM COLORING C1, COLORING C2, EDGES
      WHERE C1.n <> C2.n AND C1.c = C2.c
        AND C1.n = EDGES.f AND C2.n = EDGES.t ))
    RETURN TABLE SOLUTION AS SELECT COLORING.n, COLORS.name
      FROM COLORING, COLORS WHERE COLORING.color = COLORS.id
)
```

The `GUESS` part of the problem specification defines a new (binary) table `COLORING`, with fields `n` and `color`, as a total function from the set of `NODES` to the set of `COLORS`. The `CHECK` statement expresses the constraint an extension of `COLORING` table must satisfy to be a solution of the problem, i.e., not two distinct nodes linked by an edge are assigned the same color.

The `RETURN` statement defines the output of the problem by a query that is evaluated for an extension of the guessed table which satisfies every constraint. The user can ask for such a solution with the statement

```
SELECT * FROM Graph_Coloring.SOLUTION
```

As described in the previous subsection, if no coloring exists, the system table `Graph_Coloring.ANSWER` will contain no tuples. This can be easily checked by the user, in order to obtain only a significant `Graph_Coloring.SOLUTION` table.

Aircraft Landing. The *aircraft landing* problem [2] consists in scheduling landing times for aircraft. Upon entering within the radar range of the air traffic control (ATC) at an airport, a plane requires a *landing time* and a *runway* on which to land. The landing time must lie within a specified time window, bounded by an *earliest time* and a *latest time*, depending on the kind of the aircraft. Each plane has a most economical, preferred speed. A plane is said to be assigned its *target time*, if it is required to fly in to land at its preferred speed. If ATC requires the plane to either slow down or speed up, a cost incurs. The bigger the difference between the assigned landing time and the target landing time, the bigger the cost. Moreover, the amount of time between two landings must be greater than a specified minimum (the *separation time*) which depends on the planes involved. Separation times depend on the aircraft landing on the same or different runways (in the latter case they are smaller).

Our objective is to find a landing time for each planned aircraft, encoded in a guessed relation $LANDING$, satisfying all the previous constraints, and such that the total cost is less than or equal to a given threshold. The input database consists of the following relations:

- $AIRCRAFT(\underline{id}, target\_time, earliest\_time, latest\_time, bef\_cost, aft\_cost)$, listing aircraft planned to land, together with their target times and landing time windows; the cost associated with a delayed or advanced landing at time x is given by $bef\_cost \cdot Max[0, t - x] + aft\_cost \cdot Max[0, x - t]$, where t is the aircraft target time.
- $RUNWAY(\underline{id})$ listing all the runways of the airport.
- $SEPARATION(\underline{i, j}, interval, \underline{same\_runway})$ ($same\_runway$ is a boolean field specifying whether aircraft i and j land on the same runway or not). A tuple $\langle i, j, int, s \rangle$ means that if aircraft j lands after aircraft i, then landing times must be separated by int. There are two such values, for $same\_runway = 0$ and 1, respectively. The relation contains a tuple for all combinations of i, j, and $same\_runway$.
- $MAXCOST(c)$, containing just one tuple, the total cost threshold.

In the following specification, the search space is a total function which assigns an aircraft to a landing time (minutes after midnight) and a runway.

```
CREATE PROBLEM Aircraft_Landing (
  GUESS TABLE LANDING(aircraft, runway, time) AS
    SELECT a1.id, runway, time
    FROM TOTAL FUNCTION_TO(RUNWAY) AS runway OF AIRCRAFT a1,
         TOTAL FUNCTION_TO(0..24*60-1) AS time OF AIRCRAFT a2
    WHERE a1.id = a2.id
```

```
  // Time window constraints
  CHECK ( NOT EXISTS (
    SELECT * FROM LANDING l, AIRCRAFT a WHERE l.aircraft = a.id
      AND ( l.time > a.latest_time OR l.time < a.earliest_time )
  ))
  // Separation constraints
  CHECK ( NOT EXISTS (
    SELECT * FROM LANDING l1, LANDING l2, SEPARATION sep
    WHERE l1.aircraft <> l2.aircraft AND ((
      l1.time <= l2.time AND sep.i = l1.aircraft AND
      sep.j = l2.aircraft AND (l2.time - l1.time) < sep.interval)
    OR (l1.time > l2.time AND sep.i = l2.aircraft AND
      sep.j = l1.aircraft AND (l1.time - l2.time) < sep.interval))
      AND (( l1.runway = l2.runway AND sep.same_runway = 1 )
        OR ( l1.runway <> l2.runway AND sep.same_runway = 0 )
  )))
  // Cost constraint
  CHECK ( NOT EXISTS (
    SELECT * FROM MAXCOST WHERE MAXCOST.c < (
      SELECT SUM(cost) FROM (
        SELECT a.id, (a.bef_cost * (a.target_time - l.time)) AS cost
        FROM AIRCRAFT a, LANDING l
          WHERE a.id = l.aircraft AND l.time <= a.target
        UNION // advanced plus delayed aircraft
        SELECT a.id, (a.aft_cost * (l.time - a.target_time)) AS cost
        FROM AIRCRAFT a, LANDING l
          WHERE a.id = l.aircraft AND l.time > a.target
      ) AIRCRAFT_COST // Contains tuples <aircraft, cost>
  )))
  RETURN TABLE SOLUTION AS SELECT * FROM LANDING
)
```

5.3 NP-SQL SIMULATOR

NP-SQL SIMULATOR is an application written in Java, which works as an interface
to a traditional R-DBMS. It simulates the behavior of an NP-SQL server by
reading an input text file containing a problem specification (in the NP-SQL
language), and looking for a solution.

CREATE PROBLEM constructs are parsed, creating the new tables (corresponding to the guessed ones) and an internal representation of the search space;
ordinary SQL statements, instead, are sent directly to the DBMS. The search
space is explored, looking for an element corresponding to a solution, by posing
appropriate queries to the R-DBMS (set so as to work in main memory). As soon
as a solution is found, the results of the query specified in the RETURN statements
are accessible to the user.

In the current implementation, used mainly to check correctness of specifications, a simple-minded enumeration algorithm is used to explore the search
space. In the future, we plan to perform the exploration by performing a transla-

tion of the problem specification to a third party constraint programming system or to an instance of the propositional satisfiability problem. The latter approach has indeed been proven to be promising in [4].

6   Conclusions, Related and Future Work

In this paper we have tackled the issue of strong integration between constraint programming and up-to-date technology for storing data. In particular we have proposed constraint languages which have the ability to interact with data repositories in a standard way. To this end, we have presented *NP-Alg*, an extension of relational algebra which is specially suited for combinatorial problems. The main feature of *NP-Alg* is the possibility of specifying, via a form of non-determinism, a set of relations that can have an arbitrary extension. This allows the specification of a search space suitable for the solution of combinatorial problems, with ordinary RA expressions defining constraints. Although *NP-Alg* provides just a very simple guessing operator, many useful search spaces, e.g., permutations and functions, can be defined as syntactic sugar.

Several computational properties of *NP-Alg* have been shown, including data and combined complexity, and expressive power. Notably, the language is shown to capture exactly all the problems in the complexity class NP, which includes many combinatorial problems of industrial relevance. In the same way, we have proposed NP-SQL, a non-deterministic extension of SQL with the same expressive power of *NP-Alg*. The effectiveness of *NP-Alg* and NP-SQL both as complex query and constraint modeling languages has been demonstrated by showing several queries which specify combinatorial problems.

As for future work, we plan to increase the number of polynomial cases of *NP-Alg*, in particular considering classical results on the complexity of second-order logic. Moreover, we plan to extend both languages to account for optimization problems, and to make a significantly more sophisticated implementation of NP-SQL SIMULATOR by using efficient constraint propagation techniques (e.g., by translation into propositional satisfiability [4]), and making it able to recognize the polynomial cases.

Several query languages capable of capturing the complexity class NP have been shown in the literature. As an example, in [12] an extension of datalog (the well-known recursive query language) allowing negation are proved to have such a property. A different extension of datalog, without negation but with a form of non-determinism, is proposed in [3]. On the other hand, *NP-Alg* captures NP without recursion. Actually, recursion can be simulated by non-determinism, and it is possible to write, e.g., the transitive closure query in *NP-Alg*.

Several languages for constraint programming are nowadays available. For some of them, e.g., ECL^iPS^e [5], a traditional programming language such as PROLOG is enhanced by means of specific constructs for specifying constraints, which are then solved by highly optimized algorithms. In other modeling languages such as OPL [15] and AMPL [7], the problem is specified by means of an ad-hoc syntax. Similarly to *NP-Alg* and NP-SQL they support a clear distinction between the data and the problem description level. OPL has also a constraint programming language which allows the user to express preferences on the search methods, which is missing in the current version of NP-SQL.

References

1. S. Abiteboul, R. Hull, and V. Vianu. *Foundations of Databases.* Addison Wesley Publ. Co., Reading, Massachussetts, 1995.
2. J. Beasley, M. Krishnamoorthy, Y. Sharaiha, and D. Abramson. Scheduling aircraft landings - the static case. *Transportation Science*, 34:180–197, 2000.
3. M. Cadoli and L. Palopoli. Circumscribing DATALOG: expressive power and complexity. *Theor. Comp. Sci.*, 193:215–244, 1998.
4. M. Cadoli and A. Schaerf. Compiling problem specifications into SAT. In *Proceedings of the European Symposium On Programming (ESOP 2001)*, volume 2028 of *LNAI*, pages 387–401. Springer-Verlag, 2001.
5. ECL^iPS^e Home page. www-icparc.doc.ic.ac.uk/eclipse/.
6. R. Fagin. Generalized First-Order Spectra and Polynomial-Time Recognizable Sets. In R. M. Karp, editor, *Complexity of Computation*, pages 43–74. AMS, 1974.
7. R. Fourer, D. M. Gay, and B. W. Kernigham. *AMPL: A Modeling Language for Mathematical Programming.* International Thomson Publishing, 1993.
8. M. R. Garey and D. S. Johnson. *Computers and Intractability: A Guide to the Theory of NP-Completeness.* W.H. Freeman and Company, San Francisco, Ca, 1979.
9. G. Gottlob, P. Kolatis, and T. Schwentick. Existential second-order logic over graphs: Charting the tractability frontier. In *Proc. of FOCS 2000*. IEEE CS Press, 2000.
10. ILOG optimization suite — white paper. Available at www.ilog.com, 1998.
11. ILOG DBLink 4.1 Tutorial. Available at www.ilog.com, 1999.
12. P. G. Kolaitis and C. H. Papadimitriou. Why not negation by fixpoint? *J. of Computer and System Sciences*, 43:125–144, 1991.
13. C. H. Papadimitriou. *Computational Complexity.* Addison Wesley, Reading, MA, 1994.
14. R. Ramakrishnan. *Database Management Systems.* McGraw-Hill, 1997.
15. P. Van Hentenryck. *The OPL Optimization Programming Language.* The MIT Press, 1999.

Computational Complexity
of Propositional Linear Temporal Logics Based
on Qualitative Spatial or Temporal Reasoning

Philippe Balbiani[1] and Jean-François Condotta[2]

[1] Institut de recherche en informatique de Toulouse
118 route de Narbonne, 31062 Toulouse CEDEX 4, France
[2] Laboratoire d'informatique pour la mécanique et les sciences de l'ingénieur
BP 133, 91403 Orsay CEDEX, France

Abstract. We consider the language obtained by mixing the model of
the regions and the propositional linear temporal logic. In particular,
we propose alternative languages where the model of the regions is replaced by different forms of qualitative spatial or temporal reasoning.
In these languages, qualitative formulas describe the movement and the
relative positions of spatial or temporal entities in some spatial or temporal universe. This paper addresses the issue of the formal proof that
for all forms of qualitative spatial and temporal reasoning such that consistent atomic constraint satisfaction problems are globally consistent,
determining of any given qualitative formula whether it is satisfiable or
not is PSPACE-complete.

1 Introduction

Many real-world problems involve qualitative reasoning about space or time.
Accordingly, the development of intelligent systems that relate to spatial or
temporal information is gaining in importance. In the majority of cases, these
intelligent systems provide specialized tools for knowledge representation and
reasoning about qualitative relations between spatial or temporal entities. To
illustrate the truth of this, one has only to mention the model of the regions designed by Randell, Cui and Cohn [15] and the model of the intervals elaborated
by Allen [1]. In actual fact, there are many more models based on alternative
qualitative relations between other spatial or temporal entities, see Balbiani and
Condotta [2], Balbiani, Condotta and Fariñas del Cerro [3], Balbiani and Osmani [4], Cristani [7], Gerevini and Renz [9], Isli and Cohn [10], Ligozat [11],
Ligozat [12], Moratz, Renz and Wolter [13] and Vilain and Kautz [19]. For instance, Ligozat [12] shows how to formulate our knowledge of the relative positions of objects represented by pairs of real numbers. For this purpose, he considers the 9 jointly exhaustive and pairwise distinct atomic relations obtained by
comparing the relative positions of points in the real plane: south-west, south,
south-east, west, east, north-west, north, north-east and equality. Take another
example: Vilain and Kautz [19] demonstrate how to express our knowledge of

A. Armando (Ed.): FroCoS 2002, LNAI 2309, pp. 162–176, 2002.

the relative moments of events represented by real numbers. In this respect, they consider the 3 jointly exhaustive and pairwise distinct atomic relations obtained by comparing the relative moments of points on the real line: before, after and equality. In these models, knowledge representation and reasoning is performed through networks of constraints between spatial or temporal entities and the main issue consists in deciding consistency of such networks. This brings several researchers to the following question: what is the computational complexity of determining of any given spatial or temporal network of constraints between spatial or temporal entities whether it is consistent or not ?

Numerous applications require support for knowledge representation and reasoning about spatial and temporal relationships between moving objects. We should consider the following example: breaking up the map into its component parts, a geographer sees 2-dimensional objects and has to reason about the issue of the links between portions of space that continuously evolve as time goes by. That is the reason why several researchers made a resolution to devote themselves to the integration of spatial and temporal concepts into a single hybrid formalism. Among the hybrid formalisms for reasoning about space and time considered in computer science, there is nothing to compare with the language introduced by Wolter and Zakharyaschev [20] and obtained by mixing the model of the regions and the propositional linear temporal logic. The propositional linear temporal logic is asserting itself as one of the better known model for reasoning about program properties within the framework of the research carried out into the subject of specification and verification of reactive systems. Its combination with the model of the regions gives rise to a language of very great expressivity. Since determining of any given spatial network of constraints between regions whether it is consistent or not is in NP, see Nebel [14] and Renz and Nebel [16], whereas determining of any given formula of propositional linear temporal logic whether it is satisfiable or not is in PSPACE, see Sistla and Clarke [18], there is reason to believe that determining of any given formula of this language whether it is satisfiable or not is in PSPACE.

The one drawback is that the EXPSPACE upper bound for the complexity of the satisfiability problem for the formulas of the language introduced by Wolter and Zakharyaschev [20] does not coincide with the PSPACE-hardness lower bound. This induces us to extend the results obtained by Wolter and Zakharyaschev [20] to different forms of qualitative spatial or temporal reasoning. We aim to propose alternative languages where the model of the regions is replaced by different forms of qualitative spatial or temporal reasoning such that consistent atomic constraint satisfaction problems are globally consistent. In these languages, qualitative formulas describe the movement and the relative positions of spatial or temporal entities in some spatial or temporal universe. The requirement that consistent atomic constraint satisfaction problems are globally consistent is a sufficient condition for the fulfilment of our objective: the formal proof that determining of any given qualitative formula whether it is satisfiable or not is PSPACE-complete. Numerous forms of qualitative spatial or temporal reasoning fit this requirement, one has only to mention the models introduced by Allen [1], Balbiani and Condotta [2], Balbiani, Condotta and Fariñas del Cerro [3], Cristani [7], Ligozat [11], Ligozat [12] and Vilain and Kautz [19], and so it is reasonable to assume it. The paper is organized as follows. Before we extend the results obtained by Wolter and Zakharyaschev [20] to different forms of qualitative spatial or temporal reasoning, basic concepts relating to constraint satisfaction problems are introduced in section 2. These are the notions of networks of qualitative spatial or temporal constraints as well as solutions, consistency, partial solutions and global consistency. Section 3 deals with the basic concepts regarding the syntax and the semantics of our hybrid formalisms for reasoning about space and time. These are the notions of qualitative formulas, qualitative models as well as satisfiability. The main topic of section 4 is the proof that the question of determining of any given qualitative formula whether it is satisfiable or not requires polynomial space. Section 5 presents the concept of state to prove in section 6 that the question of determining of any given qualitative formula whether it is satisfiable or not is decidable in polynomial space.

2   Constraint Satisfaction Problems

Networks of constraints between spatial or temporal entities have been shown to be useful in formulating our knowledge of the relative positions of the objects that occupy space or in formulating our knowledge of the relative moments of the events that fill time. Within the framework of the research carried out in the domain of spatial or temporal reasoning, the main issue consists in deciding consistency of such networks. For our purposes we may only consider atomic constraint satisfaction problems, i.e., structures of the form $(\mathcal{X}, \mathcal{R})$ where $\mathcal{X}$ is a finite set of variables and $\mathcal{R}$ is a function with domain $\mathcal{X} \times \mathcal{X}$ and range a finite set ATO of atomic relations. The finite set ATO constitutes a list of jointly exhaustive and pairwise distinct atomic relations between positions or moments in some spatial or temporal universe VAL.

Example 1. Within the context of qualitative spatial reasoning in terms of points, see Ligozat [12], ATO consists of 9 atomic relations, sw, s, se, w, e, nw, n, ne and $=$. In this model of reasoning, VAL is the set of all pairs of real numbers.

Example 2. Within the context of qualitative temporal reasoning in terms of points, see Vilain and Kautz [19], ATO consists of 3 atomic relations, $<$, $>$ and $=$. In this model of reasoning, VAL is the set of all real numbers.

A solution of the atomic constraint satisfaction problem $(\mathcal{X}, \mathcal{R})$ is a function $\imath$ with domain $\mathcal{X}$ and range VAL such that for all $X, Y \in \mathcal{X}$, $\imath(X)$ and $\imath(Y)$ satisfy the atomic relation $\mathcal{R}(X, Y)$ in VAL. We shall say that the network $(\mathcal{X}, \mathcal{R})$ is consistent iff it possesses a solution. Deciding consistency of networks of atomic constraints between spatial or temporal entities constitutes the source of several problems in computer science. The thing is that those who tackled these problems proposed numerous algorithms for reasoning about space and time. For the most part, the proof that these algorithms are sound and complete is based on the notion of global consistency. A partial solution of the network $(\mathcal{X}, \mathcal{R})$ with respect to a subset $\mathcal{X}'$ of $\mathcal{X}$ is a function $\imath$ with domain $\mathcal{X}'$ and range VAL such that for all $X, Y \in \mathcal{X}'$, $\imath(X)$ and $\imath(Y)$ satisfy the atomic relation $\mathcal{R}(X, Y)$ in VAL. The atomic constraint satisfaction problem $(\mathcal{X}, \mathcal{R})$ is globally consistent if any partial solution can be extended to a solution. In the majority of cases, including the models introduced by Allen [1], Balbiani and Condotta [2], Balbiani, Condotta and Fariñas del Cerro [3], Cristani [7], Ligozat [11], Ligozat [12] and Vilain and Kautz [19]:

- Consistent networks of atomic constraints are globally consistent.

However this rule allows for a few exceptions, like the models introduced by Balbiani and Osmani [4], Gerevini and Renz [9], Isli and Cohn [10], Moratz, Renz and Wolter [13] and Randell, Cui and Cohn [15]. Our aim is to propose alternative languages to the language developed by Wolter and Zakharyaschev [20] where the model of the regions is replaced by different forms of qualitative reasoning about space and time which satisfy the rule.

3   Syntax and Semantics

Adapted from Wolter and Zakharyaschev [20], we define the set of all qualitative formulas as follows:

$$f ::= P(\bigcirc^m x, \bigcirc^n y) \mid \neg f \mid (f \vee g) \mid (f \mathbf{U} g);$$

where P ranges over the set ATO, m, n range over the set $\mathbb{N}$ of all integers and x, y range over the set VAR. Our intended interpretation of $(f \mathbf{U} g)$ is that "f holds at all following time points up to a time at which g holds". The other standard connectives are defined by the usual abbreviations. In particular, $\mathbf{F} f$ is $(\top \mathbf{U} f)$ and $\mathbf{G} f$ is $\neg(\top \mathbf{U} \neg f)$. The informal meaning of $\mathbf{F} f$ is that "there is a time point after the reference point at which f holds" whereas the informal meaning of $\mathbf{G} f$ is "f holds at all time points after the reference point". We follow the standard rules for omission of the parentheses. Our intended interpretation of atomic formula $P(\bigcirc^m x, \bigcirc^n y)$ is that "atomic relation P holds between the value of entity x in m units of time and the value of entity y in n units of time".

Example 3. Within the context of qualitative spatial reasoning in terms of points, see Ligozat [12], describing the movement and the relative positions of points x, y which move in a plane, qualitative formulas $\mathbf{G}(s(x, \bigcirc x) \vee w(x, \bigcirc x))$, $\mathbf{G}(e(y, \bigcirc y) \vee n(y, \bigcirc y))$ and $\mathbf{F}(s(x, y) \vee w(x, y))$ mean that x will always move to the north or to the east, y will always move to the west or to the south and a moment of time will come when x is to the south of y or x is to the west of y.

Example 4. Within the context of qualitative temporal reasoning in terms of points, see Vilain and Kautz [19], describing the movement and the relative positions of points x, y which move in a straight line, qualitative formulas $\mathbf{G}(x < \bigcirc x)$, $\mathbf{G}(y > \bigcirc y)$ and $\mathbf{F}(x = y)$ mean that x will always move to its right, y will always move to its left and a moment of time will come when x and y are in the same place.

Let f be a qualitative formula. The set of all individual variables in f will be denoted $var(f)$. The set of all subformulas of f will be denoted $SF(f)$. Let us be clear that there is strictly less than $Card(SF(f))$ $\mathbf{U}$-formulas in $SF(f)$. We define the size $| f |$ of f as follows:

- $| P(\bigcirc^m x, \bigcirc^n y) | = \max\{m, n\}$;
- $| \neg f | = | f |$;
- $| f \vee g | = \max\{| f |, | g |\}$;
- $| f\mathbf{U}g | = \max\{| f |, | g |\}$.

The number of occurrences of symbols in f will be denoted $length(f)$. It is well worth noting that $Card(var(f)) < length(f)$, $Card(SF(f)) < length(f)$ and $| f | < length(f)$. The set of all atomic formulas which individual variables are in $var(f)$ and which sizes are less than or equal to $| f |$ will be denoted $AF(f)$. The proof of the following lemma is simple and we do not provide it here.

Lemma 1. *Let f be a qualitative formula. Then $Card(AF(f)) = Card(ATO) \times Card(var(f))^2 \times (| f | +1)^2$.*

A function ϵ with domain $VAR \times \mathbb{N}$ and range the set VAL will be defined to be a qualitative model. The set VAL is the spatial or temporal universe in which the spatial or temporal entities of our language move. We define the relation "qualitative formula f is true at integer i in qualitative model ϵ", denoted $\epsilon, i \models f$, as follows:

- $\epsilon, i \models P(\bigcirc^m x, \bigcirc^n y)$ iff $P(\epsilon(x, i + m), \epsilon(y, i + n))$;
- $\epsilon, i \models \neg f$ iff $\epsilon, i \not\models f$;
- $\epsilon, i \models f \vee g$ iff $\epsilon, i \models f$ or $\epsilon, i \models g$;
- $\epsilon, i \models f\mathbf{U}g$ iff there is an integer k such that $i \leq k$, $\epsilon, k \models g$ and for all integers j, if $i \leq j$ and $j < k$ then $\epsilon, j \models f$.

An alternative formulation is "qualitative model ϵ satisfies qualitative formula f at integer i".

Example 5. Within the context of qualitative spatial reasoning in terms of points, see Ligozat [12], qualitative model ϵ of figure 1 satisfies qualitative formula $((s(x, \bigcirc x) \vee w(x, \bigcirc x)) \wedge (e(y, \bigcirc y) \vee n(y, \bigcirc y)))\mathbf{U}(s(x, y) \vee w(x, y))$ at integer 0.

Example 6. Within the context of qualitative temporal reasoning in terms of points, see Vilain and Kautz [19], qualitative model ϵ of figure 2 satisfies qualitative formula $((x < \bigcirc x) \wedge (y\bigcirc y))\mathbf{U}(x = y)$ at integer 0.

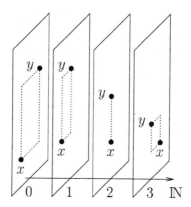

Fig. 1. A qualitative model based on qualitative spatial reasoning in terms of points.

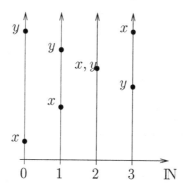

Fig. 2. A qualitative model based on qualitative temporal reasoning in terms of points.

Qualitative **U**-formula $f\mathbf{U}g$ will be defined to be fulfilled between integers i and j in qualitative model ϵ if $i \leq j$, $\epsilon, i \models f\mathbf{U}g$ and there is an integer k such that $i \leq k$, $k \leq j$ and $\epsilon, k \models g$. Qualitative formula f will be defined to be satisfiable if there is a qualitative model ϵ such that $\epsilon, 0 \models f$. The following equations specify which qualitative formulas are to count as formulas of, respectively, $\mathcal{L}_0(\mathbf{U})$ and $\mathcal{L}_1(\mathbf{U})$:

$$f ::= P(x, y) \mid \neg f \mid (f \vee g) \mid (f\mathbf{U}g);$$
$$f ::= P(\bigcirc^m x, \bigcirc^n y) \mid \neg f \mid (f \vee g) \mid (f\mathbf{U}g).$$

For the time being, let us mention outcomes of the results obtained by Wolter and Zakharyaschev [20] as regards the problem of determining of any given qualitative formula whether it is satisfiable or not: determining of any given formula of $\mathcal{L}_0(\mathbf{U})$ whether it is satisfiable or not is in $PSPACE$ whereas determining of any given formula of $\mathcal{L}_1(\mathbf{U})$ whether it is satisfiable or not is in $EXPSPACE$. Incidentally, we must not forget that the results obtained by Wolter and Zakharyaschev [20] regard the complexity of propositional linear temporal logics based on qualitative spatial reasoning in terms of regions. This brings us to the question of whether the results obtained by Wolter and Zakharyaschev [20] can be extended to different forms of qualitative spatial or temporal reasoning. What we have in mind is to prove the following important theorem for all forms of qualitative spatial and temporal reasoning in which consistent atomic constraint satisfaction problems are globally consistent.

Theorem 1. *Determining of any given qualitative formula whether it is satisfiable or not is PSPACE-complete.*

We outline how theorem 1 will be proved, but leave the details to the following sections. Firstly, we show how the question of determining of any given formula of propositional linear temporal logic whether it is satisfiable or not can be linearly reduced to the question of determining of any given formula of $\mathcal{L}_0(\mathbf{U})$ whether it is satisfiable or not. Secondly, we show how the question of determining of any given formula of $\mathcal{L}_1(\mathbf{U})$ whether it is satisfiable or not can be solved by means of a polynomial-space bounded nondeterministic algorithm.

4   Lower Bound

We first prove a simple theorem.

Theorem 2. *Determining of any given formula of $\mathcal{L}_0(\mathbf{U})$ whether it is satisfiable or not is PSPACE-hard.*

Proof. We define the set of all formulas of propositional linear temporal logic as follows:

$$f ::= p \mid \neg f \mid (f \vee g) \mid (f\mathbf{U}g);$$

where p ranges over a countable set of atomic formulas. Assuming that the set of all atomic formulas in propositional linear temporal logic is arranged in some determinate order $p_1, \ldots, p_N, \ldots$, assuming that the set of all individual variables in $\mathcal{L}_0(\mathbf{U})$ is arranged in some determinate order $x_1, y_1, \ldots, x_N, y_N, \ldots$, we define a linear function t that assigns to each formula f of propositional linear temporal logic the formula $t(f)$ of $\mathcal{L}_0(\mathbf{U})$ as follows:

- $t(p_N) = (x_N = y_N)$;
- $t(\neg f) = \neg t(f)$;
- $t(f \vee g) = t(f) \vee t(g)$;
- $t(f\mathbf{U}g) = t(f)\mathbf{U}t(g)$.

The reader may easily verify that a formula f of propositional linear temporal logic is satisfiable iff the formula $t(f)$ of $\mathcal{L}_0(\mathbf{U})$ is satisfiable. Seeing that determining of any given formula of propositional linear temporal logic whether it is satisfiable or not is *PSPACE*-hard, see Sistla and Clarke [18], we therefore conclude that determining of any given formula of $\mathcal{L}_0(\mathbf{U})$ whether it is satisfiable or not is *PSPACE*-hard.

We still have to prove that determining of any given formula of $\mathcal{L}_1(\mathbf{U})$ whether it is satisfiable or not is in *PSPACE*. In this respect, the concept of state will be of use to us.

5 f-States

Let ϵ be a qualitative model and i be an integer. Let $\widehat{\epsilon}_i$ be the function that assigns to each formula f of $\mathcal{L}_1(\mathbf{U})$ the set $\widehat{\epsilon}_i(f)$ of all atomic formulas true at i in ϵ which individual variables are in $var(f)$ and which sizes are less than or equal to $\mid f \mid$. Let $\widetilde{\epsilon}_i$ be the function that assigns to each formula f of $\mathcal{L}_1(\mathbf{U})$ the set $\widetilde{\epsilon}_i(f)$ of all subformulas of f true at i in ϵ. Let $\overline{\epsilon}_i$ be the function that assigns to each formula f of $\mathcal{L}_1(\mathbf{U})$ the structure $(\widehat{\epsilon}_{i-|f|}(f), \ldots, \widehat{\epsilon}_i(f), \widetilde{\epsilon}_i(f))$. In the case that $i <\mid f \mid$, we put:

$$\overline{\epsilon}_i(f) = (\underbrace{\emptyset, \ldots, \emptyset}_{|f|-i \text{ times}}, \widehat{\epsilon}_0(f), \ldots, \widehat{\epsilon}_i(f), \widetilde{\epsilon}_i(f)).$$

We first observe a simple lemma.

Lemma 2. *Let ϵ be a qualitative model, i be an integer and f be a formula of $\mathcal{L}_1(\mathbf{U})$. Assuming that the set of all variables in $var(f)$ is arranged in some determinate order $x_1, \ldots, x_N$, let n_1, n_2 be integers and l_1, l_2 be integers such that $n_1 \in \{1, \ldots, N\}$, $n_2 \in \{1, \ldots, N\}$, $l_1 \in \{i-\mid f \mid, \ldots, i\}$ and $l_2 \in \{i-\mid f \mid, \ldots, i\}$. Then there is exactly one atomic relation P such that for some integer k, $k \in \{i-\mid f \mid, \ldots, i\}$, $l_1 - k \in \{0, \ldots, \mid f \mid\}$, $l_2 - k \in \{0, \ldots, \mid f \mid\}$ and $P(\bigcirc^{l_1-k}x_{n_1}, \bigcirc^{l_2-k}x_{n_2}) \in \widehat{\epsilon}_k$.*

Proof. It is certain that there is an atomic relation P such that $P(\epsilon(x_{n_1}, l_1), \epsilon(x_{n_2}, l_2))$. Let k be $\min\{l_1, l_2\}$. The reader may easily verify that $k \in \{i-\mid f \mid, \ldots, i\}$, $l_1 - k \in \{0, \ldots, \mid f \mid\}$, $l_2 - k \in \{0, \ldots, \mid f \mid\}$ and $P(\bigcirc^{l_1-k}x_{n_1}, \bigcirc^{l_2-k}x_{n_2}) \in \widehat{\epsilon}_k$. If there is an atomic relation Q such that for some integer l, $l \in \{i-\mid f \mid, \ldots, i\}$, $l_1 - l \in \{0, \ldots, \mid f \mid\}$, $l_2 - l \in \{0, \ldots, \mid f \mid\}$ and $Q(\bigcirc^{l_1-l}x_{n_1}, \bigcirc^{l_2-l}x_{n_2}) \in \widehat{\epsilon}_l$ then $Q(\epsilon(x_{n_1}, l_1), \epsilon(x_{n_2}, l_2))$ and $P = Q$.

Let ω be the function that assigns to each formula f of $\mathcal{L}_1(\mathbf{U})$ the integer:

$$Card(ATO)^{Card(var(f))^2 \times (|f|+1)^3} \times 2^{Card(SF(f))}.$$

It is well worth noting that for all formulas f of $\mathcal{L}_1(\mathbf{U})$ and for all qualitative models ϵ, the range of the function that assigns to each integer i the structure $\overline{\epsilon}_i(f)$ contains strictly less than $\omega(f)$ elements. These elements are special cases of the concept of state. Let f be a formula of $\mathcal{L}_1(\mathbf{U})$. A structure:

$$(\widehat{S}_{-|f|}, \ldots, \widehat{S}_0, \widetilde{S}_0);$$

where $\widehat{S}_{-|f|}, \ldots, \widehat{S}_0$ are subsets of $AF(f)$ and $\widetilde{S}_0$ is a subset of $SF(f)$ will be defined to be a f-state. Assuming that the set of all variables in $var(f)$ is arranged in some determinate order $x_1, \ldots, x_N$, we will always suppose that for all integers n_1, n_2 and for all integers l_1, l_2, if $n_1 \in \{1, \ldots, N\}$, $n_2 \in \{1, \ldots, N\}$, $l_1 \in \{-\mid f \mid, \ldots, 0\}$ and $l_2 \in \{-\mid f \mid, \ldots, 0\}$ then, according to lemma 2, there is exactly one atomic relation P such that for some integer k, $k \in \{-\mid f \mid, \ldots, 0\}$, $l_1 - k \in \{0, \ldots, \mid f \mid\}$, $l_2 - k \in \{0, \ldots, \mid f \mid\}$ and $P(\bigcirc^{l_1-k}x_{n_1}, \bigcirc^{l_2-k}x_{n_2}) \in \widehat{S}_k$. The interesting result is that the structure $(\widehat{S}_{-|f|}, \ldots, \widehat{S}_0)$ can be linked with the atomic constraint satisfaction problem $(\mathcal{X}, \mathcal{R})$ defined as follows:

- Let $\mathcal{X}$ be $\{X_{1,-|f|}, \ldots, X_{1,0}, \ldots, X_{N,-|f|}, \ldots, X_{N,0}\}$;
- For all integers n_1, n_2 and for all integers l_1, l_2, if $n_1 \in \{1, \ldots, N\}$, $n_2 \in \{1, \ldots, N\}$, $l_1 \in \{-|f|, \ldots, 0\}$ and $l_2 \in \{-|f|, \ldots, 0\}$ then let $\mathcal{R}(X_{n_1,l_1}, X_{n_2,l_2})$ be the only atomic relation P such that for some integer k, $k \in \{-|f|, \ldots, 0\}$, $l_1 - k \in \{0, \ldots, |f|\}$, $l_2 - k \in \{0, \ldots, |f|\}$ and $P(\bigcirc^{l_1-k} x_{n_1}, \bigcirc^{l_2-k} x_{n_2}) \in \widehat{S}_k$.

f-state $(\widehat{S}_{-|f|}, \ldots, \widehat{S}_0, \widetilde{S}_0)$ will be defined to be consistent if the atomic constraint satisfaction problem $(\mathcal{X}, \mathcal{R})$ linked with the structure $(\widehat{S}_{-|f|}, \ldots, \widehat{S}_0)$ as above is consistent and:

- If $P(\bigcirc^m x, \bigcirc^n y) \in SF(f)$ then $P(\bigcirc^m x, \bigcirc^n y) \in \widetilde{S}_0$ iff $P(\bigcirc^m x, \bigcirc^n y) \in \widehat{S}_0$;
- If $\neg g \in SF(f)$ then $\neg g \in \widetilde{S}_0$ iff $g \notin \widetilde{S}_0$;
- If $g \vee h \in SF(f)$ then $g \vee h \in \widetilde{S}_0$ iff $g \in \widetilde{S}_0$ or $h \in \widetilde{S}_0$.

f-state $(\widehat{S}_{-|f|}, \ldots, \widehat{S}_0, \widetilde{S}_0)$ will be defined to be **U**-consistent with respect to f-state $(\widehat{T}_{-|f|}, \ldots, \widehat{T}_0, \widetilde{T}_0)$ if $\widehat{T}_{-|f|} = \widehat{S}_{-|f|+1}$, $\ldots$, $\widehat{T}_{-1} = \widehat{S}_0$ and:

- If $g \mathbf{U} h \in SF(f)$ then $g \mathbf{U} h \in \widetilde{S}_0$ iff $h \in \widetilde{S}_0$ or $g \in \widetilde{S}_0$ and $g \mathbf{U} h \in \widetilde{T}_0$.

6 Upper Bound

In accordance with the chain of reasoning put forward by Sistla and Clarke [18], one can establish the following remarkable lemmas for all forms of qualitative spatial and temporal reasoning such that consistent atomic constraint satisfaction problems are globally consistent.

Lemma 3. *Let ϵ be a qualitative model, i, j be integers and f be a formula of $\mathcal{L}_1(\mathbf{U})$ such that $i < j$ and $\overline{\epsilon}_i(f) = \overline{\epsilon}_j(f)$. Then there is a qualitative model ϵ' such that for all integers k, if $k < i$ then $\widehat{\epsilon'}_k(f) = \widehat{\epsilon}_k(f)$ and if $k \geq i$ then $\widehat{\epsilon'}_k(f) = \widehat{\epsilon}_{k+j-i}(f)$. Added to that, for all integers k, if $k < i$ then $\widetilde{\epsilon'}_k(f) = \widetilde{\epsilon}_k(f)$ and if $k \geq i$ then $\widetilde{\epsilon'}_k(f) = \widetilde{\epsilon}_{k+j-i}(f)$.*

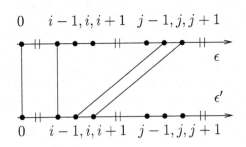

Fig. 3. The relationship between qualitative models ϵ and ϵ' in lemma 3.

Proof. If $\mid f \mid = 0$ then let ϵ' be a function with domain $VAR \times \mathbb{N}$ and range the set VAL defined as follows. For all integers k, if $k < i$ then for all individual variables x in $var(f)$, let $\epsilon'(x,k)$ be $\epsilon(x,k)$. For all integers k, if $k \geq i$ then for all individual variables x in $var(f)$, let $\epsilon'(x,k)$ be $\epsilon(x,k+j-i)$. It is beyond all doubt that ϵ' satisfies the required conditions. If $\mid f \mid \geq 1$ then the previous function ϵ' might not satisfy the required conditions. In that case we let ϵ' be a function with domain $VAR \times \mathbb{N}$ and range the set VAL defined as follows, see figure 3. For all integers k, if $k < i$ then for all individual variables x in $var(f)$, let $\epsilon'(x,k)$ be $\epsilon(x,k)$. For all integers k, if $k \geq i$ then assuming that the set of all individual variables in $var(f)$ is arranged in some determinate order x_1, ..., x_N, let $\epsilon'(x_1,k)$, ..., $\epsilon'(x_N,k)$ be the values defined as follows. Let us consider the atomic constraint satisfaction problem $(\mathcal{X}_k, \mathcal{R}_k)$ defined as follows:

- Let $\mathcal{X}_k$ be $\{X_{1,k-|f|}, \ldots, X_{1,k}, \ldots, X_{N,k-|f|}, \ldots, X_{N,k}\}$;
- For all integers n_1, n_2 and for all integers l_1, l_2, if $n_1 \in \{1,\ldots,N\}$, $n_2 \in \{1,\ldots,N\}$, $l_1 \in \{k- \mid f \mid, \ldots, k\}$ and $l_2 \in \{k- \mid f \mid, \ldots, k\}$ then let $\mathcal{R}_k(X_{n_1,l_1}, X_{n_2,l_2})$ be the only atomic relation P such that $P(\epsilon(x_{n_1}, l_1 + j - i), \epsilon(x_{n_2}, l_2 + j - i))$.

Obviously, the constraint satisfaction problem $(\mathcal{X}_k, \mathcal{R}_k)$ is consistent. Hence, it is globally consistent. All this goes to show that given the values $\epsilon'(x_1, k- \mid f \mid)$, ..., $\epsilon'(x_1, k-1)$, ..., $\epsilon'(x_N, k- \mid f \mid)$, ..., $\epsilon'(x_N, k-1)$ such that:

- For all integers n_1, n_2 and for all integers l_1, l_2, if $n_1 \in \{1,\ldots,N\}$, $n_2 \in \{1,\ldots,N\}$, $l_1 \in \{k- \mid f \mid, \ldots, k-1\}$ and $l_2 \in \{k- \mid f \mid, \ldots, k-1\}$ then $\epsilon'(x_{n_1}, l_1)$ and $\epsilon'(x_{n_2}, l_2)$ satisfy the constraint $\mathcal{R}_k(X_{n_1,l_1}, X_{n_2,l_2})$;

there are values $\epsilon'(x_1,k)$, ..., $\epsilon'(x_N,k)$ such that:

- For all integers n_1, n_2 and for all integers l_1, l_2, if $n_1 \in \{1,\ldots,N\}$, $n_2 \in \{1,\ldots,N\}$, $l_1 \in \{k- \mid f \mid, \ldots, k\}$ and $l_2 \in \{k- \mid f \mid, \ldots, k\}$ then $\epsilon'(x_{n_1}, l_1)$ and $\epsilon'(x_{n_2}, l_2)$ satisfy the constraint $\mathcal{R}_k(X_{n_1,l_1}, X_{n_2,l_2})$.

It is beyond all doubt that ϵ' satisfies the required conditions.

Lemma 4. *Let ϵ be a qualitative model, i, j be integers and f be a formula of $\mathcal{L}_1(\mathbf{U})$ such that $i < j$, $\overline{\epsilon}_i(f) = \overline{\epsilon}_j(f)$ and every $\mathbf{U}$-formula in $\widetilde{\epsilon}_i(f)$ is fulfilled between i and j in ϵ. Then there is a qualitative model ϵ' such that for all integers k, if $k < j$ then $\widehat{\epsilon'}_k(f) = \widehat{\epsilon}_k(f)$ and if $k \geq j$ then $\widehat{\epsilon'}_k(f) = \widehat{\epsilon'}_{k+i-j}(f)$. Added to that, for all integers k, if $k < j$ then $\widetilde{\epsilon'}_k(f) = \widetilde{\epsilon}_k(f)$ and if $k \geq j$ then $\widetilde{\epsilon'}_k(f) = \widetilde{\epsilon'}_{k+i-j}(f)$. ϵ' is said to be a periodic qualitative model with starting index i and starting period j.*

Proof. If $\mid f \mid = 0$ then let ϵ' be a function with domain $VAR \times \mathbb{N}$ and range the set VAL defined as follows. For all integers k, if $k < j$ then for all individual variables x in $var(f)$, let $\epsilon'(x,k)$ be $\epsilon(x,k)$. For all integers k, if $k \geq j$ then for all individual variables x in $var(f)$, let $\epsilon'(x,k)$ be $\epsilon'(x,k+i-j)$. It is beyond

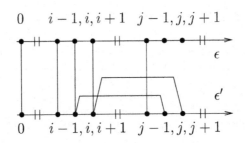

Fig. 4. The relationship between qualitative models ϵ and ϵ' in lemma 4.

all doubt that ϵ' satisfies the required conditions. If $\mid f \mid \geq 1$ then the previous function ϵ' might not satisfy the required conditions. In that case we let ϵ' be a function with domain $VAR \times \mathbb{N}$ and range the set VAL defined as follows, see figure 4. For all integers k, if $k < j$ then for all individual variables x in $var(f)$, let $\epsilon'(x, k)$ be $\epsilon(x, k)$. For all integers k, if $k \geq j$ then assuming that the set of all individual variables in $var(f)$ is arranged in some determinate order x_1, ..., x_N, let $\epsilon'(x_1, k)$, ..., $\epsilon'(x_N, k)$ be the values defined as follows. Let us consider the atomic constraint satisfaction problem $(\mathcal{X}_k, \mathcal{R}_k)$ defined as follows:

- Let $\mathcal{X}_k$ be $\{X_{1,k-|f|}, \ldots, X_{1,k}, \ldots, X_{N,k-|f|}, \ldots, X_{N,k}\}$;
- For all integers n_1, n_2 and for all integers l_1, l_2, if $n_1 \in \{1, \ldots, N\}$, $n_2 \in \{1, \ldots, N\}$, $l_1 \in \{k- \mid f \mid, \ldots, k\}$ and $l_2 \in \{k- \mid f \mid, \ldots, k\}$ then let $\mathcal{R}_k(X_{n_1, l_1}, X_{n_2, l_2})$ be the only atomic relation P such that $P(\epsilon'(x_{n_1}, l_1 + i - j), \epsilon'(x_{n_2}, l_2 + i - j))$.

Obviously, the constraint satisfaction problem $(\mathcal{X}_k, \mathcal{R}_k)$ is consistent. Hence, it is globally consistent. All this goes to show that given the values $\epsilon'(x_1, k- \mid f \mid)$, ..., $\epsilon'(x_1, k - 1)$, ..., $\epsilon'(x_N, k- \mid f \mid)$, ..., $\epsilon'(x_N, k - 1)$ such that:

- For all integers n_1, n_2 and for all integers l_1, l_2, if $n_1 \in \{1, \ldots, N\}$, $n_2 \in \{1, \ldots, N\}$, $l_1 \in \{k- \mid f \mid, \ldots, k - 1\}$ and $l_2 \in \{k- \mid f \mid, \ldots, k - 1\}$ then $\epsilon'(x_{n_1}, l_1)$ and $\epsilon'(x_{n_2}, l_2)$ satisfy the constraint $\mathcal{R}_k(X_{n_1, l_1}, X_{n_2, l_2})$;

there are values $\epsilon'(x_1, k)$, ..., $\epsilon'(x_N, k)$ such that:

- For all integers n_1, n_2 and for all integers l_1, l_2, if $n_1 \in \{1, \ldots, N\}$, $n_2 \in \{1, \ldots, N\}$, $l_1 \in \{k- \mid f \mid, \ldots, k\}$ and $l_2 \in \{k- \mid f \mid, \ldots, k\}$ then $\epsilon'(x_{n_1}, l_1)$ and $\epsilon'(x_{n_2}, l_2)$ satisfy the constraint $\mathcal{R}_k(X_{n_1, l_1}, X_{n_2, l_2})$.

It is beyond all doubt that ϵ' satisfies the required conditions.

The reasoning behind the proof of lemma 3 and the proof of lemma 4 deserves especial consideration, for the simple reason that it makes use of the fact that within the form of qualitative temporal reasoning in terms of intervals we have considered, consistent atomic constraint satisfaction problems are globally consistent. Combining lemma 3 with lemma 4, we obtain the following theorem.

Theorem 3. *Let f be a formula of $\mathcal{L}_1(\mathbf{U})$ such that f is satisfiable. Then there is a qualitative model ϵ and there are integers i, j such that $i < j$, ϵ is a periodic qualitative model with starting index i and starting period j, $i < \omega(f)$, $j - i < Card(SF(f)) \times \omega(f)$ and $\epsilon, 0 \models f$.*

Proof. Let $\epsilon^{(0)}$ be a qualitative model such that $\epsilon^{(0)}, 0 \models f$. The reader may easily verify that there are integers $i^{(0)}$, $j^{(0)}$ such that:

- $i^{(0)} < j^{(0)}$, $\overline{\epsilon^{(0)}}_{i^{(0)}}(f) = \overline{\epsilon^{(0)}}_{j^{(0)}}(f)$ and every $\mathbf{U}$-formula in $\widetilde{\epsilon^{(0)}}_{i^{(0)}}(f)$ is fulfilled between $i^{(0)}$ and $j^{(0)}$ in $\epsilon^{(0)}$.

If $i^{(0)} \geq \omega(f)$ then there are integers k, l such that $k < l$, $l \leq i^{(0)}$ and $\overline{\epsilon^{(0)}}_k(f) = \overline{\epsilon^{(0)}}_l(f)$. By applying lemma 3, we infer from this that there is a qualitative model $\epsilon^{(1)}$ such that $\epsilon^{(1)}, 0 \models f$ and there are integers $i^{(1)}$, $j^{(1)}$ such that:

- $i^{(1)} < j^{(1)}$, $\overline{\epsilon^{(1)}}_{i^{(1)}}(f) = \overline{\epsilon^{(1)}}_{j^{(1)}}(f)$, every $\mathbf{U}$-formula in $\widetilde{\epsilon^{(1)}}_{i^{(1)}}(f)$ is fulfilled between $i^{(1)}$ and $j^{(1)}$ in $\epsilon^{(1)}$ and $i^{(1)} < i^{(0)}$.

Applying this reduction as far as possible, we gather from this that there is a qualitative model $\epsilon^{(2)}$ such that $\epsilon^{(2)}, 0 \models f$ and there are integers $i^{(2)}$, $j^{(2)}$ such that:

- $i^{(2)} < j^{(2)}$, $\overline{\epsilon^{(2)}}_{i^{(2)}}(f) = \overline{\epsilon^{(2)}}_{j^{(2)}}(f)$, every $\mathbf{U}$-formula in $\widetilde{\epsilon^{(2)}}_{i^{(2)}}(f)$ is fulfilled between $i^{(2)}$ and $j^{(2)}$ in $\epsilon^{(2)}$ and $i^{(2)} < \omega(f)$.

If $j^{(2)} - i^{(2)} \geq Card(SF(f)) \times \omega(f)$ then there are integers k, l such that $i^{(2)} \leq k$, $k < l$, $l \leq j^{(2)}$, $\overline{\epsilon^{(2)}}_k(f) = \overline{\epsilon^{(2)}}_l(f)$ and for all $\mathbf{U}$-formulas $g\mathbf{U}h$ in $\widetilde{\epsilon^{(2)}}_{i^{(2)}}(f)$ and for all integers m, if $k < m$ and $m < l$ then $\epsilon^{(2)}, m \not\models h$. By applying lemma 3, we infer from this that there is a qualitative model $\epsilon^{(3)}$ such that $\epsilon^{(3)}, 0 \models f$ and there are integers $i^{(3)}$, $j^{(3)}$ such that:

- $i^{(3)} < j^{(3)}$, $\overline{\epsilon^{(3)}}_{i^{(3)}}(f) = \overline{\epsilon^{(3)}}_{j^{(3)}}(f)$, every $\mathbf{U}$-formula in $\widetilde{\epsilon^{(3)}}_{i^{(3)}}(f)$ is fulfilled between $i^{(3)}$ and $j^{(3)}$ in $\epsilon^{(3)}$, $i^{(3)} < \omega(f)$ and $j^{(3)} - i^{(3)} < j^{(2)} - i^{(2)}$.

Applying this reduction as much as possible, we gather from this that there is a qualitative model $\epsilon^{(4)}$ such that $\epsilon^{(4)}, 0 \models f$ and there are integers $i^{(4)}$, $j^{(4)}$ such that:

- $i^{(4)} < j^{(4)}$, $\overline{\epsilon^{(4)}}_{i^{(4)}}(f) = \overline{\epsilon^{(4)}}_{j^{(4)}}(f)$, every $\mathbf{U}$-formula in $\widetilde{\epsilon^{(4)}}_{i^{(4)}}(f)$ is fulfilled between $i^{(4)}$ and $j^{(4)}$ in $\epsilon^{(4)}$, $i^{(4)} < \omega(f)$ and $j^{(4)} - i^{(4)} < Card(SF(f)) \times \omega(f)$.

By applying lemma 4, we therefore conclude that there is a qualitative model ϵ and there are integers i, j such that $i < j$, ϵ is a periodic qualitative model with starting index i and starting period j, $i < \omega(f)$, $j - i < Card(SF(f)) \times \omega(f)$ and $\epsilon, 0 \models f$.

By theorem 3, we infer the following theorem.

Theorem 4. *Determining of any given formula of $\mathcal{L}_1(\mathbf{U})$ whether it is satisfiable or not is in $PSPACE$.*

Proof. To test a formula f of $\mathcal{L}_1(\mathbf{U})$ for satisfiability, we present the following nondeterministic algorithm: Guess integers i, j such that $i < j$, $i < \omega(f)$ and $j - i < Card(SF(f)) \times \omega(f)$;

   Guess a consistent f-state $(\widehat{S}_{-|f|}, \ldots, \widehat{S}_0, \widetilde{S}_0)$ such that $\widehat{S}_{-|f|} = \emptyset$, ..., $\widehat{S}_{-1} = \emptyset$ and $f \in \widetilde{S}_0$;

   $k := 0$;

   While $k < i$ do

      Guess a consistent f-state $(\widehat{T}_{-|f|}, \ldots, \widehat{T}_0, \widetilde{T}_0)$ such that $(\widehat{S}_{-|f|}, \ldots, \widehat{S}_0, \widetilde{S}_0)$ is U-consistent with respect to $(\widehat{T}_{-|f|}, \ldots, \widehat{T}_0, \widetilde{T}_0)$;

      $(\widehat{S}_{-|f|}, \ldots, \widehat{S}_0, \widetilde{S}_0) := (\widehat{T}_{-|f|}, \ldots, \widehat{T}_0, \widetilde{T}_0)$;

      $k := k + 1$;

   $(\widehat{U}_{-|f|}, \ldots, \widehat{U}_0, \widetilde{U}_0) := (\widehat{S}_{-|f|}, \ldots, \widehat{S}_0, \widetilde{S}_0)$;

   While $k < j$ do

      For all U-formulas $g\mathbf{U}h$ in $SF(f)$, if $g\mathbf{U}h \in \widetilde{U}_0$ and $h \in \widetilde{S}_0$ then mark $g\mathbf{U}h$ in $\widetilde{U}_0$;

      Guess a consistent f-state $(\widehat{T}_{-|f|}, \ldots, \widehat{T}_0, \widetilde{T}_0)$ such that $(\widehat{S}_{-|f|}, \ldots, \widehat{S}_0, \widetilde{S}_0)$ is U-consistent with respect to $(\widehat{T}_{-|f|}, \ldots, \widehat{T}_0, \widetilde{T}_0)$;

      $(\widehat{S}_{-|f|}, \ldots, \widehat{S}_0, \widetilde{S}_0) := (\widehat{T}_{-|f|}, \ldots, \widehat{T}_0, \widetilde{T}_0)$;

      $k := k + 1$;

   Check whether for all U-formulas $g\mathbf{U}h$ in $SF(f)$, if $g\mathbf{U}h \in \widetilde{U}_0$ then $g\mathbf{U}h$ is marked in $\widetilde{U}_0$;

   Check whether $(\widehat{U}_{-|f|}, \ldots, \widehat{U}_0, \widetilde{U}_0) := (\widehat{S}_{-|f|}, \ldots, \widehat{S}_0, \widetilde{S}_0)$. Remark that the previous nondeterministic algorithm works correctly and that it is polynomial-space bounded in $length(f)$. It follows that determining of any given formula of $\mathcal{L}_1(\mathbf{U})$ whether it is satisfiable or not is in $NPSPACE$. Seeing that $NPSPACE = PSPACE$, see Savitch [17], we therefore conclude that determining of any given formula of $\mathcal{L}_1(\mathbf{U})$ whether it is satisfiable or not is in $PSPACE$.

Referring to theorem 2 and theorem 4, we easily obtain a proof of theorem 1.

7   Conclusion

We have considered the language introduced by Wolter and Zakharyaschev [20] and obtained by mixing the model of the regions and the propositional linear temporal logic. In particular, we have proposed alternative languages where the model of the regions is replaced by different forms of qualitative spatial or temporal reasoning. In these languages, qualitative formulas describe the movement and the relative positions of spatial or temporal entities in some spatial or temporal universe. On the basis of the argument displayed by Sistla and Clarke [18], we have demonstrated that for all forms of qualitative spatial and temporal reasoning in which consistent atomic constraint satisfaction problems are globally consistent, determining of any given qualitative formula whether it is satisfiable or not is $PSPACE$-complete. Much remains to be done, given that there are many ways we could extend our results. An important development in the theory of propositional linear temporal logic is the introduction of the **S** operator, the informal meaning of (f**S**g) being that "f holds at all previous time points since a time at which g holds". Therefore, we plan to investigate the question whether our line of reasoning is still valid for a propositional linear temporal logic with both **U** and **S** operators. The reasoning behind the proof of lemma 3 and the proof of lemma 4 makes use of the fact that within the form of qualitative spatial or temporal reasoning we have considered, consistent atomic constraint satisfaction problems are globally consistent. Consequently, another promising direction of research is the issue whether our line of reasoning can be adapted to the forms of qualitative spatial or temporal reasoning which does not fit this requirement. In other respects, an important development in the applications of propositional linear temporal logic is the model-checking algorithm used to determine whether a given finite-state program meets a particular correctness specification. Thus, we intend to illustrate how the model-checking algorithm works within the context of our propositional linear temporal logic based on qualitative spatial or temporal reasoning.

Acknowledgment

Special acknowledgement is heartly granted to Nathalie Chetcuti who made several helpful comments for improving the readability of the paper.

References

1. Allen, J.: Maintaining knowledge about temporal intervals. Communications of the Association for Computing Machinery **26** (1983) 832–843.
2. Balbiani, P., Condotta, J.-F.: Spatial reasoning about points in a multidimensional setting. Applied Intelligence, to appear.
3. Balbiani, P., Condotta, J.-F., Fariñas del Cerro, L.: A model for reasoning about bidimensional temporal relations. In Cohn, A., Schubert, L., Shapiro, S. (Editors): Proceedings of the Sixth International Conference on Principles of Knowledge Representation and Reasoning. Morgan Kaufmann (1998) 124–130.
4. Balbiani, P., Osmani, O.: A model for reasoning about topologic relations between cyclic intervals. In Cohn, A., Giunchiglia, F., Selman, B. (Editors): Proceedings of the Seventh International Conference on Principles of Knowledge Representation and Reasoning. Morgan Kaufmann (2000) 378–385.
5. Bennett, B.: Determining consistency of topological relations. Constraints **3** (1998) 213–225.
6. Bennett, B., Cohn, A., Wolter, F., Zakharyaschev, M.: Multi-dimensional modal logic as a framework for spatio-temporal reasoning. Applied Intelligence, to appear.
7. Cristani, M.: The complexity of reasoning about spatial congruence. Journal of Artificial Intelligence Research **11** (1999) 361–390.
8. Freuder, E.: Synthesizing constraint expressions. Communications of the Association for Computing Machinery **21** (1978) 958–966.
9. Gerevini, A., Renz, J.: Combining topological and qualitative size constraints for spatial reasoning. In Maher, M., Puget, J.-F. (Editors): Proceedings of the Fourth International Conference on Principles and Practice of Constraint Programming. Springer-Verlag, Lecture Notes in Computer Science **1520** (1998) 220–234.

10. Isli, A., Cohn, A.: A new approach to cyclic ordering of 2D orientations using ternary relation algebras. Artificial Intelligence **122** (2000) 137–187.
11. Ligozat, G.: On generalized interval calculi. In Dean, T., McKeown, K. (Editors): Proceedings of the Ninth National Conference on Artificial Intelligence AAAI Press (1991) 234–240.
12. Ligozat, G.: Reasoning about cardinal directions. Journal of Visual Languages and Computing **9** (1998) 23–44.
13. Moratz, R., Renz, J., Wolter, D.: Qualitative spatial reasoning about line segments. In Horn, W. (Editor): Proceedings of the Fourteenth European Conference on Artificial Intelligence. Wiley (2000) 234–238.
14. Nebel, B.: Computational properties of qualitative spatial reasoning: first results. In Wachsmuth, I., Rollinger, C.-R., Brauer, W. (Editors): Proceedings of the Nineteenth German Conference on Artificial Intelligence. Springer-Verlag, Lecture Notes in Artificial Intelligence **981** (1995) 233–244.
15. Randell, D., Cui, Z., Cohn, A.: A spatial logic based on regions and connection. In Nebel, B., Rich, C., Swartout, W. (Editors): Proceedings of the Third International Conference on Principles of Knowledge Representation and Reasoning. Morgan Kaufman (1992) 165–176.
16. Renz, J., Nebel, B.: On the complexity of qualitative spatial reasoning: a maximal tractable fragment of the region connection calculus. Artificial Intelligence **108** (1999) 69–123.
17. Savitch, W.: Relationships between nondeterministic and deterministic tape complexities. Journal of Computer and System Sciences **4** (1970) 177–192.
18. Sistla, A., Clarke, E.: The complexity of propositional linear temporal logics. Journal of the Association for Computing Machinery **32** (1985) 733–749.
19. Vilain, M., Kautz, H.: Constraint propagation algorithms for temporal reasoning. In Kehler, T., Rosenschein, S., Filman, R., Patel-Schneider, P. (Editors): Proceedings of the Fifth National Conference on Artificial Intelligence. American Association for Artificial Intelligence (1986) 377–382.
20. Wolter, F., Zakharyaschev, M.: Spatio-temporal representation and reasoning based on RCC-8. In Cohn, A., Giunchiglia, F., Selman, B. (Editors): Proceedings of the Seventh International Conference on Principles of Knowledge Representation and Reasoning. Morgan Kaufmann (2000) 3–14.

Exploiting Constraints
for Domain Managing in CLP(FD)

Marco Gavanelli[1], Evelina Lamma[1], Paola Mello[2], and Michela Milano[2]

[1] Dip. di Ingegneria - University of Ferrara - Via Saragat, 1 - 44100 Ferrara, Italy
{mgavanelli, elamma}@ing.unife.it
[2] DEIS - University of Bologna - Viale Risorgimento, 2 - 40136 Bologna, Italy
{pmello, mmilano}@deis.unibo.it

Abstract. Constraint Logic Programming languages on Finite Domains $CLP(FD)$ provide a declarative framework for dealing with problems in Artificial Intelligence (AI). However, in many applications, domains are not known at the beginning of the computation and must be computed. The domain computation can be time-consuming, since elements can be retrieved through an expensive acquisition process from the outer world. In this paper, we introduce a CLP language that treats domains as first-class objects, and allows the definition of domains through constraints in a $CLP(FD)$ environment. We define operations and properties on variables and domains.

The language can be implemented on top of different CLP systems, exploiting thus different semantics for domains. We state the specifications that the employed system should provide, and we show that two different CLP systems (Conjunto and {log}) can be effectively used.

1 Introduction

The Constraint Satisfaction Problem (CSP) model is a powerful tool for dealing with many problems in AI. A CSP consists of a set of variables that range on a set of domains, and are subject to a set of constraints. Constraints provide a natural way for formalizing problems in a declarative fashion, and are embedded in Constraint Logic Programming (CLP) languages.

However, one drawback of the CSP model is that all the possible information about the problem is necessary at the beginning of the computation. In particular, domains have to be fully known: if some domain elements are not known, the solving process cannot start. A possible, but inefficient, approach suggests to build a CSP containing only the available information and try to solve it; if a solution cannot be found, more information must be retrieved, and a new CSP must be built and solved from scratch.

In many real-life cases, domains are not available, and have to be computed. For example, in a vision system, domain values are features that must be synthesized from the low-level representation of the image [7]. In a planner on a network system, domains are too big to be handled [2], so only the part that will be effectively used should be acquired. Moreover, domains could be defined with

A. Armando (Ed.): FroCoS 2002, LNAI 2309, pp. 177–192, 2002.
© Springer-Verlag Berlin Heidelberg 2002

a set of relations; for instance, suppose to have three variables A, B, C that range on domains, respectively S_A, S_B and S_C, that are subject to some constraints, e.g, $S_A \subseteq S_B$ and $S_C \cap S_A = \emptyset$. In a usual computation, sets must be computed in order to obtain a CSP; then the constraint solving process can start, in a strictly sequential computation.

This process is not acceptable in many problem instances. If only some of the elements will be used in CSP resolution, computing the whole domain can be a significant waste of time.

A first effective solution to this problem is the Interactive CSP model proposed in [6]. In this model, domains can be variables, values are acquired during the solution process only when necessary, and inserted into the variable domains. Moreover, constraints can be posted to an acquisition module in order to guide value extraction and drive to possibly consistent values. This model has been successfully applied to visual recognition tasks [7] and planning [2]. It could be used to acquire domain values from the web, as suggested in [14]. Experiments on randomly-generated problems [6] show that in many instances, ICSP solving algorithms can avoid domain element acquisition steps, providing good performance in problems where information is partially specified.

In this paper, we go a step further with respect to the ICSP. Not only variables can range on partially or completely unknown domains, but domains can be seen as first class objects, expressing constraints and operations on them. We propose a CLP language that

- allows the user to handle domains as first-class objects;
- contains the ICSP model as an instance, and uses ICSP solving algorithms as propagation engines, maintaining their efficiency level;
- can be implemented on top of different existing CLP systems, proposing different possible semantics for the domain concept.

We consider a CLP system with two sorts: the Finite Domain (FD) sort plus its powerset ($\mathcal{P}_{FD}$) sort. In this setting, constraints can be imposed both on FD variables, thus pruning the search space, and on $\mathcal{P}_{FD}$ variables representing domains, thus providing information useful to synthesize domain elements.

However, while most CLP systems agree on the concepts in the FD sort, many different viewpoints have been expressed on collections of values. Depending on the given problem, different semantics can be associated with the collection concept: it could be a stream [1], a set [10] or a list [5].

For the sake of simplicity, in this work we consider the set framework as the main example. Sets are a very natural and powerful language for expressing problems, but they are usually difficult to handle efficiently. Systems have to deal with a tradeoff between expressive power and efficiency. For this reason, most systems restrict the set general semantics, i.e., they limit the description capabilities, in order to achieve tolerable computation times. For example, Conjunto [12] is aimed at solving highly combinatorial problems; it exploits efficient propagation techniques similar to those used in CLP(FD). However, it can model only problems where all the elements are known: for each domain variable a ground upper bound and a lower bound are maintained.

In our setting, we have a set computation that provides domains for a CSP. Since CSP solving is better understood and more efficiently computed than computations involving sets, an efficient algorithm would try to limit the set resolution and perform the FD computation as soon as possible, before requesting information to the set component.

The rest of the paper is organized as follows. In section 2 we give the syntax of the proposed language. In section 3 we give some examples of problems that can be fruitfully addressed with the proposed language. In section 4 we show the operational semantics of the FD sort, the domain sort and we describe propagation of constraints that link the sorts. Related work is mentioned in Section 5. Conclusions and future work follow.

2   Syntax and Declarative Semantics

In this section, we describe a constraint language which allows the user to work with unbounded domains and also specify constraints on them. The language is a two sorted first-order language on objects (e.g., integers) and domains. We define operations and constraints on finite terms (they are the usual operations and constraints of CLP(FD) languages) and on domains. The declarative semantics of the language derives directly from the semantics of CLP; for the basics see [13]. In the following, we will comply to the conventions in [13].

Intuitively, we want to provide a model for binding a CLP(FD) system with a CLP($\mathcal{X}$) system with the intended semantics that variable objects in the $\mathcal{X}$ environment provide domains for the variables in the FD world. $\mathcal{X}$ can be any sort representing collection of objects (e.g., sets, arrays, lists, streams, ...) satisfying the properties defined in section 4.1.

Given two CLP languages $\mathcal{L}_{FD}$ and $\mathcal{L}_{\mathcal{P}_{FD}}$, we define the CLP language $\mathcal{L}$ as the union of the two languages, with a further constraint $::.$ as follows:

- the signature $\Sigma = \Sigma_{FD} \cup \Sigma_{\mathcal{P}_{FD}} \cup \{ ::. \}$;
- the intended interpretation $\mathcal{D}$ keeps the original mappings in the FD and $\mathcal{P}_{FD}$ sorts; i.e., $\mathcal{D}|_{\Sigma_{FD}} = \mathcal{D}_{FD}$ and $\mathcal{D}|_{\Sigma_{\mathcal{P}_{FD}}} = \mathcal{D}_{\mathcal{P}_{FD}}$.

We suppose that for finite domains, the usual binary constraints and operations are defined (i.e., the symbols $<, \leq, +, -, \times, \ldots$ belong to Σ_{FD} and are interpreted as usual). In the domain sort, we consider unary and binary constraints, such as $\subseteq, \supseteq$ and $=$. We basically consider the following elementary operations:

- $D_1 \oplus D_2$ is used to join domains coherently with the semantics of the $\mathcal{X}$ sort;
- $D_1 \ominus D_2$ performs difference;
- $D_1 \otimes D_2$ performs intersection;

where D_1 and D_2 stand for elements of the domain sort. Thus, if we use lists or streams, the $\oplus$ operation will be concatenation; for sets it will be set union.

In our framework, we can exploit different CLP languages for the domain sort, dealing with different domain formalizations, thus achieving different expressive power and computational efficiency. We could build a two-sorted CLP system on top of a CLP dealing with *lists* [5], *sets* [9,12] or *streams* [1]. The framework we are proposing is general enough to be implemented on top of a variety of CLP languages. Of course, the obtained system inherits the advantages and drawbacks of the exploited language.

In this way, we can decide which semantics we associate with domains. For example, sets are managed in a wide variety of ways, so, if we have a combinatorial problem and need to provide high efficiency levels, we can choose Conjunto [12], while if we need higher expressive power, we may prefer {log} [9].

Finally, we introduce the constraint $X ::. S$ linking the two sorts, whose signature is $\langle FD, \mathcal{P}_{FD} \rangle$. The declarative semantics of the constraint is

$$X ::. S \leftrightarrow X \in S$$

This constraint substitutes the usual $CLP(FD)$ unary constraint linking a domain variable X to its domain when domains could not be completely specified. From the $\mathcal{P}_{FD}$ viewpoint, it replaces the set membership operator, but it is more expressive, because it allows the association of the FD and the $\mathcal{P}_{FD}$ sorts; thus, in $X ::. D$, FD constraints can be imposed on X. Clearly, when all domain values in D are known, this constraint is equivalent to the standard one, $X :: [a_1, \ldots, a_n]$.

3   Examples

In this section, we show through simple examples how the $CLP(FD + \mathcal{P}_{FD})$ framework works, and how it can be useful in addressing real problems.

3.1   A Vision System

As an example, consider a vision system which has to locate an object in a given image. The system must know a model of the object, that can be naturally given by means of constraints [7]. For instance, we can say that we recognize a picture as a rectangle because it is composed of exactly four edges, which mutually touch with a ninety-degree angle, etc. The constraint model can be:

$touch(X_1, X_2), perpendicular(X_1, X_2), same\_length(X_1, X_3), parallel(X_1, X_3),$
$touch(X_2, X_3), perpendicular(X_2, X_3), same\_length(X_2, X_4), parallel(X_2, X_4),$
$touch(X_3, X_4), perpendicular(X_3, X_4), no\_touch(X_1, X_3),$
$touch(X_4, X_1), perpendicular(X_4, X_1), no\_touch(X_2, X_4).$

Of course, in order to perform recognition, a feature extraction system is required. The primitive features (e.g., the segments) of the picture compose the variable's domains, so they must be retrieved. Since the acquisition process is very time-consuming, the number of extracted primitives should be minimized. In our framework, this problem can be addressed by stating that the variables range on the set of segments in the image, which is unknown at the beginning of the computation:

$$X_1, X_2, X_3, X_4 ::. \ Segments$$

Then, each time a segment s_i is retrieved, it will be declared a member of the domains of the FD variables, by simply stating $s_i \in Segments$.

Apart from this toy example, the language can describe very complex situations. In real world recognition, various kinds of features are employed, so we could state that a group of variables range over the set of surface patches, another on the set of segments, another on the set of angles, simply by stating:

$$S_1, S_2, \ldots, S_i \ ::. \ Segments$$
$$P_1, P_2, \ldots, P_j \ ::. \ Surfaces$$
$$A_1, A_2, \ldots, A_k \ ::. \ Angles$$

Then, we can add constraints saying that each segment should be the edge of a surface, and that each angle should be the jointure of two segments. In this way, different acquisition modules can be exploited at the same time, providing in parallel different classes of information. It is worth noting that even in human vision there are different brain parts that carry on recognition of different classes of features (e.g., horizontal and vertical lines). Moreover, when seen from a certain viewpoint, a surface may appear as a segment; in this case we can state that some variable can range on the union of the two sets:

$$S_x ::. \ Segments \oplus Surfaces.$$

If we have two cameras, we can exploit stereo-vision and infer distance information about the various objects. Of course, the two cameras will see only some objects in common, so some variables could range only on the set of objects in the intersection:

$$S_{3D} ::. \ Camera_L \otimes Camera_R.$$

3.2   Map Coloring

In a map coloring problem we have to find a color for each country in a map, such that neighboring countries have different colors. Variables represent the countries, domains contain the available colors and constraints state that neighboring countries have different colors. For example:

$$A, B, C, D ::. \ \{red, green, blue\}$$
$$A \neq B, A \neq C, A \neq D, B \neq D, C \neq D$$

In this example the palette is known (i.e., the domain $\{red, green, blue\}$). Anyway, if we want to find the palette necessary for solving the problem, we have to find a *set* such that the CSP considering it as variable domain has a solution. In our language it can be stated this way:

$$A, B, C, D ::. \ Palette$$

with the same constraints. In this case, however, the domain *Palette* is undefined at the beginning of the computation, and its elements will be interactively acquired during propagation. At the end of the computation, the set variable *Palette* will contain in its known part the colors employed to solve the problem.

4   Operational Semantics

4.1   Operational Semantics: $\mathcal{P}_{FD}$ Sort

The operational semantics on the $\mathcal{P}_{FD}$ sort is defined by the employed subsystem. Different CLP($\mathcal{P}_{FD}$) (such as Conjunto [12] and {log} [9]) detect inconsistency and perform propagation in different ways. In this section, we define properties and behaviors that the domain sort should provide in order to be exploited in our framework. Then, we show that two utterly different systems (Conjunto and {log}) can give the requested functionalities.

Since the scope of our computation is finding solutions to a CSP, we need to distinguish domain elements that can be fruitfully exploited in a CSP computation from elements that are not yet known. For this reason, we request the employed system to let the user partition each domain D_i^d into a known and an unknown part (respectively, K_i^d and U_i^d)[1], with the intended meaning that the known part contains all the ground elements that are proven to semantically belong to the domain D_i^d, while the unknown part is the rest.

Property 1. Selection of known elements: for each domain D_i^d, at every step of the computation, the set of elements that are proven to belong to the set can be distinguished. We call this set the *known domain part* K_i^d.

- In {log}, domains are given by an arbitrary collection of Prolog terms; sets can be constructed using the set constructor {.|.} plus the empty set $\emptyset$. For example, $\{1, p(2), Z, q(Y, 3)|K\}$ is a valid set. {log} satisfies Property 1; the known part is the set of ground elements that are proven to belong to a set, in our example, $\{1, p(2)\}$.
- In Conjunto, a set S is represented by two ground sets: a Least Upper Bound (LUB) and a Greatest Lower Bound (GLB), such that $GLB_S \subseteq S \subseteq LUB_S$. Conjunto satisfies Property 1 and the known part coincides with the GLB.

Property 2. Partitioning domains into a known and an unknown part:[2] for each domain D_i^d it is always possible to define a set U_i^d such that $D_i^d = K_i^d \oplus U_i^d$ and $K_i^d \cap U_i^d = \emptyset$.

- In Conjunto, the unknown domain part is simply given by the set difference $U_i^d = D_i^d \setminus K_i^d = LUB \setminus GLB$.

---

[1] We use the superscript d to keep the same symbols in all the paper. The reason will be clear in section 4.2

[2] We require this property mainly for efficiency reasons in order to avoid repeated solutions. However, this is not a critical issue.

- In {log}, each time a new element is proven to belong to the known part, we need to impose a constraint stating that the element must not belong to the new unknown part. For example, if we have a domain containing $D_i = \{p(a, X), p(Y, b)\}$ (thus $K_i^d = \emptyset$), and we prove that $p(a, b) \in D_i^d$ we have $(K_i^d)' = \{p(a, b)\}$ and $(U_i^d)' = \{p(a, X), p(Y, b)\}$; we will have thus to impose an explicit constraint stating $p(a, b) \notin (U_i^d)'$.

Property 3. Promotion of elements: It is possible to define a predicate **promote** which can select an element from the unknown domain part and synthesize or acquire enough information to let it enter the known domain part.

The **promote** predicate can be implemented in a variety of ways, depending on the addressed problem and on the $\mathcal{P}_{FD}$ sort we are exploiting. Each computation providing ground domain elements can be exploited in this predicate; however, it is more convenient to associate a computation performing time-consuming operations, as the number of calls to this predicate will be minimized. In the *stream* sort, i.e., when domains are communication channels between subsystems, the promotion is a request for a domain element to the value provider. For instance, it can be used for human interaction [19] (the user declares the domain elements) or for acquisition of information from another component. When dealing with sets, the *labeling* phase is much more complex than in a CLP(FD) computation, as it usually opens many more branches. For this reason, the labeling phase on CLP($\mathcal{P}_{FD}$) can be postponed and performed after some CLP(FD) computation has provided constraints or heuristic to be exploited. In this case, the **promote** predicate can be implemented with a labeling predicate: tentative values are given to a domain element, and are provided for the known part.

Property 4. Test/Assertion of emptiness: the **promote** predicate has to provide a 'null value' information if there are no more elements in the unknown domain part to be promoted. In other words, **promote** must be a predicate reporting *false* if there are no more consistent values.

This property is very important to test if the unknown part is empty. This is an issue when linking the two sorts and it will be discussed in section 4.3.

4.2 Operational Semantics: Finite Domains

In a $\mathcal{P}_{FD}$ computation, finding sets is the goal of the computation and they need to be considered in a strictly monotonic way. Properties that are shown by a domain at a certain step of the computation will stand for all the future computations. In particular, if an element belongs to a domain, it cannot be deleted from it.

On the other hand, FD propagation algorithms possibly prune the variable domains, and this might enter in conflict with constraints imposed on set variables representing domains.

For example, consider the constraint $D_1 \supseteq \{1, 2\}$ stating that D_1 must contain at least two values. D_1 could be also the domain of an FD variable X_1, i.e.,

X_1 ::. D_1 and there could be a constraint stating that $X_1 \neq 2$. Usual CLP(FD) propagation of $X_1 \neq 2$ would remove value 2 from the domain of X_1; this elimination is inconsistent with $D_1 \supseteq \{1, 2\}$, so we would have a failure. This failure is not correct, in fact the set of constraints $(D_1 \supseteq \{1, 2\}) \wedge (X_1 :: D_1) \wedge (X_1 \neq 2)$ is satisfiable (declaratively, :: means set membership). On the FD side we wish to delete the inconsistent element from the domain, while on the $\mathcal{P}_{FD}$ side we should not delete elements, because the domain is also a logical variable.

To cope with set variables which are also FD domains (i.e., X_i ::. D_i), each domain D_i is represented de facto by two structures:

- the *definition domain*, D_i^d, which is a set variable accessible at language level, thus, it can be defined intensionally by constraints. At every step of the computation, its state can be modified exclusively by constraints imposed on it, never by constraints imposed on the X_i variable ranging on D_i;
- the *current domain*, D_i^c, which is hidden to the user and represents the standard variable domain of an FD computation, i.e., it is the set of (possibly consistent) values the variable X_i can assume during a Finite Domain computation. In our case, however, this set is not given extensionally; some elements will be known and others will be unknown. The values it contains are limited by constraints on the FD and on the $\mathcal{P}_{FD}$ sorts.

For each domain D_i, the basic property $D_i^c \subseteq D_i^d$ is imposed at each step of the computation. With this representation, inconsistent elements can be deleted from the current domain of a variable without affecting the definition domain. Moreover, D_i^c must synthesize all the knowledge provided by the definition domain; this issue will be addressed in Section 4.3.

We want to provide the FD solver (the most efficient of the two solvers) all the available information about domains in order to allow its exploitation. On the other hand, we cannot provide all the possible information at the beginning, because it would mean performing all the hard tasks (i.e., acquisitions and propagation on collections of values) before the easy tasks. In particular, we need to distinguish the ground elements from the rest of the domain. For this reason, the current domain D_i^c of a variable X_i is also partitioned into a known (K_i^c) and an unknown part (U_i^c).

From a declarative viewpoint, constraints limit the combination of assignments of elements taken both from the known and the unknown domain parts. Operationally, they can delete from the known part elements that cannot lead to a solution and they have to filter elements in the unknown part. We impose *auxiliary constraints* on the unknown domain part that provide information on the set of elements it should contain. An auxiliary constraint can only be imposed by another constraint (it is not accessible at the language level) and its purpose is twofold. First, it forbids inconsistent elements to enter the domain, i.e., whenever new information is available, it checks the synthesized elements, and eventually deletes them. Second, it can be exploited to provide information on consistent elements, and to help the synthesis of consistent elements[3]. For example, a constraint $c(X_i, X_j)$ deletes inconsistent elements from the known domain part and imposes the auxiliary constraints $c^{u_j}(X_i, U_j^c)$ and $c^{u_i}(U_i^c, X_j)$.

Definition 1. *A constraint* $c(X_i, X_j)$ *defines two auxiliary constraints* $c^{u_i}(U_i^c, X_j)$ *and* $c^{u_j}(X_i, U_j^c)$. $c^{u_i}(U_i^c, X_j)$ *is a subset of the cartesian product* $\mathcal{P}(D_i^c) \times D_j^c$ *representing couples of compatible assignments of the subdomain* $U_i^c \subseteq D_i^c$ *and the variable* $X_i \in D_i^c$. *It is satisfied by a couple of assignments* $U_i^c = S_i \subseteq D_i^c$, $X_j = v_j$ *iff* $\forall v_i \in S_i, (v_i, v_j) \in c(X_i, X_j)$. *Thus,*

$$c^{u_i}(U_i^c, X_j) = \{(S_i, v_j) \in P(D_i^c) \times D_j^c : \forall v_i \in S_i.(v_i, v_j) \in c(X_i, X_j)\}$$

For instance, a constraint $X > 5$, where $X ::. D$ and $D = \{1, 10|U\}$, produces the new domain $\{10|U'\}$ with the imposed constraint $\forall v \in U', v > 5$.

In order to perform a propagation employing all the available information on domains, we propose an extension for the partially known case, of the concept of consistency, called *known consistency*. In this paper, we provide only the extension of node-consistency and arc-consistency; the extension to higher degrees of consistency is straightforward.

Definition 2. *A unary constraint* c *is* known node-consistent (KNC) *iff* $\forall v_i \in K_i^c$, $v_i \in c(X_i)$ *and* $K_i^c \neq \emptyset$. *A binary constraint* c *is* known arc-consistent (KAC) *iff* $\forall v_i \in K_i^c$, $\exists v_j \in K_j^c$ *s.t.* $(v_i, v_j) \in c(X_i, X_j)$ *and viceversa.*

Definition 3. *A constraint network is* known arc-consistent *iff all unary constraints are KNC and all binary constraints are KAC.*

While the concept of known consistency is similar to the concept of consistency, the algorithms that achieve them are quite different. Algorithms that achieve arc-consistency typically remove inconsistent elements from the domain; in this way, the consistent problem is equivalent to the original one. In KAC, if we only delete elements that are not supported by known elements, the new problem is not necessarily equivalent to the original one. A KAC enforcing algorithm deletes values and promotes others, so, after propagation, the known part of the domains could be shrunk or enlarged.

If a network is known consistent, it shows some interesting properties:

Lemma 1. *If a network of constraints is KNC and KAC, then the problem with the same variables ranging only on the known parts of domains is arc-consistent.*

There are many algorithms that translate a problem, P, into an equivalent problem P', with different domains, such that the new problem P' is KAC. Each algorithm will be able to detect inconsistency if a domain becomes empty.

---

[3] This possibility can provide a big speedup, but it can be exploited only if the desired result does not contain definition domains. In fact, the synthesis of elements with auxiliary constraints has an implicit influence on the $\mathcal{P}_{FD}$ computation.

Proposition 1. *Every algorithm achieving KAC is able to detect inconsistency in the same instances as an algorithm achieving AC.*

Proof. An algorithm achieving known arc-consistency computes an arc-consistent subdomain (lemma 1). Since each domain must contain at least one (known) element to be known node-consistent, then the obtained known subdomain is a non empty subset of the maximal arc-consistent subdomain.

In other words, if an arc-consistent subdomain exists, then a maximal arc-consistent subdomain exists; so if KAC does not detect inconsistency, AC would not detect inconsistency either. Arc-consistency and known arc-consistency are different properties, but, as stated by Proposition 1, they give the same consistency checking ability. The advantage in using KAC is that the check for known arc-consistency can be performed lazily, without full knowledge of all the elements in every domain; a drawback is that it performs less pruning.

In order to achieve AC, an algorithm needs to remove elements that are proven to be inconsistent. To achieve KAC, an algorithm needs to delete and to *promote* elements, i.e., to move some elements from the unknown part to the known part. To obtain a problem equivalent to the original one, only elements that satisfy all the auxiliary constraints can be promoted. Elements can then be deleted if they are shown to be inconsistent. In figure 1, an algorithm for achieving KAC is shown, based on AC-3 [16]; other algorithms could be employed as well. Our KAC algorithm is like AC-3 except for the case no $v_j \in K_j^c$ exists such that $(v_i, v_j) \in c(X_i, X_j)$. In this case, another value for K_j^c is requested by calling promote. If no value exists that is consistent with the requirements of the domains on $\mathcal{P}_{FD}$ level, v_i is pruned on the grounds that U_j^c is empty and thus v_i is without support. Otherwise, the value is recorded as support for v_i, in fact, inconsistent acquisitions are prohibited by auxiliary constraints.

Implementation of the promote predicate in each setting is a crucial issue, because it highly influences efficiency. Heuristics can be exploited to select the most promising elements to be promoted; in particular, auxiliary constraints can be used to drive the provider component. For example, in a visual search problem [7], auxiliary constraints can be passed to an acquisition module that extracts visual features (such as segments or surfaces) from an image. Auxiliary constraints can provide information to the extraction agent and focalize its attention to the most significant image parts. As noted before, this is possible because in such an application, domains are not the main result we are expecting.

Operationally, achieving KAC has some similarities with achieving *Lazy Arc Consistency* (LAC) [18]. LAC is an algorithm that finds an arc-consistent subdomain (not necessarily a maximal one) and tries to avoid the check for consistency of all the elements in every domain. KAC looks for an arc-consistent subdomain as well, but it is aimed at avoiding unnecessary information retrieval, rather than unnecessary constraint checks.

```
procedure KAC
Q ← {c(Xᵢ, Xⱼ)};
while not empty(Q)
    select and delete one constraint c(Xₖ, Xₘ) from Q;
    if REVISE(c(Xₖ, Xₘ)) then
        Q ← Q ⋃{c(Xᵢ, Xₖ) such that i ≠ k ∧ i ≠ m}
    EndIf;
EndWhile;
End KAC


function REVISE(c(Xᵢ, Xⱼ)):bool;
MODIFIED ← false;
for each vᵢ ∈ Kᵢᶜ do
    if there is no vⱼ ∈ Kⱼᶜ such that (vᵢ, vⱼ) ∈ c(Xᵢ, Xⱼ) then
        MODIFIED ← true;
        if promote(v, Uⱼᶜ)
            then Uⱼᶜ = {v|(Uⱼᶜ)'}   % The value is inserted in the domain
                                      % and considered in the known part
            else delete vᵢ from Kᵢᶜ;
        EndIf;
    EndIf;
EndFor;
return MODIFIED;
End REVISE
```

Fig. 1. KAC propagation for FD constraints

4.3   Operational Semantics: Linking the Two Sorts

Elements in the $\mathcal{P}_{FD}$ sort are not unifiable with elements in the FD sort; the sorts are linked by the constraint ::. which binds an FD variable to its domain. Intuitively, this constraint ensures that only and all the elements that belong to the domain are considered as possible values for the FD variable. Operationally, for each domain, we have a constraint stating that all the elements in the current domain also belong to the definition domain (i.e., $D_i^c \subseteq D_i^d$); moreover, we must ensure that all the useful knowledge on the definition domain is propagated to the current domain. There are two basic kinds of information we need to propagate: the known elements and the (eventual) emptiness of the unknown part. All the elements in the known part of the definition domain have to be inserted in the known part of the current domain in order to be exploited for propagation. Knowledge on the unknown domain part is important because we can exploit it for deleting elements from the definition domains, thus pruning the search space. In fact, as shown in figure 1, a domain element $v \in K_i$ can be eliminated by a binary constraint $c(X_i, X_j)$ only if we know that it is not supported by any element in the domain of X_j; as any element could be supported by unknown elements, we cannot delete it.

Finally, of course the concept of *promotion* links the two sorts: the `promote` predicate will be implemented using $\mathcal{P}_{FD}$ structures, and will be made available at the FD side in order to achieve KAC.

```
:- X ::. Dx, Y ::. Dy, Z ::. Dz, intersection(Dx,Dy,Dz), Z > X.
List new values for X: {1|Dx'}.
The following constraint should guide acquisition: Z>1
List new values for Z: {2|Dz'}.
The following constraint should guide acquisition: Z>2
List new values for X: {}.

Dx={1, 2 | _}, Dy={2 | Dy'}, Dz={2 | Dz'}
X::{1 | _}, Y::{2 | _}, Z::{2 | _}

delayed goals:
intersection(Dx,Dy,Dz)
Z>X

yes.
```

Fig. 2. Example of computation

Numeric CSP. Let us see with a simple example, how a sample problem can be described and solved in $\text{CLP}(FD+\mathcal{P}_{FD})$. With the given language, we can state in a natural way the following problem:

$$:-X ::. D_X, Y ::. D_Y, Z ::. D_Z, intersection(D_X, D_Y, D_Z), Z > X.$$

defining three variables, X, Y and Z, with constraints on them and their domains. KAC propagation can start even with domains fully unknown, i.e., when D_X, D_Y and D_Z are variables. Let us suppose that the elements are acquired through a user interaction (i.e. the $\mathcal{P}_{FD}$ sort is based on channels and the `promote` predicate is specialized for acquisition from the user) and the first element retrieved for X is 1 (Figure 2). This element is inserted in the domain of X, i.e., $D_X^d = \{1|(D_X^d)'\}$; since it is consistent with auxiliary constraints, it is also inserted in the current domain, i.e., $D_X^c = \{1|(D_X^c)'\}$. Then KAC propagation tries to find a support for this element in each domain of those variables linked by FD constraints; in our instance D_Z. A value is requested for D_Z (eventually, providing the user the imposed auxiliary constraints in order to have guided acquisition) and the user gives a (possibly consistent) value: 2. This element is inserted into the domain of Z: $D_Z^d = \{2|(D_Z^d)'\}$. Since the acquired element is consistent with auxiliary constraints, it is not deleted and it is inserted in the current domain of Z. Finally, the constraint imposed on domains can propagate, so element 2 has to be inserted in both the (definition and current) domains of Y and X, thus $D_Y^c = D_Y^d = \{2|D_Y'\}$ and $D_X^c = D_X^d = \{1, 2|D_X''\}$.

KAC propagation must now find a known support for element 2 in D_X^c, so another request is performed. If the user replies that there is no consistent element in the domain of Z, then 2 is removed from the current domain of X. It will remain in the definition domain because the element semantically belongs to the domain even if no consistent solution can exist containing it.

When KAC propagation reaches the quiescence, in each domain we know a support for each other known value.

5 Related Work

Many systems consider set objects, because sets have powerful description capabilities. In particular, some have been described as instances of the general CLP($\mathcal{X}$) framework, like {log} [10,9], CLPS [15], or Conjunto [12]. However, none of them, to our knowledge, deals with a two-sorted CLP: the only aim is finding assignments for sets.

In {log} [10,9], a set can be either the empty set $\emptyset$, or defined by a constructor with that, given a set S and an element e, returns the set composed of $S \cup \{e\}$. This language is very powerful, allowing sets and variables to belong to sets. However, the resulting unification algorithm is non-deterministic, thus, in the worst case, it has an exponential time complexity.

Conjunto [12] is a CLP language in which set variables can range on set domains. Each domain is represented by its greatest lower bound (i.e., the intersection of all the sets belonging to the set domain) and its least upper bound (i.e., the union of all the sets in the set domain). Each element in a set must be bound, sets are considered to be finite, and they cannot contain sets. These restrictions avoid the non-deterministic unification algorithm, and allow good performance results. Similar constraint sorts are called *set constraints* in some CP systems. Our framework can interface with Conjunto; the propagation is lazy and based on the greatest lower bound of the variables. Our method can provide an efficient way to integrate FD with Conjunto, mainly if the Upper Bounds of set variables contain a big number of elements.

In [4], a method for compiling constraints in CLP(FD) is described. The work is based on the idea of having a single type of constraint X in R, used to implement all the other constraints. R represents a collection of objects and can also be a user function. Thus, in clp(FD) domains are managed as first-class objects; our framework can be fruitfully implemented in systems exploiting this idea, such as, for instance, SICStus Prolog [3].

In [19], a framework is proposed to deal with interaction of the user in a logic programming environment. Our work can be used for interaction in a constraint logic programming framework; it allows the user to provide domain values. As suggested in [19], the user should not provide all the possible values at the beginning of the computation if only few of them will be effectively used. This idea can be seen as a kind of *lazy domain evaluation*. In [20] the same idea is considered; the domains of the variables are viewed as *streams* during a forward checking computation. In [8], the effectiveness of such an approach is shown. In our proposal, implementation of delayed evaluation is quite natural and simple.

In [6], the ICSP model is proposed as an extension of the CSP model. In this model, variables range on partially known domains which have a known part and an unknown part represented as a variable. Domain values are provided by an extraction module and the acquisition process is (possibly) driven by constraints. The model has been proven effective in a vision system [7], in randomly-generated problems [6] and in planning [2]. This work can be considered as the language extension of the ICSP, maintaining it as the core of the propagation engine on the FD side (thus keeping its efficiency). The ICSP can also be considered as the instance of the language considering domains as streams between subsystems.

In [17], a system is shown that considers unbound domains. In this case, a domain can contain a "wildcard" element that can be linked to any possible element. Operationally, this idea has some similarities to the ICSP, however in [6] was provided a better comprehension from the theoretical viewpoint. In the ICSP model, domains have the form of streams, with a known part plus a variable which represents semantically a collection of unknown elements, not a single unknown element.

6   Conclusions and Future Work

In this work, we presented a language belonging to the CLP class that allows to perform a constraint computation on variables with finite domains while information about domains is not fully known. Domains are considered as first-class objects and can be themselves defined by means of constraints. The obtained language belongs to the CLP class and deals with two sorts: the FD sort on finite domains and the $\mathcal{P}_{FD}$ sort for domains. We defined the concept of *known arc-consistency* and compared it with arc-consistency. We provided a propagation engine for the FD sort exploiting known arc-consistency that provides the good efficiency level described in [6] in a more general framework. The framework can be specialized in order to consider, as a $\mathcal{P}_{FD}$ sort, many different sorts representing collections of values, as sets, streams or lists. In [11] we describe the implementation on streams. In particular, the framework can be implemented on top of different systems. We presented the syntax and semantics of the language and we explained what requirements a CLP($\mathcal{P}_{FD}$) language has to satisfy to be suitable. Then, we have shown that two existing systems, Conjunto and {log}, with different expressive power and different efficiency levels, satisfy the defined specifications. Finally, we have shown some application examples.

Future work concerns implementation on top of different CLP languages, in order to study in more detail the problems and features which are inherited by the system in various environments. Finally, we want to integrate more the system, in a framework where FD variables can range either on sets (of Conjunto or {log}) or on streams.

References

1. H. Abelson, G.J. Sussman, and J. Sussman. *Structure and Interpretation of Computer Programs*. MIT Press, USA, 6 edition, 1985.
2. R. Barruffi, E. Lamma, P. Mello, and M. Milano. Least commitment on variable binding in presence of incomplete knowledge. In *Proceedings of the European Conference on Planning (ECP99)*, 1999.
3. M. Carlsson, J. Widén, J. Andersson, S. Andersson, K. Boortz, H. Nilsson, and T. Sjöland. SICStus Prolog user's manual. Technical Report T91:15, Swedish Institute of Computer Science, June 1995.
4. P. Codognet and D. Diaz. Compiling constraints in clp(FD). *Journal of Logic Programming*, 27(3):185–226, June 1996.
5. J. Cohen, P. Koiran, and C. Perrin. Meta-level interpretation of CLP(lists). In F. Benhamou and A.Colmerauer, editors, *Constraint Logic Programming - Selected Research*, pages 457–481, 1993.
6. R. Cucchiara, M. Gavanelli, E. Lamma, P. Mello, M. Milano, and M. Piccardi. Constraint propagation and value acquisition: why we should do it interactively. In T. Dean, editor, *Sixteenth International Joint Conference on Artificial Intelligence*, pages 468–477, Stockholm, Sweden, July 31 – August 6 1999. Morgan Kaufmann.
7. R. Cucchiara, M. Gavanelli, E. Lamma, P. Mello, M. Milano, and M. Piccardi. Extending CLP(FD) with interactive data acquisition for 3D visual object recognition. In *Proceedings PACLP'99*, pages 137–155, 1999.
8. M.J. Dent and R.E. Mercer. Minimal forward checking. In *Proceedings of the Sixth International Conference on Tools with Artificial Intelligence*, pages 432–438, 1994.
9. A. Dovier, C. Piazza, E. Pontelli, and G. Rossi. Sets and constraint logic programming. *ACM TOPLAS*, 22(5):861–931, 2000.
10. A. Dovier, A. Policriti, and G. Rossi. Integrating lists, multisets, and sets in a logic programming framework. In F. Baader and K. U. Schulz, editors, *Frontiers of Combining Systems: 1st International Workshop*, pages 303–320, Munich, Germany, March 1996. Kluwer Academic Publishers.
11. M. Gavanelli, E. Lamma, P. Mello, and M. Milano. Channelling information through FD domains. Technical report, LIA, DEIS, University of Bologna, 2001.
12. C. Gervet. Propagation to reason about sets: Definition and implementation of a practical language. *Constraints*, 1:191–244, 1997.
13. J. Jaffar, M.J. Maher, K. Marriott, and P. Stuckey. The semantics of constraint logic programs. *Journal of Logic Programming*, 37(1-3):1–46, 1998.
14. C.A. Knoblock, S. Minton, J.L. Ambite, M. Muslea, J. Oh, and M. Frank. Mixed-initiative, multi-source information assistants. In *Tenth International World Wide Web Conference*, pages 697–707, Hong Kong, China, May 1 – 5 2001. ACM.
15. B. Legard and E. Legros. Short overview of the CLPS system. In *3rd Int. Symposium on Programming Language Implementation and Logic Programming, PLILP91*, LNCS, pages 431–433, Passau, Germany, August 1991. Springer-Verlag.
16. A.K. Mackworth. Consistency in networks of relations. *Artificial Intelligence*, 8:99–118, 1977.
17. D. Mailharro. A classification and constraint-based framework for configuration. *Artificial Intelligence for Engineering Design, Analysis and Manufacturing*, 12:383–397, 1998.
18. T. Schiex, J.C. Régin, C. Gaspin, and G. Verfaillie. Lazy arc consistency. In *Proc. of the 13th National Conference on Artificial Intelligence and the 8th Innovative Applications of Artificial Intelligence Conference*, pages 216–221, Menlo Park, August 4–8 1996. AAAI Press / MIT Press.

19. M. Sergot. A query-the-user facility for logic programming. In P. Degano and E. Sandewall, editors, *Integrated Interactive Computing Systems*, pages 27–41. North-Holland, 1983.
20. M. Zweben and M. Eskey. Constraint satisfaction with delayed evaluation. In *IJCAI 89*, pages 875–880, Detroit, August 20–25 1989.

Tutorial:
Reasoning with, about
and for Constraint Handling Rules

Thom Fruehwirth and Slim Abdennadher

Ludwig-Maximilians-University, Munich, Germany

Abstract. Constraint reasoning finds more and more applications. The rule-based concurrent programming language Constraint Handling Rules (CHR) was introduced to ease the development of constraint reasoners. Currently several CHR libraries exist in languages such as Prolog, Haskell and Java, worldwide more than 50 projects use CHR. CHR and dozens of its constraint reasoners/solvers can be used online via the internet at http://www.pms.informatik.uni-muenchen.de/~webchr/
Over time it has become apparent that CHR and its extensions are useful for implementing reasoning systems in general, including deduction and abduction, since techniques like forward and backward chaining, bottom-up and top-down evaluation, integrity constraints, tabulation/memoization can be easily implemented and combined.
This 90 minute talk will consist of the following parts:

- Introduction of CHR by examples, giving syntax and semantics of the language.
- Reasoning with CHR: How to implement and combine reasoning systems in CHR.
- Reasoning about CHR: How to analyse CHR programs, e.g. for operational equivalence and complexity.
- Reasoning for CHR: How to automatically derive from a logical specification constraint reasoners that are executable in CHR.

A. Armando (Ed.): FroCoS 2002, LNAI 2309, p. 192, 2002.
© Springer-Verlag Berlin Heidelberg 2002

PROSPER

An Investigation into Software Architecture for Embedded Proof Engines

Thomas F. Melham

Department of Computing Science
University of Glasgow
Glasgow, Scotland, G12 8QQ
tfm@dcs.gla.ac.uk

Abstract. PROSPER is a recently-completed ESPRIT Framework IV research project that investigated software architectures for component-based, embedded formal verification tools. The aim of the project was to make mechanized formal analysis more accessible in practice by providing a framework for integrating formal proof tools inside other software applications. This paper is an extended abstract of an invited presentation on PROSPER given at FroCoS 2002. It describes the vision of the PROSPER project and provides a summary of the technical approach taken and some of the lessons learned.

PROSPER [46] is a 24 person-year LTR project supported under the ESPRIT Framework IV programme and formally completed in May 2001. The project ran for three years and conducted a relatively large-scale research investigation into new software architectures for component-based, embedded formal verification tools.

The project was a collaboration between the Universities of Glasgow, Cambridge, Edinburgh, Tübingen and Karlsruhe, and the industrial partners IFAD and Prover Technology. Glasgow was the project Coordinator, as well as the main development site for the core PROSPER software infrastructure.

1 Embedded, Component-Based Verification

The starting point for PROSPER was the proposition that mechanized formal verification might be made more accessible to non-expert users by embedding it, indeed *hiding* it, as a component inside the software applications they use. Ideally, reasoning and proof support would be made available to the end-user by encapsulating it within the interaction model and interfaces they already know, rather than making them wrestle directly with theorem provers, model checkers, or other arcane software.

By contrast, the practical results of much current formal reasoning research are typically embodied in stand-alone tools that can be operated only by experts who have deep knowledge of the tool and its logical basis. Verification tools are

A. Armando (Ed.): FroCoS 2002, LNAI 2309, pp. 193–206, 2002.

therefore often not well integrated into established design flows—e.g. into the CAD or CASE tool environments currently used for hardware design or software development.

Good evidence that this imposes serious barriers to adoption of formal reasoning by industry can be found in the arena of formal verification for hardware design. By far the most successful method is formal equivalence checking (e.g. with BDDs), where the technology is relatively push-button and well integrated by electronics design tool vendors into their normal CAD tool flows [10]. On the other hand, only very few, well-resourced, early adopters have been making effective use of model checkers or theorem provers [19,43] and wider deployment of these in future is by no means certain.

But a developer who does wish to incorporate verification inside another application, for example a CAD or CASE tool, faces a difficult choice between creating a verification engine from scratch and adapting existing tools. Developing a new verification engine is time-consuming and means expensive reimplementation. But existing tools are rarely suitable as components that can be customized for a specific verification role and patched into other programs.

In summary, at the time the PROSPER research programme was being devised (circa 1996) many promising formal reasoning tools existed, but these were typically

- not integrated into other applications,
- internally monolithic,
- driven through user-orientated interfaces, and
- operable only by expert users.

PROSPER's idea was to experiment with a framework in which formal verification tools might instead be

- integrated as embedded 'proof engines' inside other applications,
- built from components,
- driven by other software through an API, and
- operable by ordinary application-domain users, by giving user-oriented guidance.

The PROSPER project investigated this proposal by researching and developing a software *Toolkit* [21], centred around an open proof tool architecture, that allows an expert to easily and flexibly assemble customized software components to provide embedded formal reasoning support inside applications. The project originally had mainly CAD or CASE applications in mind, but its results were not really specialized to these. Indeed, one early experiment was to embed proof support within Microsoft Excel.

The primary concern of the project was *not* the logical aspects of integration or combining systems, and the PROSPER Toolkit has no special mechanisms for ensuring the soundness of translations between the logical data of different tools. Of course this is important, but it was not emphasized in the project because other work, such as the OMRS project [29], was developing systematic frameworks for treating soundness.

The remainder of this abstract gives a sketch of the technical approach taken in PROSPER and a brief account of some of the general lessons learned. Of course, other researchers have had similar ideas. There is a growing research literature on combinations of proof tools, tool integration architectures, and design tools with embedded verification—not least in the proceedings of the FroCoS workshop series [9,28,36]. A brief list of some related work is given in section 5

2   Technical Approach

Central to PROSPER's vision is the idea of a *proof engine*, a custom-built verification software component which can be operated by another program through an Application Programming Interface (API). This allows the embedded formal reasoning capability to be operated in a machine-oriented rather than human-oriented fashion.

A proof engine is expected to be specially tuned to the verification needs of the application it supports. Application requirements in general are, of course, unpredictable and in any case will vary widely. PROSPER therefore does not supply just one 'general-purpose' proof engine. Instead, the project has developed a collection of software libraries, called the PROSPER *Toolkit*, that enables a system developer to build custom proof engines as required.

Every PROSPER proof engine is constructed from a (possibly quite minimal) deductive theorem prover, with additional capabilities provided by 'plugins' created from existing, off-the-shelf, tools such as model checkers or SAT solvers. The theorem prover's command language is regarded as a kind of scripting language for managing the plugin components and orchestrating proofs. The Toolkit includes libraries, currently supporting the C, ML and Java programming languages, for implementing data and control communications between the components of a final system. A standard for this is also documented in a language-independent specification, called the PROSPER *Integration Interface* (PII), which could be implemented in other languages.

A theorem prover is placed at the centre of the architecture because this comes with ready-made concepts of logical term, theorem, and goal—essentially all the formal language infrastructure needed for managing verifications. A side benefit is that all the functionality in the theorem prover (libraries of procedures, tactics, logical theories, and so on) becomes available to a developer for inclusion in their custom proof engine. But this does not prevent the theorem proving part of a PROSPER proof engine being very lightweight, if desired.

The PROSPER Toolkit has been implemented around HOL98, a modern descendant of the HOL theorem prover [31]. HOL98 is highly modular, which suits the PROSPER approach of building up a proof engine from components (be they HOL libraries or external plugins). It also contains numerous sophisticated automatic proof procedures. HOL's command language is the functional programming language ML [42], extended with datatypes for the abstract syntax of

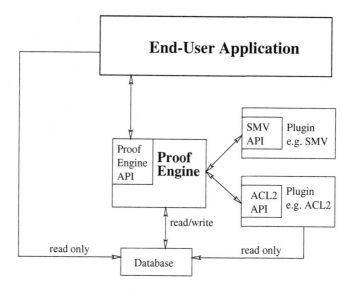

Fig. 1. A system built with the PROSPER Toolkit.

logical data and functions to support proof construction. This gives a developer a full programming language in which to create bespoke verification procedures. Proof procedures programmed in the proof engine are offered to client applications in an API.

The native formal logic of HOL is classical higher-order logic [15]. This is also supported by the PII communications infrastructure, so any formula expressible in higher-order logic can be passed between components. Many applications and plugins operate with logical data that is either already a subset of higher-order logic (e.g. first-order or propositional logic) or embeddable in it (e.g. CTL or other temporal logics [4,38]), so communication with these tools is directly supported.

The Toolkit provides code to construct several plugins based on particular external tools. These include a version of the SMV model checker [38], a version of the Prover Plug-In SAT solver of Prover Technology [50], and the circuit analysis tool AC/3 [33]. To complement these plugins, the PROSPER project provided a more tightly integrated BDD package in the implementation of ML used for proof engines [30]. Third party plugins have also been developed from ACL2 [35,51], Gandalf [34], and SVC [53]. Finally, the Toolkit includes a separate database component that duplicates the internal logical state of the theorem prover, so that plugins and applications can access theory-related data while the proof engine is busy.

The application, proof engine, database, and plugins are components integrated to produce the final system. A typical example is shown in Figure 1. In the current prototype, all these components are also separate processes that communicate in the uniform manner specified by the PII. The PROSPER architecture also includes a separate *monitor* process not shown in the diagram. This allows components to interrupt each other and the output of servers to be redirected to be handled by clients. It also includes a *name server* facility whereby components may be requested by name instead of location. This is achieved by means of a configuration file that contains component names together with information about their initialization scripts and configurations.

For a fuller account of the technical approach taken in the PROSPER Toolkit, including several illustrative examples, see [21]. Much more technical detail can also be found in the user guide [22].

3   Case Studies

PROSPER researchers undertook three main case studies to demonstrate the concept of embedded proof engines and test the Toolkit. The first was an early experiment in integrating a function that used formal proof into Microsoft Excel [41]. The second was a much larger development to add verification capabilities to the VDM-SL Toolbox [24], a CASE tool for VDM specifications marketed by project partner IFAD. The third was a hardware verification tool, driven by a novel natural language and graphical interface, that allows specifications to be checked by a proof engine that incorporates a model checker.

Excel Example. Excel is a spreadsheet package marketed by Microsoft [41]. Ordinary users are unlikely to be directly interested in mathematical proof, but they do want to check they have entered their spreadsheet formulas correctly. As a simple case study, the PROSPER Toolkit developers undertook to incorporate a 'sanity checking' function into Excel that users could employ to reassure themselves of correctness [18].

The function supplied tests the equality of the contents of two spreadsheet cells, not by comparing their current values, but by trying to verify that the two formulas underlying these cells are equal for all possible values of the input cells occurring in them. The idea is to provide ordinary users with a way of checking for errors in their spreadsheets, in cases where two cells calculated in different ways are expected always to produce the same value—for example, in financial bookkeeping applications.

When this operation is included in a spreadsheet formula, it invokes a simple proof engine to compute its result. The proof engine uses term-rewriting and a linear arithmetic decision procedure in HOL, as well as an external SAT solver to try to verify equivalence.

The prototype handled only very simple formulas, in which a small subset of the (natural number or Boolean) functions available in Excel could appear. But given this simplification, fewer than 150 lines of code and only a few days work were needed to produce a prototype, demonstrating that the basic functionality was achievable very easily using the PROSPER Toolkit.

CASE Tool Application. The IFAD VDM-SL Toolbox [24] is a software design tool that supports the specification language VDM-SL. Its capabilities include syntax checking and type checking of specifications and code generation in C++ and Java. As a major case study within PROSPER, IFAD researchers worked together with other project partners to develop and integrate a proof engine for the VDM-SL Toolbox for discharging proof obligations generated by VDM-SL type invariants.

Type invariants are undecidable in general, but in practice many of them can be dismissed by simplification and term-rewriting in combination with bounded first-order logic decision procedures. A PROSPER proof engine that supplied this reasoning capability was developed by integrating theorem proving in HOL with BDDs and the Prover Plug-In SAT solver. The resulting heuristic was found by IFAD to perform well on realistic industrial test cases.

An additional requirement was if an automatic proof attempt fails, a user must be able to intervene and guide a proof by hand. The VDM-SL Toolbox application therefore also involved a fairly large-scale development to steer the proof engine through an interactive proof management interface in the VDM-SL Toolbox.

Hardware Verification Workbench Application. The second major PROSPER case study was a Hardware Verification Workbench that served as a research platform for developing and evaluating new methods in formal hardware verification. It was designed to use external verification back-ends, rather than implement all its own proof procedures. Communication between the Hardware Verification Workbench and the proof back-ends was achieved via the PROSPER Integration Interface (PII).

One experiment done with this platform was the development of a natural language interface [32] to the Hardware Verification Workbench. This translates statements about circuits, in the normal technical language of engineers, into temporal logic formulas that a model checking plugin can verify. Of course, natural language specifications may be ambiguous. To disambiguate, timing diagrams (waveforms) are generated from output of the model checker and presented back to the engineer. In keeping with the PROSPER aim of 'hiding' the proof tool, users never have to run the model checker directly, or even see temporal logic formulas—they work only with already familiar things, namely natural language and timing diagrams.

4   Some Conclusions from PROSPER

The premise of the PROSPER project was that mechanized formal analysis could be made more accessible to users by integrating it into applications. Moreover, embedded formal proof will gain widespread use, or at least be widely experimented with, only if verification tools can be easily customized, combined, and integrated.

The research results obtained support these propositions. An effective infrastructure for building and integrating embedded, component-based proof engines was found to be technically feasible; the PROSPER Toolkit represents one possible prototype. And the general idea of embedded custom reasoning engines, giving ordinary users the power of proof, is promising enough to merit much more investigation on applications.

The experiment with Excel was very encouraging. It showed that infrastructure of the kind proposed can indeed make it easy to embed formal verification tools into other applications. The VDM-SL CASE tool example was also encouraging. The PROSPER Toolkit gave a much more controllable and effective integration of verification into IFAD's existing CASE tool product than was found in the broadly negative experience of previous, ad-hoc experiments [3]. The Hardware Verification Workbench case study also provided an intriguing and novel example, showing that formal notations could be completely hidden behind a user-oriented interface.

PROSPER aimed from the start for a single infrastructure covering both hardware and software design tool applications. In the end, the Toolkit is perhaps better suited to software design tools (CASE tools) and interactive general applications (like Excel) than the current generation of CAD tools. CAD tool flows are typically compilation or batch processing oriented, with large amounts of design data passing between tools through disk files in numerous different formats. The kind of fine-grained communications and interaction supported by the PII is less relevant here.

The PROSPER architecture places a theorem prover, implemented in ML, at the centre of every proof engine. The reasons given for this in Section 2 are sound, but the architecture is in some respects also quite awkward. ML has all the usual advantages of a functional programming language—conciseness, strong typing, and so on—and this does make it well suited as a scripting language for *orchestrating verification strategies*. But the single-threaded nature of ML[1] is something of a disadvantage in a scripting language for *coordinating the invocation of plugins and communications between them*. For example, because ML (and hence HOL) is single-threaded, the architecture needed a separate database process to allow asynchronous access by plugins to logical data.

The separate 'monitor' process mentioned in section 2 is also related to this. Extra processes were added to the architecture mainly to support two seemingly elementary capabilities—namely, the ability to interrupt a proof engine and its plugins while they are working, and the ability to divert the output streams from plugins for handling by other processes. Providing these features, expressly requested by the VDM-SL application developers at IFAD, required a surprising amount of quite tricky distributed-systems programming.

A major outcome of the project is the language-independent specification of the PROSPER Integration Interface and the implementations for ML, C, and Java. Alternative transport mechanisms were considered for logical data, such as the Extensible Markup Language (XML). Standard component architectures, such as CORBA [44], were also considered for low-level communications. Both were rejected early on in the project in favour of a custom solution, which was

---

[1] Or at least the ML underlying HOL98, namely Moscow ML.

felt in advance to be the more 'lightweight' approach. In retrospect, it may have been better to pursue standard solutions. On the other hand, it is by no means certain that much of the eventual Toolkit infrastructure would not have to have been built anyway.

Our experience with plugins was that many existing tools have command-line or user interfaces that are very difficult to separate from the underlying proof capabilities. This makes them hard to wrap up as PROSPER plugin components. It helps enormously if a tool already has a distinct and identifiable API—that is if its reasoning functionality is available through a well-documented and coherent set of entry points into the code. Good examples of such tools include the Prover Plug-In [50] and NuSMV [16].

On the logical side, the simply-typed higher-order logic implemented in HOL and supported by the PII was found to be adequate for the examples considered. This is not really a surprise—it has long been known how to embed a large range of other formalisms in this logic. Of course, PROSPER looked at only a limited range of plugins and applications; there are doubtless many other settings in which a more expressive type system (e.g. predicate subtypes as in PVS) would be strictly necessary.[2] But we would expect the infrastructure to extend quite naturally to this.

An important issue that was not investigated in depth was how to provide support for producing and presenting counter-examples in case of failed proof attempts. PROSPER focused on applications where automatic proof is possible, but this is rather idealistic. In many applications, failure of proof is likely to be frequent—not least while debugging specifications. The user then needs good feedback on why the proof attempt failed, in a form with which the user is familiar. A systematic treatment of this process and some general infrastructure support would be very valuable.

5   Related Work

Research related to PROSPER includes work on combining proof tools, tool integration architectures, and design tools with embedded verification. Only a brief list of pointers to some of the most relevant work is given here. An analysis of the relation of this research to PROSPER's approach and results can be found in an extended version of [21], to appear in the *International Journal on Software Tools for Technology Transfer.*

Combining Proof Tools. There is now a fairly large literature on combining decision procedures, and in particular model checkers, with theorem proving. The aim of this research is typically to increase the level of automation of theorem provers or extend the reach of model checkers in the face of fundamental capacity limits (or both). Early experiments include links to model-checking based on

---

[2] Partial functions in VDM seem a case in point. But these were avoided by doing some logical pre-processing within the CASE tool client itself—so HOL's logic of total functions was adequate for this example.

embeddings of the modal mu-calculus in the logics of the HOL and PVS theorem provers [4,47].

A notable example of current work is Intel's Forte system [1,2], which intimately combines Symbolic Trajectory Evaluation model checking [49] and theorem proving in a single framework. This has been used very effectively for industrial-scale formal hardware verification [45]. Another approach being investigated by Ken McMillan at Cadence Berkeley Labs is to extend the top-level of a model-checker with proof rules for abstraction and problem decomposition [39,40].

A useful summary of other recent work on combining model checking with theorem proving is given in Tomás Uribe's invited talk at FroCoS 2000 [54].

Integration Architectures. PROSPER focused more on infrastructure for tool integration in general than on developing particular tool combinations. (An exception is the work on linking BDDs into HOL98 [30].) Some other projects which also provide a generic framework for the integration of tools are listed below.

MATHWEB is a framework for distributed mathematical services provided by reasoning systems such as resolution theorem provers and computer algebra systems [25]. A special service for storing knowledge, MBASE [26], allows theory information to be shared between other services.

Ω-ANTS combines interactive and automated theorem provers using an agent-based approach [13]. Its blackboard architecture and other agent-oriented features provide flexible interaction between components.

ILF is a framework for integrating interactive and automated provers that places special emphasis on a good user interface for the automated provers [20]. The provers can be distributed and Prolog is used as a scripting language, much as ML is used in PROSPER.

TECHS is another framework which enables automated provers for first-order logic to cooperate by exchanging logical information [27].

ETI, the Electronic Tool Integration platform [52], aims to support easy and rapid comparison of tools that do similar jobs as well as rapid prototyping of combinations of tools. ETI has its own scripting and communication language, HLL, which acts much like PROSPER's combination of ML and the PII.

OMRS aims to develop an *open* architecture for integration of reasoning systems. The architecture covers three aspects: logic [29], control strategies [17], and interaction mechanisms [6].

LBA, the *Logic Broker Architecture* [7,8], is a CORBA-based infrastructure for the integration of reasoning systems. It provides location transparency, fowarding of requests to reasoning components via a registration/subscription mechanism, and provable soundness guarantees. The LBA was initially designed to be OMRS-based but has evolved into an independent entity.

SAL (Symbolic Analysis Laboratory) is a new collaborative effort that provides a framework for combining different tools to calculate properties of concurrent systems. One instance includes the PVS theorem prover as a major component [11].

Design Tools with Embedded Verification. Braun et al. argue that for formal techniques to be useful they must be integrated into the design process [14]. A primary aim of PROSPER was to support this by making it easier to link verification tools into the CASE and CAD tool environments for current software and hardware development processes. The two major PROSPER case studies described in section 3 looked at target applications of both kinds, embedding proof engines into both a commercial CASE tool and a formal hardware verification platform.

Some other projects also looking at linking formal techniques into design tools and the design process are listed below.

UniForM is a project that aims to encourage the development of reliable industrial software by enabling suitable tool-supported combinations of formal methods. The UniForM Workbench [37] is a generic framework that can be instantiated with specific tools. The project has produced a workbench for software design that gives access to the Isabelle theorem prover plus other verification tools through their command lines.

Extended Static Checking (ESC) is a software development tool using embedded verification developed at the Compaq Systems Research Center [23]. ESC uses cooperating decision procedure technology first developed in the early 1980s to analyse Java programs for static errors.

KeY is a relatively substantial research effort that aims to bridge the gap between object-oriented software engineering methods and deductive verification. The KeY system integrates a commercial CASE tool with an interactive verification system and automated deduction [5]. It aims to provide an industrial verification tool that benefits even software engineers who have little experience of formal methods.

InVeSt integrates the PVS theorem prover with the SMV model checker [12]. The combination is used as a 'proof engine', in the sense that it discharges verification conditions generated by another program external to the theorem prover.

As far as I am aware, no project other than PROSPER aims specifically to provide a general framework to support the integration of existing components with the view to producing an embeddable, customised proof engine. The closest in scope and aims is the Logic Broker Architecture.

Acknowledgments

I thank the organizers of FroCoS 2002 for their invitation to speak at the conference in Santa Margherita. Richard Boulton and Alessandro Armando kindly read and commented on an early draft of this abstract. Warm thanks are also due to the PROSPER Management Board and all the individual members of the PROSPER research team. The project could not have succeeded without their hard work and dedication to the project's vision. PROSPER was supported in part by the Commission for European Communities as LTR Project 26241 under the ESPRIT Framework IV programme.

References

1. M. D. Aagaard, R. B. Jones, and C.-J. H. Seger, 'Combining theorem proving and trajectory evaluation in an industrial environment,' in *ACM/IEEE Design Automation Conference, Proceedings* (1998), pp. 538–541.

2. M. D. Aagaard, R. B. Jones, and C.-J. H. Seger, 'Lifted-fl: A pragmatic implementation of combined model checking and theorem proving', in *Theorem Proving in Higher Order Logics*, edited by Y. Bertot, G. Dowek, A. Hirschowitz, C. Paulin, and L. Théry, Lecture Notes in Computer Science, vol. 1690 (Springer-Verlag, 1999), pp. 23–340.

3. S. Agerholm, 'Translating Specifications in VDM-SL to PVS', in *Theorem Proving in Higher Order Logics: 9th International Conference, TPHOLs'96: Turku, August 1996: Proceedings*, edited by J. von Wright, J. Grundy, and J. Harrison Lecture Notes in Computer Science, vol. 1690 (Springer-Verlag, 1999), pp. 1–16.

4. S. Agerholm and H. Skjødt, *Automating a model checker for recursive modal assertions in HOL*. Technical Report DAIMI IR-92, Computer Science Department (Aarhus University, 1990).

5. W. Ahrendt, T. Baar, B. Beckert, M. Giese, E. Habermalz, R. Hähnle, W. Menzel, and P. H. Schmitt, 'The KeY approach: Integrating object oriented design and formal verification', in *Proceedings of the 8th European Workshop on Logics in AI (JELIA)*, edited by M. Ojeda-Aciego, I. P. de Guzmán, G. Brewka, and L. M. Pereira (eds), Lecture Notes in Computer Science, vol. 1919 (Springer-Verlag, 2000), pp. 21–36,

6. A. Armando, M. Kohlhase, and S. Ranise, 'Communication protocols for mathematical services based on KQML and OMRS', in *Symbolic Computation and Automated Reasoning: The CALCULEMUS-2000 Symposium (Proceedings of the Eighth Symposium on the Integration of Symbolic Computation and Mechanized Reasoning)*, edited by M. Kerber and M. Kohlhase (A. K. Peters Ltd., 2001).

7. A. Armando and D. Zini, 'Interfacing computer algebra and deduction systems via the Logic Broker Architecture', in *Symbolic Computation and Automated Reasoning: The CALCULEMUS-2000 Symposium (Proceedings of the Eighth Symposium on the Integration of Symbolic Computation and Mechanized Reasoning)*, edited by M. Kerber and M. Kohlhase (A. K. Peters Ltd., 2001).

8. A. Armando and D. Zini, 'Towards Interoperable Mechanized Reasoning Systems: the Logic Broker Architecture', in *Proceedings of the AI*IA-TABOO Joint Workshop 'Dagli Oggetti agli Agenti: Tendenze Evolutive dei Sistemi Software'*, 29–30 May 2001, Parma, Italy (2001), pp. 70–75.

9. F. Baader and K. U. Schulz, editors, *Frontiers of Combining Systems: First International Workshop, Munich, March 1996*, Applied Logic Series, vol. 3 (Kluwer Academic Publishers, 1996).

10. L. Bening and H. Foster, *Principles of Verifiable RTL Design* (Kluwer, 2000).

11. S. Bensalem, V. Ganesh, Y. Lakhnech, C. Muñoz, S. Owre, H. Ruess, J. Rushby, V. Rusu, H. Saïdi, N. Shankar, E. Singerman, and A. Tiwari, 'An overview of SAL', in *Proceedings of the Fifth NASA Langley Formal Methods Workshop, June 2000* (Williamsburg, 2000).

12. S. Bensalem, Y. Lakhnech, and S. Owre, 'InVeSt: A tool for the verification of invariants', in *Proceedings of the 10th International Conference on Computer Aided Verification (CAV'98)*, edited by A. J. Hu and M. Y. Vardi, Lecture Notes in Computer Science, vol. 1427 (Springer-Verlag, 1998), pp. 505–510.

13. C. Benzmüller and V. Sorge, 'Ω-ANTS — An open approach at combining interactive and automated theorem proving' in *Symbolic Computation and Automated Reasoning: The CALCULEMUS-2000 Symposium (Proceedings of the Eighth Symposium on the Integration of Symbolic Computation and Mechanized Reasoning)*, edited by M. Kerber and M. Kohlhase (A. K. Peters Ltd., 2001).

14. P. Braun, H. Lötzbeyer, B. Schätz, and O. Slotosch, 'Consistent integration of formal methods', in *Tools and Algorithms for the Construction and Analysis of Systems: 6th International Conference, TACAS 2000: Berlin, March/April 2000: Proceedings*, edited by S. Graf and M. Schwartzbach, Lecture Notes in Computer Science, vol. 1785 (Springer-Verlag, 2000), pp. 48–62.

15. A. Church, 'A Formulation of the Simple Theory of Types', *Journal of Symbolic Logic*, vol. 5 (1940), pp. 56–68.

16. A. Cimatti, E. M. Clarke, F. Giunchiglia, and M. Roveri, 'NUSMV: a new Symbolic Model Verifier', in *Proceedings of the Eleventh Conference on Computer-Aided Verification (CAV'99)*, edited by N. Halbwachs and D. Peled, Lecture Notes in Computer Science, vol. 1633 (Springer-Verlag, 1999), pp. 495–499.

17. A. Coglio, 'The control component of OMRS: NQTHM as a case study', in *Proceedings of the First Workshop on Abstraction, Analogy and Metareasoning*, IRST (Trento, 1996), pp. 65–71.

18. G. Collins and L. A. Dennis, 'System description: Embedding verification into Microsoft Excel', in *Proceedings of the 17th International Conference on Automated Deduction: CADE-17*, edited by D. McAllester, Lecture Notes in Artificial Intelligence, vol. 1831 (Springer-Verlag, 2000), pp. 497–501.

19. B. Colwell and B. Brennan, 'Intel's Formal Verification Experience on the Willamette Development', in *Theorem Proving in Higher Order Logics: 13th International Conference, TPHOLs 2000: Portland, August 2000: Proceedings*, edited by M. Aagaard and J. Harrision, Lecture Notes in Computer Science, vol. 1869 (Springer-Verlag, 2000), pp. 106–107.

20. B. I. Dahn, J. Gehne, T. Honigmann, and A. Wolf, 'Integration of automated and interactive theorem proving in ILF', in *Proceedings of the 14th International Conference on Automated Deduction (CADE-14)*, edited by W. McCune, Lecture Notes in Artificial Intelligence, vol. 1249 (Springer-Verlag, 1997), pp. 57–60.

21. L. A. Dennis, G. Collins, M. Norrish, R. Boulton, K. Slind, G. Robinson, M. Gordon, and T. Melham, 'The PROSPER Toolkit', in *Tools and Algorithms for the Construction and Analysis of Systems: 6th International Conference, TACAS 2000: Berlin, March/April 2000: Proceedings*, edited by S. Graf and M. Schwartzbach, Lecture Notes in Computer Science, vol. 1785 (Springer-Verlag, 2000), pp. 78–92. An extended version of this paper is to appear in the *International Journal on Software Tools for Technology Transfer*.

22. L. Dennis, G. Collins, R. Boulton, G. Robinson, M. Norrish, and K. Slind, *The PROSPER Toolkit, version 1.4*, Part of deliverable D3.5, ESPRIT LTR Project PROSPER (26241), Department of Computing Science, University of Glasgow (April, 2001). Available as `prosper1-4.ps.gz` at `www.dcs.gla.ac.uk/prosper/toolkit/`.

23. D. L. Detlefs, K. R. M. Leino, G. Nelson, and J. B. Saxe, *Extended static checking*, Research Report 159, Compaq Systems Research Center, Palo Alto (December, 1998).

24. J. Fitzgerald and P. G. Larsen, *Modelling Systems: Practical Tools and Techniques in Software Development* (Cambridge University Press, 1998).

25. A. Franke, S. M. Hess, C. G. Jung, M. Kohlhase, and V. Sorge, 'Agent-Oriented Integration of Distributed Mathematical Services', *Journal of Universal Computer Science*, vol. 5 (1999), pp. 156–187.

26. A. Franke and M. Kohlhase, 'System description: MBASE, an open mathematical knowledge base', in *Proceedings of the 17th International Conference on Automated Deduction: CADE-17*, edited by D. McAllester, Lecture Notes in Artificial Intelligence, vol. 1831 (Springer-Verlag, 2000), pp. 455–459.

27. D. Fuchs and J. Denzinger, *Knowledge-based cooperation between theorem provers by TECHS*, SEKI-Report SR-97-11 (University of Kaiserslautern, 1997).

28. D. M. Gabbay and M. de Rijke, editors, *Frontiers of Combining Systems 2*, Studies in Logic and Computation Series (Research Studies Press, 2000).

29. F. Giunchiglia, P. Pecchiari, and C. Talcott, 'Reasoning theories: Towards an architecture for open mechanized reasoning systems', in *Frontiers of Combining Systems: First International Workshop, Munich, March 1996*, edited by F. Baader and K. U. Schulz, Applied Logic Series, vol. 3 (Kluwer Academic Publishers, 1996), pp. 157–174.

30. M. Gordon and K. F. Larsen, *Combining the Hol98 proof assistant with the BuDDy BDD package*, Technical Report 481, University of Cambridge Computer Laboratory (December, 1999).

31. M. J. C. Gordon and T. F. Melham, editors, *Introduction to HOL: A theorem proving environment for higher order logic* (Cambridge University Press, 1993).

32. A. Holt, E. Klein, and C. Grover, 'Natural language specifications for hardware verification', *Language and Computation*, vol. 1 (2000), pp. 275–282. Special issue on ICoS-1.

33. D. W. Hoffmann and T. Kropf, 'Automatic error correction of large circuits using boolean decomposition and abstraction', in *Correct Hardware Design and Verification Methods: 10th IFIP WG10.5 Advanced Research Working Conference: Bad Herrenalb, September 1999: Proceedings*, edited by L. Pierre and T. Kropf, Lecture Notes in Computer Science, vol. 1703 (Springer-Verlag, 1999), pp. 157–171.

34. J. Hurd, 'Integrating Gandalf and HOL', in *Theorem Proving in Higher Order Logics*, edited by Y. Bertot, G. Dowek, A. Hirschowitz, C. Paulin, and L. Théry, Lecture Notes in Computer Science, vol. 1690 (Springer-Verlag, 1999), pp. 311–321.

35. M. Kaufmann, P. Manolios, and J S. Moore, *Computer-Aided Reasoning: An Approach* (Kluwer Academic Publishers, 2000).

36. H. Kirchner and C. Ringeissen, editors, *Frontiers of Combining Systems: Third International Workshop, FroCoS 2000: Nancy, March 2000: Proceedings*, Lecture Notes in Artificial Intelligence, vol. 1794 (Springer-Verlag, 2000).

37. B. Krieg-Brückner, J. Peleska, E.-R. Olderog, and A. Baer, 'The UniForM Work-Bench, a universal development environment for formal methods', in *FM'99—Formal Methods*, edited by J. M. Wing, J. Woodcock, and J. Davies, vol. 2, Lecture Notes in Computer Science, vol. 1709 (Springer-Verlag, 1999), pp. 1186–1205.

38. K. L. McMillan, *Symbolic Model Checking* (Kluwer Academic Publishers, 1993).

39. K. L. McMillan, 'Verification of infinite state systems by compositional model checking', in *Correct Hardware Design and Verification Methods*, edited by L. Pierre and T. Kropf, Lecture Notes in Computer Science, vol. 1703 (Springer-Verlag, 1999), pp. 219–233.

40. K. L. McMillan, 'Parameterized Verification of the FLASH Cache Coherence Protocol by Compositional Model Checking', in *Correct Hardware Design and Verification Methods: 11th IFIP WG10.5 Advanced Research Working Conference, CHARME 2001: Livingston, Scotland, UK, September 4–7 2001: Proceed-*

ings, edited by T. Margaria and T. Melham, Lecture Notes in Computer Science, vol. 2144, (Springer-Verlag, 2001), pp. 179–195.

41. Microsoft Corporation, *Microsoft Excel*, `www.microsoft.com/excel`.

42. R. Milner, M. Tofte, R. Harper, and D. MacQueen, *The Definition of Standard ML*, revised edition (MIT Press, 1997).

43. N. Mokhoff, 'Intel, Motorola report formal verification gains', *The EE Times Online*, `www.eetimes.com/story/OEG20010621S0080`.

44. Object Management Group, *The Common Object Request Broker: Architecture and Specification*, OMG Technical Report (July 1995).

45. J. O'Leary, X. Zhao, R. Gerth, and C.-J. H. Seger, 'Formally verifying IEEE compliance of floating-point hardware', *Intel Technology Journal* (First Quarter, 1999). Available online at `developer.intel.com/technology/itj/`.

46. PROSPER: Proof and Specification Assisted Design Environments, ESPRIT Framework IV LTR Project 26241, `www.dcs.gla.ac.uk/prosper/`.

47. S. Rajan, N. Shankar, and M. Srivas, 'An integration of model checking and automated proof checking', in *Proceedings of the International Conference on Computer-Aided Verification*, Lecture Notes in Computer Science, vol. 939 (Springer-Verlag, 1995), pp. 84–97.

48. K. Schneider and D. W. Hoffmann, 'A HOL Conversion for Translating Linear Time Temporal Logic to ω-Automata', in *Proceedings of the 12th International Conference on Theorem Proving in Higher Order Logics, Nice, 14–17 September, 1999*, Lecture Notes in Computer Science, vol. 1690 (Springer-Verlag, 1999), pp. 255–272.

49. C.-J. H. Seger and R. E. Bryant, 'Formal verification by symbolic evaluation of partially-ordered trajectories', *Formal Methods in System Design*, vol. 6 (1995), pp. 147–189.

50. M. Sheeran and G. Stålmarck, 'A tutorial on Stålmarck's proof procedure for propositional logic', *Formal Methods in System Design*, vol. 16, no. 1 (2000), pp. 23–58.

51. M. Staples, *Linking ACL2 and HOL*, Technical Report 476, University of Cambridge Computer Laboratory (1999).

52. B. Steffen, T. Margaria, and V. Braun, 'The Electronic Tool Integration Platform: concepts and design', *International Journal on Software Tools for Technology Transfer*, vol. 1 (1997), pp. 9–30.

53. A. Stevenson and L. A. Dennis, 'Integrating SVC and HOL with the Prosper Toolkit', in *Supplemental Proceedings of the 13th International Conference on Theorem Proving in Higher Order Logics (TPHOLs 2000)*, OGI Technical Report CSE 00-009, Oregon Graduate Institute (August, 2000), pp. 199–206.

54. T. E. Uribe, 'Combinations of Model Checking and Theorem Proving', in *Frontiers of Combining Systems: Third International Workshop, FroCoS 2000: Nancy, March 2000: Proceedings*, edited by H. Kirchner and C. Ringeissen, Lecture Notes in Artificial Intelligence, vol. 1794 (Springer-Verlag, 2000), pp. 151–170.

Constraint-Lambda Calculi

Matthias Hölzl[1] and John N. Crossley[2],[*]

[1] Institut für Informatik, Ludwig-Maximilians-Universität,
Oettingenstraße 67, 80538 München, Germany
hoelzl@informatik.uni-muenchen.de
[2] School of Computer Science and Software Engineering, Monash University,
Clayton, Victoria 3800, Australia.
jnc@csse.monash.edu.au

Abstract. We introduce two forms of calculi that integrate constraint solving with functional programming. These are the Unrestricted, and the Restricted, Constraint-Lambda Calculi. Unlike previous attempts at combining constraint solving with lambda calculus, these are conservative extensions of traditional lambda calculi in terms of both term reduction and their denotational semantics. We establish a limited form of confluence for the unrestricted calculus and full confluence for the restricted one.

1 Introduction

Constraint programming languages combine the efficiency of dedicated constraint solvers with the (Turing complete) power of a programming language. In this paper we describe two constraint-lambda calculi. Each of these comprises a standard lambda calculus and a constraint solver. Processing of terms takes place as in a standard lambda calculus but every now and again we pass terms into the constraint store to be processed by the constraint solver. After solution, the values, when available, are returned for the appropriate variables and the processing then continues. We regard the constraint solver as a black box chosen by the user and only assume that it is closed under deduction.

An early example of such a combination of a programming language and a constraint solver is CLP($\mathfrak{R}$) (see [7]) which followed the logic programming paradigm. In [8] Luis Mandel introduced the original constrained lambda calculus following the functional programming paradigm.

In the same way as Jaffar and Lassez [7] allowed arbitrary terms for individuals, even with uninterpreted functors, Mandel's systems allowed the importation of lambda terms into the constraint solver. This causes some complications with the semantics and so we have chosen to keep the constraint store and the lambda calculus parts separate, somewhat in the style of Lim *et al.* [1].

The main contribution of the present systems is that they have a very clean and clear syntax and semantics. Indeed they are conservative extensions of the

---

[*] Special thanks to Martin Wirsing for his support, interest and extremely helpful criticism.

A. Armando (Ed.): FroCoS 2002, LNAI 2309, pp. 207–222, 2002.
© Springer-Verlag Berlin Heidelberg 2002

classical lambda calculus (see Facts 1 and 2) and this was not the case for Mandel's calculi.

The structure of this paper is as follows. In Section 2 we discuss related work. In Section 3 we introduce the syntax of constraints and then the *Unrestricted Constraint-Lambda Calculus* that augments the traditional lambda calculus (λK) with constraints. We introduce the basic definitions and revisit an example of Mandel [8]. Then, in Section 4, we show that this calculus is confluent in a certain sense, namely as a reduction system. We give an example of why confluence only holds for a certain kind of reduction in the calculus. In section 5 we introduce the *Restricted Constraint-Lambda Calculus*. This calculus has the same reduction rules as the unrestricted one but the terms are based on Church's original λI calculus. We show that this is confluent in the traditional sense. Finally, in Section 6 we note that these calculi are conservative extensions of the traditional lambda calculi and extend the traditional denotational semantics.[1]

2   Related Work

The original linking of constraints with a declarative programming language was with logic programming in CLP($\Re$) developed by Jaffar and Lassez [7] and the latest such language is *HAL*, see e.g. [5].

There have been a number of languages integrating both logic and functional programming with constraint solving, such as the language *Falcon* (**F**unctional and **l**ogic language with **con**straints) which is defined in terms of guarded functional rewrite rules and relations defined over functional expressions, developed by John Darlington, Yi-ke Guo and Helen Pull, see [4]. Semantically, *Falcon* uses SLD resolution where constraint solving is used instead of unification. Such languages, therefore, not only incorporate constraints and a kind of functional language but, by doing so much, they sacrifice the transparency that is found in our approach.

Lambda-Prolog is a strongly typed logical language based on higher-order hereditar(il)y Harrop formulae. It does not provide built-in facilities for defining recursive lambda expressions, but β-reduction of simply typed terms is included in the language. *Lambda-Prolog* was developed by Dale Miller and Gopalan Nadathur (see e.g. [12]).

Mozart-Oz is a multi-paradigm language that integrates concurrent-constraint-logic, functional and object-oriented programming. It is based on the ρ and γ calculi and described in [14]. *Oz* provides logic variables, constraints and programmable search mechanisms as well as first-class functions with lexical scope and nested syntax.

Alice is a new programming language developed by Gert Smolka at the University of Saarbrücken. It is based on Standard *ML* but contains extensions for the support of concurrent, distributed and constraint programming. Constraint

---

[1] The treatment of disjunctions greatly influenced the present work and is dealt with in [6] and a paper in preparation while an implementation will be dealt with in a third paper in preparation. Details for both may currently be found in [6].

problems are given as nullary functions that "post" constraints. These are then passed to search engines.

Curry is a programming language that combines functional and logic programming features and offers lazy evaluation. *Curry* provides a built-in equality constraint and its constraint solver can be extended by a standardized interface to external constraint solvers. External constraint solvers cannot compute values in the language, they can only communicate via the entailment of constraints.

There are two systems that are closest to ours and link constraints and lambda calculus (or the corresponding programming language, *Lisp*).

Screamer is an extension to *Common Lisp* that permits the addition of backtracking and constraint-solving to the language. However there seems to have been no theoretical basis provided for this language. It was developed by David McAllester and Jeffrey Mark Siskind (see [11]) and was one of the major influences for this work.

The Constrained Lambda Calculus by Luis Mandel is a combination of the untyped lambda calculus with constraints. It is described in [8,2,10,3] and [9]. There are three variants of this calculus: A simple propositional calculus, the first-order calculus, that allows the specification of variables whose value is only computed by a constraint-solver, and the disjunctive constrained lambda calculus that allows constrained variables to have more than one solution. In the constrained lambda calculi a term $\{C\}M$ represents a term subject to the constraint C. However, in Mandel's calculi the constraints may themselves include (constrained) lambda terms. This means that constraint stores are not opaque but participate in the lexical scoping of the lambda calculus. This syntactical approach has the disadvantage that the constraint solver has to be able to deal with bound variables and (probably) complicated lambda terms *inside* constraints. In addition Mandel's eleven reduction rules allow the movement of constraints across predicates (and functions) resulting in very complicated syntax. For example, $P(\{C_1\}M, \{C_2\}N)$ reduces to $\{C_1, C_2\}P(M, N)$. These aspects contrast with our approach where the constraint solver operates only on pure constraints (see rule (CI) below, section 3) and we only require a total of three rules.

The Tiny Constraint Functional Logic Language of Mück *et al.* in [13] which was influenced by Mandel *et al.*'s work differs significantly from the present work in two respects. 1. it is very restricted in the substitution of lambda terms for (constraint) variables and 2. it already includes non-deterministic choice which, for us, corresponds to the disjunctive extension (see footnote 1).

3   The Unrestricted Constraint-Lambda Calculus

A constraint can be thought of as a relation that holds between entities from a fixed domain. We only consider constraint domains on which a notion of equality, denoted by =, is given. Typical constraint domains are the real numbers with addition, multiplication and equality, or the set of all integers.

A *constraint language* comprises a countable set, $\mathcal{C}$, of *individual constants*, a countable set, $\mathcal{V}$, of *constraint variables*, a countable set, $\mathcal{F}$, of *function letters* of fixed arities, and a countable set, $\mathcal{P}$, of *predicate symbols*, again with fixed arities. The set $\mathcal{T}$ of *constraint terms* over a constraint-language is inductively defined in the usual way.

Definition 1. *If P is a predicate letter with arity n and $t_1, \ldots, t_n$ are constraint terms, then $P(t_1, \ldots, t_n)$ is an* atomic constraint. *A constraint is a finite conjunction $(C_1 \wedge C_2 \wedge \ldots \wedge C_n)$ of atomic constraints. The conjunction of two constraints is the conjunction of all their atomic constraints. Satisfaction of a constraint for a particular domain is defined in the obvious way.*

The unrestricted constraint-lambda calculus which we now define is an extension of the usual lambda calculus.

A *constraint store* is regarded as a collection of formulae. Two constraint stores are regarded as equal if their logical consequences are the same and we shall only be concerned with formulae, principally equations, provable from a constraint store S.

Constraint-lambda terms are like standard lambda terms but they now include notations for constraint-variables and they also may include a notation for the store of constraints. *General constraint terms (GCT)* are augmented terms of the constraint language. Constraint-variables may appear as part of a constraint-lambda term or as part of a general constraint term. This makes it possible to transfer values from the constraint store to lambda terms. Similarly, a lambda term may appear inside a constraint term. Having lambda terms inside constraints allows us to compute values in the lambda calculus and introduce them as part of a constraint. These terms have to be reduced to constraint terms before being passed to the constraint-solver. *General constraints (GC)* comprise primitive constraints and conjunctions of constraints, defined in terms of general constraint terms instead of the usual constraint terms. They correspond to the notion of constraint in the previously defined constraint-language but are slightly more general since they may include lambda terms as constituents.

Similarly to the notation in Mandel's calculi, a constrained-lambda term is of the form $\{C\}M$ where C is a constraint (that may be absent) and M is a (constrained)lambda term. We use the letters C for general constraints and t for general constraint terms. These terms may be modified by sub- or super-scripts.

The grammar of constraint-lambda terms is

$\Lambda ::= x \mid X \mid c \mid f(\Lambda, \ldots, \Lambda) \mid \lambda x.\Lambda \mid \Lambda\Lambda \mid \{GC\}\Lambda$ and for general constraints is $GC ::= P(GCT, \ldots, GCT) \mid (GC \wedge GC)$. For general constraint terms it is $GCT ::= \Lambda$.

The generalized constraint terms are exactly the same as the constraint-lambda terms. Nevertheless we consider it important to distinguish these two sets since the set of *pure* constraint-lambda terms and *pure* constraint terms, which we now define, are disjoint.

We call a constraint-lambda term *pure* if it contains no subterm of the form $\{C\}M$; we call a constraint term *pure* if it contains no lambda term, i.e., if the only constraint-lambda terms it contains are constraint variables, constants or applications of function-symbols to pure constraint terms. A constraint C is called a *pure constraint*, if every constraint term appearing in C is pure.

Free and bound variables and substitution are defined in a straightforward way (see [6] for full details). We identify terms that are only distinguished by the names of bound variables, e.g., we regard the terms $\lambda x.M$ and $\lambda y.(M[x/y])$ as equal, provided y does not appear in M. This means that we do not need to introduce an α-reduction rule.

We now define the reduction rules for the (single-valued) unrestricted constraint-lambda calculus. "Single-valued" means that substitution only occurs when a constraint variable can only take a unique value. (Multiple values are dealt with in [6] and our paper in preparation.) Because of its simplicity this calculus is a good starting point for the investigation of our calculi.

Reduction rules for the single-valued unrestricted constraint-lambda calculus are defined on pairs (M, S) consisting of a constraint-lambda term and a store. Nevertheless we shall abuse notation by speaking of "reducing a constraint lambda term" when the store is obvious or irrelevant.

A constraint store is either a set of constraints or the inconsistent store: $\otimes$. We assume that for every element of the constraint domain there is a distinguished or *canonical name* (cf. [8]). The store will then automatically entail e.g. $X = cn$ if it entails $X = t$ and $t = cn$, where cn is a canonical name.

The only operation on constraint stores we shall use is the addition of a new constraint, C, to a store, denoted by $S \oplus C$ where $S \oplus C = S \cup \{C\}$ if $S \cup \{C\}$ is consistent, $= \otimes$ otherwise. For the present we shall assume that all constraint stores are consistent. Moreover we shall assume that the adding constraints monotonically increases the store.

There are three rules: The first rule is the usual beta-reduction familiar from the lambda calculus. The other two allow information to flow from the constraint-lambda term into the constraint store and *vice versa*.

Definition 2 (Reduction rules). *We say that a constraint-lambda term M is reducible with store S if one of the rules (β), (CI) or (CS), below, is applicable to the pair (M, S). We write $(M, S) \to (M', S')$ where S' is the resulting store. We say M is reducible (or M is a redex), if, for all stores S, there is a store S', such that (M, S) is reducible to (M', S'). We write $M \to M'$ in this case.*

We call a sequence of zero or more reduction steps $(M_1, S_1) \to (M_2, S_2), \ldots, (M_{n-1}, S_{n-1}) \to (M_n, S_n)$ a reduction sequence and abbreviate it by $(M_1, S_1) \to^* (M_n, S_n)$. We write $M \to^* M'$ as an abbreviation for $\forall S.\exists S'.(M, S) \to^* (M', S')$.

1. Beta-reduction.
$$((\lambda x.M)N, S) \to (M[x/N], S). \tag{β}$$

E.g. if we have the integers as constraint domain, $(\lambda x.x + 1)\,5 \to 5 + 1$.

2. Constraint Introduction. When a pure constraint appears in a term, we can add this constraint to the constraint store and remove it from the lambda expression:

$$(\{C\}M, S) \to (M, S \oplus C) \quad \text{if } C \text{ is a pure constraint.} \tag{CI}$$

For example $(\{X < 7\}X, \{X > 2\}) \to (X, \{X < 7, X > 2\})$. (The appearance of lambda terms inside constraints is merely a syntactical device to allow the lambda calculus to provide values to the constraint solver.)

3. Constraint Substitution. This next rule allows us to substitute values computed by the constraint solver into the lambda term provided they are unique:

$$(X, S) \to (M, S) \quad \text{if } S \vdash X = M. \qquad (CS)$$

This rule allows us to reduce $(X, \{X < 5, X > 3\})$ to $(4, \{X < 5, X > 3\})$ over the constraint domain of integers. It is often convenient to restrict this rule to terms not containing constraint variables, since otherwise there may be infinite reduction sequences whenever a constraint of the form $X = Y$ is provable in the constraint theory. Thus we could have: $(X, \{X = Y\}) \to (Y, \{X = Y\}) \to (X, \{X = Y\}) \to \cdots$.

Closure. We now take the closure of these reductions. We give a few examples.

$$\text{if } (M, S) \to (M', S'), \text{ then } (\lambda x.M, S) \to (\lambda x.M', S'),$$
$$\text{and similarly } (f(M_1, \ldots, M, \ldots, M_n), S) \to (f(M_1, \ldots, M', \ldots, M_n), S'),$$
$$(MN, S) \to (M'N, S'),$$
$$\text{and } (\{C[x/M]\}N, S) \to (\{C[x/M']\}N, S').$$

As usual if M is a term such that no reduction rule is applicable to a subterm of M for a given store S, then we say that M is in *normal form for the store S*. If M is in normal form for all stores S, we say that M is in *normal form*.

Fact 1. *The unrestricted constraint-lambda is a conservative extension of the traditional lambda calculus* (λK).

This is clear since every lambda term can be interpreted as a constraint-lambda term and the only reduction rule that then applies is beta-reduction.

3.1   Example. Mandel's Triangle Example Revisited

We consider a constraint solver for the real numbers that can solve quadratic equations, etc. and consider this triangle (cf. [8], p. 49). By Pythagoras' Theorem we have $p^2 + h^2 = b^2$ and $(a - p)^2 + h^2 = c^2$. Every 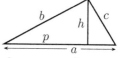 solution has to satisfy the triangle inequality: $a < b + c$, $b < c + a$ and $c < a + b$. Having computed p and h from these equations, we obtain the area as the sum of the areas of the small right-angled triangles $ph/2 + (a - p)h/2$.

We write x_a, x_b and x_c for the variables representing the lengths of a, b and c. We use the upper case variables X_p and X_h for p and h because their values are computed by the constraint solver. This leads to the following program that is, in fact, a restricted constraint-lambda term (see below Section 5).

$$\lambda x_a x_b x_c . \{X_p^2 + X_h^2 = x_b^2 \land (x_a - X_p)^2 + X_h^2 = x_c^2 \land X_h > 0 \land$$
$$x_a < x_b + x_c \land x_b < x_c + x_a \land x_c < x_b + x_a\}$$
$$((\lambda y_1 y_2 . \{y_1 > 0 \land y_2 > 0\} y_1 \times y_2 / 2) X_p X_h +$$
$$(\lambda y_1 y_2 . \{y_1 > 0 \land y_2 > 0\} y_1 \times y_2 / 2)(x_a - X_p) X_h)$$
$$5 \quad 4 \quad 3$$

By performing three β-reductions and one (CI)-step we obtain

$$((\lambda y_1 y_2.\{y_1 > 0 \ \wedge \ y_2 > 0\} y_1 \times y_2/2) X_p X_h +$$
$$(\lambda y_1 y_2.\{y_1 > 0 \ \wedge \ y_2 > 0\} y_1 \times y_2/2)(5 - X_p) X_h)$$

By performing three β-reductions and one (CI)-step we obtain

$$((\lambda y_1 y_2.\{y_1 > 0 \ \wedge \ y_2 > 0\} y_1 \times y_2/2) X_p X_h +$$
$$(\lambda y_1 y_2.\{y_1 > 0 \ \wedge \ y_2 > 0\} y_1 \times y_2/2)(5 - X_p) X_h)$$

with a constraint store containing $X_p^2 + X_h^2 = 4^2 \ \wedge \ (5 - X_p)^2 + X_h^2 = 3^2 \ \wedge$ $X_h > 0 \ \wedge \ 5 < 4 + 3 \ \wedge \ 4 < 3 + 5 \ \wedge \ 3 < 4 + 5$. Then, because the constraint solver can solve quadratic equations, the constraint store entails

$$X_h = 2.4 \text{ and } X_p = 1.8. \tag{$\triangle$}$$

We can then β-reduce the constraint-lambda term to

$$(\{X_p > 0 \ \wedge \ X_h > 0\} X_p \times X_h/2) + (\{\{(5 - X_p) > 0 \ \wedge \ X_h > 0\}(5 - X_p) \times X_h/2)$$

with the same constraint store. Next we reduce the term using (CI) to

$$X_p \times X_h/2 + (5 - X_p) \times X_h/2.$$

Finally we use (CS) (twice) on X_p and X_h utilizing $(\triangle)$ so that we obtain the numerical expression $1.8 \times 2.4/2 + (5 - 1.8) \times 2.4/2$ and therefore 6 as the final solution (using the canonical name 6 for the numerical expression).

4 Confluence of the Unrestricted Constraint-Lambda Terms as a Reduction System

There is a significant difference between the rules (β) and (CI) on the one hand and (CS) on the other: the first two rules only depend on the syntactical structure of the term, while the constraint-substitution rule (CS) depends on the constraint store and the logical consequences of the constraint system.

It is not possible to have confluence in the traditional sense for the unrestricted calculus because different reductions can lead to different constraint stores. Consider the pair $((\lambda x.X)(\{X = cn\}M), \emptyset)$, where the constraint store is initially empty. This can be reduced in two different ways. In the first the final store contains $X = cn$ but in the second the store remains empty and it is not possible to carry out any further reduction. Thus we have the reductions:

$$((\lambda x.X)(\{X = cn\}M), \emptyset) \rightarrow ((\lambda x.X)M, \{X = cn\}) \qquad \text{by } (CI)$$
$$\rightarrow (X, \{X = cn\}) \qquad \text{by } \beta\text{-reduction}$$
$$(*) \qquad \qquad \rightarrow (cn, \{X = cn\}) \qquad \text{by } (CS)$$

but we also have

$$(**) \quad ((\lambda x.X)(\{X = cn\}M), \emptyset) \rightarrow (X, \emptyset) \text{ by } \beta\text{-reduction},$$

and there is no way to reduce $(*)$ and $(**)$ to a common pair (N, S').

Note that the constraint store may contain different sets of constraints at different stages of the the reduction so that, while a constraint substitution may not be possible at some reduction step, it may become possible later.

We therefore introduce a restricted notion of confluence where the term obtained is the same in the final pair but the stores may be different.

First we say that a sequence of reductions can be *restricted to store S* if we only need to use information from store S in applications of (CS).

Definition 3. *A constraint-lambda calculus is said to be* confluent as a reduction system *if: For each pair of reduction sequences* $(M, S) \to^* (M_1, S_1)$ *and* $(M, S) \to^* (M_2, S_2)$ *such that both can be restricted to store S, then there exist a term N and stores* S_1', S_2' *such that* $(M_1, S_1) \to^* (N, S_1')$ *and* $(M_2, S_2) \to^* (N, S_2')$.

Observe that (*) above cannot be restricted to store $\emptyset$ but, of course, (**) can.

It is not straightforward to show confluence of constraint-lambda calculi using the usual method of critical pairs, since the constraint-lambda calculi are conditional rewrite systems and the (CS)-rule does not satisfy the usual preconditions for such systems. We prefer to show one-sided local confluence with a labelled reduction system. This technique is sufficient to establish confluence as a reduction system for the unrestricted constraint-lambda calculus and it can easily be adapted to the restricted calculus (see below Theorem 2).

Theorem 1. *The unrestricted constraint-lambda calculus is confluent as a reduction system.*

The proof involves proving an analogue of the Strip Lemma. In the present case this means that if there are two reductions of a constraint-lambda term, $(M, S) \to (N_1, S_1)$ and $(M, S) \to^* (N_2, S_2)$, then there are stores S_1', S_2' and a term N such that $(N_1, S_1) \to^* (N, S_1')$ and $(N_2, S_2) \to^* (N, S_2')$. We do *not* suppose that two reduction paths ending in the same term also result in the same store.

We "remember" the redex L that we reduce in the single reduction step $M \to N_1$ by labelling L in the term M. We then trace L through the reductions from M to N_2 and show that we can reduce the "residuals" of L in N_2. We do this by defining *indexed constraint-lambda terms*, Λ^*, by

$$\Lambda^* = x \mid X \mid X^* \mid c \mid f(\Lambda^*, \ldots, \Lambda^*) \mid \lambda x.\Lambda^* \mid \lambda^* x.\Lambda^* \mid \Lambda^* \Lambda^* \mid \{C\}\Lambda^* \mid \{C\}^* \Lambda^*$$

Terms of the form X^*, $\lambda^* x.M$ and $\{C\}^* M$ are called *labelled terms*. The definition of generalized constraint terms is extended to include indexed terms as well: $GCT := \Lambda^*$. The labelled terms are used for the proof of the Strip Lemma to "remember" where the single reduction step from M to N_1 took place and to trace this reduction step through the reduction sequence $M \to^* N_2$. We can then obtain the common reduct N by reducing all the labelled terms still present in N_2.

We then add to the rules in Definition 2:

$$((\lambda^* x.M)N, S) \to (M[x/N], S), \qquad\qquad (\beta^*)$$

$$(\{C\}^* M, S) \to (M, S \oplus C), \text{ if } C \text{ is a pure constraint}, \qquad (CI^*)$$

$$\text{and } (X^*, S) \to (cn, S), \text{ if } S \vdash X = cn. \qquad\qquad (CS^*)$$

Let M be an indexed term, S a constraint store, and X a constraint variable such that $S \vdash X = cn$ for some canonical name cn. If X appears in M, we can use rule (CS) on the store S to reduce X to cn. If we obtain a term M' from M by replacing some occurrences of X by X^* we say that M' is obtained from M by *labelling the subterm X with store*[2] S.

If M has a subterm $L = (\lambda x.L_1)L_2$ and M' is obtained from M by replacing some occurrences of L by the term $(\lambda^* x.L_1)L_2$, we again say that M' is obtained from M by *labelling the subterm L with store S*. Since in cases such as this L is reducible for every store, we sometimes say M' is obtained from M by labelling. Similarly if a subterm $\{C\}M$ is replaced by $\{C\}^*M$.

We now have a series of lemmata whose proofs may be found in [6].

Lemma 1. *If $x \neq y$ and is not free in L, then $M[x/N][y/L] = M[y/L][x/N[y/L]]$.*

Recall that we are only considering applications of rule (CS) when the constraint variable for which we substitute a value is uniquely determined. Thus, if we have some store S for which $S \vdash X = M$, then no other value can be introduced for X. From this we conclude that if we have reduction sequences $(M, S) \to^* (M_1, S_1)$ and $(M, S) \to^* (M_2, S_2)$ that can both be restricted to store S, then every (CS) reduction performed in one of the sequences is either already performed in the other sequence or can still be performed on the result of the other sequence.

Lemma 2. *Let M^* be an indexed term that can be obtained from a constraint-lambda term M by labelling with store S. Then every labelled subterm of M^* is reducible with store S.*

Lemma 3. *Let M^* be an indexed term that can be obtained from a constraint-lambda term by labelling with store S, and let $(M^*, S) \to^* (M', S')$. Then every labelled subterm of M' is reducible with store S'.*

For every indexed constraint-lambda term M and every store S we define a constraint-lambda term $\epsilon_S(M)$ by induction on the structure of M as follows:

$$\epsilon_S(MN) := \epsilon_S(M)\epsilon_S(N) \qquad \text{if } M \neq \lambda^* x.L$$

$$\epsilon_S((\lambda^* x.M)N) := \epsilon_S(M)[x/\epsilon_S(N)]$$

$$\epsilon_S(\{C\}^* M) := \epsilon_S(M)$$

$$\epsilon_S(X^*) := cn \text{ if } S \vdash X = cn.$$

---

[2] The store is important for this definition since we assume that all labelled terms are redexes and we might not be able to derive the equation $X = cn$ for a store $S' \subsetneq S$.

On all other terms $\epsilon_S(M)$ operates transparently, e.g. $\epsilon_S(\lambda x.M) := \lambda x.\epsilon_S(M)$ and $\epsilon_S(\{C\}M) := \{\epsilon_S(C)\}\epsilon_S(M)$. In many cases the store S will be obvious from the context or not important so we omit it.

We also have to define an appropriate store. Again $S_\epsilon(M)$ leaves the store unchanged except in the following cases:

$$S_\epsilon(MN) := S_\epsilon(M) \cup S_\epsilon(N) \qquad S_\epsilon(C_1 \wedge C_2) := S_\epsilon(C_1) \cup S_\epsilon(C_2)$$
$$S_\epsilon(\{C\}M) := S_\epsilon(C) \cup S_\epsilon(M) \quad S_\epsilon(f(t_1,\ldots,t_n)) := S_\epsilon(t_1) \cup \cdots \cup S_\epsilon(t_n)$$
$$S_\epsilon(\{C\}^*M) := S_\epsilon(M) \oplus C \quad S_\epsilon(P(t_1,\ldots,t_n)) := S_\epsilon(t_1) \cup \cdots \cup S_\epsilon(t_n)$$

Lemma 4. *Let M_1, M_2 be constraint-lambda terms with $(M_1, S_1) \to^* (M_1', S_1')$ and $(M_2, S_2) \to^* (M_2', S_2')$. If S_1, $S_2 \subseteq S$, then $M_1[x/M_2]$ is reducible to $M_1'[x/M_2']$ with store S.*

Lemma 5. *Let S be a store and M^* an indexed term that can be obtained from a constraint-lambda term M by labelling with store S. Then M^* is reducible to $\epsilon_S(M)$ with store S.*

For every indexed term M, the term $|M| \in \Lambda$ is defined by replacing each labelled subterm by the corresponding unlabelled term, e.g., $|\lambda^*x.\lambda^*y.xy| = \lambda x.\lambda y.xy$.

The previous lemma guarantees that we can obtain $\epsilon_S(M)$ by performing reductions if M is obtained by labelling. The following lemma shows that, if we can perform a reduction between labelled terms, we can also perform a reduction between the corresponding unlabelled terms, and *vice versa*.

Lemma 6.   *1. Let M, N be constraint-lambda terms with $(M, S) \to^* (N, S')$, and let M' be obtained from M by labelling (i.e., $M = |M'|$). Then there exists a term N' such that N' can be obtained from N by labelling and $(M', S) \to^* (N', S')$.*
   2. For all indexed terms M', N' with $(M', S) \to^* (N', S')$ we have $(|M'|, S) \to^* (|N'|, S')$.

Lemma 7. *Let M, N be indexed terms where M is obtained by labelling a constraint-lambda term with store S and $(M, S) \to (N, S')$. Then $\epsilon(M)$ is reducible to $\epsilon(N)$ using store $S_\epsilon(M)$, i.e., $\exists S''.(\epsilon(M), S_\epsilon(M)) \to^* (\epsilon(N), S'')$.*

Lemma 8. *Let M, N be indexed terms where M is obtained by labelling a constraint-lambda term and let $(M, S) \to^* (N, S')$ be a reduction sequence that can be restricted to store S. Then $\epsilon(M)$ is reducible to $\epsilon(N)$ using store $S_\epsilon(M)$, i.e., $\exists S''.(\epsilon(M), S_\epsilon(M)) \to^* (\epsilon(N), S'')$.*

Lemma 9. *For an indexed constraint-lambda term M the following holds: For every store S such that M is a labelling for $|M|$ with store S, there exists a store S' such that $(|M|, S) \to^* (\epsilon_S(M), S')$.*

Lemma 10 (Strip Lemma). *Let S be a store. For all constraint-lambda terms M, M', N, with $(M, S) \to (M', S')$ and $(M, S) \to^* (N, S'')$, where both reductions can be restricted to S, there exist stores S_1 and S_2 and a term N' with $(M', S') \to^* (N', S_1)$ and $(N, S'') \to^* (N', S_2)$.*

This immediately yields Theorem 1.

5   The Restricted Constraint-Lambda Calculus

The *unrestricted* constraint-lambda calculus is based on the λK-calculus. The *restricted* constraint-lambda calculus offers the same reduction rules, but the set of pure lambda terms is restricted to λI-terms only (see the next paragraph). This eliminates the problems with "disappearing" constraints.

The set of *restricted constraint-lambda terms* is defined just like the set of unrestricted constraint-lambda terms except that if M is a restricted constraint-lambda term then $\lambda x.M$ is a restricted constraint-lambda term only if x actually appears in, and is free in, M. The sets of *extended constraints* and *extended constraint terms* are defined similarly to the sets of general constraints and general constraint terms, but with restricted constraint-lambda terms in place of general constraint terms (see above Section 3). We write $M \in \Lambda_I$ if M is a restricted constraint-lambda term.

We use the same reduction rules and the same conventions as for the unrestricted constraint-lambda calculus. Most importantly, we use the variable convention. Then, as for the unrestricted constraint-lambda calculus (Fact 1), we have:

Fact 2. *The restricted constraint-lambda calculus is a conservative extension of the λI calculus.*

The terms of the restricted constraint-lambda calculus satisfy certain properties that are not necessarily true of unrestricted terms.

Lemma 11.   *1. $\forall x.M, N \in \Lambda_I \implies M[x/N] \in \Lambda_I$,*
2. $\lambda x.M \in \Lambda_I \implies$ free variables of $((\lambda x.M)N)$ = free variables of $(M[x/N])$,
3. $M \in \Lambda_I, M \to^* N \implies N \in \Lambda_I$, and
4. $M \in \Lambda_I, M \to^* N \implies$ free variables of M = free variables of N.

Lemma 12. *The restricted constraint-lambda calculus is confluent as a reduction system.*

The proof of this lemma is identical to the proof for the unrestricted constraint-lambda calculus, since the two systems share the same reduction rules and the restricted constraint-lambda calculus is closed under these reductions.

In the restricted constraint-lambda calculus we can no longer "lose" constraints, since terms such as $(\lambda x.Y)(\{C\}z)$ that lead to problems in the case of the unrestricted constraint-lambda calculus are no longer allowed. This can be seen from the following lemmata which are strengthened results of Lemmata 7 and 8 for the unrestricted constraint-lambda calculus.

Lemma 13. *Let M, N be indexed terms where M is obtained by labelling a constraint-lambda term with store S and $(M, S) \to (N, S')$. Then $\epsilon(M)$ is reducible using store $S_\epsilon(M)$ and there exists a unique store S'' such that $(\epsilon(M), S_\epsilon(M)) \to^* (\epsilon(N), S'')$ and $(N, S') \to^* (\epsilon(N), S'')$, and in particular $S' \subseteq S''$.*

Lemma 14. *Let M, N be indexed terms where M is obtained by labelling a constraint-lambda term and let $(M, S) \to^* (N, S')$ be a reduction sequence. Then $\epsilon(M)$ is reducible with store $S_\epsilon(M)$ and there exists a unique store S'' such that $(\epsilon(M), S_\epsilon(M)) \to^* (\epsilon(N), S'')$ and $(N, S') \to^* (\epsilon(N), S'')$, and in particular $S' \subseteq S''$.*

Lemma 15 (Strengthened Strip Lemma). *For all constraint-lambda terms M, M', N and for all stores S, S_1, S_2 with $(M, S) \to (M', S_1)$ and $(M, S) \to^* (N, S_2)$, there exists a term N' and a unique store S' with $(M', S_1) \to^* (N', S')$ and $(N, S_2) \to^* (N', S')$.*

Then the proof of Theorem 1 immediately yields

Theorem 2. *The restricted constraint-lambda calculus is confluent.*

Corollary 1. *Normal forms are unique: If a term M of the restricted constraint-lambda calculus has normal forms N_1 and N_2, then $N_1 = N_2$.*

5.1   Inconsistent Stores and the Single-Valued Calculus

The single-valued constraint-lambda calculi can be extended to allow for inconsistent constraint stores. If we add the special constraint-lambda term $\bot$ and the reduction rule

$$(M, \otimes) \to \bot \qquad\qquad (\bot)$$

to the restricted constraint-lambda calculus it remains confluent: If $(M, S) \to^* (M_1, S_1)$ and $(M, S) \to^* (M_2, \otimes)$, then the confluence of the restricted constraint-lambda calculus ensures that (M_1, S_1) can be further reduced to $(M_1', \otimes)$ for some term M_1'. Both terms can then be reduced to the common reduct $(\bot, \otimes)$.

6   Denotational Semantics

We let E denote the semantic domain of the constraint-lambda terms. The denotational semantics are defined in such a way that each model for the usual lambda calculus can be used as a model for the constraint-lambda calculus provided that the model is large enough to allow an embedding $emb : D \to E$ of the underlying constraint domain D into E. This is usually the case for the constraint domains appearing in applications.

As usual we have an isomorphism $E \to E \simeq E$. We denote environments by η (a mapping from lambda variables to E). We can then define a semantic valuation from the set of constraint terms, $\mathcal{T}$, into D which we call $val : \mathcal{T} \to D$. We shall write val' for $emb \circ val : \mathcal{T} \to E$.

We associate a pure lambda term with every constraint-lambda term by replacing all constraint variables with lambda variables. Let M be a constraint-lambda term with constraint variables $\{X_1, \ldots, X_n\}$ and let $\{x_1, \ldots, x_n\}$ be a set of distinct lambda variables not appearing in M. Then the *associated constraint-variable free term*, $cvft(M)$, is the term

$$\lambda x_1 \ldots \lambda x_n.(M[X_1/x_1] \ldots [X_n/x_n])$$

We separate the computation of a constraint-lambda term into two steps. First we collect all constraints appearing in the term and compute all the lambda terms contained therein in the appropriate context. Then we apply the associated constraint-variable free term to the values computed by the constraint-solver to obtain the value of the constraint-lambda term.

For a constraint-lambda term M and store S we set

1. $\mathfrak{D}_\eta$ as the denotation of a constraint-lambda term in an environment η when the constraints are deleted from the term.[3]
2. The function $\mathfrak{C}^C$ collects all the constraints appearing in the constraint-lambda term T and evaluates the lambda expressions contained within these constraints. The superscript C on $\mathfrak{C}$ denotes the context that is recursively generated.

The semantics of a single-valued constraint-lambda term with respect to a store S is defined as

$$[\![(M, S)]\!] = \{\mathfrak{D}_\eta(cvft(M)v_1 \ldots v_n) \mid S \cup \mathfrak{C}^\circ(M) \vdash X_1 = v_1, \ldots, X_n = v_n\}$$

where $\mathfrak{D}$ defines the usual semantics for pure lambda terms and ignores constraints contained within a term. The superscript $\circ$ on $\mathfrak{C}$ indicates that we are starting with the empty context and building up $\mathfrak{C}$ as we go into the terms. The environment η is supposed to contain bindings for the free variables of M.

Intuitively this definition means that the semantics of a single-valued constraint-lambda term is obtained as the denotation of the lambda term when all constraints are removed from the term and all constraint-variables are replaced by their values. In particular we have (by footnote 3):

Fact 3. *The denotational semantics of a pure lambda term is the same as in the traditional denotational semantics.*

---

[3] Therefore, for pure constraint-lambda terms, $\mathfrak{D}_\eta$ represents the usual semantics.

The denotation of a constraint-lambda term in an environment η, $\mathfrak{D}_\eta$, is defined as follows:[4]

$$
\begin{aligned}
\mathfrak{D}_\eta(\lambda x.M) &= \lambda v.\mathfrak{D}_{\eta[x/v]}(M) \\
\mathfrak{D}_\eta(x) = \eta(x) \qquad \mathfrak{D}_\eta(MN) &= \mathfrak{D}_\eta(M)\mathfrak{D}_\eta(N) \\
\mathfrak{D}_\eta(c) = val'(c) \qquad \mathfrak{D}_\eta(\{C\}M) &= \mathfrak{D}_\eta(M) \\
\mathfrak{D}_\eta(f(M_1,\ldots,M_n)) &= val'(f)(\mathfrak{D}_\eta(M_1),\ldots,\mathfrak{D}_\eta(M_n))
\end{aligned}
$$

When evaluating lambda terms nested inside constraints, we are only interested in results that are pure constraints, since the constraint solver cannot handle any other terms. Therefore we identify all other constraint-lambda terms with the failed computation.

We can now show that the semantics of a constraint-lambda term is compatible with the reduction rules.

Lemma 16. *For all environments η and all terms M, N, we have*

$$
\mathfrak{D}_\eta(M[x/N]) = \mathfrak{D}_{\eta[x/\mathfrak{D}_\eta(N)]}(M).
$$

Theorem 3 (Correctness of the Denotational Semantics). *Let M and M' be restricted constraint-lambda terms such that $(M, S) \to (M', S')$. Then*
1. for every environment η, we have $\mathfrak{D}_\eta(cvft(M)) = \mathfrak{D}_\eta(cvft(M'))$, and
2. $[\![(M, S)]\!] = [\![(M', S')]\!]$.

For unrestricted constraint-lambda terms we may lose a constraint during the reduction and then one of two things can happen. 1. We can still compute a single value for each constraint variable and then we get the same result as if we had entered that constraint into the store (since we are assuming there are no inconsistencies), or 2. there is at least one constraint variable for which we no longer obtain a single value. Then, in the denotational semantics, we get the empty set as the value of the term. Therefore Theorem 3 also holds for the unrestricted calculus provided we replace = by $\supseteq$ in item 2.

Theorem 4. *The denotational semantics is compatible with the reduction rules for both the restricted and the unrestricted constraint-lambda calculi.*

7   Conclusions and Future Work

We have introduced the unrestricted constraint-lambda calculus and the restricted constraint-lambda calculus in a simple and transparent fashion which, unlike previous attempts at defining combinations of constraint solvers and

---

[4] Notice that the semantic function $\mathfrak{D}$ is only applied to constraint-variable-free terms and that it does not recurse on constraints, therefore there is no need to define it on constraints or constraint terms. Furthermore the interpretations of a constant, when regarded as part of a lambda term or as part of a constraint, coincide, as is to be expected.

lambda calculi, makes them conservative extensions of the corresponding traditional lambda calculi.

The interface between the constraint store and the lambda terms ensures clarity and the smooth movement of information into and out of the constraint store.

We have shown that the unrestricted constraint-lambda calculus satisfies a restricted, but natural, confluence property, namely that it is confluent as a reduction system, and we have proved that the restricted constraint-lambda calculus is confluent in the usual sense so its normal forms are unique.

In addition, the denotational semantics of each of the theories is a simple, conservative, extension of the standard denotational semantics of the corresponding lambda calculus.

In papers in preparation we add disjunction and multiple solutions to the system and also describe our implementation of these calculi in the language *Dylan*.

References

1. John Newsome Crossley, Pierre Lim, and Peter John Stuckey. Interface logic programming. *Australian Computer Journal*, 21(2):49–55, 1989.
2. John Newsome Crossley, Luis Mandel, and Martin Wirsing. Una extensión de constraints al cálculo lambda. In *Segundo Congreso de Programación Declarativa, ProDe '93, Blanes, Girona, Spain, September 29-30, October 1 1993*, pages 203–16. 1993. In Spanish.
3. John Newsome Crossley, Luis Mandel, and Martin Wirsing. First-order constrained lambda calculus. In *Frontiers of Combining Systems, First International Workshop*, number 3 in Applied Logics, pages 339–356. Kluwer Academic Publishers, 1996.
4. John Darlington, Yi-ke Guo, and Helen Pull. Introducing constraint functional logic programming. Technical report, Imperial College, Febuary 1991.
5. Bart Demoen, María García de la Banda, Warren Harvey, Kim Marriott, and Peter Stuckey. An overview of *HAL*. In *Proceedings of Principles and Practice of Constraint Programming*, pages 174–188. Asociation for Computing Machinery, 1999.
6. Matthias Hölzl. *Constraint-Lambda Calculi: Theory and Applications*. PhD thesis, Ludwig-Maximilians-Universität, München, 2001.
7. Joxan Jaffar and Jean-Louis Lassez. Constraint logic programming. In *Conference Record, 14th Annual ACM Symposium on Principles of Programming Languages, Munich, West Germany, 21-23 Jan 1987*, pages 111–119. Association for Computing Machinery, 1987.
8. Luis Mandel. *Constrained Lambda Calculus*. PhD thesis, Ludwig-Maximilians-Universität, München, 1995.
9. Luis Mandel and María Victoria Cengarle. The disjunctive constrained lambda calculus. In Dines Bjørner, Manfred Broy, and Igor Vasilevich Pottosin, editors, *Perspectives of Systems Informatics, (2nd. International Andrei Ershov Memorial Conference, Proceedings)*, volume 1181 of *Lecture Notes in Computer Science*, pages 297–309. Springer Verlag, 1996.

222 Matthias Hölzl and John N. Crossley

10. Luis Mandel, Martin Wirsing, and John Newsome Crossley. Cálculo lambda de primer orden con constraints y la propiedad Church-Rosser. In *Primer Congreso Argentino de Ciencias de la Computacion, CACIC'95 Proceedings, Bahia Blanca, Argentina*, pages 493–504. Universaidad Nacional de Sur, 1995. In Spanish.
11. David McAllester and Jeffrey Mark Siskind. Nondeterministic Lisp as a substrate for constraint logic programming. In *Proceedings AAAI*, pages 133–138, July 1993.
12. Dale Miller and Gopalan Nadathur. An overview of λ-prolog. In R. Kowalski and K. Bowen, editors, *Proceedings of the Fifth International Conference on Logic Programming*, pages 810–827, 1988.
13. Andy Mück, Thomas Streicher, and Hendrik C.R. Lock. A tiny constraint functional logic language and its continuation semantics. In Donald Sannella, editor, *Programming languages and systems – ESOP'94, 5th European Symposium on Programming, Edinburgh, U.K., April 11–13, 1994 Proceedings*, volume 788 of *Lecture Notes in Computer Science*, pages 439–453, Berlin, 1994. Springer-Verlag.
14. Gert Smolka. A foundation for higher-order concurrent constraint programming. In Jean-Pierre Jouannaud, editor, *1st International Conference on Constraints in Computational Logics*, volume 845 of *Lecture Notes in Computer Science*, pages 50–72, Berlin, 1994. Springer-Verlag.

Labelled Deduction
over Algebras of Truth-Values[*]

João Rasga[1], Amílcar Sernadas[1], Cristina Sernadas[1], and Luca Viganò[2]

[1] CLC, Dep. de Matemática, IST, Av. Rovisco Pais, 1049-001 Lisbon, Portugal
`www.cs.math.ist.utl.pt/s84.www/cs/{jfr,acs,css}.html`
`jfr,acs,css@math.ist.utl.pt`
[2] Institut für Informatik, Universität Freiburg, Georges-Köhler-Allee 52,
D-79110 Freiburg, Germany
`www.informatik.uni-freiburg.de/~luca`
`luca@informatik.uni-freiburg.de`

Abstract. We introduce a framework for presenting non-classical logics in a modular and uniform way as labelled natural deduction systems. The use of algebras of truth-values as the labelling algebras of our systems allows us to give generalized systems for multiple-valued logics. More specifically, our framework generalizes previous work where labels represent worlds in the underlying Kripke structure: since we can take multiple-valued logics as meaning not only finitely or infinitely many-valued logics but also power-set logics, our framework allows us to present also logics such as modal, intuitionistic and relevance logics, thus providing a first step towards fibring these logics with many-valued ones.

1 Introduction

Context. *Labelled Deduction* is an approach to presenting different logics in a uniform and natural way as Gentzen-style deduction systems, such as natural deduction, sequent or tableaux systems; see, for instance, [2,3,8,9,11,16,21]. It has been applied, for example, to formalize and reason about dynamic "state-oriented" properties, such as knowledge, belief, time, space, and resources, and thereby formalize deduction systems for a wide range of non-classical logics, such as modal, temporal, intuitionistic, relevance and other substructural logics. The intuition behind Labelled Deduction is that the *labelling* (sometimes also called prefixing, annotating or subscripting) allows one to explicitly encode additional information, of a semantic or proof-theoretical nature, that is otherwise implicit in the logic one wants to capture. To illustrate this, take the simple, standard example of modal logics, where the additional information encoded into the syntax usually comes from the underlying Kripke semantics: instead of considering a modal formula φ, we can consider the *labelled formula* $x : \varphi$, which intuitively means that φ holds at the world denoted by x within the underlying Kripke structure (i.e. model). We can also use labels to specify the way in which the

---

[*] Work partially supported by *Fundação para a Ciência e a Tecnologia*, Portugal.

A. Armando (Ed.): FroCoS 2002, LNAI 2309, pp. 222–239, 2002.
© Springer-Verlag Berlin Heidelberg 2002

different worlds are related in the Kripke structures; for example, we can use the formula xRy to specify that the world denoted by y is accessible from that denoted by x. A modal labelled natural deduction system over this extended language is then obtained by giving inference rules for deriving labelled formulae, introducing or eliminating formula constructors such as implication $\sqsupset$ and modal necessity $\Box$, and by defining a suitable *labelling algebra*, which governs the inferences of formulae *about* labels, such as xRy.

Labelled deduction systems are *modular* for families of logics, such as the family of normal modal logics, in that to capture logics in the family we only need to vary appropriately the labelling algebra, while leaving the language and the rules for the formula constructors unchanged. Labelled deduction systems are also *uniform*, in that the same philosophy and technique can be applied for different, unrelated logic families. More specifically, changes in the labelling, i.e. in how formulae are labelled and with what labels (as we might need labels that are structurally more complex than the simple equivalents of Kripke worlds), together with changes in the language and rules, allow for the formalization of systems for non-classical logics other than the modal ones. For instance, labels can also be employed to give Gentzen-style systems for many-valued logics; in this case labels are used to represent the set of truth-values of the particular logic, which can be either the unit interval $[0,1]$ on the rational numbers or a finite set of rational numbers of the form $\{0, \frac{1}{n-1}, \ldots, \frac{n-2}{n-1}, 1\}$, e.g. the set $\{0, 0.5, 1\}$ that is used in 3-valued Gödel logic (see Example 3 and note that in this paper we employ falsum $\bot$ and verum $\top$ instead of 0 and 1). For examples of many-valued labelled deduction systems, mostly tableaux systems, see [1,6,7,13,14]. In these systems, the labelled formula $x : \varphi$ intuitively means that the formula φ has truth-value x; or, when x is a set of truth-values as in the "sets-as-signs" approach, it means that φ has one of the values in x. The inference rules and the labelling algebra of a system then essentially mirror the truth-tables of the formula constructors of the corresponding logic.

Contributions. We here introduce a framework for presenting non-classical logics in a modular and uniform way as labelled natural deduction systems. The main idea underlying our approach is the use of *algebras of truth-values* as the labelling algebras of our systems, which allows us to give generalized systems for *multiple-valued logics*. More specifically, our framework generalizes previous work, including our own [3,16,21], on labelled deduction systems where labels represent worlds in the underlying Kripke structures, and this generalization is illustrated by the following observation: since we can take multiple-valued logics as meaning not only finitely or infinitely many-valued logics but also *power-set logics*, i.e. logics for which the denotation of a formula can be seen as a set of worlds, our framework allows us to give systems also for logics such as modal, intuitionistic and relevance ones. In a nutshell, the novelty of our approach with respect to previous approaches based on labelling is that we can capture all these different logics *within the same formalism*. (It is interesting to note that this also provides a first, large, step towards the *fibring* [4,12] of these logics with many-valued ones; we have begun [15] investigating in this direction as part of our research program on fibring of logics [16,18,19,22].)

The fact that the labels constitute an algebra of truth-values means that we can have operations on truth-values, and that formula constructors can be associated with these operations. To this end, the syntax of our systems defines operators that build labels as terms of truth-values, and uses these "complex" labels to build two kinds of formulae: (i) *labelled formulae*, which are built by prefixing "standard", unlabelled, formulae with a label (and with an infix operator : or ::), and (ii) *truth-value formulae*, which are equalities and inequalities between labels. For labels β, β_1, β_2 and a formula φ, the semantic intuition behind these formulae is as follows: $\beta : \varphi$ means that the value of φ is equal to that of the truth-value term β, $\beta :: \varphi$ means that the value of φ is greater than or equal to that of β, $\beta_1 = \beta_2$ means that the value of β_2 is equal to that of β_1, and $\beta_1 \leq \beta_2$ means that the value of β_2 is greater than or equal to that of β_1.

A system for a particular logic comprises then inference rules that define how these formulae can be derived, e.g. "basic" rules expressing the properties of :, ::, = and $\leq$, rules defining how the formula constructors are introduced and eliminated and how this is reflected in the associated label operators, and rules defining properties of these operators. For example, the modal constructor $\Box$ is associated with the label operator $\check{\Box}$, and different modal logics are obtained modularly, by varying the properties of (i.e. adding or deleting rules for) $\check{\Box}$.

We give here introduction and elimination rules for general formula constructors, which subsume, as special cases, non-classical constructors like necessity or intuitionistic, relevant, or many-valued implication, as well as classical (i.e. material) implication and classical conjunction and disjunction. We then consider three particular kinds of labelled deduction systems that can be expressed within our framework: (i) *exhaustive systems* where each formula constructor is associated with a truth-value operator of the same arity, (ii) *well-behaved systems* where the arity of the operator is less than or equal to the arity of the associated constructor, and for each constructor there are both introduction and elimination rules, and (iii) *finitely-valued systems* where the rules capture the truth-tables of formula constructors, as is common in systems for finitely-valued logics. As examples, we give systems for modal and relevance logics (which provide the basis for systems for other non-classical logics such as intuitionistic logic), and systems that capture many-valued logics, e.g. the 3-valued Gödel logic.

As exemplified in the intuitive explanations above, the semantics of our systems is given by structures interpreting both formulae and labels as truth-values, and checking if the relationship between them complies with the labelling, e.g. for the labelled formula $\beta : \varphi$ if the value of φ is indeed that of β. Rather than simply proving soundness and completeness for a particular system, we analyze soundness and completeness in the general context of our framework. That is, we establish the conditions under which our systems are sound and complete with respect to the algebraic semantics for the corresponding logics.

Organization. In §2 we introduce our general labelled deduction systems on algebras of truth-values, and in §3 we consider some special systems. In §4 we focus on semantics and define interpretation systems, and in §5 we establish conditions for soundness and completeness. In §6 we draw conclusions and discuss related and future work. Note that discussions and proofs have been shortened or omitted altogether; a detailed account is given in [15].

2   Labelled Deduction Systems

We define the language of our labelled deduction systems (LDSs), specifying how to build labels, formulae and judgements, and then define inference rules and derivations. We then consider the case of exhaustive LDSs, which is important for establishing completeness (as each LDS can be transformed into an exhaustive one).

2.1   Truth-Value Labels and Formulae

The use of terms of truth-values as labels allows us to build two kinds of formulae, namely (i) labelled formulae, obtained by prefixing "standard", unlabelled, formulae with a label (and with an infix operator : or ::), and (ii) truth-value formulae, which are equalities and inequalities between labels. To define these formulae, we introduce the general concept of signature, and then define a truth-value signature as the composition of a signature for formulae with one for labels.

A *signature* is a pair $\langle F, S \rangle$ where $F = \{F_k\}_{k \in \mathbb{N}}$ is a family of sets of *constructors* (F_k is the set of constructors of arity k) and S is a set of *meta-variables*. The set of propositions over a signature is the free algebra $L(\langle F, S \rangle)$ where the 0-ary operations are the elements of $F_0 \cup S$ and, for $k > 0$, the k-ary operations are the elements of F_k.

Definition 1. *A truth-value signature TVS is a tuple* $\Sigma = \langle C^f, \Xi^f, C^v, \Xi^v, D \rangle$ *where* $\langle C^f, \Xi^f \rangle$ *and* $\langle C^v, \Xi^v \rangle$ *are signatures with* $\mathbf{t} \in C_0^f$, $\top \in D$ *and* $D \subseteq C_0^v$.

The elements of the sets C_k^f and C_k^v are the *formula constructors of arity* k and the *truth-value operators of arity* k, respectively, where the *true* $\mathbf{t}$ is a 0-ary constructor. The elements of Ξ^f and Ξ^v are *schema formula variables* and *schema truth-value variables*, respectively. The elements of D are the *distinguished elements*, i.e. the designated elements of the set of truth-values; D is not empty and contains at least the top element (verum) $\top$. We call the elements of $L(\langle C^f, \Xi^f \rangle)$ *formulae* and the elements of $L(\langle C^v, \Xi^v \rangle)$ *truth-value terms*.

Definition 2. *Given a TVS* Σ, *truth-value terms* $\beta, \beta_1, \beta_2 \in L(\langle C^v, \Xi^v \rangle)$, *and a formula* $\varphi \in L(\langle C^f, \Xi^f \rangle)$, *the equalities* $\beta_1 = \beta_2$ *and the inequalities* $\beta_1 \leq \beta_2$ *are truth-value formulae, and* $\beta : \varphi$ *and* $\beta :: \varphi$ *are labelled formulae. We denote by* $L(\Sigma)$ *the set of truth-value and labelled formulae, and call its elements* composed *formulae.*

We employ the following notation: φ and γ are formulae in $L(\langle C^f, \Xi^f \rangle)$, β is a truth-value term in $L(\langle C^v, \Xi^v \rangle)$, ξ is a schema formula variable in Ξ^f, δ is a schema truth-value variable in Ξ^v, and ψ and η are composed formulae in $L(\Sigma)$. All these variables may be annotated with subscripts.

2.2   Deduction Systems and Derivations

A LDS allows us to infer a composed formula in $L(\Sigma)$ from a set of composed formulae in $L(\Sigma)$ or, in other words, to infer judgements.

Definition 3. *A judgement* J *over a TVS* Σ *is a triple* $\langle \Theta, \eta, \Upsilon \rangle$, *written* $\Theta \, / \, \eta \triangleright \Upsilon$ *(or* $\Theta \, / \, \eta$ *if* $\Upsilon = \emptyset$), *where* $\Theta \subseteq L(\Sigma)$, $\eta \in L(\Sigma)$ *and* $\Upsilon \subseteq \Xi^v$.

The set of composed formulae Θ and the composed formula η are the *antecedent* and the *consequent* of the judgement, respectively, and the schema truth-value variables in the set Υ are the *fresh* variables of the judgement. As will become clear when we will give rules for formula constructors, e.g. in Definition 10 and in Example 1, the fresh variables allow us to impose constraints on substitutions and thereby express universal quantification over truth-values.

In order to prove assertions using hypotheses, we need to say when a judgement follows (i.e. can be derived) from a set of judgements. Hence, we now introduce inference rules and then define generically a "basic" LDS that can be extended to systems for particular non-classical logics.

Definition 4. *A rule* r *over a TVS* Σ *is a pair* $\langle \{J_1, \ldots, J_k\}, J \rangle$, *graphically*

$$\frac{J_1 \cdots J_k}{J} \; r \, ,$$

where $J_1, \ldots, J_k, J$ *are judgements, and* J *is such that* $\Theta = \emptyset$ *and* $\Upsilon = \emptyset$.

Definition 5. *A labelled deduction system* LDS *is a pair* $\langle \Sigma, R \rangle$, *where* Σ *is a TVS and* R *is a set of rules including at least the following rules:*

$$\frac{\delta_1 \leq \delta_2 \quad \delta_2 :: \xi}{\delta_1 :: \xi} \; ::_I \, , \qquad \frac{\delta_1 :: \xi \quad \delta_2 : \xi}{\delta_1 \leq \delta_2} \; ::_E \, , \qquad \frac{\delta_1 = \delta_2 \quad \delta_2 : \xi}{\delta_1 : \xi} \; :_I \, , \qquad \frac{\delta : \xi}{\delta :: \xi} \; :_E \, ,$$

$$\frac{}{\delta \leq \delta} \; \leq_r \, , \qquad \frac{\delta_1 \leq \delta_2 \quad \delta_2 \leq \delta_3}{\delta_1 \leq \delta_3} \; \leq_t \, , \qquad \frac{\delta_1 \leq \delta_2 \quad \delta_2 \leq \delta_1}{\delta_1 = \delta_2} \; =_I \, , \qquad \frac{\delta_1 = \delta_2}{\delta_1 \leq \delta_2} \; =_E \, ,$$

$$\frac{\delta_2 = \delta_1}{\delta_1 = \delta_2} \; =_s \, , \qquad \frac{\delta_1 = \delta_1' \quad \cdots \quad \delta_k = \delta_k'}{o(\delta_1, \ldots, \delta_k) = o(\delta_1', \ldots, \delta_k')} \; =_{cong} \, , \qquad \frac{}{\delta \leq \top} \; \top \, , \qquad \frac{}{\top : t} \; t \, ,$$

where $k \in \mathbb{N}$, $o \in C_k^v$, $\delta, \delta_1, \ldots, \delta_k, \delta_1', \ldots, \delta_k' \in \Xi^v$ *and* $\xi \in \Xi^f$.

LDSs for particular logics are obtained by fixing a particular TVS Σ and adding rules to the ones in Definition 5, which establish minimal properties on labelling, common to all our LDSs. So, $\leq_r$ and $\leq_t$ establish that $\leq$ is reflexive and transitive, $=_s$ establishes that $=$ is symmetric, $=_I$ and $=_E$ introduce and eliminate $=$, and together with $=_{cong}$ they say that $=$ constitutes a congruence relation. The rules $::_I$, $::_E$ and $:_I$ define conditions that $::$ and $:$ should obey, relating labelled and truth-value formulae. Similarly to $=_E$, rule $:_E$ relates $:$ to $::$ (intuitively because if the value of ξ is equal to δ, i.e. $\delta : \xi$ holds, then a fortiori it is greater than or equal to it, i.e. $\delta :: \xi$ holds). The rule $\top$ says that "top" is the greatest element, and the rule **t** says that the true **t** is a formula corresponding to $\top$. Note also that, as we indicate below, other rules about $:$, $::$, $=$ and $\leq$ can be derived, such as the rules for the reflexivity and transitivity of $=$.

To define derivations in our LDSs, we introduce additional terminology and notation. A *substitution* is a pair $\sigma = \langle \sigma^f, \sigma^v \rangle$, where $\sigma^f : \Xi^f \to L(\langle C^f, \Xi^f \rangle)$ and $\sigma^v : \Xi^v \to L(\langle C^v, \Xi^v \rangle)$ are maps from schema variables to formulae and truth-value terms, respectively. Given a composed formula $\psi \in L(\Sigma)$, we denote by $\psi\sigma$ the composed formula that results from ψ by the simultaneous substitution of each ξ by $\sigma(\xi) = \sigma^f(\xi)$ and of each δ by $\sigma(\delta) = \sigma^v(\delta)$. By extension, $\Psi\sigma$ denotes the set consisting of $\psi\sigma$ for all $\psi \in \Psi$. Given a set of schema truth-value variables $\{\delta_1, \ldots, \delta_k\} \subseteq \Xi^v$, we say that the substitutions σ_1 and σ_2 are $\{\delta_1, \ldots, \delta_k\}$-*co-equivalent*, in symbols $\sigma_1 \equiv_{\{\delta_1, \ldots, \delta_k\}} \sigma_2$, iff $\sigma_1^f = \sigma_2^f$ and $\sigma_1^v(\delta) = \sigma_2^v(\delta)$ for each $\delta \in \Xi^v$ such that $\delta \notin \{\delta_1, \ldots, \delta_k\}$. We use $label(\Theta)$ to denote the set of all schema truth-value variables in a set of composed formulae Θ.

Definition 6. *A judgement J is derivable from a set Ω of judgements in a LDS $\langle \Sigma, R \rangle$, in symbols $\Omega \vdash_{\langle \Sigma, R \rangle} J$, iff there is a finite sequence of judgements $J_1, \ldots, J_n$ such that J_n is J and, for $l = 1, \ldots, n$, either*

1. *J_l is an axiom Ax, that is of the form $\psi_1, \ldots, \psi_m, \eta / \eta \rhd \Upsilon$; or*
2. *there are a rule $r' = \langle \{\Theta_1' / \eta_1' \rhd \Upsilon_1', \ldots, \Theta_k' / \eta_k' \rhd \Upsilon_k'\}, \eta' \rangle$ in R and substitutions $\sigma, \sigma_1, \ldots, \sigma_k$ such that $\eta_l = \eta'\sigma$ and for each $i = 1, \ldots, k$ there is $\Theta_i / \eta_i \rhd \Upsilon_i$ in $J_1, \ldots, J_{l-1}$ such that $\Theta_i = \Theta_l \cup \Theta_i'\sigma_i$, $\eta_i = \eta_i'\sigma_i$, $\Upsilon_i'\sigma_i \subseteq \Upsilon_i$ and $\Upsilon_i \setminus \Upsilon_i'\sigma_i = \Upsilon_l$, $label(\Theta_l) \cap \Upsilon_i'\sigma_i = \emptyset$, $\sigma_i \equiv_{\Upsilon_i'} \sigma$ and $\sigma_i(\delta) \notin (\Xi^v \setminus \{\delta\})\sigma_i$ for each $\delta \in \Upsilon_i'$; or*
3. *there is $\Theta / \eta \rhd \Upsilon \in \Omega$ and a substitution σ with $\sigma \equiv_\Upsilon id$ such that $\Theta\sigma \subseteq \Theta_l$, $label(\Theta \cup \{\eta\})\sigma \cap \Upsilon_l \subseteq \Upsilon\sigma$ and η_l is $\eta\sigma$ (where id is the pair of identity substitutions on Ξ^f and Ξ^v).*

The judgements $\Theta_l / \eta_l \rhd \Upsilon_l$ and $\Theta_i / \eta_i \rhd \Upsilon_i$ for $i = 1, \ldots, k$ in condition 2 constitute a rule, referred to as an instance of r' *by the substitutions $\sigma, \sigma_1, \ldots, \sigma_k$.*

Definition 7. *We say that a composed formula $\eta \in L(\Sigma)$ is inferred from a set of composed formulae $\Psi \subseteq L(\Sigma)$ in a LDS $\langle \Sigma, R \rangle$, in symbols $\Psi \vdash_{\langle \Sigma, R \rangle} \eta$, iff there are $\psi_1, \ldots, \psi_n \in \Psi$ such that $\vdash_{\langle \Sigma, R \rangle} \psi_1, \ldots, \psi_n / \eta$. When there is no risk of confusion we will simply write $\Psi \vdash \eta$.*

We say that a formula φ is a theorem of a LDS $\langle \Sigma, R \rangle$ with set D of designated truth-values whenever $\vdash_{\langle \Sigma, R \rangle} \delta : \varphi$ or $\vdash_{\langle \Sigma, R \rangle} \delta :: \varphi$ for some $\delta \in D$.

A rule $\langle \{J_1, \ldots, J_k\}, J \rangle$ is a *derived rule* in a LDS $\langle \Sigma, R \rangle$ iff $J_1, \ldots, J_k \vdash_{\langle \Sigma, R \rangle} J$. We will use derived rules like primitive ones. For example, among others, from the rules in Definition 5 we can derive in any LDS the rules for the reflexivity and transitivity of equality for labels ($=_r$ follows straightforwardly by the reflexivity $\leq_r$ of $\leq$ and $=_t$ follows by the transitivity $\leq_t$ of $\leq$ and the symmetry $=_s$ of $=$):

$$\frac{}{\delta = \delta} =_r \qquad \text{and} \qquad \frac{\delta_1 = \delta_2 \quad \delta_2 = \delta_3}{\delta_1 = \delta_3} =_t .$$

We give example derivations in the next section; we conclude this one by defining exhaustive systems, in which each formula constructor c is associated with a truth-value operation symbol $\overline{c}$ of the same arity.

Definition 8. *An* exhaustive LDS *is a triple* $\langle \Sigma, R, \dot{-}\rangle$ *such that: (i)* $\langle \Sigma, R \rangle$ *is a LDS, (ii)* $\dot{-}$ *is a family* $\{\dot{-}_k\}_{k \in \mathbb{N}}$ *of maps where* $\dot{-}_k : C_k^f \to C_k^v$ *for* $k \geq 1$, *and* $\dot{-}_0 : C_0^f \cup \Xi^f \to C_0^v \cup \Xi^v$ *with* $\overline{c}_0 \in C_0^v$ *and* $\overline{\xi}_0 \in \Xi^v$, *and (iii)* R *includes* $\dfrac{}{\overline{\xi} : \xi} \, \dot{-}$.

It is then easy to derive the following rules in any exhaustive LDS:

$$\frac{\delta = \overline{\xi}}{\delta : \xi} \; :_{I_2} \, , \qquad \frac{\delta : \xi}{\delta = \overline{\xi}} \; :_{E_2} \, , \qquad \frac{\delta \leq \overline{\xi}}{\delta :: \xi} \; ::_{I_2} \, , \qquad \frac{\delta :: \xi}{\delta \leq \overline{\xi}} \; ::_{E_2} \, .$$

Given a formula φ, $\overline{\varphi}$ denotes the term in $L(\langle C^v, \Xi^v \rangle)$ inductively induced by $\dot{-}$, and for a labelled formula $\beta : \varphi$, $\overline{\beta : \varphi}$ denotes the truth-value formula $\beta = \overline{\varphi}$. That is, $\dot{-}$ corresponds to $=$. Similarly for $\beta :: \varphi$, where $\ddot{-}$ corresponds to $\leq$.

By induction on the length of derivations we can then show that if $\Theta \vdash_{\langle \Sigma, R \rangle} \eta$ then $\overline{\Theta} \vdash_{\langle \Sigma, R, \dot{-}\rangle} \overline{\eta}$ where $\langle \Sigma, R, \dot{-}\rangle$ is the exhaustive LDS induced by $\langle \Sigma, R \rangle$.

3   Special Deduction Systems

In our LDSs we can formalize formula constructors that are common to several multiple-valued logics. One such constructor is conjunction, which, interpreted as a binary meet, is common to classical, intuitionistic, relevance, Gödel and many other logics. Another example is implication, in all its variants ranging from material to intuitionistic to relevance or to other non-classical, substructural implications. In fact, our framework allows us to define general introduction and elimination rules that encompass formula constructors in several logics like modal, intuitionistic and relevance logics thus obtaining the counterpart of the rules in [21], where the labels represent worlds in the underlying Kripke structures. To formalize this, we now introduce well-behaved systems, which are based on a stronger definition of signature than the simple one given above.

3.1   Well-Behaved Deduction Systems

A well-behaved signature associates, by means of the operation $\dot{-}$, each formula constructor of arity k with a truth-value operator of arity n with $n \leq k$. For instance, the unary constructor $\square$ is associated with the unary operator $\check{\square}$, while the binary "local" constructor $\wedge$ for conjunction is associated with the unary operator $\check{\wedge}$ (see the examples below).

Definition 9. *A* well-behaved signature *is a tuple* $\langle \Sigma, \dot{C}^f, \dot{-}\rangle$, *where* Σ *is a TVS* $\dot{C}^f = \{\dot{C}_k^f\}_{k \in \mathbb{N}^+}$ *with* $\dot{C}_k^f \subseteq C_k^f$, *and* $\dot{-} : \cup_{k \in \mathbb{N}^+} C_k^f \to \cup_{k \in \mathbb{N}^+} C_k^v \cup \{\top\}$ *such that if* $c \in C_k^f$ *then* $\check{c} \in C_n^v$ *with* $n \leq k$.

To illustrate the intuition behind $\dot{-}$ and $\dot{C}^f$, let us first define a well-behaved LDS as a system that is based on a well-behaved signature, and that has an introduction and an elimination rule for each constructor in C^f (as is usual for *natural* deduction systems; see, e.g., [20]).

Definition 10. *A well-behaved labelled deduction system is a LDS* $\langle \Sigma, R \rangle$, *where* Σ *is a well-behaved signature and* R *includes the rules:*

- *for each* $c \in \dot{C}_k^f$ *where* $\check{c} \in C_n^v$, $\boldsymbol{\delta} = \delta_1, \ldots, \delta_{n-1}$, $\boldsymbol{\xi} = \xi_1, \ldots, \xi_{n-1}$, *and* $i = n, \ldots, k$

$$\frac{\boldsymbol{\delta} :: \boldsymbol{\xi} \,/\, \check{c}(\delta, \boldsymbol{\delta}) :: \xi_j \,\triangleright\, \delta, \; j = n, \ldots, k}{\delta :: c(\xi_1, \ldots, \xi_k)} \; c_I \,, \qquad \frac{\delta :: c(\xi_1, \ldots, \xi_k) \quad \boldsymbol{\delta} :: \boldsymbol{\xi}}{\check{c}(\delta, \boldsymbol{\delta}) :: \xi_i} \; c_{E^i} \,,$$

- *for each* $c \in C_k^f \setminus \dot{C}_k^f$ *where* $\check{c} \in C_n^v$, $\boldsymbol{\delta} = \delta_1, \ldots, \delta_n$, $\boldsymbol{\xi} = \xi_1, \ldots, \xi_n$ *and* $i = n+1, \ldots, k$

$$\frac{\delta \leq \check{c}(\boldsymbol{\delta}) \quad \boldsymbol{\delta} :: \boldsymbol{\xi} \quad \delta :: \xi_i}{\delta :: c(\xi_1, \ldots, \xi_k)} \; c_{I^i} \,,$$

$$\frac{\delta :: c(\xi_1, \ldots, \xi_k) \quad [\delta \leq \check{c}(\boldsymbol{\delta}), \boldsymbol{\delta} :: \boldsymbol{\xi} \,/\, \delta' :: \xi', \; if \, n \neq 0] \quad \delta :: \xi_j \,/\, \delta' :: \xi', \; j = n+1, \ldots, k}{\delta' :: \xi'} \; c_E,$$

where, for $\boldsymbol{\delta} = \delta_1, \ldots, \delta_l$ *and* $\boldsymbol{\xi} = \xi_1, \ldots, \xi_l$, *the vector* $\boldsymbol{\delta} :: \boldsymbol{\xi}$ *stands for the* l *hypothesis formulae* $\delta_1 :: \xi_1 \, \cdots \, \delta_l :: \xi_l$, *and* $\delta \leq \check{c}(\boldsymbol{\delta})$ *stands for* $\delta \leq \check{c}(\delta_1, \ldots, \delta_l)$. *Observe also that* $[\delta \leq \check{c}(\boldsymbol{\delta}), \boldsymbol{\delta} :: \boldsymbol{\xi} \,/\, \delta' :: \xi', \; if \, n \neq 0]$ *indicates that this judgement does not appear in the rule when* $n = 0$ *(e.g. as in the case of disjunction).*

The introduction and elimination rules of Definition 10 are general and cover a large number of constructors and logics. The constructors in $\dot{C}_k^f$ are those that have a "universal" nature, such as necessity $\square$ and classical, intuitionistic and relevant implications $\sqsupset$, as well as conjunction $\wedge$. For instance, recall that in the Kripke semantics a modal formula $\square \varphi$ holds at a world x iff for *all* worlds y, xRy implies that φ holds at y. Similarly, intuitionistic implication is universal since to be satisfied in a Kripke world it has to be satisfied in *all* the accessible worlds, and it is locally implicative for each world. Analogously, the constructors in $C_k^f \setminus \dot{C}_k^f$ are those that have an "existential" nature, such as modal possibility $\Diamond$, relevant fusion $\circ$, and disjunction $\vee$.

To illustrate this further, we give examples of well-behaved LDSs for power-set logics, i.e. logics for which the denotation of a formula can be seen as a set of worlds. In particular, we give a LDS for the normal modal logic K [5] and one for the basic positive relevance logic B^+ [10,17]. We first need one additional definition, namely that of a local constructor, which allows us to identify the constructors whose evaluation in the corresponding Kripke-style semantics only depends on one world (and is thus "local" to that world), such as classical implication, conjunction and disjunction.

Definition 11. *A constructor* $c \in \dot{C}_k^f$ *in a well-behaved LDS* $\langle \Sigma, R \rangle$ *is local iff* $\check{c} \in C_n^v$ *and* R *includes the following rules (where* $\boldsymbol{\delta} = \delta_1, \ldots, \delta_{n-1}$*)*

$$\frac{}{\delta \leq \check{c}(\delta, \boldsymbol{\delta})} \; U_1 \qquad and \qquad \frac{}{\check{c}(\delta, \boldsymbol{\delta}) \leq \delta} \; U_2 \,.$$

Example 1. The *modal system* $\mathcal{L}(K)$ is a well-behaved LDS $\langle \Sigma, R \rangle$ where Σ is a well-behaved signature such that

- $C_1^f = \dot{C}_1^f = \{\Box\}$, $C_2^f = \dot{C}_2^f = \{\sqsupset\}$, $\mathbf{f}, \mathbf{t} \in C_0^f$ and $C_k^f = \emptyset$ for $k \geq 3$,
- $\bot, \top \in C_0^v$, $C_1^v = \{\breve{\Box}\}$, $C_2^v = \{\breve{\sqsupset}\}$ and $C_k^v = \emptyset$ for $k > 2$,
- $\sqsupset$ is a local constructor (so that the rules U_1 and U_2 hold for $\breve{\sqsupset}$),
- $D = \{\top\}$,

and R includes the rules $\dfrac{}{\bot :: \xi} \bot^f$, $\dfrac{}{\bot \leq \delta} \bot^v$, and $\dfrac{}{\bot : \mathbf{f}} \mathbf{f}_I$.

The rules for the operators $\Box$ and $\sqsupset$ of the system $\mathcal{L}(K)$ are thus the following instances of the rules in the Definitions 10 and 11:

$$\dfrac{\breve{\Box}\delta :: \xi}{\delta :: \Box\xi} \Box_I, \quad \dfrac{\delta :: \Box\xi}{\breve{\Box}\delta :: \xi} \Box_E, \quad \dfrac{\delta :: \xi_1 / \delta :: \xi_2}{\delta :: \xi_1 \sqsupset \xi_2} \sqsupset_I, \quad \dfrac{\delta :: \xi_1 \sqsupset \xi_2 \quad \delta :: \xi_1}{\delta :: \xi_2} \sqsupset_E .$$

The intuition behind the additional rules of $\mathcal{L}(K)$ is the following: $\bot^f$ and $\bot^v$ define $\bot$ as the least element of the set of truth-values in $\mathcal{L}(K)$, and $\mathbf{f}_I$ says that the *false* $\mathbf{f}$ is indeed false. As usual for modal logics, negation is a derived constructor, i.e. $\neg\varphi$ abbreviates $\varphi \sqsupset \mathbf{f}$, and so is $\Diamond$, which abbreviates $\neg\Box\neg$.

That our system $\mathcal{L}(K)$ indeed represents the logic K will become clear below when defining the algebraic semantics (which allows us to show that the system is sound and complete with respect to it), but we can already observe that our system is justified, albeit informally, by the way in which one can obtain a modal algebra from a Kripke structure [5]. As another informal justification for $\mathcal{L}(K)$, observe that it is straightforward to derive the axioms and rules of the standard Hilbert system $H(K)$ [5]. For instance, we can show that the normality axiom $\Box(\xi_1 \sqsupset \xi_2) \sqsupset ((\Box\xi_1) \sqsupset (\Box\xi_2))$ is a theorem of $\mathcal{L}(K)$ as follows:

$$\dfrac{\dfrac{\dfrac{\top :: \Box(\xi_1 \sqsupset \xi_2), \top :: \Box\xi_1 / \top :: \Box(\xi_1 \sqsupset \xi_2)}{\top :: \Box(\xi_1 \sqsupset \xi_2), \top :: \Box\xi_1 / \breve{\Box}\top :: \xi_1 \sqsupset \xi_2} \Box_E \quad \dfrac{\top :: \Box(\xi_1 \sqsupset \xi_2), \top :: \Box\xi_1 / \top :: \Box\xi_1}{\top :: \Box(\xi_1 \sqsupset \xi_2), \top :: \Box\xi_1 / \breve{\Box}\top :: \xi_1} \Box_E}{\dfrac{\dfrac{\top :: \Box(\xi_1 \sqsupset \xi_2), \top :: \Box\xi_1 / \breve{\Box}\top :: \xi_2}{\top :: \Box(\xi_1 \sqsupset \xi_2), \top :: \Box\xi_1 / \top :: \Box\xi_2} \Box_I}{\dfrac{\top :: \Box(\xi_1 \sqsupset \xi_2) / \top :: (\Box\xi_1) \sqsupset (\Box\xi_2)}{\top :: \Box(\xi_1 \sqsupset \xi_2) \sqsupset ((\Box\xi_1) \sqsupset (\Box\xi_2))} \sqsupset_I} \sqsupset_I} \sqsupset_E}{} .$$

where the top instances are labelled Ax.

Labelled equivalents of the necessitation rule and of modus ponens can be derived similarly, e.g.

$$\dfrac{\dfrac{\dfrac{}{\top :: \xi / \breve{\Box}\top \leq \top} \top \quad \dfrac{}{\top :: \xi / \top :: \xi} Ax}{\top :: \xi / \breve{\Box}\top :: \xi} ::_I}{\top :: \xi / \top :: \Box\xi} \Box_I .$$

Compare our system here with the labelled deduction systems where labels are worlds in a Kripke structure, e.g as in [3,16,21] and [2,11]: the unary operator $\breve{\Box}$ corresponds at the algebraic level to the accessibility relation of the Kripke semantics. In fact, our system $\mathcal{L}(K)$ is modular, as it directly mirrors the modularity of modal logics: all we have to do is add rules expressing properties of $\breve{\Box}$, and thereby corresponding to properties of the accessibility relation of the underlying Kripke semantics (and thus also to axioms of the corresponding Hilbert axiomatization). For instance, to get a LDS for the modal logic $S4$ we only have to add the rules

$$\frac{}{\delta \le \tilde{\Box}\delta} \; T \qquad \text{and} \qquad \frac{\delta \le \tilde{\Box}\delta' \quad \delta' \le \tilde{\Box}\delta''}{\delta \le \tilde{\Box}\delta''} \; 4 \, .$$

We can then show that the Hilbert axiom $\Box\xi \sqsupset \xi$, corresponding to the reflexivity of the Kripke accessibility relation [5], can be derived in our LDS for T, i.e. in the system extending $\mathcal{L}(K)$ with the rule T, and that $\Box\xi \sqsupset \Box\Box\xi$ is a theorem of $\mathcal{L}(K)$ extended with the rule 4.

Example 2. The *basic positive relevance system* $\mathcal{L}(B^+)$ is a well-behaved LDS $\langle \Sigma, R \rangle$ where Σ is a well-behaved signature such that

- $\dot{C}_2^f = \{\wedge, \sqsupset\}$, $C_2^f = \{\wedge, \sqsupset, \vee\}$, $\mathbf{t} \in C_0^f$ and $C_k^f = \emptyset$ for $k \ge 3$ and $k = 1$,
- $\wedge$ is a local constructor, and $\check{\vee} = \top$,
- $\top \in C_0^v$, $C_1^v = \{\check{\wedge}\}$, $C_2^v = \{\tilde{\sqsupset}\}$, and $C_k^v = \emptyset$ for $k \ge 3$,
- $D = \{\top\}$,

and R includes the rules $\quad \dfrac{\delta :: \xi}{\tilde{\sqsupset}(\top, \delta) :: \xi} \; her \quad$ and $\quad \dfrac{}{\delta \le \tilde{\sqsupset}(\top, \delta)} \; iden \, .$

The rules for the operators $\sqsupset, \wedge, \vee$ of $\mathcal{L}(B^+)$ are thus the following instances of the rules in the Definition 10 (for example, $\wedge_I$ is an instance of the rule c_I since $\wedge$ is local and $\check{\wedge}$ is unary):

$$\frac{\delta_1 :: \xi_1 / \tilde{\sqsupset}(\delta, \delta_1) :: \xi_2 \triangleright \delta_1}{\delta :: \xi_1 \sqsupset \xi_2} \; \sqsupset_I \, , \quad \frac{\delta :: \xi_1 \sqsupset \xi_2 \quad \delta_1 :: \xi_1}{\tilde{\sqsupset}(\delta, \delta_1) :: \xi_2} \; \sqsupset_E \, , \quad \frac{\delta :: \xi_1 \quad \delta :: \xi_2}{\delta :: \xi_1 \wedge \xi_2} \; \wedge_I \, ,$$

$$\frac{\delta :: \xi_1 \wedge \xi_2}{\delta :: \xi_i} \; \wedge_{E^i} \, , \quad \frac{\delta :: \xi_i}{\delta :: \xi_1 \vee \xi_2} \; \vee_{I^i} \, , \quad \frac{\delta :: \xi_1 \vee \xi_2 \quad \delta :: \xi_1 / \delta' :: \xi' \quad \delta :: \xi_2 / \delta' :: \xi'}{\delta' :: \xi'} \; \vee_E.$$

Note that the rules *her* and *iden* capture the hereditary and identity properties of the ternary compossibility relation of the Kripke semantics of relevance logics [10,17]. The use of fresh variables in the rule $\sqsupset_I$ for the introduction of relevant implication $\sqsupset$ also mirrors the Kripke semantics, namely the evaluation clause of $\sqsupset$ in terms of the compossibility relation: the rule says that $\delta :: \xi_1 \sqsupset \xi_2$ holds whenever for an arbitrary δ_1 the antecedent $\delta_1 :: \xi_1$ yields the consequent $\tilde{\sqsupset}(\delta, \delta_1) :: \xi_2$, which in turn says that the value of ξ_2 is greater than or equal to the value of the arbitrary (due to the arbitrariness of δ_1) term $\tilde{\sqsupset}(\delta, \delta_1)$.

As for modal logics, an intuitive justification for the LDS $\mathcal{L}(B^+)$ can be obtained by showing that we can derive the axioms and rules of the corresponding Hilbert system $H(B^+)$ for basic positive relevance logic [10,17,21], e.g.

$$\cfrac{\cfrac{\cfrac{\dfrac{}{\delta :: \xi_1 / \delta :: \xi_1} \; Ax}{\delta :: \xi_1 / \tilde{\sqsupset}(\top, \delta) :: \xi_1} \; her}{\delta :: \xi_1 / \tilde{\sqsupset}(\top, \delta) :: \xi_1 \vee \xi_2} \; \vee_{I^1}}{\top :: \xi_1 \sqsupset (\xi_1 \vee \xi_2)} \; \sqsupset_I \quad .$$

Similarly, we can prove both $\top :: (\xi_1 \wedge (\xi_2 \vee \xi_3)) \sqsupset ((\xi_1 \wedge \xi_2) \vee (\xi_1 \wedge \xi_3))$ and $\top :: \xi_1 \sqsupset \xi_2, \top :: \xi_3 \sqsupset \xi_4 / \top :: (\xi_2 \sqsupset \xi_3) \sqsupset (\xi_1 \sqsupset \xi_4)$.

Similar to the case of modal logics, other logics in the relevance family (up to the notable examples of the relevance logic R and, perhaps even more importantly, of intuitionistic logic) are obtained by extending $\mathcal{L}(B^+)$ with rules formalizing other properties of the truth-value operator $\check{\sqsupset}$, e.g. its transitivity.

3.2   Finitely-Valued Deductive Systems

We now consider systems for finitely many-valued logics; in particular, we give a system for the 3-valued Gödel logic with one distinguished element [13]. In fact, our framework allows us to impose that a LDS has a finite number of values in a very simple way: we just need to require the set C_0^v of operation symbols of arity zero to have as many elements as we want.

Definition 12. *Let $Var(\eta)$ denote the set of elements of Ξ^v that occur in the composed formula η, and let $Var(\Theta)$ denote the set $\cup_{\eta \in \Theta} Var(\eta)$. A finitely-valued LDS is an exhaustive LDS $\langle \Sigma, R, \check{\sqsupset} \rangle$ such that C_0^v is finite and R includes*

$$\frac{\eta_1, \ldots, \eta_n / \psi}{\eta_1{}_{\beta_1 \ldots \beta_k}^{\delta_1 \ldots \delta_k}, \ldots, \eta_n{}_{\beta_1 \ldots \beta_k}^{\delta_1 \ldots \delta_k} / \psi_{\beta_1 \ldots \beta_k}^{\delta_1 \ldots \delta_k}} \; val_I \; (\text{with } \beta_1 \ldots \beta_k \in C_0^v),$$

$$\frac{\eta_1{}_{\beta_1 \ldots \beta_k}^{\delta_1 \ldots \delta_k}, \ldots, \eta_n{}_{\beta_1 \ldots \beta_k}^{\delta_1 \ldots \delta_k} / \psi_{\beta_1 \ldots \beta_k}^{\delta_1 \ldots \delta_k} \; for \; every \; \beta_1 \ldots \beta_k \; in \; C_0^v}{\eta_1, \ldots, \eta_n / \psi} \; val_E,$$

where $\eta_1, \ldots, \eta_n, \psi$ are composed formulae and $Var(\{\eta_1, \ldots, \eta_n, \psi\}) = \{\delta_1, \ldots, \delta_k\}$. A k-LDS is a finitely-valued LDS such that the cardinality of C_0^v is k.

The rule val_E states that to derive a formula we have to derive it by considering all the possible instances of schema truth-value variables with elements in C_0^v. The rule val_I states the inverse.

Example 3. The 3-*valued Gödel LDS* $\mathcal{L}(G)$ is a 3-LDS $\langle \Sigma, R \rangle$ where Σ is such that

- $C_1^f = \{\neg\}$, $C_2^f = \{\sqsupset\}$, and $C_k^f = \emptyset$ for $k \geq 3$ and $k = 0$,
- $C_0^v = \{\bot, 0.5, \top\}$, $C_1^v = \{\check{\neg}\}$, $C_2^v = \{\check{\sqsupset}\}$, and $C_k^v = \emptyset$ for $k \geq 3$,
- $D = \{\top\}$,

and R includes the rules $\dfrac{}{\check{\neg}\delta = \delta\check{\sqsupset}\bot} \; \check{\neg}_I$, $\dfrac{}{\bot :: \xi} \; \bot^f$, $\dfrac{}{\bot \leq \delta} \; \bot^v$, and

$$\frac{\delta_1 \leq \delta_2}{\delta_1 \check{\sqsupset} \delta_2 = \top} \; \check{\sqsupset}_{I^1}, \qquad \frac{\delta_1 = 0.5 \quad \delta_2 = \bot}{\delta_1 \check{\sqsupset} \delta_2 = \bot} \; \check{\sqsupset}_{I^2}, \qquad \frac{\delta_1 = \top}{\delta_1 \check{\sqsupset} \delta_2 = \delta_2} \; \check{\sqsupset}_{I^3},$$

$$\frac{\delta_1 \check{\sqsupset} \delta_2 = \top}{\delta_1 \leq \delta_2} \; \check{\sqsupset}_{E^1}, \quad \frac{\delta_1 \check{\sqsupset} \delta_2 = \bot \quad \delta_1 = 0.5}{\delta_2 = \bot} \; \check{\sqsupset}_{E^2}, \quad \frac{\delta_1 \check{\sqsupset} \delta_2 = \delta \quad \delta_1 = \top}{\delta = \delta_2} \; \check{\sqsupset}_{E^3}.$$

Observe that the rules $\check{\sqsupset}_{I^i}$ and $\check{\sqsupset}_{E^i}$ actually capture the entries of the truth-table for 3-valued Gödel implication

$\check{\sqsupset}$	$\bot$	0.5	$\top$
$\bot$	$\top$	$\top$	$\top$
0.5	$\bot$	$\top$	$\top$
$\top$	$\bot$	0.5	$\top$

For instance, that $\delta = \top\overline{\sqsupset}0.5$ yields $\delta = 0.5$ can then be shown as follows:

$$\cfrac{\overline{\delta = \top\overline{\sqsupset}0.5\,/\,\delta = \top\overline{\sqsupset}0.5}\;Ax \qquad \cfrac{\cfrac{\overline{\delta = \top\overline{\sqsupset}0.5\,/\,\top = \top}\;=_r}{\delta = \top\overline{\sqsupset}0.5\,/\,\top\overline{\sqsupset}0.5 = 0.5}\;\overline{\sqsupset}_{I3}}{}}{\cfrac{}{\delta = \top\overline{\sqsupset}0.5\,/\,\delta = 0.5}}\;=_t\;.$$

To illustrate the rule val_E at work, we show that the Heyting chain axiom $((\xi_1 \sqsupset \xi_2) \sqsupset \bot) \sqsupset (\xi_2 \sqsupset \xi_1)$, i.e. $(\xi_1 \sqsupset \xi_2) \vee (\xi_2 \sqsupset \xi_1)$, is a theorem of $\mathcal{L}(\mathrm{G})$:

$$\cfrac{\cfrac{\cfrac{\cfrac{\cfrac{\cfrac{\overline{\bot \leq 0.5}\;\bot^v}{(\bot\overline{\sqsupset}0.5) = \top}\;\overline{\sqsupset}_{I1}}{\top = (\bot\overline{\sqsupset}0.5)}\;=_s}{\top \leq (\bot\overline{\sqsupset}0.5)}\;=_E}{(\bot\overline{\sqsupset}0.5) = \top}\;=_I}{\cfrac{}{}}}{\ddots}$$

$$\cfrac{\overline{(\bot\overline{\sqsupset}0.5) \leq \top}\;\top \quad \cfrac{(\bot\overline{\sqsupset}0.5) = \top}{\cfrac{((\bot\overline{\sqsupset}0.5) \sqsupset \bot) = \bot}{((\bot\overline{\sqsupset}0.5) \sqsupset \bot) \leq \bot}\;=_E}\;\overline{\sqsupset}_{I3} \qquad \cfrac{\overline{\bot \leq (0.5\overline{\sqsupset}\bot)}\;\bot^v}{}}{\cfrac{((\bot\overline{\sqsupset}0.5) \sqsupset \bot) \leq (0.5\overline{\sqsupset}\bot)}{\cfrac{((\bot\overline{\sqsupset}0.5) \sqsupset \bot)\overline{\sqsupset}(0.5\overline{\sqsupset}\bot) = \top}{\cfrac{\top = ((\bot\overline{\sqsupset}0.5) \sqsupset \bot)\overline{\sqsupset}(0.5\overline{\sqsupset}\bot)}{\top \leq ((\bot\overline{\sqsupset}0.5) \sqsupset \bot)\overline{\sqsupset}(0.5\overline{\sqsupset}\bot)}\;=_E}\;=_s}\;\overline{\sqsupset}_{I1}}\;\leq_t}$$

$$\cfrac{\top \leq ((\overline{\xi}_1\overline{\sqsupset}\overline{\xi}_2) \sqsupset \bot)\overline{\sqsupset}(\overline{\xi}_2\overline{\sqsupset}\overline{\xi}_1) \qquad \cdots}{\top :: ((\xi_1 \sqsupset \xi_2) \sqsupset \bot) \sqsupset (\xi_2 \sqsupset \xi_1)}\;::_2 \qquad val_E$$

where the elided cases are similar to the one displayed (with $\overline{\xi}_1 = \bot$ and $\overline{\xi}_2 = 0.5$).

4   Interpretation Systems

The structure for a signature is an algebra providing the interpretation of formula constructors and truth-value operators.

Definition 13. *A* structure *for a signature* Σ *(or* Σ-*structure for short) is a tuple* $\mathcal{B} = \langle B, B_0, \leq, [\cdot]^f, [\cdot]^v \rangle$, *where* $\langle B, \leq, [\cdot]^f \rangle$ *is a pre-ordered algebra for the formula constructors* C^f, $\langle B, \leq, [\cdot]^v \rangle$ *is a pre-ordered algebra for the truth-value operators* C^v, $B_0 \subseteq B$ *and* B_0 *has a top element* $\top$. *A structure for an exhaustive signature* Σ *is a* Σ-*structure such that* $[c]^f = [\overline{c}]^v$.

The elements of the set B are the truth-values and those of B_0 are the distinguished truth-values; in most cases, B_0 is a singleton set, but there are many-valued logics that have more than one distinguished element (see [7]). The other components of $\mathcal{B}$ provide the denotations of the constructors and operators, e.g. $[\cdot]^f$ is a family of maps $[c]_k^f : B^k \to B$ for each $c \in C_k^f$, and similarly for $[\cdot]^v$.

For the modal signatures we now introduce structures that are based on generalized Kripke frames $\langle W, G, R \rangle$, where W is a set of worlds, $G \subseteq \wp W$ is a set of sets of worlds and R is a binary accessibility relation on worlds (see [5]).

Example 4. Each generalized Kripke frame $\langle W, G, R \rangle$ induces a structure for a modal signature, as defined in Example 1, as follows:

- B is G with W as $\top$ and $\emptyset$ as $\bot$, and $B_0 = \{\top\}$;
- $[\check{\Box}]^v(b) = \{u \in W \mid wRu, \text{ for some } w \in b\}$;
- $[\mathbf{t}]^f = \top$ and $[\mathbf{f}]^f = \bot$;
- $[\sqsupset]^f(b_1, b_2) = (W \setminus b_1) \sqcup b_2$;
- $[\Box]^f(b) = \{w \in W \mid w \in [\check{\Box}]^v(b)\}$.

Each such structure is of course a modal algebra.

Similarly, the structures for the basic positive relevance signature are based on the algebras associated with the relational structures $\langle W, R \rangle$ for relevance logic, where R is a ternary compossibility relation on worlds in W (see [10,17]).

Example 5. Each relational structure $\langle W, R \rangle$ induces a structure for the basic positive relevance signature of Example 2 as follows:

- B is $\wp W$ with W as $\top$, and $B_0 = \{\top\}$;
- $[\check{\sqsupset}]^v(b, b_1) = \{w_2 \in W \mid Rww_1w_2 \text{ for some } w \in b \text{ and } w_1 \in b_1\}$;
- $[\mathbf{t}]^f = \top$;
- $[\wedge]^f(b_1, b_2) = b_1 \cap b_2$;
- $[\sqsupset]^f(b_1, b_2)$ is the greatest set b such that for every $b' \subseteq W$ if $b' \subseteq b_1$ then $[\check{\sqsupset}]^v(b, b') \subseteq b_2$;
- $[\vee]^f(b_1, b_2) = b_1 \cup b_2$.

Example 6. A structure $\mathcal{B}$ for the 3-valued Gödel signature Σ of Example 3 is defined as follows:

- $\langle B, \leq \rangle$ is a total order with a top $\top$ and a bottom $\bot$ and $B = \{\bot, b, \top\}$, and $B_0 = \{\top\}$;
- $\langle B, [\cdot]^f \rangle$ and $\langle B, [\cdot]^v \rangle$ are 3-valued Gödel algebras such that $[c]^f = [\overline{c}]^v$ for each $c \in \{\neg, \sqsupset\}$, $[\bot]^v = \bot$, $[\top]^v = \top$ and $[0.5]^v = b$.

For more details about Gödel algebras see [13].

In the sequel, we will sometimes omit the reference to the arity of the constructors and operators in order to make the notation lighter.

Definition 14. *An* interpretation system *is a pair* $\mathcal{I} = \langle \Sigma, M \rangle$ *where* Σ *is a signature and* M *is a class of structures for* Σ.

Definition 15. *Let* $\mathcal{B} = \langle B, B_0, \leq, [\cdot]^f, [\cdot]^v \rangle$ *be a* Σ*-structure. An* assignment α *over* $\mathcal{B}$ *is a pair* $\langle \alpha^f, \alpha^v \rangle$ *such that* $\alpha^f : \Xi^f \to B$ *and* $\alpha^v = \Xi^v \to B$.

The interpretation of formulae *over* $\mathcal{B}$ *and* α *is a map* $[\![\cdot]\!]_\alpha^{\mathcal{B}} : L(\langle C^f, \Xi^f \rangle) \to B$ *inductively defined as follows:*

- $[\![c]\!]_\alpha^{\mathcal{B}} = [c]^f$, *whenever* $c \in C_0^f$;
- $[\![\xi]\!]_\alpha^{\mathcal{B}} = \alpha^f(\xi)$, *whenever* $\xi \in \Xi^f$;
- $[\![c(\varphi_1, \ldots, \varphi_k)]\!]_\alpha^{\mathcal{B}} = [c]^f([\![\varphi_1]\!]_\alpha^{\mathcal{B}}, \ldots, [\![\varphi_k]\!]_\alpha^{\mathcal{B}})$, *whenever* $c \in C_k^f$ *and* $\varphi_1, \ldots, \varphi_k$ $\in L(\langle C^f, \Xi^f \rangle)$ *for* $k \in \mathbb{N}$.

The interpretation of truth-value terms *over $\mathcal{B}$ and α is a map* $\llbracket . \rrbracket_\alpha^\mathcal{B} : L(\langle C^v,$
$\Xi^v \rangle) \to B$ *inductively defined as follows:*

- $\llbracket o \rrbracket_\alpha^\mathcal{B} = [o]^v$, *whenever* $o \in C_0^v$;
- $\llbracket \delta \rrbracket_\alpha^\mathcal{B} = \alpha^v(\delta)$, *whenever* $\delta \in \Xi^v$;
- $\llbracket o(\beta_1, \ldots, \beta_k) \rrbracket_\alpha^\mathcal{B} = [o]^v(\llbracket \beta_1 \rrbracket_\alpha^\mathcal{B}, \ldots, \llbracket \beta_k \rrbracket_\alpha^\mathcal{B})$, *whenever* $o \in C_k^v$ *and* $\beta_1, \ldots, \beta_k \in$
  $L(\langle C^v, \Xi^v \rangle)$ *for* $k \in \mathbb{N}$.

We say that $\mathcal{B}$ and α satisfy a composed formula ψ, in symbols $\mathcal{B}, \alpha \Vdash \psi$, iff

- $\llbracket \beta \rrbracket_\alpha^\mathcal{B} = \llbracket \varphi \rrbracket_\alpha^\mathcal{B}$ *whenever ψ is $\beta : \varphi$;*
- $\llbracket \beta \rrbracket_\alpha^\mathcal{B} \leq \llbracket \varphi \rrbracket_\alpha^\mathcal{B}$ *whenever ψ is $\beta :: \varphi$;*
- $\llbracket \beta_1 \rrbracket_\alpha^\mathcal{B} \bullet \llbracket \beta_2 \rrbracket_\alpha^\mathcal{B}$ *whenever ψ is $\beta_1 \bullet \beta_2$ with $\bullet \in \{=, \leq\}$.*

To introduce satisfaction of judgements, we define *co-equivalent assignments* with respect to a set of schema truth-value variables as follows: $\alpha_1 \equiv_{\{\delta_1, \ldots, \delta_k\}} \alpha_2$ iff $\alpha_1^v(\delta) = \alpha_2^v(\delta)$ for every $\delta \in \Xi^v \setminus \{\delta_1, \ldots, \delta_k\}$ and $\alpha_1^f = \alpha_2^f$.

Definition 16. *A structure $\mathcal{B}$ and an assignment α satisfy $\Theta / \eta \rhd \delta_1, \ldots, \delta_k$, in symbols $\mathcal{B}, \alpha \Vdash \Theta / \eta \rhd \delta_1, \ldots, \delta_k$, iff for every assignment α' with $\alpha' \equiv_{\{\delta_1, \ldots, \delta_k\}} \alpha$, $\mathcal{B}, \alpha' \Vdash \eta$ whenever $\mathcal{B}, \alpha' \Vdash \psi$ for every $\psi \in \Theta$.*

A structure $\mathcal{B}$ validates a rule $\langle \{J_1, \ldots, J_k\}, J \rangle$ iff for every assignment α over $\mathcal{B}$ we have $\mathcal{B}, \alpha \Vdash J$ whenever $\mathcal{B}, \alpha \Vdash J_i$ for each $i = 1, \ldots, k$.

A composed formula $\eta \in L(\Sigma)$ is entailed by $\Theta \subseteq L(\Sigma)$ in a LDS $\langle \Sigma, R \rangle$, in symbols $\Theta \vDash_{\langle \Sigma, R \rangle} \eta$, iff $\mathcal{B}, \alpha \Vdash \Theta / \eta$ for every Σ-structure $\mathcal{B}$ and assignment α. When there is no risk of confusion we will simply write $\Theta \vDash \eta$.

5   Soundness and Completeness

Rather than focussing on particular systems and logics, we will now analyze soundness and completeness in the general context of our framework. We first introduce the concept of logic system and then identify the conditions under which a logic system is sound and complete.

Definition 17. *A logic system is a tuple $\langle \Sigma, R, M \rangle$ where $\langle \Sigma, R \rangle$ is a LDS and $\langle \Sigma, M \rangle$ is an interpretation system. An* exhaustive logic system $\langle \Sigma, R, \doteq, M \rangle$ *is a logic system based on an exhaustive LDS.*

Definition 18. *Let $\Theta \subseteq L(\Sigma)$ and $\eta \in L(\Sigma)$. A logic system is* sound *iff $\Theta \vDash \eta$ whenever $\Theta \vdash \eta$, and it is* complete *iff $\Theta \vdash \eta$ whenever $\Theta \vDash \eta$.*

We can prove soundness by showing that every Σ-structure in M satisfies all the instances of the inference rules in $\langle \Sigma, R \rangle$. By a simple case analysis we have:

Proposition 1. *Let $\langle \Sigma, R, M \rangle$ (or $\langle \Sigma, R, \doteq, M \rangle$) be a logic system. If a Σ-structure validates a rule in R, then it validates all instances of that rule.*

We can then show by induction that:

Theorem 1. *A logic system $\langle \Sigma, R, M \rangle$ (or $\langle \Sigma, R, \vdots, M \rangle$) is sound whenever every Σ-structure in M validates all rules of R.*

For example, the Σ-structures for modal signatures, as introduced in Example 4, validate the rules of $\mathcal{L}(K)$, the Σ-structures of Example 5 for basic positive relevance signatures validate the rules of $\mathcal{L}(B^+)$, and the Σ-structures of Example 6 for 3-valued Gödel signatures validate the rules of $\mathcal{L}(\mathrm{G})$.

For completeness, we consider exhaustive LDSs; this is by no means a restriction since, as we argued in Section 2, it is always possible to get an exhaustive system out of a LDS. The proof of completeness follows a standard approach [5] by defining the induced Lindenbaum-Tarski algebra for maximally consistent sets and showing that this algebra validates the rules. The next definition adapts the standard definition to introduce the notion of maximality of a set of composed formulae with respect to a composed formula.

Definition 19. *Let $\langle \Sigma, R, \vdots \rangle$ be an exhaustive LDS. A set Θ of composed formulae is maximal with respect to a composed formula $\eta \in L(\Sigma)$ iff (i) $\Theta \not\vdash \eta$ and (ii) for any Θ' such that $\Theta \subset \Theta'$ we have $\Theta' \vdash \eta$. We say Θ is maximally consistent iff Θ is maximal with respect to η for some $\eta \in L(\Sigma)$.*

In the proof of completeness (cf. Theorem 2 below), it is necessary to extend a set Θ_0 of composed formulae, with $\Theta_0 \not\vdash \eta$ for some $\eta \in L(\Sigma)$, to a set Θ maximal with respect to η. The details of this construction, of course, depend on the particular logic we are considering, which might be a common modal logic or some not so common non-classical logic. (For examples of similar constructions for labelled deduction systems based on Kripke-style semantics see [3,16,21].) So, here we only illustrate the main ideas underlying the construction.

Definition 20. *An exhaustive LDS $\langle \Sigma, R, \vdots \rangle$ induces, for every (maximally) consistent set $\Theta \subseteq L(\Sigma)$ of composed formulae, the Lindenbaum-Tarski algebra $\lambda \tau_\Theta = \langle B, B_0, \leq_\Theta, [.]^f, [.]^v \rangle$ where*

- $B = L(\langle C^v, \Xi^v \rangle)$, *and* $B_0 = D$;
- $\leq_\Theta$ *is such that* $b_1 \leq_\Theta b_2$ *iff* $b_1 \leq b_2 \in \Theta$;
- $[c]^f(b_1, \ldots, b_n) = \bar{c}(b_1, \ldots b_n)$;
- $[o]^v(b_1, \ldots, b_n) = o(b_1, \ldots, b_n)$.

Note that the construction of the Lindenbaum-Tarski algebra is as expected, and that exhaustiveness is required to define the denotations of the constructors over tuples of truth-values. The following two propositions are useful in establishing the completeness of logic systems under some conditions (namely, exhaustiveness and fullness, which we will formalize below).

Proposition 2. *Let $\langle \Sigma, R, \vdots \rangle$ be an exhaustive LDS and $\Theta \subseteq L(\Sigma)$ a maximally consistent set of composed formulae . Then, for any assignment α and substitution σ_α such that $\overline{\sigma_\alpha^f(\delta)} = \alpha^f(\delta)$ and $\overline{\sigma_\alpha^v(\xi)} = \alpha^v(\xi)$ we have:*

1. $b : \varphi \in \Theta$ *iff* $b \leq_\Theta \overline{\varphi}$ *and* $\overline{\varphi} \leq_\Theta b$, *and* $b :: \varphi \in \Theta$ *iff* $b \leq_\Theta \overline{\varphi}$*;*

2. $[\![\varphi]\!]_\alpha^{\lambda\tau_\Theta} = \overline{\varphi\sigma_\alpha}$ *and* $[\![b]\!]_\alpha^{\lambda\tau_\Theta} = b\sigma_\alpha$*;*

3. $\lambda\tau_\Theta\alpha \Vdash \eta$ *iff* $\eta\sigma_\alpha \in \Theta$*;*

4. $\lambda\tau_\Theta\alpha \Vdash \Psi / \eta \vartriangleright \Upsilon$ *iff* $\Theta \cup \Psi\sigma_{\alpha'} \vdash \eta\sigma_{\alpha'}$*, for any assignment* α' *with* $\alpha' \equiv_\Upsilon \alpha$.

Next we prove that the Lindenbaum-Tarski algebra validates the rules.

Proposition 3. *Let* $\langle \Sigma, R, \dot{\cdot} \rangle$ *be an exhaustive LDS and* Θ *a maximally consistent set of composed formulae. Then the induced algebra* $\lambda\tau_\Theta$ *validates all rules of* R.

Proof. Let α be an assignment over $\lambda\tau_\Theta$, σ_α a substitution related to α according to Proposition 2, and $r = \langle \{\Theta_1 / \eta_1 \vartriangleright \Upsilon_1, \ldots, \Theta_k / \eta_k \vartriangleright \Upsilon_k\}, \eta \rangle \in R$. Assume $\lambda\tau_\Theta\alpha \Vdash \Theta_i / \eta_i \vartriangleright \Upsilon_i$ for every $i \in \{1, \ldots, k\}$. Then, by Proposition 2, for any assignment α' with $\alpha' \equiv_{\Upsilon_i} \alpha$ we have $\Theta \cup \Theta_i\sigma_{\alpha'} \vdash \eta_i\sigma_{\alpha'}$. So $\vdash \Theta \cup \Theta_i\sigma_{\alpha'} / \eta_i\sigma_{\alpha'}$. Hence, using rule r we have that $\vdash \Theta / \eta\sigma_\alpha$. Thus $\Theta \vdash \eta\sigma_\alpha$, and since Θ is maximal then $\eta\sigma_\alpha \in \Theta$. So, again by Proposition 2, we have $\lambda\tau_\Theta\alpha \Vdash \eta$.   QED

To prove completeness we need to require that our exhaustive systems are full, in the sense that the Lindenbaum-Tarski algebras are among the structures that we consider.[1]

Definition 21. *An exhaustive logic system* $\langle \Sigma, R, \dot{\cdot}, M \rangle$ *is* full *iff* $\lambda\tau_\Theta \in M$ *for every maximally consistent set* $\Theta \subseteq L(\Sigma)$.

Theorem 2. *Every full exhaustive logic system is complete.*

Proof. Let $\langle \Sigma, R, \dot{\cdot}, M \rangle$ be a full exhaustive logic system. Assume $\Theta_0 \not\vdash \eta$. Then $\eta \notin \Theta$ where Θ is an extension of Θ_0 maximal with respect to η. So, by Proposition 2, we have that $\lambda\tau_\Theta \, id \not\Vdash \eta$. Since $\lambda\tau_\Theta \in M$, then $\Theta_0 \not\vDash \eta$.   QED

With these general results at hand, it is not difficult to prove the soundness and completeness of particular systems, such as the ones we considered above.

6   Concluding Remarks

We have given a framework for presenting non-classical logics in a modular and uniform way as labelled natural deduction systems, where the use of algebras of truth-values as the labelling algebras of our systems, as opposed to the more customary labelling based on Kripke semantics, allows us to give generalized systems for multiple-valued logics. In the tradition of Labelled Deduction for many-valued logics [1,6,7,13,14] and for modal, relevance and other power-set logics [2,3,8,9,11,16,21], our systems make use of labels to give natural deduction

---

[1] Note that it is always possible to make full an exhaustive logic system by considering all Σ-structures that validate the rules, and that soundness is preserved by the closure for fullness.

rules for a large number of formula constructors. The novelty of our approach is that these constructors, and thus the logics they appear in, are all captured within the same formalism. This also opens up the possibility of investigating many-valued variants of power-set logics, and, more generally, their fibring [4,12], as we have already begun [15] to do as part of our research program on fibring of logics and of their deduction systems [16,18,19,22]. As future work, we plan to investigate also extensions to the first-order case of the propositional multiple-valued logics we considered here.

References

1. M. Baaz, C. G. Fermüller, G. Salzer, and R. Zach. Labeled calculi and finite-valued logics. *Studia Logica*, 61(1):7–33, 1998.
2. D. Basin, M. D'Agostino, D. M. Gabbay, S. Matthews, and L. Viganò, editors. *Labelled Deduction*. Kluwer Academic Publishers, 2000.
3. D. Basin, S. Matthews, and L. Viganò. Natural deduction for non-classical logics. *Studia Logica*, 60(1):119–160, 1998.
4. P. Blackburn and M. de Rijke. Why combine logics? *Studia Logica*, 59:5–27, 1997.
5. P. Blackburn, M. de Rijke, and Y. Venema. *Modal Logic*. Cambridge University Press, 2001.
6. L. Bolc and P. Borowik. *Many-Valued Logics I*. Springer-Verlag, 1992.
7. W. Carnielli. Systematization of finite many-valued logics through the method of tableaux. *Journal of Symbolic Logic*, 52(2):473–493, 1987.
8. M. D'Agostino and D. M. Gabbay. A Generalization of Analytic Deduction via Labelled Deductive Systems I: Basic Substructural Logics. *Journal of Automated Reasoning*, 13(2):243–281, 1994.
9. M. D'Agostino, D. M. Gabbay, R. Hähnle, and J. Posegga, editors. *Handbook of Tableau Methods*. Kluwer Academic Publishers, 1999.
10. J. M. Dunn. Relevance logic and entailment. In D. M. Gabbay and F. Guenthner, editors, *Handbook of Philosophical Logic III*, pp. 117–224. D. Reidel Publ. Co, 1986.
11. D. M. Gabbay. *Labelled Deductive Systems*, volume 1. Clarendon Press, 1996.
12. D. M. Gabbay. *Fibring Logics*. Oxford University Press, 1999.
13. S. Gottwald. *A Treatise on Many-Valued Logics*. Research Studies Press, 2001.
14. R. Hähnle. Tableaux for many-valued logics. In D'Agostino et al. [9], pp. 529–580.
15. J. Rasga, A. Sernadas, C. Sernadas, and L. Viganò. Fibring deduction systems labelled with truth-values. Technical report, Section of Computer Science, Department of Mathematics, Instituto Superior Técnico, Lisboa, Portugal, to appear.
16. J. Rasga, A. Sernadas, C. Sernadas, and L. Viganò. Fibring labelled deduction systems. *Journal of Logic and Computation*, to appear.
17. G. Restall. Relevant and substructural logics. In D. M. Gabbay and J. Woods, editors, *Handbook of the History and Philosophy of Logic*. To appear.
18. A. Sernadas, C. Sernadas, and C. Caleiro. Fibring of logics as a categorial construction. *Journal of Logic and Computation*, 9(2):149–179, 1999.
19. A. Sernadas, C. Sernadas, C. Caleiro, and T. Mossakowski. Categorial fibring of logics with terms and binding operators. In M. de Rijke and D. M. Gabbay, editors, *Frontiers of Combining Systems 2*, pp. 295–316. Research Studies Press, 2000.
20. A. Troelstra and H. Schwichtenberg. *Basic Proof Theory*. Cambridge University Press, 1996.

21. L. Viganò. *Labelled Non-Classical Logics*. Kluwer Academic Publishers, 2000.
22. A. Zanardo, A. Sernadas, and C. Sernadas. Fibring: Completeness preservation. *Journal of Symbolic Logic*, 66(1):414–439, 2001.

A Temporal × Modal Approach
to the Definability of Properties of Functions

Alfredo Burrieza and Inma P. de Guzmán

Facultad de Filosofía, E.T.S.I. Informática
Universidad de Málaga
Campus de Teatinos. 29071 Málaga, Spain
burrieza@uma.es
guzman@ctima.uma.es

Abstract. This work is focused on the study of temporal × modal logics. These logics have been traditionally used in several fields such as
causation, the theory of actions, conditionals and others. In this paper
we study the representation of properties of functions of interest because of their possible computational interpretations. The semantics is
exposed in an algebraic style, and the definability of the basic properties
of the functions is analysed. We introduce minimal systems for linear
time with total functions. Moreover, completeness proofs are offered for
this minimal system. Finally, $T \times W$-validity and Kamp-validity in comparison with functional validity are discussed.

keyword: $T \times W$-semantics, functional semantics, definability, completeness.

1 Introduction

In recent years, several combinations of tense and modality $(T \times W$-
logics) have been introduced. The main interest of this investigation is
focused on fields as causation, the theory of action and others (see
[BP90,Bel96,Che92,Kus93,TG81,Rey97,Tho84]). However, our interest for this
type of combinations is in the field of Mathematics and Computer Science. To
this respect, the combinations of modal and tense operators is mentioned, for
example, in [Rey97] as a suitable tool to treat parallel processes, distributed
systems and multiagents.

In this paper we present a new type of frames, which we call *functional
frames*. The interest of this approach is that it allows to study the definability
of basic properties of the theory of functions (such as being injective, surjective,
increasing, decreasing, etc.) and, in addition, it is a general purpose tool for stu-
dying logics containing modal and temporal operators. Traditional approaches in
this field are Thomason's $T \times W$-*frames* and also *Kripke's frames*, and both are
special cases of the approach we introduce here, in the sense that, if we consider
the restrictions imposed on the $T \times W$ (Kamp)-models in [Tho84], then every
$T \times W$(Kamp)-model has an equivalent functional model (i.e. the same formulas

A. Armando (Ed.): FroCoS 2002, LNAI 2309, pp. 239–254, 2002.
© Springer-Verlag Berlin Heidelberg 2002

are valid in both models). If those restrictions are ignored, as in [Zan96], then for all $T \times W$(Kamp)-frame there exists an equivalent functional frame. The most remarkable differences between the functional approach and the previous ones are commented below:

- In a $T \times W$ frame, the flow of time is shared by all the worlds. In a Kamp frame each world has its own flow of time, although for two different worlds the time can coincide up to an instant. In a functional frame each world has its own flow of time and it is not required that flows of time for different worlds have to be neither totally nor partially isomorphic.
- In both $T \times W$-frames and Kamp-frames the flow of time is strictly linear. In this paper, we will also use linear time in our functional frames.
- It is typical in both, $T \times W$ frames and Kamp's frames, that worlds are connected by equivalence relations defined for their respective temporal orders and, as a consequence, the axioms of the modal basis of S5 are valid for our operators of necessity and possibility. In our approach there is more flexibility, the inter-world accessibility is defined by partial functions, called *accessibility functions*. These functions allows us to connect the worlds and so, to compare the measure of different courses of time in several ways.
- The equivalence relations are used in previous approaches to establish which segments of different temporal flows are to be considered as the same history. This way, it is possible to define the notion of *historical necessity*. This can also be made using functional frames, as it will be shown, but in addition, functions allows to define situations which do not require, neither partial nor total, isomorphisms between temporal flows.

More concretely, a type of frame is proposed, which we call functional frames, where each frame is characterized by the following:

1. A nonempty set W of worlds. Each $w \in W$ is a label of an associated temporal strict linear order, denoted by T_w.
2. A nonempty set of pairwise disjoint strict linear orderings, indexed by W.
3. A set of partial functions (accessibility functions), with the characteristic that at most one accessibility function is defined between two orders.

An example follows:

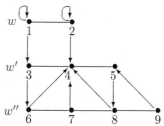

$W = \{w, w', w''\}$; the linear temporal flows: $(T_w, <_w), (T_{w'}, <_{w'}), (T_{w''}, <_{w''})$, where $T_w = \{1_w, 2_w\}, T_{w'} = \{3_{w'}, 4_{w'}, 5_{w'}\}$ and $T_{w''} = \{6_{w''}, 7_{w''}, 8_{w''}, 9_{w''}\}$. There are four accessibility functions:

$$\xrightarrow{w\ w} : T_w \to T_w; \quad \xrightarrow{w\ w'} : T_w \to T_{w'}; \quad \xrightarrow{w'\ w''} : T_{w'} \to T_{w''} \text{ and } \xrightarrow{w''\ w'} : T_{w''} \to T_{w'}$$

defined as follows:

$$\xrightarrow{w\,w} = id_{T_w}; \quad \xrightarrow{w\,w'} (1_w) = 3_{w'}, \quad \xrightarrow{w\,w'} (2_w) = 4_{w'};$$

$$\xrightarrow{w'\,w''} (3_{w'}) = 6_{w''}, \quad \xrightarrow{w'\,w''} (5_{w'}) = 8_{w''};$$

$$\xrightarrow{w''\,w'} (6_{w''}) = \xrightarrow{w''\,w'} (7_{w''}) = \xrightarrow{w''\,w'} (8_{w''}) = 4_{w'}, \quad \xrightarrow{w''\,w'} (9_{w''}) = 5_{w'}.$$

The paper is structured as follows: in Section 2 we define the functional semantics for the language $L_{T \times W}$. In Section 3 we analyze the definability of the basic properties of the functions. In Section 4 we introduce minimal axiomatic systems for $L_{T \times W}$ and its completeness proofs are given. In Section 5 we prove that the $T \times W$-frames and the $Kamp$-frames are particular cases of our approach. Finally, in Section 6, future work is outlined.

2   The Logic $L_{T \times W}$

The alphabet of $L_{T \times W}$ is defined as follows:

- a denumerable set, $\mathcal{V}$, of propositional variables;
- the logic constants $\top$ and $\bot$, and the classical connectives $\neg$ and $\rightarrow$;
- the temporal connectives G and H, and the modal connective $\square$.

The well-formed formulae (wffs) are generated by the construction rules of classical logic adding the following rule: If A is a wff, then GA, HA and $\square A$ are wffs. We consider, as usual, the connectives $\wedge$, $\vee$ F, P and $\Diamond$ to be defined connectives. The connectives G and H have their usual readings, but $\square A$ has the following meaning: "A is true at every accessible present" (in the above example, the accessible present for 1_w is $\{1_w, 3_{w'}\}$, etc.).

Definition 1. *We define a* **functional frame** *(or simply a frame) for $L_{T \times W}$ as a tuple $(W, \mathcal{T}, \mathcal{F})$, where W is a nonempty set (set of labels for a set of temporal flows), $\mathcal{T}$ is a nonempty set of strict linear orders, indexed by W, specifically:*

$$\mathcal{T} = \{(T_w, <_w) \mid w \in W\} \text{ such that if } w \neq w', \text{ then } T_w \cap T_{w'} = \varnothing;$$

$\mathcal{F}$ is a set of non-empty functions, called **accessibility functions**, *such that:*

a) *each function in $\mathcal{F}$ is a partial function from T_w to $T_{w'}$, for some $w, w' \in W$.*
b) *for an arbitrary pair $w, w' \in W$, there is (in $\mathcal{F}$) at most one accessibility function from T_w to $T_{w'}$, denoted by $\xrightarrow{w\,w'}$.*

We will denote $\mathcal{F}_w = \{\xrightarrow{w\,w'} \in \mathcal{F} \mid w' \in W\}$. Then $\mathcal{F} = \bigcup_{w \in W} \mathcal{F}_w$. The elements t_w of the disjoint union $Coord_\Sigma = \bigoplus_{w \in W} T_w$ are called **coordinates**.

Definition 2. *A* **functional model** *on Σ is a tuple $\mathcal{M} = (\Sigma, h)$, where Σ is a functional frame and h is a function, $h : L_{T \times W} \longrightarrow 2^{Coord_\Sigma}$, called a* **functional interpretation**, *satisfying:*

$h(\bot) = \varnothing; h(\top) = Coord_\Sigma; h(\neg A) = Coord_\Sigma \setminus h(A);$
$h(A \rightarrow B) = (Coord_\Sigma \setminus h(A)) \cup h(B);$

$h(\square A) = \{t_w \in Coord_\Sigma \mid \mathcal{F}_w(t_w) \subseteq h(A)\};$
$h(GA) = \{t_w \in Coord_\Sigma \mid (t_w, \rightarrow) \subseteq h(A)\};$
$h(HA) = \{t_w \in Coord_\Sigma \mid (\leftarrow, t_w) \subseteq h(A)\}.$

Definition 3. *Let A be a formula in $L_{T \times W}$. Then, A is true at t_w if $t_w \in h(A)$. A is said to be* **valid in the functional model** *(Σ, h) if $h(A) = Coord_\Sigma$. If A is valid in every functional model on Σ, then A is said to be* **valid in the frame** *Σ, and denote it by $\models_\Sigma A$. If A is valid in every frame, then A is said to be* **valid***, and denote it by $\models A$. Let $\mathbb{K}$ be a class of frames, if A is valid in every frame Σ such that $\Sigma \in \mathbb{K}$, then A is said to be* **valid with respect to $\mathbb{K}$***.*

3   Definability in $L_{T \times W}$

Definition 4. *Let $\mathbb{J}$ be a class of frames and let $\mathbb{K} \subseteq \mathbb{J}$. We say that $\mathbb{K}$ is $L_{T \times W}$-* **definable** *in (or relative to) $\mathbb{J}$ if there exists a set Γ of formulas in $L_{T \times W}$ such that for every frame $\Sigma \in \mathbb{J}$, we have that $\Sigma \in \mathbb{K}$ if and only if every formula of Γ is valid in Σ. If $\mathbb{J}$ is the class of all frames, we say that $\mathbb{K}$ is $L_{T \times W}$-definable.*

Let P be a property of functions (injectivity, etc) and $\mathbb{K}$ the class of all frames whose functions have the property P. We say that P is $L_{T \times W}$-definable if $\mathbb{K}$ is $L_{T \times W}$-definable.

Due to lack of space, the following theorem is stated without proof.

Theorem 1.

(0) $\mathbb{K}_0 = \{(W, \mathcal{T}, \mathcal{F}) \mid \mathcal{F}$ *is a class of total functions*$\}$ *is $L_{T \times W}$-definable and the formula $\square(A \wedge GA \wedge HA) \rightarrow (G\square A \wedge H\square A)$ defines $\mathbb{K}_0$.*

(1) $\mathbb{K}_1 = \{(W, \mathcal{T}, \mathcal{F}) \mid \mathcal{F}$ *is a class of total injective functions*$\}$ *is $L_{T \times W}$-definable and the formula $\square(GA \wedge HA) \rightarrow (G\square A \wedge H\square A)$ defines $\mathbb{K}_1$.*

(2) $\mathbb{K}_2 = \{(W, \mathcal{T}, \mathcal{F}) \mid \mathcal{F}$ *is a class of surjective functions*$\}$ *is $L_{T \times W}$-definable and the formula $(G\square A \wedge H\square A) \rightarrow \square(GA \wedge HA)$ defines $\mathbb{K}_2$.*

(3) $\mathbb{K}_3 = \{(W, \mathcal{T}, \mathcal{F}) \mid \mathcal{F}$ *is a class of total increasing functions*$\}$ *is $L_{T \times W}$-definable and the set $\{\square(A \wedge GA) \rightarrow G\square A, \square(A \wedge HA) \rightarrow H\square A\}$ defines $\mathbb{K}_3$.*

(4) $\mathbb{K}_4 = \{(W, \mathcal{T}, \mathcal{F}) \mid \mathcal{F}$ *is a class of total strictly increasing functions*$\}$ *is $L_{T \times W}$-definable and the set $\{\square GA \rightarrow G\square A, \; \square HA \rightarrow H\square A\}$ defines $\mathbb{K}_4$.*

(5) $\mathbb{K}_5 = \{(W, \mathcal{T}, \mathcal{F}) \mid \mathcal{F}$ *is a class of total decreasing functions*$\}$ *is $L_{T \times W}$-definable and the set $\{\square(A \wedge GA) \rightarrow H\square A, \square(A \wedge HA) \rightarrow G\square A\}$ defines $\mathbb{K}_5$.*

(6) $\mathbb{K}_6 = \{(W, \mathcal{T}, \mathcal{F}) \mid \mathcal{F}$ *is a class of total strictly decreasing functions*$\}$ *is $L_{T \times W}$-definable and the set $\{\square GA \rightarrow H\square A, \square HA \rightarrow G\square A\}$ defines $\mathbb{K}_6$.*

(7) $\mathbb{K}_7 = \{(W, \mathcal{T}, \mathcal{F}) \mid \mathcal{F}$ *is a class of total constant functions*$\}$ *is $L_{T \times W}$-definable and the formula $\square A \rightarrow (G\square A \wedge H\square A)$ defines $\mathbb{K}_7$.*

4   Minimal Axiomatic Systems for $L_{T \times W}$

4.1   The System $\mathcal{S}_{T \times W}$ -Tot

This system has the following axiom schemes:

1. All tautologies of the classical propositional logic, $\mathcal{PL}$.
2. Those of the minimal system of propositional linear temporal logic $\mathcal{Kl}$.
3. The characteristic axiom schema of the modal propositional logic $\mathcal{K}$.
4. The axiom schema *(Tot)*: $\Box(A \wedge GA \wedge HA) \to (G\Box A \wedge H\Box A)$

The rules of inference are those of $\mathcal{Kl} + \mathcal{K}$:

   (MP) $A, A \to B \vdash B$; (RG) $A \vdash GA$; (RH) $A \vdash HA$ and (RN) $A \vdash \Box A$

Theorem 2. *The following formulas are theorems in $\mathcal{S}_{T \times W}$ -Tot:*
   T1: $F\Box A \to \Box(A \vee FA \vee PA)$.   *T2:* $P\Box A \to \Box(A \vee FA \vee PA)$.

Completeness Theorem for $\mathcal{S}_{T \times W}$ -Tot: The proof of soundness is standard. We focus our attention on the completeness proof and adopt the usual definitions of a *consistent (maximal)* set of formulas. In the following, we abbreviate *maximal consistent set* as *mc-set*. On the other hand, by $\mathcal{S}$ we mean any axiomatic system for $L_{T \times W}$ which is an extension of $\mathcal{Kl} + \mathcal{K}$ (in particular, the system $\mathcal{S}_{T \times W}$ -Tot). Familiarity with the basic properties of *mc*-sets in classical propositional systems is assumed.

Definition 5. *Let Γ_1 and Γ_2 be mc-sets in $\mathcal{S}$, then we define:*
$\Gamma_1 \prec_T \Gamma_2$ *iff* $\{A \mid GA \in \Gamma_1\} \subseteq \Gamma_2$; $\Gamma_1 \prec_W \Gamma_2$ *iff* $\{A \mid \Box A \in \Gamma_1\} \subseteq \Gamma_2$.

The following lemma is standard in modal and tense logic.

Lemma 1. *Let Γ_1, Γ_2 and Γ_3 be mc-sets in $\mathcal{S}$, then we have:*

(a) $\Gamma_1 \prec_T \Gamma_2$ *iff* $\{PA \mid A \in \Gamma_1\} \subseteq \Gamma_2$ *iff* $\{FA \mid A \in \Gamma_2\} \subseteq \Gamma_1$.
(b) $\Gamma_1 \prec_W \Gamma_2$ *iff* $\{\Diamond A \mid A \in \Gamma_2\} \subseteq \Gamma_1$.
(c) (Lindenbaum's Lemma) Any consistent set of formulas in $\mathcal{S}$ can be extended to an mc-set in $\mathcal{S}$.
(d) If $FA \in \Gamma_1$, there exists an mc-set $\Gamma_2 \in \mathcal{S}$ such that $\Gamma_1 \prec_T \Gamma_2$ and $A \in \Gamma_2$.
(e) If $PA \in \Gamma_1$, there exists an mc-set $\Gamma_2 \in \mathcal{S}$ such that $\Gamma_2 \prec_T \Gamma_1$ and $A \in \Gamma_2$.
(f) If $\Diamond A \in \Gamma_1$, there exists an mc-set $\Gamma_2 \in \mathcal{S}$ such that $\Gamma_1 \prec_W \Gamma_2$ and $A \in \Gamma_2$.
(g) If $\Gamma_1 \prec_T \Gamma_2$ and $\Gamma_2 \prec_T \Gamma_3$, then $\Gamma_1 \prec_T \Gamma_3$.
(h) If $\Gamma_1 \prec_T \Gamma_2$ and $\Gamma_1 \prec_T \Gamma_3$, then $\Gamma_2 = \Gamma_3$ or $\Gamma_2 \prec_T \Gamma_3$ or $\Gamma_3 \prec_T \Gamma_2$.

The following lemma is specific to our system for total functions.

Lemma 2. *Let $\Gamma_1, \Gamma_2, \Gamma_3$ be mc-sets in $\mathcal{S}_{T \times W}$ -Tot, then we have:*

(a) If $\Gamma_1 \prec_T \Gamma_2$ and $\Gamma_1 \prec_W \Gamma_3$, then there exists an mc-set in $\mathcal{S}_{T \times W}$ -Tot, Γ_4, such that $\Gamma_2 \prec_W \Gamma_4$ and, either $\Gamma_3 = \Gamma_4$ or $\Gamma_3 \prec_T \Gamma_4$ or $\Gamma_4 \prec_T \Gamma_3$.

(b) If $\Gamma_1 \prec_T \Gamma_2$ and $\Gamma_2 \prec_W \Gamma_3$, then there exists an mc-set in $\mathcal{S}_{T \times W}$ -Tot, Γ_4, such that $\Gamma_1 \prec_W \Gamma_4$ and, either $\Gamma_3 = \Gamma_4$ or $\Gamma_3 \prec_T \Gamma_4$ or $\Gamma_4 \prec_T \Gamma_3$.

Proof. We prove (a). The proof of (b) is similar. Assume that $\Gamma_1 \prec_T \Gamma_2$ and $\Gamma_1 \prec_W \Gamma_3$. To construct Γ_4, it suffices to prove that one of the following conditions is satisfied:

(i) $\Gamma_2 \prec_W \Gamma_3$. In this case, we obtain the result because $\Gamma_4 = \Gamma_3$.

(ii) $\{A \mid \Box A \in \Gamma_2\} \cup \{A \mid GA \in \Gamma_3\}$ is consistent. Now, Lindenbaum's lemma guarantees that there exists at least one mc extension, Γ_4, of the set $\{A \mid \Box A \in \Gamma_2\} \cup \{A \mid GA \in \Gamma_3\}$ which trivially satisfies $\Gamma_2 \prec_W \Gamma_4$ and $\Gamma_3 \prec_T \Gamma_4$.

(iii) $\{A \mid \Box A \in \Gamma_2\} \cup \{A \mid HA \in \Gamma_3\}$ is consistent. Lindenbaum's lemma again guarantees that there exists at least one mc extension, Γ_4, of the set $\{A \mid \Box A \in \Gamma_2\} \cup \{A \mid HA \in \Gamma_3\}$ which satisfies $\Gamma_2 \prec_W \Gamma_4$ and $\Gamma_4 \prec_T \Gamma_3$.

If we assume that none of the conditions i)–iii) holds, we have:

a) there exists a formula $\Box A \in \Gamma_2$ such that $A \notin \Gamma_3$;

b) there are $B_1, \ldots, B_{n_1} \in \{A \mid \Box A \in \Gamma_2\}, C_1, \ldots, C_{m_1} \in \{A \mid GA \in \Gamma_3\}$ such that $\vdash \neg(B_1 \wedge \ldots \wedge B_{n_1} \wedge C_1 \wedge \ldots \wedge C_{m_1})$;

c) there are $D_1, \ldots, D_{n_2} \in \{A \mid \Box A \in \Gamma_2\}, E_1, \ldots, E_{m_2} \in \{A \mid HA \in \Gamma_3\}$ such that $\vdash \neg(D_1 \wedge \ldots \wedge D_{n_2} \wedge E_1 \wedge \ldots \wedge E_{m_2})$.

Thus, we have:

$B = B_1 \wedge \ldots \wedge B_{n_1}$, with $\Box B \in \Gamma_2$; $C = C_1 \wedge \ldots \wedge C_{m_1}$, with $GC \in \Gamma_3$;

$D = D_1 \wedge \ldots \wedge D_{n_2}$, with $\Box D \in \Gamma_2$; $E = E_1 \wedge \ldots \wedge E_{m_2}$, with $HE \in \Gamma_3$.

Now, from $\vdash \neg(B \wedge C)$, we obtain $\vdash \Box B \to \Box \neg C$ and (since $\Box B \in \Gamma_2$) $\Box \neg C \in \Gamma_2$. Similarly, from $\vdash \neg(D \wedge E)$, we obtain $\Box \neg E \in \Gamma_2$. Thus, $\Box(A \wedge \neg C \wedge \neg E) \in \Gamma_2$ and, since $\Gamma_1 \prec_T \Gamma_2$, we obtain $F\Box(A \wedge \neg C \wedge \neg E) \in \Gamma_1$. Therefore, by $(T1)$ in theorem 2, we obtain:

$$\Box((A \wedge \neg C \wedge \neg E) \vee F(A \wedge \neg C \wedge \neg E) \vee P(A \wedge \neg C \wedge \neg E)) \in \Gamma_1$$

Henceforth, by the definition of $\prec_W$, either (1) $A \wedge \neg C \wedge \neg E \in \Gamma_3$ or (2) $F(A \wedge \neg C \wedge \neg E) \in \Gamma_3$ or (3) $P(A \wedge \neg C \wedge \neg E) \in \Gamma_3$. However, $A \notin \Gamma_3$ is contrary to (1); $GC \in \Gamma_3$ is contrary to (2), and $HE \in \Gamma_3$ is contrary to (3). Since we obtain a contradiction in any case, one of these conditions i)–iii) is satisfied.

Definition 6. *Let $\Sigma = (W, \mathcal{T}, \mathcal{F})$ be a frame. A* **trace** *of Σ is any function $\Phi_\Sigma : Coord_\Sigma \longrightarrow 2^{\mathcal{L}_{T \times W}}$ such that, for all t_w, the set $\Phi_\Sigma(t_w)$ is an mc-set.*

Definition 7. *Let Φ_Σ be a trace of $\Sigma = (W, \mathcal{T}, \mathcal{F})$. Φ_Σ is called:*

temporally coherent *if, for all $t_w, t'_w \in Coord_\Sigma$:*

$$\text{if } t'_w \in (t_w, \to), \text{ then } \Phi_\Sigma(t_w) \prec_T \Phi_\Sigma(t'_w)$$

modally coherent *if, for all $t_w, t'_{w'} \in Coord_\Sigma$:*

$$\text{if } t'_{w'} \in \mathcal{F}_w(t_w), \text{ then } \Phi_\Sigma(t_w) \prec_W \Phi_\Sigma(t'_{w'})$$

coherent *if it is temporally coherent and modally coherent.*

prophetic *if it is temporally coherent and for all $A \in L_{T \times W}$ and all t_w:*

(1)   *if $FA \in \Phi_\Sigma(t_w)$, there exists a $t'_w \in (t_w, \to)$ such that $A \in \Phi_\Sigma(t'_w)$*

historic *if it is temporally coherent and for all $A \in L_{T \times W}$ and all t_w:*

(2)   if $PA \in \Phi_\Sigma(t_w)$, there exists a $t'_w \in (\leftarrow, t_w)$ such that $A \in \Phi_\Sigma(t'_w)$

possibilistic if it is modally coherent and for all $A \in L_{T \times W}$ and all t_w,:

(3)   if $\Diamond A \in \Phi_\Sigma(t_w)$, there exists a $t'_{w'} \in \mathcal{F}_w(t_w)$ such that $A \in \Phi_\Sigma(t'_{w'})$.

The conditional (1) (resp., (2) or (3)) is called a prophetic (historic or possibilistic) **conditional for** Φ_Σ **with respect to** FA, $(PA$ **or** $\Diamond A)$ **and** t_w.

Definition 8. Let Φ_Σ be a trace of $\Sigma = (W, \mathcal{T}, \mathcal{F})$. Φ_Σ is called **total** if it is coherent and Σ satisfies the following property: for all $t_w, t'_w, t'_{w'} \in Coord_\Sigma$

(4)   if $t'_{w'} \in \mathcal{F}_w(t_w)$ and $t'_w \neq t_w$, then there exists $t''_{w'} \in \mathcal{F}_w(t'_w)$ [1]

(4) is called **a total conditional for** Φ_Σ **with respect to** t_w, t'_w, **and** $t'_{w'}$. Φ_Σ is called **total-full** if it is prophetic, historic, possibilistic, and total.

Definition 9. Let W be a denumerable infinite set and $T = \bigcup_{w \in W} T_w$, where T_w is a denumerable infinite set, for each $w \in W$. We consider the class, Ξ, of frames, $(W', \mathcal{T}', \mathcal{F}')$, such that W' is a nonempty finite subset of W and $\mathcal{T}' = \{(T'_w, <'_w) \mid w \in W'\}$ where T'_w is a nonempty finite subset of T_w.

For $\Sigma_1 = (W_1, \mathcal{T}_1, \mathcal{F}_1)$ and $\Sigma_2 = (W_2, \mathcal{T}_2, \mathcal{F}_2)$ in Ξ we say that Σ_2 is **an extension of** Σ_1 if: (i) $W_1 \subseteq W_2$; (ii) either $\mathcal{T}_1 \subset \mathcal{T}_2$ or for every $(T_w, <_w) \in \mathcal{T}_1$, the set $\mathcal{T}_2$ contains a flow wich extends $(T_w, <_w)$ and (iii) either $\mathcal{F}_1 \subset \mathcal{F}_2$ or for every $\xrightarrow{w\,w'} \in \mathcal{F}_1$, the set $\mathcal{F}_2$ contains a function which extends $\xrightarrow{w\,w'}$.

Definition 10. Let Ξ be as in definition 9 and let $\Phi_{\Sigma'}$ be a trace of a frame $\Sigma' = (W', \mathcal{T}', \mathcal{F}') \in \Xi$.

I) Let the prophetic conditional be:

(1)   if $FA \in \Phi_{\Sigma'}(t_w)$, there exists a $t'_w \in (t_w, \rightarrow)$ such that $A \in \Phi_{\Sigma'}(t'_w)$

We say that it is **inactive**, if its antecedent is not fulfilled, that is, if one of the following conditions is satisfied: (i) $t_w \notin Coord_{\Sigma'}$ and (ii) $t_w \in Coord_{\Sigma'}$ but $FA \notin \Phi_{\Sigma'}(t_w)$. We say that the conditional (1) is **active**, if its antecedent is fulfilled but its consequent is not, that is, $t_w \in Coord_{\Sigma'}$ and $FA \in \Phi_{\Sigma'}(t_w)$, but there is no $t'_w \in (t_w, \rightarrow)$ such that $A \in \Phi_{\Sigma'}(t'_w)$. We say that (1) is **exhausted**, if its consequent is fulfilled, i.e. there exists a $t'_w \in (t_w, \rightarrow)$ such that $A \in \Phi_{\Sigma'}(t'_w)$.

II) Let the historic conditional be:

(2)   if $PA \in \Phi_{\Sigma'}(t_w)$, there exists a $t'_w \in (\leftarrow, t_w)$ such that $A \in \Phi_{\Sigma'}(t'_w)$

We say that it is **inactive**, if its antecedent is not fulfilled, that is, if one of the following conditions is satisfied: (i) $t_w \notin Coord_{\Sigma'}$ and (ii) $t_w \in Coord_{\Sigma'}$ but $PA \notin \Phi_{\Sigma'}(t_w)$. We say that the conditional (2) is **active**, if its antecedent is fulfilled but its consequent is not, that is, $t_w \in Coord_{\Sigma'}$ and $PA \in \Phi_{\Sigma'}(t_w)$, but there is no $t'_w \in (\leftarrow, t_w)$ such that $A \in \Phi_{\Sigma'}(t'_w)$. We

---

[1] That is, Φ_Σ is called *total* when is a coherent trace of a total frame.

say that (2) *is* **exhausted**, *if its consequent is fulfilled, i.e. there exists a* $t'_w \in (\leftarrow, t_w)$ *such that* $A \in \Phi_{\Sigma'}(t'_w)$.

III) *Let the possibilistic conditional be:*

(3)   *if* $\Diamond A \in \Phi_{\Sigma'}(t_w)$, *there exists a* $t'_{w'} \in \mathcal{F}'_w(t_w)$ *such that* $A \in \Phi_{\Sigma'}(t'_{w'})$

We say that it is **inactive**, *if its antecedent is not fulfilled, that is, if one of the following conditions is satisfied:* (i) $t_w \notin Coord_{\Sigma'}$ *and* (ii) $t_w \in Coord_{\Sigma'}$ *but* $\Diamond A \notin \Phi_{\Sigma'}(t_w)$. *We say that the conditional* (3) *is* **active**, *if its antecedent is fulfilled but its consequent is not, that is,* $t_w \in Coord_{\Sigma'}$ *and* $\Diamond A \in \Phi_{\Sigma'}(t_w)$, *but there is no* $t'_{w'} \in \mathcal{F}'_w(t_w)$ *such that* $A \in \Phi_{\Sigma'}(t'_{w'})$. *We say that* (3) *is* **exhausted**, *if its consequent is fulfilled, that is, there exists a* $t'_{w'} \in \mathcal{F}'_w(t_w)$ *such that* $A \in \Phi_{\Sigma'}(t'_{w'})$.

IV) *Let the total conditional be:*

(4)   *if* $t'_{w'} \in \mathcal{F}'_w(t_w)$ *and* $t'_w \neq t_w$, *then there exists* $t''_{w'} \in \mathcal{F}'_w(t'_w)$

We say that it is **inactive**, *if its antecedent is not fulfilled, that is, if one of the following conditions is satisfied:* (i) *something* $(t_w, t'_w$ *or* $t'_{w'})$ *is not in* $Coord_{\Sigma'}$; (ii) $t'_{w'} \notin \mathcal{F}'_w(t_w)$; (iii) $t'_w = t_w$. *We say that the conditional* (4) *is* **active**, *if its antecedent is fulfilled but its consequent is not, that is,* $t_w, t'_w, t'_{w'} \in Coord_{\Sigma'}$, $t'_{w'} \in \mathcal{F}'_w(t_w)$, $t'_w \neq t_w$, *but* $t''_{w'} \in \mathcal{F}'_w(t'_w)$ *does not exist. We say that* (4) *is* **exhausted**, *if its consequent is fulfilled, i.e.* $t''_{w'} \in \mathcal{F}'_w(t'_w)$ *exists.*

Lemma 3 (trace lemma). *Let* Φ_Σ *be a total-full trace of* $\Sigma = (W, \mathcal{T}, \mathcal{F})$ *and let* h *be a functional interpretation assigning each propositional variable,* p, *the set* $h(p) = \{t_w \in Coord_\Sigma \mid p \in \Phi_\Sigma(t_w)\}$. *Then, for any wff,* A, *we have*

$$h(A) = \{t_w \in Coord_\Sigma \mid A \in \Phi_\Sigma(t_w)\}$$

In order to prove the completeness theorem, for each consistent formula A we will construct (using the class, Ξ, of frames in definition 9) a total frame $\Sigma = (W, \mathcal{T}, \mathcal{F})$ and a total-full trace Φ_Σ, so that $A \in \Phi_\Sigma(t_w)$ for some $t_w \in Coord_\Sigma$. To do this, we will define an enumeration of elements in T as defined in definition 9: $T = \bigcup_{i \in \mathbb{N}} T_{w_i}; T_{w_i} = \{t_{(i,j)} \mid j \in \mathbb{N}\}$ and an enumeration of wffs of $L_{T \times W}$: $A_0, A_1, \ldots, A_n, \ldots$ Therefore, we have a code number for each prophetic conditional (historic conditional, etc.) :

- The code number of the prophetic conditional

"if $FA \in \Phi_{\Sigma'}(t_w)$, there exists a $t'_w \in (t_w, \rightarrow)$ such that $A \in \Phi_{\Sigma'}(t'_w)$"

is $2 \cdot 11^i \cdot 13^j \cdot 17^k$, where i is the index of FA and (j, k) is the index of t_w.

- The code number of the historic conditional

"if $PA \in \Phi_{\Sigma'}(t_w)$, there exists a $t'_w \in (\leftarrow, t_w)$ such that $A \in \Phi_{\Sigma'}(t'_w)$"

is $3 \cdot 11^i \cdot 13^j \cdot 17^k$, where i is the index of PA and (j, k) is the index of t_w.

- The code number of the possibilistic conditional

"if $\Diamond A \in \Phi_{\Sigma'}(t_w)$, there exists a $t'_{w'} \in \mathcal{F}'_w(t_w)$ such that $A \in \Phi_{\Sigma'}(t'_{w'})$"

is $5 \cdot 11^i \cdot 13^j \cdot 17^k$, where i is the index of $\Diamond A$ and (j, k) is the index of t_w.

-The code number of the total conditional

"if $t'_{w'} \in \mathcal{F}'_w(t_w)$ and $t'_w \neq t_w$, then there exists $t''_{w'} \in \mathcal{F}'_w(t'_w)$"

is the tuple $(7 \cdot 13^j \cdot 17^k, 7 \cdot 13^j \cdot 17^{k'}, 7 \cdot 13^{j'} \cdot 17^{k''})$, where (j, k) is the index of t_w, (j, k') is the index of t'_w, and (j', k'') is the index of $t'_{w'}$.[2]

Now, given a consistent formula A, the constructions of Σ and Φ_Σ go step by step as follows: We begin with a finite frame $\Sigma_0 = (W_0, \mathcal{T}_0, \mathcal{F}_0)$ and a trace Φ_{Σ_0}, where: $W_0 = \{w_0\}$, $\mathcal{T}_0 = \{(\{t_{(0,0)}\}, \varnothing)\}$, $\mathcal{F}_0 = \varnothing$ and $\Phi_{\Sigma_0}(t_{(0,0)}) = \Gamma_0$, where Γ_0 is an mc-consistent set containing A. Assume that $\Sigma_n = (W_n, \mathcal{T}_n, \mathcal{F}_n)$ and Φ_{Σ_n} are defined. Then, Σ_{n+1} and $\Phi_{\Sigma_{n+1}}$ are defined as follows:

- If all conditionals are not active, then $\Sigma_{n+1} = \Sigma_n$, $\Phi_{\Sigma_{n+1}} = \Phi_{\Sigma_n}$ and the construction is finished.
- In other case, i.e., if there are prophetic conditionals (or historic, possibilistic, etc.) for Φ_{Σ_n} with respect to FA (respectively, PA or $\Diamond A$) and t_w, or there is a total conditional for Φ_{Σ_n} with respect to t_w, t'_w, and $t'_{w'}$ which are active, then we choose the conditional with the lowest code number and the lemma below ensures that there exists an extension Σ_{n+1} of Σ_n and an extension $\Phi_{\Sigma_{n+1}}$ of Φ_{Σ_n} so that this conditional for $\Phi_{\Sigma_{n+1}}$ is exhausted.

The result is a sequence of finite frames $(W_0, \mathcal{T}_0, \mathcal{F}_0), ..., (W_n, \mathcal{T}_n, \mathcal{F}_n), ...$, whose union is Σ, and a sequence of corresponding traces $\Phi_{\Sigma_0}, \Phi_{\Sigma_1}, ..., \Phi_{\Sigma_n}, ...$ whose union is Φ_Σ. Each finite frame of the above sequence satisfies the condition of linearity of orders and each trace of it is coherent, but in general, it fails to be prophetic, historic, possibilistic or total. However, as we shall show, Σ is such that Φ_Σ is total-full. Thus, A is verified by the trace lemma.

Lemma 4 (Exhausting lemma). *Let Ξ be as in definition 9, Φ_{Σ_n} a coherent trace of $\Sigma_n = (W_n, \mathcal{T}_n, \mathcal{F}_n) \in \Xi$, and suppose that there is a prophetic (historic, possibilistic or total) conditional for Φ_{Σ_n} which is active. Then there exists a coherent trace $\Phi_{\Sigma_{n+1}}$, an extension of Φ_{Σ_n}, such that this conditional is a conditional for $\Phi_{\Sigma_{n+1}}$ which is exhausted.*

Proof. Let Φ_{Σ_n} be a coherent trace of $\Sigma_n = (W_n, \mathcal{T}_n, \mathcal{F}_n)$ in Ξ, and let

(1) if $FA \in \Phi_{\Sigma_n}(t_w)$, there exists $t'_w \in (t_w, \rightarrow)$ such that $A \in \Phi_{\Sigma_n}(t'_w)$

a prophetic conditional for Φ_{Σ_n} with respect to FA and t_w, which is active. In this case, the proof is a simple adaptation of the one offered in (Burguess, 1984), by induction on the number l of successors of $t_w \in T_w$: since (1) is active, we obtain that $FA \in \Phi_{\Sigma_n}(t_w)$, but there is no coordinate $t'_w \in (t_w, \rightarrow)$ such that $A \in \Phi_{\Sigma_n}(t'_w)$. Then, by lemma 1, we have that there is some mc-set Γ such that $\Phi_{\Sigma_n}(t_w) \prec_T \Gamma$ and $A \in \Gamma$. We want to extend the function Φ_{Σ_n}, assign Γ to a new coordinate t'_w and preserve the linear order and coherence of the trace. The result will be a new frame $\Sigma_{n+1} = (W_{n+1}, \mathcal{T}_{n+1}, \mathcal{F}_{n+1}) \in \Xi$ and a trace $\Phi_{\Sigma_{n+1}}$. For this, we consider the number l of successors of t_w in T_w. Thus, if $l = 0$:

---

[2] Given a conditional for Φ_Σ, if we simply replace the label Σ with Σ' so that $\Sigma \subseteq \Sigma'$, we have a conditional for $\Phi_{\Sigma'}$ but with the same code number as the conditional for Φ_Σ. Then we can say that in both cases we refer to the same conditional.

- $W_{n+1} = W_n$.
- $\mathcal{T}_{n+1} = (\mathcal{T}_n - \{(T_w, <_w)\}) \cup \{(T'_w, <'_w)\})$, where $T'_w = T_w \cup \{t'_w\}$, and $<'_w = <_w \cup \{(t_w, t'_w)\} \cup \{(t_{1_w}, t'_w) \mid t_{1_w} <_w t_w\}$
- $\mathcal{F}_{n+1} = \mathcal{F}_n$ and $\Phi_{\Sigma_{n+1}} = \Phi_{\Sigma_n} \cup \{(t'_w, \Gamma)\}$

If $l > 0$, we assume that for any natural number $m < l$ the construction is well-defined and consider the case l. We reason as follows: let t^*_w be the successor of t_w in T_w. Clearly, $\neg A \in \Phi_{\Sigma_n}(t^*_w)$; in other case, the conditional should be exhausted. If $FA \in \Phi_{\Sigma_n}(t^*_w)$, the case is resolved by inductive hypothesis. If not, that is, if $\neg FA \in \Phi_{\Sigma_n}(t^*_w)$, then by (h) in lemma 1, we obtain that $\Gamma \prec_T \Phi_{\Sigma_n}(t^*_w)$. Thus, we have $\Phi_{\Sigma_n}(t_w) \prec_T \Gamma \prec_T \Phi_{\Sigma_n}(t^*_w)$. Then:

- $W_{n+1} = W_n$
- $\mathcal{T}_{n+1} = (\mathcal{T}_n - \{(T_w, <_w)\}) \cup \{(T'_w, <'_w)\}$, where $T'_w = T_w \cup \{t'_w\}$ and $<'_w = <_w \cup \{(t_w, t'_w), (t'_w, t^*_w)\} \cup \{(t_{1_w}, t'_w) \mid t_{1_w} <_w t_w)\} \cup \{(t'_w, t_{1_w}) \mid t^*_w <_w t_{1_w}\}$
- $\mathcal{F}_{n+1} = \mathcal{F}_n$ and $\Phi_{\Sigma_{n+1}} = \Phi_{\Sigma_n} \cup \{(t'_w, \Gamma)\}$.

In both cases, $l = 0$ and $l > 0$, the ítem (g) in lemma 1 allows us to conclude that $\Phi_{\Sigma_{n+1}}$ is coherent and the proof is complete.

The proof for a historic conditional is similar. Assume a possibilistic conditional for Φ_{Σ_n} with respect to $\Diamond A$ and t_w:

(2)   if $\Diamond A \in \Phi_{\Sigma_n}(t_w)$, there exists a $t'_{w'} \in \mathcal{F}_w(t_w)$ such that $A \in \Phi_{\Sigma_n}(t'_{w'})$

is active. Then, $\Diamond A \in \Phi_{\Sigma_n}(t_w)$ but there is no $t'_{w'} \in \mathcal{F}_w(t_w)$ with $A \in \Phi_{\Sigma_n}(t'_{w'})$. We know – by item f) in lemma 1 – that there exists an mc-set, Γ, such that $\Phi_{\Sigma_n}(t_w) \prec_W \Gamma$ and $A \in \Gamma$; then we require a new flow of time $T_{w'}$ with a coordinate $t'_{w'}$ associated with Γ so that $t'_{w'} \in \mathcal{F}_w(t_w)$. That is:

- $W_{n+1} = W_n \cup \{w'\}$
- $\mathcal{T}_{n+1} = \mathcal{T}_n \cup \{(T_{w'}, <_{w'})\}$, where $T_{w'} = \{t'_{w'}\}$ and $<_{w'} = \varnothing$
- $\mathcal{F}_{n+1} = \mathcal{F}_n \cup \{\overset{w\ w'}{\longrightarrow}\}$, where $\overset{w\ w'}{\longrightarrow} = \{(t_w, t'_{w'})\}$ and $\Phi_{\Sigma_{n+1}} = \Phi_{\Sigma_n} \cup \{(t'_{w'}, \Gamma)\}$.

It is easy to see that $\Phi_{\Sigma_{n+1}}$ is coherent.

Now, assume a total conditional for Φ_{Σ_n} with respect to t_w, t'_w and $t'_{w'}$:

(3)   if $t'_{w'} \in \mathcal{F}_w(t_w)$ and $t'_w \neq t_w$, then there exists $t''_{w'} \in \mathcal{F}_w(t'_w)$

is active. Then, $t'_{w'} \in \mathcal{F}_w(t_w)$ and $t'_w \neq t_w$, but $t''_{w'} \in \mathcal{F}_w(t'_w)$ does not exist. Therefore, we must fix an image for t'_w. We have either $t'_w \in (t_w, \to)$ or $t'_w \in (\leftarrow, t_w)$. Now, by hypothesis with respect to Φ_{Σ_n}, we have $\Phi_{\Sigma_n}(t_w) \prec_W \Phi_{\Sigma_n}(t'_{w'})$ and either $\Phi_{\Sigma_n}(t_w) \prec_T \Phi_{\Sigma_n}(t'_w)$ or $\Phi_{\Sigma_n}(t'_w) \prec_T \Phi_{\Sigma_n}(t_w)$. In any case, by lemma 2, there is an mc-set, Γ, such that $\Phi_{\Sigma_n}(t'_w) \prec_W \Gamma$ and one of the following conditions is satisfied: (1) $\Phi_{\Sigma_n}(t'_{w'}) = \Gamma$; (2) $\Phi_{\Sigma_n}(t'_{w'}) \prec_T \Gamma$; (3) $\Gamma \prec_T \Phi_{\Sigma_n}(t'_{w'})$.

In all cases, we have $W_{n+1} = W_n$. Moreover:

a) If condition 1 above holds, then
- $\mathcal{T}_{n+1} = \mathcal{T}_n$;
- $\mathcal{F}_{n+1} = (\mathcal{F}_n - \{\overset{w\ w'}{\longrightarrow}\}) \cup \{\overset{w\ w'}{\longrightarrow}'\}$, where $\overset{w\ w'}{\longrightarrow}' = \overset{w\ w'}{\longrightarrow} \cup \{(t'_w, t'_{w'})\}$
- $\Phi_{\Sigma_{n+1}} = \Phi_{\Sigma_n}$

Clearly, $\Phi_{\Sigma_{n+1}}$ is coherent.

b) If condition 2 above holds, then we consider $\{t_{i_{w'}} \mid 1 \le i \le n\} = (t'_{w'}, \rightarrow)$ i.e., the number n of successors of $t'_{w'}$ in the flow $T_{w'}$. If $n = 0$, then we choose a new coordinate $t''_{w'}$ to be associated to Γ and we have:

- $\mathcal{T}_{n+1} = (\mathcal{T}_n - \{(T_{w'}, <_{w'})\}) \cup \{(T'_{w'}, <'_{w'})\}$, where $T'_{w'} = T_{w'} \cup \{t''_{w'}\}$ and
  $<'_{w'} = <_{w'} \cup \{(t'_{w'}, t''_{w'})\} \cup \{(t^*_{w'}, t''_{w'}) \mid t^*_{w'} <_{w'} t'_{w'}\}$.
- $\mathcal{F}_{n+1} = (\mathcal{F}_n - \{\overset{w\ w'}{\longrightarrow}\}) \cup \{\overset{w\ w'}{\longrightarrow}'\})$, where $\overset{w\ w'}{\longrightarrow}' = \overset{w\ w'}{\longrightarrow} \cup \{(t'_w, t''_{w'})\}$ (†)
- $\Phi_{\Sigma_{n+1}} = \Phi_{\Sigma_n} \cup \{(t''_{w'}, \Gamma)\}$.   (†)

Now, using lemma 1 again, the proof of the coherence of $\Phi_{\Sigma_{n+1}}$ is complete. If $\{t_{i_{w'}} \mid 1 \le i \le n\} = (t'_{w'}, \rightarrow)$ is not empty, i.e., $n > 0$, we take into account the immediate successor of $t'_{w'}$, namely $t_{1_{w'}}$. Now, as $\Phi_{\Sigma_n}(t'_{w'}) \prec_T \Phi_{\Sigma_n}(t_{1_{w'}})$, by item (h) of lemma 1, we have three cases:

(i) $\Phi_{\Sigma_n}(t_{1_{w'}}) = \Gamma$;   (ii) $\Gamma \prec_T \Phi_{\Sigma_n}(t_{1_{w'}})$;   (iii) $\Phi_{\Sigma_n}(t_{1_{w'}}) \prec_T \Gamma$.

Case (i) is the same as condition 1 above but with $t_{1_{w'}}$ instead of $t'_{w'}$. Case (ii) means that $\Phi_{\Sigma_n}(t'_{w'}) \prec_T \Gamma \prec_T \Phi_{\Sigma_n}(t_{1_{w'}})$. We select a new coordinate $t''_{w'}$ to be associated with Γ. Therefore:

- $\mathcal{T}_{n+1} = (\mathcal{T}_n - \{(T_{w'}, <_{w'})\}) \cup \{(T'_{w'}, <'_{w'})\}$, where $T'_{w'} = T_{w'} \cup \{t''_{w'}\}$ and
  $<'_{w'} = <_{w'} \cup \{(t'_{w'}, t''_{w'}), (t''_{w'}, t_{1_{w'}})\} \cup \{(t^*_{w'}, t''_{w'}) \mid t^*_{w'} <_{w'} t'_{w'}\} \cup$
  $\{(t''_{w'}, t^*_{w'}) \mid t_{1_{w'}} <_{w'} t^*_{w'}\}$
- $\mathcal{F}_{n+1}$ and $\Phi_{\Sigma_{n+1}}$ are defined as in (†) above.

Again item (g) in lemma 1 completes the proof of the coherence of $\Phi_{\Sigma_{n+1}}$. Case (iii) lead us to consider the immediate successor of $t_{1_{w'}}$, namely $t_{2_{w'}}$, and we proceed similarly.

By iterating this operation at most n times, we fix the image of t'_w associating an mc-set to it, preserving coherence and linearity.

c) If the condition 3 above holds, the treatment is similar to condition 2. This completes the proof of the exhausting lemma.

Finally we can enunciate the following theorem.

Theorem 3 (Completeness theorem for $\mathcal{S}_{T \times W}$-Tot). *If a formula A is valid in the class of frames $\{(W, \mathcal{T}, \mathcal{F}) \mid \mathcal{F}$ is a class of total functions$\}$, then A is a theorem of $\mathcal{S}_{T \times W}$-Tot.*

5 $T \times W$-Validity, Kamp-Validity, and Functional Validity

Now, we analyze the relation of $T \times W$-validity and Kamp-validity to functional validity. As we shall see, the functional context introduced is a generalization of the $T \times W$ and $Kamp$ contexts. Specifically, we can generate a functional model, $\mathcal{M}_{Func}$, from a $T \times W$ (resp. Kamp model), $\mathcal{M}_{T \times W}$ (resp. $\mathcal{M}_{Kamp}$) and prove the equivalence between $\mathcal{M}_{Func}$ and $\mathcal{M}_{T \times W}$ (resp, $\mathcal{M}_{Kamp}$).

5.1 $T \times W$-Validity and Functional Validity

Definition 11. *A $T \times W$-frame is a quadruple $\Sigma_{T \times W} = (T, <, W, \approx)$ consisting of:*

1. *A nonempty set T ("time-points").*
2. *A strict linear order $<$ on T.*
3. *A nonempty set W ("worlds" or "histories").*
4. *A family $\approx = \{\approx_t\}_{t \in T}$ of equivalence relations $\approx_t$ on W such that the following condition is satisfied: "if $w \approx_{t_1} w'$ and $t_2 < t_1$, then $w \approx_{t_2} w'$".*
   The expression $w \approx_t w'$ is read "w and w' share the same history up to (and inclusively) t".

Definition 12. *A $T \times W$-model is a tuple $\mathcal{M}_{T \times W} = (\Sigma_{T \times W}, h^\dagger)$ where $\Sigma_{T \times W}$ is a $T \times W$-frame and $h^\dagger$ is a function assigning each atomic formula, p, a subset of $T \times W$ and satisfying:*

$$\text{if } w \approx_t w', \text{then } (t, w) \in h^\dagger(p) \text{ iff } (t, w') \in h^\dagger(p) \quad (*)$$

$h^\dagger$ is recursively extended to $\mathcal{L}_{T \times W}$ treating truth-functional connectives in the usual way. The modal and temporal connectives run as follows:

$h^\dagger(GA) = \{(t, w) \in T \times W \mid \bigcup_{t' \in (t, \rightarrow)} (t', w) \subseteq h^\dagger(A)\};$
$h^\dagger(HA) = \{(t, w) \in T \times W \mid \bigcup_{t' \in (\leftarrow, t)} (t', w) \subseteq h^\dagger(A)\};$
$h^\dagger(\Box A) = \{(t, w) \in T \times W \mid \bigcup_{w' \in [w]_{\approx_t}} (t, w') \subseteq h^\dagger(A)\};$

where $[w]_{\approx_t}$ denotes the equivalence class of w for the relation $\approx_t$.

Generating a Functional Model from a $T \times W$-Model. A functional frame, $(W^*, \mathcal{T}, \mathcal{F})$, is generated from a $T \times W$-frame, $(T, <, W, \approx)$, as follows:

1. $W^* = W$.
2. $\mathcal{T}$ is the set of all $(T_w, <_w)$ such that for each $w \in W$, $(T_w, <_w)$ is an isomorphic copy of $(T, <)$. The copy of t in T_w will be denoted t_w. Thus, if $w \neq w'$, t_w and $t_{w'}$ are considered different.
3. $\mathcal{F}$ is the class $\{\overset{w \ w'}{\longrightarrow} \mid w, w' \in W^*\}$, where $\overset{w \ w'}{\longrightarrow}$ is defined as follows: if there exists t_0 such that $w \approx_{t_0} w'$, then the domain of $\overset{w \ w'}{\longrightarrow}$ is $\{t_w \in T_w \mid w \approx_t w'\}$ and, for each $t_w \in T_w$, $\overset{w \ w'}{\longrightarrow}(t_w) = t_{w'}$.

   As a consequence of the properties of the equivalence relations, we have:
   (a) $id_{T_w} \in \mathcal{F}_w$, for all $w \in W^*$; (b) if $\overset{w \ w'}{\longrightarrow} \in \mathcal{F}_w$, then $\overset{w \ w'}{\longrightarrow}{}^{-1} \in \mathcal{F}_{w'}$ and (c) $\mathcal{F}$ is closed under composition of functions.

The following lemma (whose proof is trivial) ensures that, in the above construction, $\approx$ is determined by $\mathcal{F}$:

Lemma 5. *Let $(T, <, W, \approx)$ be a $T \times W$-frame and let $\Sigma = (W^*, \mathcal{T}, \mathcal{F})$ be a functional frame generated from $(T, <, W, \approx)$ as defined. Then, if $w, w' \in W$ and $t \in T$, we have that $w \approx_t w'$ if and only if $t_{w'} \in \mathcal{F}_w(t_w)$*[3].

Now we restrict the notion of a model given in definition 2.

---

[3] Where t_w is the copy of t at T_w and $t_{w'}$ is the copy of t at $T_{w'}$.

Definition 13. *Let* $\Sigma = (W, \mathcal{T}, \mathcal{F})$ *the functional frame generated from a* $T \times W$ *-frame. We define a functional model on* Σ *as a tuple* $\mathcal{M} = (\Sigma, h)$ *as in definition 2 with the following restriction for* h*: for all atoms* $p \in \mathcal{V}$ *and all* $t_w, t'_{w'} \in Coord_{\Sigma}$ *such that* $t'_{w'} \in \mathcal{F}_w(t_w)$*, we have*

$$t_w \in h(p) \quad \text{if and only if} \quad t'_{w'} \in h(p) \qquad (**)$$

Lemma 6. *Let* $\mathcal{M}_{T \times W} = (T, <, W, \approx, h^\dagger)$ *a* $T \times W$ *-model on the* $T \times W$ *-frame,* $U = (T, <, W, \approx)$*,* $\Sigma = (W, \mathcal{T}, \mathcal{F})$ *the functional frame generated from* U*, and let* $\mathcal{M} = (\Sigma, h)$ *as in definition 13. Then, if the following condition is satisfied*

$$t_w \in h(p) \text{ if and only if } (t, w) \in h^\dagger(p)$$

we have for all formula A*:*

$$t_w \in h(A) \text{ if and only if } (t, w) \in h^\dagger(A).$$

Proof. By structural induction on A.

Now, the following result is immediate:

Theorem 4. *A is* $T \times W$ *-valid in a* $T \times W$ *-frame, U, if and only if A is valid in the functional frame generated from U, according to restriction (**) established in definition 13.*[4]

5.2   Kamp-Validity and Functional Validity

Definition 14. *A Kamp-frame is a quadruple* $\Sigma_{Kamp} = (T, W, <, \approx)$ *consisting of:*

1. *A nonempty set* T *("time-points").*
2. *A nonempty set* W *("worlds" or "histories").*
3. *A family* $< = \{<_w |\ w \in W\}$ *of binary relations on* T*, where each* $<_w$ *is a strict linear order on a subset* $T_w \subseteq T$ *and* $\bigcup_{w \in W} T_w = T$*.*
4. *A family* $\approx = \{\approx_t\}_{t \in T}$ *of equivalence relations* $\approx_t$ *on* W *such that the following conditions are satisfied:*
   (a) *if* $w \approx_t w'$ *then:* $\{t \in T_w \cap T_{w'} | t_1 \in T_w\ |\ t_1 <_w t\} = \{t_1 \in T_{w'}\ |\ t_1 <_{w'} t\}$
   (b) *if* $w \approx_t w'$ *and* $t' <_w t$*, then* $w \approx_{t'} w'$
   As in the $T \times W$ *-frames, the expression* $w \approx_t w'$ *is read "w and w' share the same history up to (and inclusively) t".*

Definition 15. *A **Kamp-model** is a tuple* $\mathcal{M}_{Kamp} = (\Sigma_{Kamp}, h^\dagger)$ *where* Σ_{Kamp} *is a Kamp-frame and* $h^\dagger$ *is a function assigning each atomic formula,* p*, a subset of* $T \times W$ *and satisfying:*

$$\text{if } w \approx_t w', \text{ then } (t, w) \in h^\dagger(p) \text{ if and only if } (t, w') \in h^\dagger(p)$$

$h^\dagger$ *is recursively extended to* $\mathcal{L}_{T \times W}$ *treating truth-functional connectives in the usual way. The modal and temporal connectives run as follows:*

---

[4]   If we eliminate the restriction (*) on the definition 12, as in [Zan96], we obtain the same result established by theorem 4 but without the corresponding restriction on the functional frames in definition 13.

$h^\dagger(GA) = \{(t,w) \in T \times W \mid \bigcup_{t' \in (t, \rightarrow)} (t', w) \subseteq h^\dagger(A)\};$

$h^\dagger(HA) = \{(t,w) \in T \times W \mid \bigcup_{t' \in (\leftarrow, t)} (t', w) \subseteq h^\dagger(A)\};$

$h^\dagger(\Box A) = \{(t,w) \in T \times W \mid \bigcup_{w' \in [w]_{\approx_t}} (t, w') \subseteq h^\dagger(A)\};$

  where $[w]_{\approx_t}$ denotes the equivalence class of w for the relation $\approx_t$.

Generating a Functional Model from a $Kamp$-Model. We generate a functional frame, $\Sigma = (W^*, \mathcal{T}, \mathcal{F})$, from a $Kamp$-frame, $\Sigma_{Kamp} = (T, W, <, \approx)$, as follows:

1. $W^* = W$.
2. $\mathcal{T} = \bigcup_{w \in W} (T_w^*, <_w^*)$, where for each $(T_w, <_w)$ in Σ_{Kamp}, $(T_w^*, <_w^*)$ is a copy of $(T_w, <_w)$, so that if $w, w' \in W$ and $w \neq w'$, then $T_w^* \cap T_{w'}^* = \varnothing$. The copy of $t \in T = \bigcup_{w \in W} T_w$ is denoted t_w^*. Thus, if $t \in T_w \cap T_{w'}$, then there is a copy t_w^* of t in T_w^* and a copy $t_{w'}^*$ of t in $T_{w'}^*$.
3. $\mathcal{F}$ is the class $\{\xrightarrow{w \ w'} \mid w, w' \in W^*\}$, where $\xrightarrow{w \ w'}$ is defined as follows:

   if there exists $t_0 \in T$ such that $w \approx_{t_0} w'$, then the domain of $\xrightarrow{w \ w'}$ is $\{t_w^* \in T_w^* \mid w \approx_t w'\}$ and, for each $t_w^* \in T_w^*$, $\xrightarrow{w \ w'} (t_w^*) = t_{w'}^*$.

   As a consequence of the properties of the equivalence relations, we have:
   (a) $id_{T_w^*} \in \mathcal{F}_w$ for all $w \in W^*$; (b) if $\xrightarrow{w \ w'} \in \mathcal{F}_w$, then $\xrightarrow{w \ w'}{}^{-1} \in \mathcal{F}_{w'}$ and (c) $\mathcal{F}$ is closed under composition of functions.

The following lemma ensures that, in the construction, $\approx$ is determined by $\mathcal{F}$:

Lemma 7. *Let $(T, W, <, \approx)$ be a $Kamp$-frame and let $\Sigma = (W^*, \mathcal{T}, \mathcal{F})$ a functional frame generated from $(T, W, <, \approx)$ as defined. Then, if $w, w' \in W$ and $t \in T$, we have that: $w \approx_t w'$ if and only if $t_{w'}^* \in \mathcal{F}_w(t_w^*)$.*

The rest follows step-by-step as in $T \times W$-frames.

6   Future Work: Some Remarks about Incompleteness

In this section, we show that if we want to obtain complete minimal systems with respect to the classes of frames with injective (surjective, etc.) functions, then, in general, we cannot follow the method given in section 4, that is, it is not sufficient (as a standard generalization) to consider the method of adding successively to the basis of $\mathcal{K}l + \mathcal{K}$ the formulae introduced in the section defining these classes. In consequence, deeper study is required which we shall consider as future work. As an example, we shall show that adding the formula
$$(Tot\text{-}Inj) \qquad \Box(GA \wedge HA) \to (G\Box A \wedge H\Box A)$$
as axiom schema to the basis of $\mathcal{K}l + \mathcal{K}$ is not sufficient to obtain a complete system with respect to the class of frames with total injective functions and, indeed, taking into account that this class is defined by $(Tot\text{-}Inj)$, the system $\mathcal{K}l + \mathcal{K} + (Tot\text{-}Inj)$ is incomplete in a wider sense, that is, there is no class $\mathbb{K}$ of

functional frames such that the theorems of that system are precisely the valid formulas in $\mathbb{K}$. For the incompleteness of $\mathcal{K}l + \mathcal{K} + (Tot\text{-}Inj)$ we shall prove that there is a formula valid in the class of functional frames with total injective functions which is not a theorem of it. Let X be the formula

$$F(\square A \wedge F\square B) \rightarrow \square[F(A \wedge FB) \vee F(FA \wedge B) \vee (FA \wedge PB) \vee$$
$$(PA \wedge FB) \vee P(A \wedge PB) \vee P(PA \wedge B)]$$

Now, it is sufficient to prove the following conditions:

1. The formula X is valid in the class of all functional frames with total injective functions.
2. There is a model of $\mathcal{K}l + \mathcal{K} + (Tot\text{-}Inj)$ in which X is not valid.

The proof of 1 is easy. For 2, we define a new type of frame for $L_{T \times W}$. Let $\Psi = (W, \mathcal{T}, \mathcal{F}^\bullet)$ where W and $\mathcal{T}$ are as in definition 1 but $\mathcal{F}^\bullet$ is a set of correspondences, called *accessibility correspondences*, such that:

a) each correspondence in $\mathcal{F}^\bullet$ is a correspondence from T_w to $T_{w'}$ for some $w, w' \in W$.
b) for an arbitrary pair $w, w' \in W$, there is (in $\mathcal{F}^\bullet$) at most one accessibility correspondence from T_w to $T_{w'}$, denoted $\phi_{ww'}$.
   We will denote $\mathcal{F}_w^\bullet = \{\phi_{ww'} \in \mathcal{F}^\bullet \mid w' \in W\}$. Then, $\mathcal{F}^\bullet = \bigcup_{w \in W} \mathcal{F}_w^\bullet$.

The set of coordinates of a frame $\Psi = (W, \mathcal{T}, \mathcal{F}^\bullet)$, denoted $\mathcal{C}oord_\Psi$, is defined as in definition 2.

A **correspondence model** on a frame $\Psi = (W, \mathcal{T}, \mathcal{F}^\bullet)$ is a tuple $(\Psi, h^\bullet)$, where $h^\bullet$ is a function: $h^\bullet : L_{T \times W} \longrightarrow 2^{\mathcal{C}oord_\Psi}$, satisfying the usual conditions for the boolean and temporal connectives, and the specific condition:

$$h^\bullet(\square A) = \{t_w \in \mathcal{C}oord_\Psi \mid \mathcal{F}_w^\bullet(t_w) \subseteq h^\bullet(A)\}$$

The notions of valid formula in a correspondence model, valid formula in a correspondence frame, and valid formula are defined in a standard way.

Now, let the following correspondence frame be:

- $W = \{w, w'\}$;
- $\mathcal{T} = \{(T_w, <_w), (T_{w'}, <_{w'})\}$, where
    - $T_w = \{1_w, 2_w, 3_w\}$, $<_w = \{(1_w, 2_w), (1_w, 3_w), (2_w, 3_w)\}$;
    - $T_{w'} = \{4_{w'}, 5_{w'}\}$, $<_{w'} = \{(4_{w'}, 5_{w'})\}$;
- $\mathcal{F}^\bullet = \{\phi_{ww'}\}$, where $\phi_{ww'}(1_w) = \phi_{ww'}(2_w) = \phi_{ww'}(3_w) = T_{w'}$

Now we consider an arbitrary model, $\mathcal{M}$, on this frame, i.e., an arbitrary interpretation function $h : \mathcal{V} \longrightarrow 2^{\{1_w, 2_w, 3_w, 4_{w'}, 5_{w'}\}}$.

To verify that $\mathcal{M}$ is a model of $\mathcal{K}l + \mathcal{K} + (Tot\text{-}Inj)$ it suffices to show the validity of its axioms in $\mathcal{M}$. Details of proofs are omitted.

On the other hand, $\mathcal{M}$ falsifies X at 1_w. Thus, we conclude that X is not a theorem of $\mathcal{K}l + \mathcal{K} + (Tot\text{-}Inj)$ as required.

References

Bel96.   Belnap, N: Agents in branching time, In *Logic and Reality: Essays in Pure and Applied Logic, in Memory of Arthur Prior*, edited by B. J. Copeland, pp. 239-71 Oxford University Press, Oxford, 1996.

BP90.   Belnap, N. and Perloff, M: Seeing to it that: A canonical form of agentives, In *Knowledge Representation and Defeasible Reasonings*, ed. by H.E. Kyburg, R.P. Loui, and G.N. Carlson, Kluwer Academic Publishers, Dordrech, 1990.

Bur84.   Burgess, J.P: Basic Tense Logic, In *Handbook of Philosophical Logic, vol 2: Extensions of Classical Logic*, edited by D. Gabbay and F. Guenthner, pp. 89-133. Reidel, Dorchecht, 1984.

Che92.   Chellas, B: Time and Modality in the Logic of Agency, *Studia Logica*, 51: 485-517, 1992.

Kus93.   Kuschera, V.F: Causation, *Journal of Philosophical Logic*, 22: 563-88, 1993.

Rey97.   Reynolds, M: A decidable temporal logic of parallelism, *Notre Dame Journal of Formal Logic*, 38: 419-36, 1997.

Tho84.   Thomason, R.H: Combinations of tense and modality, In *Handbook of Philosophical Logic, Vol.2: Extensions of Classical Logic*, edited by D. Gabbay and F. Guenthner, pp. 135-65. Reidel, Dordrecht, 1984.

TG81.   Thomason, R.H., Gupta, A: A theory of conditionals in the context of branching time, in *Ifs: Conditionals, Belief, Decision, Chance and Time*, edited by W. Harper, R. Stalnaker, and G. Pearce, pp. 299-322. Reidel, Dordrecht, 1981.

Zan86.   Zanardo, A: On the Characterizability of the frames for the Unpreventability of the Present and the Past, *Notre Dame Journal of Formal Logic*, 27: 556-64, 1986.

Zan96.   Zanardo, A: Branching-time logic with quantification over branches: the point of view of modal logic, *The Journal of Symbolic Logic*, 61: 1-39, 1996.

Author Index

Lecture Notes in Artificial Intelligence (LNAI)

Lecture Notes in Computer Science